Home Safety Desk Reference

By
Dr. Ted Ferry

Foreword by Peter Couden

Home Safety Desk Reference

By

Dr. Ted Ferry

Foreword by Peter Couden

CAREER PRESS
180 Fifth Avenue
P.O. Box 34
Hawthorne, NJ 07507
1-800-CAREER-1
201-427-0229 (outside U.S.)
FAX: 201-427-2037

HOME SAFETY DESK REFERENCE

ISBN 1-56414-137-3, $16.95

Cover design by A Good Thing, Inc.

Printed in the U.S.A. by Book-mart Press

To order this title by mail, please include price as noted above, $2.50 handling per order, and $1.00 for each book ordered. Send to: Career Press, Inc., 180 Fifth Ave., P.O. Box 34, Hawthorne, NJ 07507

Or call toll-free 1-800-CAREER-1 (Canada: 201-427-0229) to order using VISA or MasterCard, or for further information on books from Career Press.

Library of Congress Cataloging-in-Publication Data

Ferry, Ted S.
    Home safety desk reference / by Ted Ferry ; foreword by Peter
Couden.
        p.   cm.
    Includes index.
    ISBN 1-56414-137-3 $16.95
    1. Home accidents--Prevention--Handbooks, manuals, etc.
2. Product safety--Handbooks, manuals, etc.   I. Title.
TX150.F47   1994
643'.028'9--dc20   94-22506
                                                                         CIP

CONTENTS

FOREWORD

Living safely is a basic human need that should be approached responsibly from infancy through adulthood. Unfortunately, this need is too often taken for granted until an individual, family or friend becomes a victim.

The home and common family activities can present dangers that, if not recognized and countered, may cause death, injury or property damage. Further, the home environment usually presents a comfortable and protective feeling that tends to mask risks and hazards. It takes a thinking person to combine common sense with acquired knowledge to ensure that safety is an unconscious part of everyday living.

Why should you as a responsible individual be concerned? The latest figures available from the National Safety Council indicate that, each year, twice as many deaths and disabling injuries occur at home than in the workplace. These are not mysterious accidents. They are caused by falls, poisoning, fires and suffocation. The news media reports them every day and yet they continue.

The Consumer Product Safety Commission states that 1 million injuries related to sports and recreation are treated each year as hospital emergencies. The bicycle is involved in more than half of these injuries. These figures only add to the millions of unreported home injuries that occur. Individual effort and more information is needed to reverse these yearly trends.

Home Safety Desk Reference is a practical guide that can be useful to you and your family, as well as businesses and organizations. It can be used as a reference or given as a caring gift. Because an employee injured at home still has an impact on the work force, companies may wish to include it as a part of their off-the-job safety program. The sensible information included here covers not only commonly used products, equipment and activities, but situations that contain elements of danger or risk.

I am writing this foreword as a former student and friend of the author. It is an honor to introduce this book as it was to be selected by him to teach his graduate class at the University of Southern California. While working as a safety manager for a public utility, his teachings in safety management and accident investigation served as a practical guide to my safety program. *Home Safety Desk Reference* was completed shortly before Mr. Ferry's death and it was important to his family that this valuable resource be made available, and that it be updated as necessary. The book is readable, contains real-life situations and can be immediately useful. The information collected from a multitude of reputable sources relieves the reader from seeking brochures, booklets and fact sheets from individual companies or government agencies. The complete bibliographies allow further inquiries, if necessary.

Ted Ferry has created a primer on living safely. *Home Safety Desk Reference* contains something for everyone and will be a valuable addition to the family or professional reference library. This book provides the information. You must place it in practice.

James Peter Couden
Safety Management and Education

PREFACE

The home can be hazardous and challenging to the good life. Home workshop tools, kitchen appliances, home-based sports activities, flammable clothes, aerosol cans, house cleaners and many other things combine to make the home a most hazardous place, worse than most workplaces.

Home Safety Desk Reference is about improving your lifestyle. We discuss many products that are a blessing for the homemaker and a source of fun, pleasure and relaxation. We point out their hazards and how to protect against them. You will find how to turn the dangers to your advantage for a long, injury-free life.

While the book aims at you, the consumer, emphasis is on protecting the younger child, so much so that a subtitle could easily be, "Making Your Home Safe for Children." Yet, we recognize the older and impaired user of consumer products as well.

Wherever practical, we advise on buying a product, its safe use, maintenance and storage—often in checklist format. With concern for the environment, you'll often find how to dispose of a product safely.

Home Safety Desk Reference is a good shelf reference, something to keep handy, next to the cookbooks, dictionaries and how-to guides. Refer to it often, particularly when you are ready to buy a product, or want to make your home safer for your children, yourself or older or handicapped occupants.

There has been much research on home hazards, particularly those products that cause the most injuries and the most problems. Much material in this book stems from work of the Consumer Product Safety Commission (CPSC). In its search to make the home a haven, the CPSC does more than any other group to make the home safe. While many staff members freely gave advice and assistance, special help came from Jerry Bjork, of the Seattle Field Office.

The National Safety Council was a frequent source of valuable information as well.

J.C. Smith and her University of Southern California staff did the original drafting. B. Lynn Beattie, M.D., Head, Division of Geriatric Medicine, University Hospital, University of British Columbia, Vancouver, British Columbia, Canada, reviewed Appendix 8 on Senior Affairs.

New consumer products enter the market by the tens of thousands each year. Products constantly improve, change and become more reliable. Each new product and each product improvement brings change—and each change may bring a new hazard, even while eliminating an old one. No truer or better advice exists than "Let the buyer (and user) beware!"

INTRODUCTION

When you consider that nearly every home is a work and recreational center, it should not be surprising to find that it is so dangerous. This book cannot survey all of the activities and consumer household products, but those that are presented here have potential accident and injury sources beyond our normal expectations.

You will find not only the potential hazards and the correct use of consumer products covered in this book, but also hints on buying and keeping products in safe condition. A bargain may be a bad buy if it later brings grief. A beautiful, clear-glass door, can shatter, cut and disable. Ask any builder about the bandaged people who come in to buy a safety glazed or tempered glass door after such an encounter.

When the subject of safety comes up, the average person thinks of work or traffic safety or sometimes sports. Seldom do we think of the less dramatic home safety. Because the home is private and seldom open for inspection, it is largely exempt from our concern about accidents. Further, it is only in recent years that there has been good data on home accidents. And it is still incomplete.

It continues to amaze us to find that we accidentally kill twice as many people at home as at work. Somehow it doesn't register that, year after year, falls are the number two cause of accidental deaths, right behind motor vehicles. Or that three times as many people receive disabling injuries from home mishaps as from highway accidents.

There has been progress in many areas of home safety. The fatality rate is lower.

The increase in hazards from new convenience products is somewhat offset by safer products and a wider awareness of some causes of accidents in the home. The causes are the same as for accidents in the workplace. That is, there are always unsafe acts and unsafe conditions, or both.

Organization

Home Safety Desk Reference has six sections and the Appendices. Each section has an introductory paragraph or two. These sections include:

1. **The Very Young** (with emphasis on the infant and youngster in the home). Products discussed range from baby carriages and cribs, to toys and walkers.

2. **Recreation.** This section deals with consumers of all ages. Some products such as darts (they are banned) get only a mention, while others receive considerable space.

3. **Homemaking.** Personal use items, packaging, canning, home maintenance products and housewares are covered in this section.

4. **Home Furnishings.** Included in this section are many appliances, home heating and such diverse products as carpets and smoke detectors.

5. **Fixing and Maintaining the Home.** This section covers areas from home construction to the garage, yard and garden. Subjects range from air quality

problems to lawnmowers, and from plastics to aerosols and hammers.

6. **Regulating Safety.** This section discusses the idea of consumer product hazard identification and control, mostly by regulation and voluntary standards. It covers the general background and importance of consumer safety and then moves into the serious business of hazardous products.

7. **Appendices.** We advise you to scan the Appendices early on. Included is a thorough discussion of fire and electricity basics that relates to testing and using consumer products. There are several safety checklists for a final check on some home consumer products and on home safety. The last appendix briefly addresses pets and their hazards, safety and health in the home.

Marketers say that people first look at a book or magazine different ways. Some riffle the pages like a deck of cards, while others start from the back and move forward. We suggest this: First, look at the Contents for a general picture of the topics. Then, go to the Appendices, near the back of the book. Next, pick any consumer product and see if it is in the index and on what page. Try it with two or three products. Not all will be listed. It would take several volumes to deal with *all* consumer products. However you will find listed most products that are used in or around the average home.

THE VERY YOUNG

This section of the *Home Safety Desk Reference* emphasizes safety for the infant, toddler and growing child. With it, we begin coverage of the safety needs of the consumer cycle, which starts with the very young.

It is important to recognize that what is safe and healthy for the adult is not always safe and healthy for the youngster. To experience the home from a child's point of view, you need to crawl on your stomach or hands and knees. It is a different world from the perspective of the nursery and developing years.

CHAPTER 1

THE SAFE NURSERY

Why start with the nursery in a book on safety in our daily lives? It is where safe home living should start.

From the onset of a child's life, products meant for him or her—cribs, playpens, toys, walkers, high-chairs, etc.—should be selected with safety in mind. Parents and caretakers of infants and young children need to know the potential hazards in the child's environment: hazards from the misuse of products or from products that are not well-designed.

CRIBS

Every year, 150 to 200 infants die in crib accidents in the United States. Another 40,000 are hurt seriously enough for treatment by a doctor.

Selecting new cribs

1. Buy cribs with corner posts less than 1/16 inch in height. Corner post extensions are a catch point for children's necklaces or cords around the neck.

2. If you buy bumper pads for the crib make sure they:
   - Fit around the entire crib.
   - Tie or snap into place.
   - Have at least six straps.
   - Use bumpers until the baby can pull up to a standing position, then remove them so the baby will not use them to climb out of the crib.

3. To keep your baby from chewing on the bumper pad straps or becoming caught in them, trim off any excess length. Use bumpers until the baby can pull up to a standing position, then remove them so the baby will not use them to climb out of the crib.

4. Buy a crib with as narrow a space as possible between the slats. Take a tape measure with you when you shop to be certain that slats are no more than 2 3/8 inches apart.

5. Be sure the mattress you buy fits the crib very snugly. An infant can suffocate if his or her head or body becomes wedged between the mattress and crib sides. If you can fit more than two fingers between the mattress and the crib, the mattress is too small.

6. Buy a crib with a latch or lock for the side that can't be easily tripped.

7. Buy a crib with as large a distance as possible between the top of the side rail and the mattress support. This discourages your baby from trying to climb out. Most crib accidents occur when infants fall while climbing out of the crib.

8. Check the crib's metal parts and the edges of the crib frame for sharp or rough edges.

9. Be aware that any decorative cutout areas might entrap a child's head. These often are found between the corner posts and the robe rail (the horizontal piece along the top of the crib).

10. Examine the crib for stability. Look for strength in the frame and headboard, a secure fitting mattress support structure and a label saying that the crib meets CPSC crib standards.

11. Remove all plastic wrapping and destroy it at once. Before throwing the plastic away, tie it in knots. Children

have suffocated while playing with plastic wrap. Never use thin plastic cleaning or trash bags as mattress covers. The plastic film may cling to children's faces and suffocate them.

Buying or using a second-hand crib

1. Note the guidelines listed under *Selecting new cribs*, as well as those that follow.
2. Make sure all hardware is present and in good condition.
3. When you erect the crib, make sure all pieces of the crib attach securely and the mattress fits snugly.
4. Check wood joints to make sure they are not coming apart.
5. If the crib has decorative knobs or tall extensions on the corner posts, remove them or cut them off flush with the top of the head and foot boards. Sand off splinters and sharp corners.
6. Some older crib and foot board designs may allow an infant's head to get caught between the corner post and the rail along the top of the crib or in other headboard openings. This could lead to strangulation. Look for a crib design either without the curved openings or corner posts, or one in which the opening is too large for the head to become caught in it.
7. Check to see that the slats are no more than 2 3/8 inches apart to avoid strangulation. You should not use a crib that does not meet this requirement. If you must, secure bumper pads around the entire crib and snap or tie in place with at least six straps. Cut off any excess length. Never use a crib with missing slats. Be sure that all slats fasten tightly in place.
8. Use a mattress that fits snugly. If you cannot replace a mattress with one that fits snugly, and you must continue to use the crib, roll large towels and place them between the mattress and crib

sides for a tighter fit. Fill the openings completely.

9. Buy a crib with as large a distance as possible between the top of the side rail and the mattress support. This discourages your baby from trying to climb out. Most crib accidents occur when infants fall while climbing out of the crib.
10. If you paint or refinish a crib, use only high quality household enamel paint or finishes that are labeled nontoxic. Let it dry thoroughly so there are no residual fumes. Do not use old paints you have around the house, especially if they are several years old. They may still contain a high level of lead additive. The labels on paint cans may recommend that you do not use that paint for cribs.

If you already have a crib or are refurbishing an antique

1. Note all the above guidelines for new and second-hand cribs.
2. Check the general condition of the crib. Is anything missing? Be sure that all slats and bolts and other fasteners are in place. Check with the manufacturer, if possible, for replacement parts.

No matter what the age of your crib

1. Set the mattress at its lowest position when your child can pull up to a standing position.
2. Don't leave any toys or other articles in the crib that your child can use to help him or herself climb out.
3. Don't keep your child in the crib once the height of the side rail is less than three quarters of your child's height.
4. Replace damaged teething rails. They can cut your child's mouth.
5. Don't use the crib as a playpen.
6. If you put crib extenders on the side rails, they should not make the side rails taller than the crib end panels. The extenders should have no easily

removable nuts or bolts and slats should be narrowly spaced.

7. Make sure all bolts and screws fit tightly.

8. Make sure the mattress support hanger securely fits the hanger on the post or corner.

9. See *Crib safety tips*.

Remember: These are only precautions. Children are ingenious. There is no substitute for close parental supervision.

Preventing strangulations in cribs that need repair. Here are two examples of the problem:

- A 5-month-old infant died when he was caught between the mattress and the crib side rail. A support hanger on the mattress frame had come off the hook attached to the crib and panel or corner post, creating a space in which the infant's head became entrapped.

- A 6-month-old infant became entrapped and suffocated when screws securing the side rail pulled loose from the corner post of the crib, creating a space between the rail and the mattress. A missing bolt caused a side rail to separate from the mattress, and the baby became caught in a space between the mattress and side rail.

Accidents such as these occur when hardware that holds together parts of the crib work loose, come apart or break. On some cribs, the design allows the mattress support hanger to come out of the supporting hook easily, which causes the mattress to drop to one side. This can happen when changing the sheets, raising or lowering the side drop or simply when the baby moves in the crib. In some cases, wood screws pull out of the wood, machine screws and nuts work loose and hooks which support the mattress bend or break. Note these guidelines when buying a crib or checking one that you now have.

Safety tips

1. If you place a crib next to a window, make sure that there are no drapery or blind cords within the child's reach.

2. Never hang any stringed object, such as a toy on a string or a laundry bag, on the corner post or nearby where a child could become caught in it and strangle. This has happened frequently. If you have toys with cords or elastic for hanging, cut off the strings. Never put a loop of ribbon or cord around a child's neck to hold a pacifier, or for any other reason.

3. Always lock the side rail in its raised position as soon as your child can stand. Adjust the mattress to its lowest position and remove the bumper pads or large toys. An active toddler will use anything to climb out of the crib.

4. When you child reaches 35 inches in height, he or she has outgrown the crib and should sleep in a bed. A crib is not a playpen.

5. Never use thin plastic cleaning or trash bags as mattress covers. The plastic film may cling to a child's face and cause suffocation.

6. Check the crib and replace any missing parts such as screws, bolts or mattress support hangers before placing your child in it. Make sure all screws and bolts are tight. Replace any screw in a wood part that you cannot tighten. On cribs where the mattress support is suspended by hangers and hooks on the end panels, check often to be sure they are still connected.

CRIB TOYS

Crib gyms and other brightly colored toys that stretch across or attach to the crib can be a hazard for active or older babies.

1. Be sure to install all crib gyms securely at both ends to prevent them from being pulled down into the crib.

2. Remove the crib gyms from the crib when the baby is 5 months or older, or can push up on the hands and knees.

3. Keep toys that hang from a string over a crib or playpen out of reach of a child.

4. Do not use crib toys with protrusions that could catch on clothing or other items around an infant's neck.

5. Children can strangle when they become entangled in ribbons or streamers hanging from wall decorations near the crib. Such decorations should be kept away from cribs and anywhere children might reach them.

Rattles. Children choke to death on rattles, by partially swallowing or sucking on them, or by falling with rattles in their mouths. Squeeze toys and teethers cause similar incidents. The squeeze toys often have handles small enough to lodge in a baby's throat and obstruct the airway.

New rattles must be large enough so they will not lodge in an infant's throat. They should be made so they will not separate into small pieces that can be swallowed or inhaled. The largest size rattle known to have become caught in a baby's mouth had an end that measured 1 5/8 inches across.

Small balls. Although persons of all ages choke on small balls (as large as 1 1/2 inches), most victims are under 5 years of age. Small balls meant for children under 3 are banned, but there remains concern about round toys or parts of toys that size. Keep small balls and other smooth, round objects away from those who put objects in their mouths, which includes all infants and most youngsters.

Pacifiers. Deaths have occurred from children choking on pacifiers and from strangulation by cords or ribbons that tie pacifiers around children's necks.

To protect against this, a pacifier must be nearly two inches wide to prevent it from blocking the child's windpipe if it is sucked into the child's mouth. Two ventilation holes allow air passage. Pacifiers must *not* have a ribbon or string attached. Look for sturdy construction when buying. Check to see that the nipple portion cannot separate from the mouth guard. The mouth guard itself should be firm, but not brittle.

Stuffed mobiles. Stuffed animal mobiles are a hazard when hung within an infant's reach. The cord on which the animal hangs from the corner posts or is strung across the crib can cause strangulation. Keep the mobile entirely out of reach or remove the cords and springs.

BABY GATES

Baby gates at the top of stairs or in open doorways prevent toddlers from falling or entering unsafe areas. But some baby gates are dangerous.

Accordion-style baby gates create strangulation and entrapment hazards. These gates have V-shaped openings along the top and bottom edges and diamond shaped openings between the slats. When toddlers try to climb through or over the gate, they may become trapped in the V-shaped or diamond shaped openings.

Selection

1. Choose a gate with a straight top edge or an accordion-style gate with small V- and diamond-shaped openings. Entrance to V-shapes should be no more than 1 1/2 inches in wide to prevent head entrapment.

2. Be sure the baby gate anchors firmly in the doorway or stairway it blocks. Children can push gates over and fall down the stairs.

3. Gates retained by an expanding pressure bar should be placed with the bar on the side away from the child. A pressure bar may be used by a child as a toehold to climb over the gate.

4. Do not use old-style gates with large V- and diamond-shaped openings.

Choose styles of baby gates that have straight edge tops and bottoms and rigid mesh screens, or *small* V-shaped or diamond-shaped openings.

Expandable enclosures

Circular wooden enclosures that expand accordion-style have the same strangulation and entrapment hazards as the accordion-style gates. Avoid accordion-style expandable enclosures with V-shaped or diamond-shaped openings.

HIGH CHAIRS

In one recent year, 7,000 youngsters received emergency treatment for high chair accidents. Most were under 4 years old. Nearly 25 percent were 1 year or younger, a very susceptible age group. Most of these patients received treatment in emergency rooms and were released. Common high chair mishaps can be very serious.

Falls from the chair. Falls are the most frequent high chair accident. They occur when straps are not used and when children are not closely supervised.

In infants under 1 year of age, the skull provides only slight protection to the rapidly growing brain. If the head strikes in a fall (particularly from a higher surface such as a high chair) the injury can be serious enough to block a child's normal development.

Many falls result from failure to use and secure safety devices...

- A 5-month-old girl suffered a contusion of the scalp when she fell from her high chair onto a concrete patio. The chair's restraining straps were not being used.

...and the failure to supervise children in a high chair...

- An 11-month-old girl fractured her skull in a high chair fall, though both the tray and a seat belt were in use. She unfastened the buckle of the belt, stood up and fell out.

...and the failure of the product to operate properly.

- A 17-month-old boy was treated for a head wound after he pushed the tray from the high chair and fell, striking the tray. A catch that locked the tray in place did not work properly.

The high chair tray may come loose if it does not lock because it is worn or poorly made. Often it gives way when it is not fastened correctly. Even a properly locked tray is scant protection if the child learns to detach it.

Two different restraints are common on high chairs:

1. A crotch strap, fastened to the tray and the chair, that runs between the legs of the child to prevent slipping under the tray. A crotch strap that fastens to the tray is no safe guard if the tray detaches. And a small, active child might move to one side of the strap and slip through.

2. A belt that fastens across the waist to prevent falls and deter standing up in the chair. The waist strap gives some safety if the tray comes loose, but it is not foolproof. Children can squirm out of waist straps, break them and learn to unbuckle them.

Restraining straps should withstand a 45-pound pull for at least 10 seconds. Unfortunately, you can only guess at this force.

Reducing the risk of falls

1. When buying a high chair, check the safety devices carefully. Compare the sturdiness of straps and belts on different models. Babies are often surprisingly strong. Remember that these restraints must be used at all times. If

a certain strap or belt is hard for you to fasten, there is a good chance you may not use it. Finally, check the tray and straps of the chair to be sure they are undamaged and work correctly.

2. Lock the tray tightly in place each time you place the child in the high chair. If a tray no longer locks properly, repair or replace it promptly.

3. Always use all restraining straps. Fasten the waist belt as soon as the child is in the chair. Unfasten it only to remove the child. This can prevent a fall during moments when the tray is not attached.

4. Never allow a child to stand up in a high chair.

5. Don't stray too far from a child in a high chair—especially if the child can unfasten safety straps or loosen the tray.

6. If you own a high chair without effective safety straps, buy a safety harness for your child. It offers good protection when attached to the chair.

7. If the seat of a high chair is slippery, make it more slip-resistant by attaching rough-surfaced adhesive strips to it.

Fall or collapse of the high chair. Another common high chair accident occurs when the chair collapses or falls. When a high chair falls, it is often because the child is boisterous. The child pushes off with the hands or feet from the table, stands up in the high chair or rocks it back and forth. Some chairs fall when older brothers or sisters climb on them. If a chair stands against a force of 15 pounds, it is probably acceptable. This is slightly more force than a toddler exerts. The less stable a high chair is, the more likely it is that a fall can occur.

- A 19-month-old boy received a head laceration when he pushed off from the kitchen table and his high chair tipped back and fell.

- A 11-month-old boy received a head laceration after his high chair collapsed. He had been sitting in the folding chair and kicking, causing the locking device to release.

To avoid such accidents:

1. Select a sturdy high chair with a wide base for stability. Always place the high chair on a level surface. Nearly all high chairs sold today have splayed legs or a wide base for stability.

2. Chairs that fold out of the way for storage or travel are the norm. Most have locking devices so that they do not collapse. When you open a chair it should lock automatically and stay open, even if you push on it fairly hard. Be sure that the locking device is secure each time you set up the chair. Many locks will not withstand the forces applied when folding them. If the chair remains standing for extended periods, check the locking device periodically, especially if your child is very active. Folding devices sometimes become worn with use and do not work properly.

3. Discourage children from being too active in the high chair. Don't let them stand in a high chair. Sounds like an impossible task, doesn't it? Nevertheless, the child should be taught that the high chair is not playground equipment.

4. Keep the high chair far enough away from the table or counter that a child can't push away from it. Hook-on chairs, which are used frequently in restaurants, can be forced away from tables by active youngsters pushing with their feet. The tabletop to which the chair fastens should be at least half an inch thick (for enough support), not glass (could shatter) and the table itself must be very steady. This rules out pedestal tables that can rock too easily.

5. When a high chair is not in use, put it in the corner and out of the way. An empty chair can fall if a child tries to climb into it without help or pulls on the chair to stand or maintain balance. If it folds, put it where it cannot be knocked over easily. Don't lean it against a wall.

Buying a chair—wood or plastic?

Many accidents occur when the tray is worn. Imagine the wear and tear on the tray after a year of daily fastening and un-fastening and locking and unlocking. Add to that the abuse from constant banging with utensils. No tray will hold up undam-aged after being dropped and scratched, but some will wear better than others.

Plastic seems to hold up better than wood. The plastic tray also seems to have a better shape to hold more food, retain cups and plates and to hold spilled liquids. Plastic chairs do not splinter and are easier to clean than wood. Finally, plastic seats are softer. If you buy a wooden chair you can also probably buy padded inserts for the chair. Be certain that the inserts work with the chair's restraint system and other features.

If you buy a second-hand high chair, check the condition of the straps, their attachment and that they work properly. If the chair does not have adequate safety straps, contact the manufacturer for re-placements.

Small parts a hazard. Plastic caps over the ends of metal tubes, and stickers and labels are a choking hazard. A de-termined child can loosen or pry them off. The best defense is to peel off stickers and labels and remove tags before use. Now and then check the chair for small parts that could be swallowed if they came loose.

Pinching and entrapment. A final hazard involves the pinching or catching

of part of a child's body—usually a fin-ger—by a high chair part.

• A 2-month-old girl lacerated her finger when it was caught in the tray locking mechanism.

The best way to avoid these accidents is to check the location of your child's hands when you attach or detach the tray. Be sure they are up and out of the way, not in the tray mechanism. See that there are no sharp areas on the locking device. These can make an injury much more severe.

Safety tips

1. Use the restraining straps. Remember that the feeding tray is not a good re-straint.
2. Be sure that the locking device on a folding high chair locks each time you set up the chair and that the tray locks properly in place.
3. Never allow a child to stand up in a high chair and do not stray too far from a child in a high chair—especially if the child shows an ability to undo safety straps.
4. Keep the chair far enough away from a table, counter or other surface so that a child cannot push off from it.
5. Don't let children play around a high chair or climb into it without help.
6. Don't let older children hang onto a high chair with a baby in it. This could cause the high chair to fall.

PLAYPENS

The most severe hazards involve drop-side mesh playpens and mesh cribs that can be left with a side in the down posi-tion. When one side is down, the mesh hangs loosely. This forms a pocket or gap between the edge of the floor panel and the side. Infants, including newborns, have rolled into these pockets and suffocated. Newer, mesh-sided playpens with drop sides carry labels that warn parents to never leave an infant in the pen with a side down. Older mesh playpens or cribs that do not have these warning labels may still be in use.

When buying

1. Look for mesh netting with very small openings.
2. Space between slats on a wooden playpen should not be more than 2 3/8 inches wide.

Buying or using a second-hand playpen

1. Check the slat spacing on older, wooden playpens. The space between slats should not be more than 2 3/8 inches wide.
2. Check vinyl- or fabric-covered top rails of playpens for holes and tears. If the material is vinyl, a teething child may chew off pieces and choke.

Safety tips

1. Never leave an infant in a mesh playpen or crib with the drop-side down. Infants have rolled into the space between the mattress and the loose mesh side and suffocated. Even when a child is not in the playpen, leave the drop-side up. Children may try to climb into a playpen and cut or pinch their fingers on the unlocked hinge device.
2. Remove large toys, bumper pads or boxes from inside playpens. Children can climb out on them.
3. Avoid tying any decorative items across the top of the playpen. They are a strangulation hazard.
4. If toys must be hung from the sides, the cords should be short enough that they won't wrap around a child's neck.
5. Children may use the top rail of the playpen for teething. Check vinyl- or fabric-covered rails often for holes and

tears. A teething child may chew off pieces and choke.
6. If staples fasten the mesh side to the floor plate, make sure none are loose.
7. Check the mesh and its connection to the top rail for loose threads. There have been reports of entanglements in stitching that unraveled.
8. Never use a playpen with holes in the mesh sides. These could entrap a child's head and cause strangulation.
9. Do not use the playpen once the baby can climb over the side.

RATTLES, SQUEEZE TOYS, TEETHERS

Since 1978, the law has required that rattles be large enough that they cannot become caught in an infant's throat, and made so they will not separate into small pieces that can be inhaled or swallowed.

Rattles have been swallowed partially or have been forced into the throats of children as young as 15 months. Squeeze toys and teethers are involved in similar incidents because the handles are small enough to lodge in a baby's throat and obstruct the airway.

An infant's mouth and throat are very flexible and can stretch to hold larger shapes than one might expect. The largest rattle known to have lodged in an infant's mouth/throat had an end that measured 1 5/8 inches in diameter.

Safety tips

1. Check all rattles, squeeze toys and teethers for small ends that could extend into the back of the baby's mouth. If you feel that the toy may be too small for safety, throw it away.
2. Take rattles, squeeze toys, teethers and other small objects out of the crib or playpen when the baby sleeps.
3. Like pacifiers, never fasten teethers around a baby's neck.

TOY CHESTS

Chests for storing toys take many forms: trunks, footlockers, blanket chests, deacon's benches and similar items. Most have vertically opening, hinged lids, and require the same precautions as regular toy chests.

In a 1-year period, more than 2,600 persons injured in accidents involving toy boxes and toy chests were treated in emergency rooms. Nearly 70 percent were children under the age of 4. Though the number injured may not seem high, the seriousness of these accidents has made toy box/toy chest hazards an area of great concern. In the U.S., at least 33 fatalities and two cases of permanent brain damage have resulted from the lids of toy chests falling on children's heads or necks. Most victims were under 2 years old.

Most toy chest injures involve bruises and cuts. Most occur when a child falls against the corner or edge of the box, a problem common to much furniture.

Toy boxes and chests with hinged lids present serious hazards. There is the danger that the heavy lid may fall with great force on a child. If it falls on the back of the neck or the head and traps the head inside, the child may not be able to get free.

Accidents happen when children use chests to pull themselves up, causing the lids to fall from the upright position, or when they try to open the lids themselves. Children who have reached over and into a chest when the lid dropped, have either fallen on their heads or had their necks trapped.

- A 2-year-old boy received a head laceration when he ran through his cluttered room, tripped on a toy block and struck the corner of his heavy wooden toy chest.
- A 1-year-old girl suffered cuts on her hand when the lid of her toy chest fell on it as she tried to reach her toys.

- A 13-month-old boy died of asphyxiation when his head was trapped inside his toy box by the fallen lid.

Another less frequent, but potentially fatal hazard is suffocation. These accidents happen when children climb into toy chests to hide or sleep. Because the chests have poor ventilation, children can suffocate.

Selection. If you plan to purchase a toy box or toy chest, or if you already own such a product, here is some advice:

1. If you buy a chest or box with a hinged lid, be sure that the lid is lightweight. It should have a flat inner surface and a device to hold it open in a raised position. It should not slam shut of its own weight. There is some evidence that a lid with protrusions or recessed areas on the inner side make it harder for a child to get free if the lid closes accidentally. Make sure that the device holding the lid open cannot pinch.
2. Check for rough or sharp edges on all metal parts and for splinters and other rough areas on wooden boxes. Rounded and padded edges and corners may prevent some injuries and reduce the severity of others.
3. The toy box or chest should be well-ventilated. This means ventilation holes in the lid and at least one side near the top. There should also be ventilation holes near the top on two opposite sides, or the product should have a lid that cannot close all the way.
4. Make certain that the lid of the toy chest does not have a latch. You should not be able to lock the lid of the toy box or chest.

Use of toy chests

1. Don't put the box in a heavily traveled area.
2. Caution children against running or roughhousing near it.

3. Keep the area toy chest area as free from clutter as possible to avoid falls.

4. Don't add to the hazard by making the footing underneath insecure. For example, don't use throw rugs on a waxed floor or place toy chests near stairways.

5. If you own a toy chest with lid that may be hazardous (one that is free falling, heavy, has a recessed inner surface or will not hold an open position) or if the box is ventilated poorly, remove the hazard by removing the lid. If this is impractical, install a lid support that holds the lid open in any position. Look for a lid support, such as a spring-loaded device, that does not require periodic adjustment.

Maintenance of toy chests

1. Check regularly to see that the device that holds the lid open works. It may need adjustment or repair.

2. Examine the box from time to time to see if it has developed rough edges or if protection such as padding has deteriorated.

3. In many households, the toy box or toy chest is homemade. Check your homemade chest for the above hazards.

WALKERS

Most baby walker accident victims are children under 2 years of age. Most injuries are to the head.

- A 2-year-old girl was trying to move herself from the wood floor onto the carpet. The wheels of the baby walker caught on the edge of the carpet and caused the walker to tip. She cut her lip and bruised her forehead when she fell.

- A little boy scooted along the floor after his mother who left him to go downstairs. The boy slid his baby walker to the edge of the staircase and fell down the stairway. He received a concussion.

- As a little girl's mother lifted her out of the X-frame walker, the frame collapsed and the child's fingers were pricked and cut by the sharp edges.

Accident patterns. An estimated 20,000 children receive emergency room treatment for baby walker injuries each year. Some communities and states have become so alarmed over walker mishaps that they have legislated against their sale. Almost all the victims are under two years of age. The above cases depict these accident patterns with baby walkers.

1. Tipping over. Many baby walkers can tip over easily when the child attempts to move from a floor to a rug, over a door threshold or onto any uneven surface (such as a gravel driveway or the lawn). Baby walkers also can tip over when the child leans to one side or attempts to pick up a toy.

2. Falling down stairs. Children in baby walkers can move to the edge of stairs and then fall down. This often happens when parents leave children alone and the stairs unguarded. Always use a guard fence at the stop of stairs to prevent falls. Baby walkers do not replace parental supervision.

3. Finger entrapment. Fingers can be pinched when lifting children in and out of some older X-frame baby walkers. The frame acts like a pair of scissors when it closes and can cut a child's skin. A rule for walkers/jumpers bans any exposed parts that can amputate, crush, cut, break or bruise a child's fingers or toes. This includes X-frame walkers, coil-spring baby bounders and walkers with holes or tubes that can injure a finger or toe.

Always remember that a baby walker gives your child new, exciting mobility before the child knows what is dangerous. This requires more supervision and an awareness of hazards, such as carpet edges, stairs and pinch points.

Selection of walkers

1. If you buy an X-frame baby walker, look for protective covers over accessible coil springs, spacers between scissoring parts and locking devices to keep the X-frame from collapsing.
2. Buy a baby walker with a wheel base that is both wider and longer than the frame of the walker itself, so that it will be stable. Stability prevents tipping. Look for plastic sleeves over coil springs. Metal parts should have no sharp edges or points.

Use of walkers

1. There have been several infant deaths when young children have peeled off and choked on plastic labels and decals. Pull off and throw away plastic labels and decals, but do not remove permanent paper warning labels.
2. Keep your infant and baby walker on flat, smooth surfaces—away from carpets, door thresholds and other obstructions. These can cause the walker to tip over.
3. Place guards at the tops of all stairways to prevent children and baby walkers from falling down the stairs.
4. Keep doors closed so children cannot slide baby walkers toward the stairs.
5. Watch your child to avoid accidents.

Safety tips

1. Place guards at the top of all stairways or keep stairway doors closed to prevent falls.
2. Use baby walkers only in areas where there are smooth surfaces.
3. Remember that walkers are not baby sitters.

BACK CARRIERS

An infant back carrier makes it easier to go shopping, walking or hiking with a baby. However, you should not use framed back carriers before a baby is 4 to 5 months old. At that age, the baby's neck can withstand jolts and not sustain a neck injury.

Buying a back carrier

1. Buy one to match the baby's size and weight. Try it on with the baby in it and check for:
   - Enough depth to support the baby's back.
   - Leg openings small enough to keep the baby from slipping out.
   - Leg openings large enough to avoid chafing the baby's legs.
2. Look for sturdy materials with strong stitching or large, heavy duty snaps to prevent the baby from slipping out.
3. Look for a back carrier with padded covering over the metal frame near the baby's face to protect the baby from bumps.

Safety tips

1. Restraining straps are vital. Children may stand up or try to climb out of the carriers. Always use the straps.
2. Be sure the child's fingers are clear when folding the joints.
3. Check frames for sharp edges, points or rough surfaces.
4. Check the carrier periodically for ripped seams, missing or loose snaps, frayed seats or straps. Repair them promptly or discard the carrier.
5. If leaning over or stooping, bend from the knees instead of the waist to prevent the baby from falling out of the back carrier and to keep from straining your back.
6. Don't give food to a child in a back carrier food. You cannot see if the child is choking while he or she is on your back.

BASSINETS AND CRADLES

The most frequent accidents involving bassinets and cradles are the result of children falling when the bottom of the bassinet or cradle breaks or when it tips or collapses.

Buying a bassinet or cradle

1. Look for a bassinet or cradle with a sturdy bottom and wide, stable base.
2. Follow the manufacturer's guidelines on the weight and size of babies who can safely use the bassinet or cradle.

Safety tips

1. Check the screws and bolts periodically to see if they are tight.
2. If the product has legs that fold for storage, make sure that the locks ensure that the legs do not fold while in use.
3. Mattresses and padding should be firm and smooth. Never use pillows.
4. Trim decorative bows and ribbons short and stitch them securely to prevent strangulation.

CARRIER SEATS

A carrier seat (infant seat) is not a child auto seat. It is to carry the infant from one place to another. Most carrier seat injuries occur when infants fall out of carrier seats, or when carrier seats fall while the infants are in them. Active infants can move or tip carrier seats by pushing off other objects with their feet.

Safety tips

1. The carrier needs a wide, sturdy base for stability.
2. Stay within arm's reach of the baby when the carrier seat is on tables, counters, couches and chairs.
3. If the carrier seat does not have non-skid feet, attach rough adhesive strips to the underside.

4. Always use the safety belts.
5. If the carrier seat has wire support devices that snap on the back, check for security. These can pop out causing the seat to collapse.
6. Remember that a carrier seat is not a substitute for an infant or child car seat. It should never be used in an automobile.

CHANGING TABLES

Most changing tables injuries occur when children fall from the table to the floor. Look for a table with safety straps and always use them. In the instant it takes to turn to reach for diapers and pins, an active baby can roll over and fall. A table with a guard rail offers some protection, but do not leave a baby unattended.

DIAPER PAILS

Young children get into everything. There are many reports of children who reached diaper pail cake deodorizers and ate them. There are also reports of children who fell head first into diaper pails and drowned. Keep diaper pails tightly closed and out of the reach of young children.

BUCKETS

Buckets filled with water present a special hazard to small children. In one recent 2-year period, there were 67 bucket drowning deaths. Most of these drownings were in 5 gallon buckets or containers used for mopping floors or for other household chores.

A young child's curiosity, combined with the ability to crawl and pull up can lead to danger. Most victims of bucket drownings are between 8 months and 1 year of age. In the last four months of his or her first year, a child learns to walk, at first gaining support by holding onto objects and then by taking unsteady free steps. Though suddenly more mobile, the child still is awkward and top-heavy. Drownings occur when children or toddlers crawl to a bucket filled with mop water or other liquids for household chores. They pull themselves up and lean forward to play in the water. When they topple in, they cannot free themselves and drown.

The 5 gallon bucket is particularly dangerous (even when only partly filled). It's heavier weight makes it more stable than a smaller bucket. It is unlikely to tip over when a child uses it to pull up. The 5 gallon containers are about half the height of these infants. With several gallons of water they weigh more than most children of that age.

Prevention

1. Never leave any bucket of water unattended where children may reach it.
2. Be alert that others tending your children—friends, relatives, baby sitters and care givers—know of the hazard.
3. Empty any large containers immediately after use.
4. When taking a break from a tasks requiring a bucket, put it out of the reach of children.
5. If large containers must be around a home with small children, order free warning labels by calling 1-800-282-5385, the Coalition for Container Safety.

HOOK-ON CHAIRS

Hook-on chairs replace high chairs and attach to the edges of tables. They can be hazardous when children fall out of them, dislodge them from the table or push off from a table.

Safety tips

1. Avoid placing the chair where the child's feet can push off and dislodge the chair from the table.
2. The restraining straps should be easy to use and they should fasten around the child when in the chair.
3. A chair with a clamp that locks it onto the table offers more safety.

4. Don't leave a child unattended.

PACIFIERS

The regulation on pacifiers provides good safety guidelines:

1. Pacifiers must be strong enough that they will not come apart into small pieces on which a baby could choke or suffocate.
2. Pacifier guards or shield must be large and firm enough to prevent drawing the pacifier entirely into a baby's mouth.
3. Pacifier guards or shields must have ventilation holes to make it possible to breathe if the baby gets the pacifier shield into its mouth.
4. Pacifiers cannot be sold with a string, ribbon, cord or yarn attached. They must have this label: "Warning—Do not tie pacifier around child's neck as it presents a strangulation danger."

Safety tips

1. Never fasten a pacifier or other items around your baby's neck. Children can catch the cord or ribbon on crib corner posts, pieces of furniture and even doorknobs.
2. Pacifiers may deteriorate with age, exposure to food, sunlight, etc. Inspect them often and discard them quickly if you notice a change in texture, tears, holes or weakening.

QUICK CHECKLIST

This checklist is a quick guide only. It does not replace reading more on the product in other sections of this book, or getting information from other sources. Proper and safe use is still a parent/user responsibility.

Yes/No

Back carriers

1. Carrier has restraining strap to secure child. ___
2. Leg openings small enough to prevent child from slipping out. ___
3. Leg openings large enough to prevent chafing. ___
4. Frames have no pinch points in the folding mechanism. ___
5. Carrier has padded covering over metal frame near baby's face. ___

Bassinets and cradles

1. Bassinet/cradle has a sturdy bottom and a wide base for security. ___
2. Bassinet/cradle has smooth surface. ___
3. No protruding staples or other hardware that could injure the baby. ___
4. Legs have strong, effective locks to prevent folding while in use. ___

Carrier seats

1. Carrier seat has a wide, sturdy, stable base. ___
2. Carrier has non-skid feet to keep from slipping. ___
3. Support devices lock securely. ___
4. Carrier seat has crotch and waist strap. ___
5. Buckle or strap is easy to use. ___

Changing tables

1. Table has safety straps to prevent falls. ___
2. Table has drawers or shelves that are easily reached without leaving the baby unattended. ___

Cribs

1. Slats are no more than 2 3/8 inches apart. ___
2. No slats are missing or cracked. ___
3. Mattress fits snugly, leaving less than two fingers space between edge of mattress and crib side. ___
4. Mattress support attaches securely to the head and foot boards. ___
5. Corner posts are no higher than 1/16 inch to prevent entanglement. ___
6. There are no cutouts in head and foot boards to allow head entrapment. ___
7. Drop-side latches cannot be easily released by the baby. ___
8. Drop-side latches securely hold sides in raised position. ___
9. All screws and bolts that secure components of crib together are present and tight. ___

Crib toys

1. Crib toys have no strings longer than 12 inches to prevent entanglement. ___
2. Crib gym or other toys suspended over the crib have devices that securely fasten to the crib to prevent from being pulled into the crib. ___
3. Parts of toys are not small enough to be a choking hazard. ___

Gates and enclosures

1. Gate or enclosure has a straight top edge. ___
2. Openings in gate are too small to entrap a child's head. ___
3. Gate has a pressure bar or other fastener that will resist forces exerted by a child. ___

High chairs

1. High chair restraining straps are independent of tray. ___
2. Tray locks securely. ___
3. Buckle on waist strap is easy to fasten and unfasten. ___
4. High chair has a wide stable base. ___
5. High chair has caps or plugs on tubing that are firmly attached and cannot be pulled off and choke a child. ___

6. If it is a folding high chair, it has an effective locking device. ___

Hook-on chairs

1. Hook-on chair has a restraining strap to secure the child. ___
2. Chair has a clamp that locks onto the table for added security. ___
3. Chair has caps and plugs on tubing that are firmly attached and cannot be pulled off and choke a child. ___
4. Chair has a warning never to place chair where child can push off with feet. ___

Pacifiers

1. Pacifier has no attached yarn, cord or string. ___
2. Shield is large enough and firm enough that it cannot be drawn into child's mouth. ___
3. Guard or shield has ventilation holes so baby can breathe if shield does go into mouth. ___
4. Pacifier nipple has no holes or tears that might cause it to break off in baby's mouth. ___

Playpens

1. Drop-side mesh playpen or mesh crib has warning label about never leaving a side in down position. ___
2. Playpen mesh has small weave (less than ¼ inch openings). ___
3. Mesh has no loose threads or tears. ___
4. Mesh attaches securely to top rail and floor plate. ___
5. Top rail has no tears or holes. ___
6. Wooden playpen has slats spaced no more than 2 3/8 inches apart. ___
7. If staples are used in construction, they are firmly installed and none are missing or loose. ___

Rattles / squeeze toys / teethers

1. Rattles and teethers have handles too large to lodge in baby's throat. ___
2. Rattles have sturdy construction that will not cause them to break apart in use. ___
3. Squeeze toys do not contain a squeaker that could detach and choke a baby. ___
4. Squeeze toys are not less than 1 5/8 inches in diameter and with long handles. (Cut out a hole 1 5/8" in diameter to use as a guide.) ___

Strollers

1. Stroller has a wide base to prevent tipping. ___
2. Seat belt and crotch belt are securely fastened to frame. ___
3. Seat belt buckle is easy to fasten and unfasten. ___
4. Brakes securely lock the wheel(s). ___
5. Shopping basket is low on the back and located directly over or in front of the rear wheels. ___

Toy chests

1. Toy chest has no latch to entrap child within chest. ___
2. Toy chest has a spring-loaded lid support that will not require periodic adjustment and supports the lid in any position to prevent lid slam. ___
3. Chest has ventilation holes or spaces in front or sides, or under lid. ___

Walkers

1. Walker has a wide wheel base for stability. ___
2. Walker has plastic sleeves over coil springs to avoid cuts. ___
3. Seat attaches securely to walker frame. ___
4. There are no X-frames that could pinch. ___

General household safety tips

1. Lock "danger" items—medicines, toxic bleaches, oven and drain cleaners, paint solvents, polishes and waxes in secure places, out of children's sight and reach. Don't leave these items under a sink or in plain view. Buy items in child-resistant containers.

2. Keep all thin, plastic wrapping materials, such as dry cleaning, produce and trash bags away from children.

3. Guard against electrical shocks. Cover unused electrical outlets with safety caps. Unplug electric hair rollers, curling irons and hair dryers when not in use. Children have been electrocuted by hairdryers, left plugged in, that fell into bathtubs or sinks.

4. Keep young children out of the bathroom unless you watch them closely. Children can drown or scald in very small amounts of water. Since 1973 about 400 children have drowned in bathtubs, basins, hot tubs, showers and jacuzzis, in as little as six inches of water. This usually happens after falling in head first. If you use a baby "supporting ring" device while bathing baby, be aware that the suction cups may suddenly release. The baby can then tip over or may slip between the legs of the device and drown. The baby may also slip between the legs of the device and become caught under the ring. Never leave a baby or young child unattended in a bathtub.

5. Keep children away from open windows to prevent falls. Don't depend on screens. They are there to keep insects out, not children in. Keep away from windows furniture on which a child can climb to a window sill or seat.

6. Infant bean bag pillows have been implicated in at least 30 infant deaths. Plans are underway to ban their sale. The pillows, manufactured by at least 10 companies, are similar. Most have loose filled, plastic-foam pellet filling, covered by a quilted material. Infants sink their head into the quilted cover and are unable to lift their heads or call out. Sometimes the loose bag have been pulled over their heads. All manufacturers have agreed to stop making the product. If a bean bag pillow is still in your home, discard it immediately.

SUMMARY

We see that the home is a dangerous place for children and that most hazards are under the control of parents or other residents. Actually, the hazards of home are not so neatly divided. Any hazard in the home may pose dangers for children. The contents of Chapter 2 focus on more child-specific hazards and their backgrounds.

SAFETY RECAP

1. Be certain there is not room between a frame and mattress, or pad, to trap an infant.

2. Don't use crib toys on which infants and small children in cribs or playpens might get caught.

3. Baby gates are needed, but some of them by design are hazardous.

4. A solid highchair with a plastic tray may be best, but it must be used as directed to be safe.

5. Net playpens, properly used, are best.

6. Don't buy toys small enough to be swallowed.

7. Buy toy chests with smooth edges, non-toxic paint and lids that cannot fall or otherwise harm children.

8. Purchase walkers that have no pinch points and will remain upright under all circumstances. Recognize that they make the baby highly mobile and are not baby sitters.

9. Use nursery equipment and toys as they were meant to be used.

10. Keep large buckets closed and away from small children.

11. Use the checklist in this chapter to check your home's safety.

BIBLIOGRAPHY

"Addendum, CPSC Publication Number 202," *The Safe Nursery*, Consumer Product Safety Commission, February 1989, November 1990.

"Ask Dr. Mark," *Family Safety and Health*, Chicago: National Safety Council, Winter 1992-1993, p. 4.

"Avoid the Danger," Washington, DC: Coalition for Container Safety.

"Baby Rattles," *Product Safety Fact Sheet, No. 86*, U.S. Consumer Product Safety Commission, December 1984.

"Baby Walkers," *Product Safety Fact Sheet, No. 66*, U.S. Consumer Product Safety Commission, 1981.

"Children Can Strangle When They Become Entangled in Wall Decorations," *Consumer Product Safety Alert*. U.S. Consumer Product Safety Commission, March 1992.

"CPSC Issues Warning that Choking on Small Balls Can be Fatal to Young Children," *Consumer Product Safety Alert*, U.S. Consumer Product Safety Commission, April 1988.

"CPSC Warns Consumers of Suffocation Danger Associated With Children's Balloons," *Consumer Product Safety Alert*, August 1988.

"CPSC Warns Consumers of Dangers With Infant Rattles," *Consumer Product Safety Alert*, U.S. Consumer Product Safety Commission, May 1985.

"CPSC Warns Consumers of Dangers With Mesh Drop-Side Playpens and Portable Cribs," *Consumer Product Safety Alert*, U.S. Consumer Product Safety Commission, July 1985.

"CPSC Warns Consumers of Dangers With Toy Chest Lids," *Consumer Product Safety Alert*, U.S. Consumer Product Safety Commission, February 1985.

"CPSC Warns of Strangulation with Crib Toys," *Consumer Product Safety Alert*, U.S. Consumer Product Safety Commission, July 1986.

"CPSC Warns Parents About Infant Strangulations by Failure of Crib Hardware," *Consumer Product Safety Alert*, U.S. Consumer Product Safety Commission, January 1985.

"Crib Safety—Keep Them on the Safe Side," *Product Safety Fact Sheet, No. 43*, U.S. Consumer Product Safety Commission, October 1985.

"Follow Up—A Ban on Deadly Infant Cushions," *Consumer Reports*, February 1991, p. 75.

"High Chairs," *Product Safety Fact Sheet, No. 79*, U.S. Consumer Product Safety Commission, September 1985.

"High Chairs: Which Ones Are Safer? Which Ones Hold Up?," *Consumer Reports*, October 1990, pp. 649-651.

Ignelzi, R. J., "Kid's Car Safety is a Critical Matter," *The Journals*, Seattle, WA, March 9-18, p. 20.

"Infant Falls," *Product Safety Fact Sheet, No. 20.*, U.S. Consumer Product Safety Commission, 1980.

Jones, Sandy and Werner Freitag, Guide to Baby Products, 3rd Ed., Yonkers, NY: Consumer Reports Books, 1991, pp. 45-60.

"Large Buckets Are Drowning Hazards For Young Children," *Consumer Product Safety Alert*, U.S. Consumer Product Safety Commission, July 1989.

"Pacifiers," U.S. Consumer Product Safety Commission.

"Some Baby Gates are Dangerous, Others are Safer," *Consumer Product Safety Alert*, U.S. Consumer Product Safety Commission, July 1987.

"Strings, Cords, and Necklaces Can Strangle Infants," *Consumer Product Safety Alert*, U.S. Consumer Product Safety Commission, July 1990.

"Stuffed Animal Mobiles Recalled," *Consumer Product Safety Alert*, U.S. Consumer Product Safety Commission, August 1987.

"The ABC's of Child Safety," C.L. Bete Co.

"The Safe Nursery," Washington, DC: U.S. Consumer Product Safety Commission, 1989, 18 pages.

"Tips for Baby's Safety (pamphlet)," Washington, DC: U.S. Consumer Product Safety Commission, September 1985.

"Toy Boxes and Toy Chests," *Product Safety Fact Sheet, No. 4*, U.S. Consumer Product Safety Commission, July 1984.

CHAPTER 2

DANGEROUS YEARS FOR CHILDREN

As a companion chapter to Chapter 1, this chapter addresses the safety of older children. The first step in protecting children is understanding their skills and abilities at various ages.

CHILD SKILLS

Each year as many as 15,000 children die in accidents. Many of those deaths could be prevented by purchasing the appropriate children's toys, furniture and equipment, and by remembering a few common sense rules.

Ages 0-1

1. Never leave a baby alone on a table or in a bathtub.
2. Use a firm mattress, but not a pillow, in a crib.
3. Never use a lead-based paint on toys and children's furniture.
4. Keep small objects away from children.
5. Use harnesses on high chairs.
6. Keep children away from stoves.

Ages 1-2

1. Secure cabinets and doors, as children this age are able to open some doors.
2. Toddlers can climb, so be aware of open windows, and watch children closely around swimming pools.
3. Take special care to keep knives and appliances out of reach.

4. Children are able to open cans and bottles, so keep them out of reach and be informed about poisons.

Ages 2-3

1. Install hand rails on stairways.
2. Block stairways with gates.
3. Avoid throw rugs and toys on which children can slip or trip.
4. Don't allow children to run with things in their mouths.
5. Watch for weakened and broken toys and keep them out of use.
6. Explain safe activity to children.

Ages 3-4

1. Because children this age are developing skills, teach the safe way to ride tricycles, throw balls, climb trees and use tools.
2. Avoid placing television sets or other items on top of bookcases or other furniture that can tip over if children try to reach by climbing on shelves or drawers.

INFANT FALLS

Accidental falls are the leading cause of hospitalizations and emergency care visits for infants and young children. Most falls are minor, but some can be severe. The younger the child and the higher the fall, the more likely it is that the injury will be serious.

The skull of an infant is quite fragile in the first few months of life and, unfortunately, it is the infant's head that is most likely to strike the floor or any object in a fall. A head injury at this age can cause permanent damage.

- A 5-month-old girl fell from a kitchen table while her mother was dressing her. The mother dropped a shirt and while picking it up, the baby rolled off the table, striking her head on a radiator. The baby suffered a skull fracture.

- A 1-year-old boy fractured his left arm after he fell out of his crib onto a carpeted floor. The side rail of the crib was lowered.

How do you protect your children from falls from high places? The best way to prevent many falls is to avoid leaving children unattended anywhere. Always keep a constant watch when you have a child on a bed, sofa, counter top, dressing table or similar piece of furniture.

Use guard fences to block flights of stairs to children too young to use them safely. Windows pose a special problem because a small child can squeeze through a window opening as small as 5 inches. You can buy window guards at most hardware stores, but not block windows that provide access to fire escapes. Screens will not prevent falls, so keep children and furniture on which they can climb away from windows.

CHILD'S ABILITIES/INTERESTS

Knowing the abilities and interests of the average child in an age group can help you select appropriate toys. Here, abilities and interests of each age group are classified as physical, mental and social. Simply select the age group in which you're interested and choose a toy that fits the physical and mental abilities or social interests of that age group. You'll find more specific suggestions listed in the references.

Young infants, birth to 6 months:

1. Physical: Visual focus matures; follows objects with eyes; learns to localize sounds and turns to see them; gains control of hands; discovers feet; begins to sit with support; rolling, rocking and bouncing.

2. Mental: Explores with eyes and ears; starts to use hands and feet; enjoys creating own effects; becomes aware of novelty and strangeness in people and objects; develops preferences; imitates simple movements; starts to do one thing at a time.

3. Social: Develops special interest in some people; smiles; quiets on contact; seeks attention; knows different people; coos and gurgles; plays with sounds; listens to voices.

4. Safety summary for toys: Nontoxic materials; no sharp or pointed edges; safe for mouthing; nonbreakable, with no glass or brittle plastic; no small parts to lodge in throat, ears or nose; no electrical parts.

Older infants, 7 to 12 months:

1. Physical: Begins to sit alone; creeps and crawls; pulls to a stand and walks alone; moves about; holds onto furniture; grasps objects with finger and thumb; wants to do things with objects; enjoys bath play, kicking and splashing; holds objects with one hand and manipulates with other.

2. Mental: Develops interest in appearing and disappearing people and things; interest in containers, dropping objects, exploring and operating simple mechanisms; bangs, pushes, pulls, twists, squeezes, shakes, throws, open/shuts, empties and fills; remembers people and things; new interest in picture books.

3. Social: May fear strangers or react badly to change; watches and imitates others; sensitive to social approval; wants attention;

enjoys simple games like peek-a-boo; plays with language; knows own name; likes to appear and disappear, play with empty containers, search for things and explore.

4. Safety summary for toys: See summary for young infants.

Young toddlers, 1-year-olds:

1. Physical: Endless exercise of physical skills; lugs, dumps, pushes, pulls, piles, empties and fills; likes to climb; kicks; more tries at manipulation; interested in many small objects; strings large beads; uses screw motion.

2. Mental: Displays interest in cause/effect and in mechanisms; very curious; likes action toys; combines objects, builds blocks and stacks; likes hidden objects and simple puzzles; marks on paper; groups similar toys; points; enjoys water and sand play.

3. Social: Enjoys mostly solitary play; tries adult tasks; shows affection for others; likes being read to and interactive games.

4. Safety summary for toys: Sturdy; not likely to break into small pieces and strong enough for child to stand on; nontoxic materials; no sharp edges or points; too large to lodge in throat, ears or nose; no detachable small parts or parts that can pinch or entrap small fingers, toes or hair; no easily exposed straight pins, sharp wires or nails in construction; no electrical parts.

Older toddlers, 2-year-olds:

1. Physical: Skilled at simple, large muscle tasks; much physical testing; throws and retrieves; pushes self on wheeled objects; better hand and finger coordination plays with small objects; likes to do somersaults and rough and tumble play.

2. Mental: Interested in attributes of articles; can match similar objectives; plays with patterns and sequences;

displays counting skills; solves problems in head, likes creative activities and fantasy play.

3. Social: Remains interested primarily in parents; plays cooperatively with others; uses language; engages in game-like interactions and pretend play with others; enjoys hearing simple stories; desires independence.

4. Safety summary for toys: See summary for young toddlers.

Preschoolers, ages 3 to 5 years:

1. Physical: Runs, jumps, climbs, balances, rolls, gallops and hangs; likes risks; increases finger control; picks up small objects; builds with expertise; interested in ball games; likes acrobatics and outdoor play.

2. Mental: Familiar with common shapes and colors; interested in number activities, matching/sorting; draws pictures; solves problems in head; makes plans and follows; produces designs and pictures that mean something; interested in science, animals and time; prefers realism; interested in dramatic plays; begins to be goal-oriented.

3. Social: Shares, takes turns and is cooperative and conforming; likes group pretend play and simple board games; is not ready for competition; displays sex differentiation in play roles.

4. Safety summary for toys: Not likely to break easily into small pieces, with no glass or brittle plastic or glass; nontoxic materials, with no sharp points or edges; no electrical parts, unless supervised by adult.

Primary school children, ages 6 to 8 years:

1. Physical: Displays large muscle abilities and interested in related sports; not ready for competition; displays small muscle development as in drawing and sewing, practice in target games.

2. Mental: Reads, spells, prints; does simple math and tells time; interested in nature and collecting things; likes tricks and models; likes to produce finished art, models, crafts and sewing.

3. Social: Interested in peers; prefers same-sex games; plays cooperatively and interested in fair play; likes dramatics, cops and robbers; develops wider community interests.

4. Safety summary for toys: No sharp points or edges; no electrical parts, without adult supervision; appropriate safety equipment and apparel.

Older school children, ages 9 to 12 years:

1. Physical: Interested in and ready for most sports; enjoys dexterity games, complex constructions and models; displays small muscle ability for formal dance, arts and crafts.

2. Mental: Plays and carries out activities on own; displays independent thinking and individual differences; evaluates ideas and people, interested in hobbies, collections, stories and plays, gadgets, inventions and computers; shows increased ability to arrange, classify and generalize.

3. Social: Works cooperatively; participates in clubs and groups; likes complex card and table games, dramatics; interested in wider community.

4. Safety summary for toys: Appropriate safety equipment and apparel for activities; no electrical parts, without adult supervision.

TOYS

Skates, tricycles, toy trucks, cars and airplanes, toy boats, wagons and balls are among children's favorite playthings. But, each year about 150,000 people receive emergency room treatment for injuries associated with toys.

Falls are the most common accident. However, many serious injuries result from children swallowing small parts or placing tiny toys in noses and ears, exploding gas-powered toys, flammable products and sharp edges. Some toys, especially electrically operated ones, can be extremely hazardous for young users. The dangers include electric shocks and burns, especially if the toy has a heating element. Many mechanical hazards are common to toys, such as sharp edges, points and dangerous moving parts.

The Toy Manufacturers of America, Inc., founded in 1916, is the trade association for U.S. producers and importers of toys. One of TMA's main activities is an ongoing toy assurance program. TMA points to nearly 60 years of safety affiliation with the National Safety Council, the National Bureau of Standards, the American National Standards Institute (ANSI) and the American Society for Testing and Materials (ASTM). Together, the TMA and the Consumer Product Safety Commission (CPSC), have taken leadership roles in developing toy safety standards.

The CPSC, spending more than half its annual budget on children, has issued regulations that specify manufacturing, construction and performance requirements meant to reduce the risk of injury from toys. These regulations are incorporated in the industry's voluntary standard, ASTM F963. This standard covers toys, but bicycles and home playground equipment have their own standards. The regulations give certain labeling requirements. Some important requirements are:

Mechanical

1. The product must have enclosures strong and rigid enough to preserve the safety and integrity of various electrical parts in normal use, even with any foreseeable abuse.

2. Any potentially hazardous moving parts will be enclosed or guarded to minimize the chance of accidental contact.

3. The product must have strong handles and knobs that will not crack or break off, even when abused.

4. If it has pressurized enclosures (such as steam chambers), it will be equipped with an automatic pressure-relief valve that will discharge in the safest possible direction.

5. Toy sewing machines must minimize the chance of a needle piercing a child's finger.

Electrical

1. All live electrical parts must be securely enclosed. These enclosures must be designed so they cannot be opened with ordinary household tools such as screwdriver or pliers. This does not apply, for obvious reasons, to the housings of replaceable light bulbs.

2. Switches, motors, transformers and the like must be mounted to prevent any nonfunctional movement and possible damage.

3. Heating elements must be supported and prevented from making contacts that might produce shock hazards.

4. Products must not be designed for use with water unless the electrical components are in a sealed chamber completely separate from the water reservoir (as in toy steam engines).

5. Products that need cleaning with a wet cloth must be designed to prevent seepage of water into electrically active areas that might produce hazardous conditions.

6. Electrical plugs require a finger/thumb grasping area and a safety shield to protect small fingers from accidentally touching energized prongs when the toy plugs into a wall outlet.

Thermal. There is a regulation that specifies maximum temperatures and reliable electrical construction for electrically operated toys. Such toys must bear warning labels stating they are not recommended for children under a certain age. If the toy has a heating element, the manufacturer may not say that the toy is for a child under 8. More comprehensive standards apply to "children-under-eight toys."

1. Products must not exceed maximum surface temperature requirements. These temperatures are based on accessibility of a particular surface, its function and its composition. A surface to which a child cannot gain access, for instance, can reach a higher temperature than a knob or carrying handle.

2. Containers for holding molten compounds and hot liquids must be designed to minimize spills. No container should melt or become deformed when heated.

Testing. Rigorous testing insures that products conform to these requirements in ordinary use and during foreseeable abuse. Toys are dropped, subjected to compression forces and run for long periods of time. Motors are overloaded, pressure-relief valves are blocked and handles and knobs crushed. This is only part of the punishment that these products undergo to simulate the treatment that they might receive from a child. All products must still comply with safety requirements after this testing.

Labeling. The requirements specify that certain precautionary information will be in the labels on children's electrical products. The labeling should help buyers choose the appropriate toy for a child's age group, and warn of potential hazards. Each product package must carry a cautionary message and a minimum age requirement. No item with a heating element may be recommended for children under 8 years of age. Some hobby items, such as wood burning kits, reach very high temperatures and are exempt from certain maximum surface temperature regulations. These items are not for children under 12 years of age. Certain areas of the product itself must also have labels:

1. Accessible surfaces that exceed specified maximum temperatures must carry a warning of the danger.
2. Toys with replaceable electric lights must carry a warning of the maximum safe wattage for a replacement bulb and a notice to disconnect the plug before changing the bulb.
3. Nonreplaceable lights will be so marked.
4. Products not meant to be immersed in water must carry a notice to that effect.

Instructions. All cautionary statements that appear on a toy or its package must also appear in the instructions that must accompany it. These instructions must cover all aspects of safe use and maintenance. They must advise parents to examine the product periodically to be sure it is in safe working order. These requirements help assure that electrically operated products for children will be as safe as expected. But this solves only part of the problem. Before we can reduce injuries from electrical toys, adults must buy these products selectively. They must oversee their use in the home, and repair or discard them at the first sign of deterioration.

Selection. Do not buy a toy for a child too young to use it. Always check the age recommendation. If a label reads "Not recommended for children under 8 years of age," this does not mean that every 8-year-old child is mature enough to operate it. You must still consider an individual child's capabilities. Plug-in electrical toys should carry the Underwriters Laboratories mark. Battery-operated toys eliminate shock and cord hazards.

Use. Read the instructions with the product carefully and then read them with any child who will be using the product. Be sure that the child knows how to use the item safely, understands the instructions and warning labels and knows the hazards of misusing the toy. Keep the instructions with the toy or in a safe place where they can be found easily.

Supervision. Supervise the use of an electrical product. The amount of supervision again is a matter of judgment. Consider both the maturity of the child and the nature of the toy. For example, there is a great difference between a 2-year-old playing with an electric football game and a 9-year-old using a toy oven. Be sure that the plug of an electrical product fits snugly into wall outlets or (if they must be used) extension cord receptacle. No prongs should be exposed. Teach children always to disconnect an electrical appliance by grasping the plug, not by pulling on the cord. Keep infants and toddlers out of the area where an electrical toy is being used.

Storage. Immediately after use, all electrical toys should be put in dry storage areas out of the reach of younger children.

Maintenance and disposal. Deterioration of electrically operated toys can present many hazards. It is necessary to check their condition periodically. Be alert for broken parts, frayed cords and damage to enclosures of wiring and other protected parts. Preventive maintenance is critical for those products manufactured many years ago.

Only an adult or responsible older child should replace a light bulb on an electrical toy. The replacement bulb must be of the proper wattage and the plug disconnected for the change.

On wooden toys, edges that might become sharp or surfaces covered with splinters should be sanded smooth. When repainting toys, avoid using leftover paint, since older paints may contain more lead than newer paints. Check outdoor toys for rust or weak parts that could become hazardous. Discard at once any product that is so severely damaged that proper repairs cannot be made.

BANNED TOYS

There is authority to ban from sale in the U.S. hazardous toys and other children's products with the following features:

1. Toy rattles containing rigid wires, sharp points or loose, or small objects that could become exposed and cause cuts, punctures or other injuries.
2. Any toy with noise-making parts that could be removed by a child and swallowed or inhaled.
3. Lawn darts and other sharp pointed items for outdoor use that could cause puncture wounds, unless they include cautionary language, proper directions and warnings. They cannot be sold by toy stores or stores dealing largely in toys and other children's articles.
4. Any doll, stuffed animal or similar toy with parts that could become exposed and cause cuts, punctures or other similar injuries.
5. Caps for use with toy guns that cause noise above a certain level. Others may have a label "Warning—Do not fire closer than one foot to the ear."
6. "Baby bouncers" and similar articles that support very young children while sitting, walking or bouncing, which could cause injury to the child such as pinching, cutting or bruising.
7. Toys known as clacker balls (ceramic balls connected by ropes) that could break off or fracture, causing injury. Later versions made of plastic are not banned.

Suggestions

Each year 5,000 new toys enter the marketplace. A typical holiday season will find 150,000 different kinds of toys for sale in a million retail outlets. It is impossible for you to examine every toy and visit each sales outlet. It is impossible for parents, relatives and older sisters and brothers to check every new toy, as well as old toys, for hazards. Here are some guidelines:

1. Buy toys that suit the skills and abilities of the child. Avoid toys that are too complex for young children.
2. Look for labels that give age recommendations or safety information, such as "nontoxic."
3. Watch out for toys that have sharp edges, small parts or sharp points. Avoid toys that produce extremely loud noises that can damage hearing and propelled objects that can injure eyes.
4. Explain to the child how to use toys properly and safely.
5. Always supervise young children while they play.
6. Insist that be put their toys away so won't be broken and to avoid tripping or falling on them.

Examine toys periodically so that repairs can be made or broken toys discarded.

The right toy for the right age. The Consumer Product Safety Commission (CPSC) has printed guides to selecting the appropriate toys for a child's age. They are in the bibliography. Order from the CPSC without charge. The following material comes from those publications.

Interested parties. Three parties have major roles in deciding the right toy to buy for a child between birth and 12 years of age. They are the government, the toy industry and parents.

What the government does:

1. For all ages
   - No shock or thermal hazards in electrical toys.
   - Lead in paint limited.
   - No toxic materials in toys.
2. Under age 3
   - Unbreakable—will withstand uses and abuse.
   - No small parts or pieces that could become lodged in the throat.
   - Infant rattles large enough not to become lodged in the throat and constructed so as not to separate into small pieces.
3. Under age 8
   - No electrically operated toys with heating elements.
   - No sharp points on toys.
   - No sharp edges on toys.
4. Classifies toys by five age groups
   - Young infants (birth to 6 months).
   - Older infants (7 to 12 months).
   - Young toddlers (1 year olds).
   - Older toddlers (2 year olds).
   - Preschoolers (ages 3, 4 and 5).
5. Classifies toys by five categories
   - Active. Push and pull and ride-on toys, outdoor gym equipment, sports equipment.
   - Manipulative. Construction toys, puzzles.
   - Make believe. Dolls, puppets, transportation toys.
   - Creative. Musical instruments, arts and crafts, audio-visual equipment.
   - Learning. Games, skill-development toys, books.

What the industry does with the voluntary toy safety standard:

1. Puts age and safety labels on toys.
2. Puts warning labels on crib gyms advising that they should be removed from the crib when babies can raise on hands and knees (to prevent strangling).
3. Assures that toy chest lids will stay open in any position to which they are raised and not fall unexpectedly.
4. Makes strings on crib and playpen toys no longer than 12 inches, so cords cannot become wrapped around children's necks.

What a parent can do:

1. Look for and read age and safety labels on toys.
2. Explain and/or show children how to use toys properly and safely.
3. Keep toys intended for older children away from younger children, who could be injured by them.
4. Check all toys periodically for breakage and potential hazards. Repair damaged toys and immediately discard dangerous toys.
5. Store toys safely and teach children to do so also. Check toy boxes and shelves for safety.

Summary of points to consider in buying toys:

1. Choose playthings suitable for the child's age and abilities.
2. Buy items that are flame-retardant or flame-resistant, washable and nontoxic.
3. Throw away plastic wrappings right away.
4. Read the instructions. Make sure the toy's proper use is clear to you and the child.
5. Buy the safety equipment appropriate for a toy or activity. For example: buy a helmet with a bike; knee and shoulder pads and helmet with a skateboard; and goggles with a chemistry set. Wear or use safety equipment when playing with a child.
6. Make sure ride-on toys are the right size for the child. If they are too small

they'll be unstable; if they are too big, they'll be hard to control.

7. Watch for these toy dangers:
   - Sharp edges. New toys for children under 8 years must have no sharp edges, but toys can break.
   - Small parts. Choking kills more children under 6 than any other home accident. Children can choke on anything small enough to fit in their mouths but large enough to lodge in their throats: chunks of hot dogs, grapes, carrots and pieces of toys. New toys should not have pieces that can be swallowed, but check all toys, especially older toys that may break.
   - Loud noises. Read labels for safe use of toys that make noise to avoid damage to hearing.
   - Cords and strings. These can become wrapped around a child's neck. Remove crib gyms from the crib once the child can pull up on hands and knees. Never attach toys with strings more than 12 inches long to crib gyms or playpens.
   - Sharp points. Toys for older children may have sharp points that can injure a small child. Stuffed toys may have wires inside them that will protrude if the toy comes apart.
   - Propelled objects. Make sure children know how to use projectile toys that shoot objects, such as arrows, into the air. Children should never play with adult hobby or sport equipment. Arrows used by children should have soft cork tips, rubber suction cups or other protective tips to prevent injury. Check to make sure the protective tips are secure and that the toy cannot fire other things, such as pencils.
   - Inappropriate for age. Follow the age guidelines on toys. Older children should never leave their toys where younger children can reach them. Rubber balloons are not to be used by children under 3. Uninflated balloons and pieces of broken balloons are the leading cause of suffocation in children.
   - Electric toys. Make sure electrical toys meet the standards described in this book. Toys with heating elements acceptable for children over 8, when used under adult supervision.
   - Small toys. Be sure that toys for infants are too large to swallow. See that foam toys are too big to be swallowed even when they are completely compressed.

8. Store toys in a safe place. Keep toys requiring adult supervision under lock and key. All toys should be put away when they are not in use so they won't be a hazard. Store toys for older children on shelves out of reach of little ones. If you must have a toy chest, be sure the lid is removable or has a spring-loaded support so that it cannot drop on a child. Toy chests should have ventilation holes and open easily from the inside.

9. Frequently check toys for damage. Check wooden toys for splinters or sharp edges and sand them when necessary. Check outdoor toys for rust. If you repaint toys, use new paint. Old paint may have hazardous levels of lead or other chemicals. If a toy cannot be fixed, throw it away immediately.

10. Provide a safe place for play indoors and out. Watch for things that children can trip over, fall from or bump into. Always supervise children closely when they are playing in or around water. Assemble home playground equipment correctly, making sure it is anchored firmly on a level surface of grass or wood chips. Set safety rules for play on all play equipment and enforce them. Teach children to be especially careful near traffic and on the neighborhood

streets. They should not walk or ride their bikes, skateboards or other wheeled toys across streets.

PREVENTING SUFFOCATION AND CHOKING

Suffocation and choking claim many young victims. Infants do not have the physical strength to get out of some suffocation and choking situations and youngsters try to put most things in their mouths.

Balloons. There have been several instances of deaths caused by choking on balloons. Most victims are under the age of 6. Some children suck uninflated balloons into the their mouths while trying to inflate them. In other situations, children have chewed or sucked on uninflated balloons. Also, when a balloon breaks, pieces can be drawn into the mouth. Many inflated balloons easily mold into shapes that go into a child's mouth. These parts also mold easily into the shape of the mouth or throat, cutting off all air. A fully inflated balloon offers little danger for children. But, because of the suffocation danger, children under 6 years should not play with balloons without strict supervision.

Choking, itself, is the fourth leading cause of death in younger children, especially those under the age of 3. Here are some steps to avoid these tragic deaths.

Suffocation

1. Avoid using plastic packaging such as cleaning or trash bags as mattress covers.
2. Be very careful that children do not lay on beds on which they can fall into the sides or the bed covers can drape about them.
3. Keep pillows and soft toys out of the crib. Do not hang things where the child can pull them down over the face.
4. Don't allow ribbons or cords to be placed around a child's neck.
5. Don't use the bean bag type of pillows.
6. Don't leave children in a mesh playpen with the drop side down.
7. Don't let young children play on recliner chairs. It is possible for a child to get his or her head caught in the space between the chair seat and leg rest. The child's weight allows the leg rest to close on the youngster.
8. Don't allow children under 6 to play with balloons while unsupervised.
9. Do not use accordion-style safety gates if the openings are large enough for a child's head or if the top of the gate can catch on a child's clothing.
10. Check to be sure that there are no chests with lids or refrigerators that might close on children seeking a cozy place to play.

Choking

1. When buying toys, look at the label or box for the suggested age range. A toy that is suitable for a 5-to-7-year-old could be a choking hazard to a younger child.
2. Check toys often to be certain that they don't have loose parts.
3. Cut up foods like hot dogs or grapes into pieces that can be easily swallowed.
4. Don't give younger children foods like hard candies, nuts, raisins, grapes, popcorn or foods with pits and seeds.
5. Avoid giving children raw food like raw carrots that cannot be easily chewed.
6. Keep floor areas clean and clear of small items that could be swallowed. Children can choke on such things as safety pins, nails, tacks, screws, marbles, jewelry and small batteries.

For children under 1 year:

1. Place the baby on your forearm, face down and with head down. Rest your forearm on your thigh for support.

2. Use the heel of your hand to hit the baby four times on the back, high between the shoulder blades.

3. If this does not work, support the baby's head and place the baby on his back on your thigh with the head lower than the trunk. Give four chest thrusts with two fingers on the breast bone, between the nipples.

4. Repeat this back and front sequence until the airway opens or until medical help arrives.

For children over 1 year:

Standing behind the child, wrap your arms around the child's waist. Make a fist of one hand. Place the thumb of the fist against the child's abdomen, a little above the navel and below the breastbone. Grab your fist with the other hand and press the fist into the abdomen with a quick, upward thrust.

For foreign object in the nose. Sneeze out the object by sniffing pepper or tickling the other nostril. Do not try to probe for the article, as that can push the article into the nose. Consult a doctor.

For foreign object in the ear. If the object cannot be seen or easily dislodged, consult a doctor. Do not try to get it out with a pin, toothpick or other slender object. It is easy to damage the ear canal or eardrum.

STROLLERS AND CARRIAGES

In a typical year, emergency rooms treat about 11,500 children under 5 years old for injuries involving strollers and carriages. Select nursery equipment that is appropriate for the child's age. Have your child sit in each stroller you consider.

Buying a stroller

1. Choose a stroller and carriage with a wide base to prevent tipping, even when the baby leans over the side. If the seat reclines, make sure that the stroller does not tip backward when the baby lies down.

2. If a stroller has a shopping basket to carry packages, it should be low on the back of the stroller and in front of, or directly over, the rear wheels. Avoid hanging pocketbooks and shopping over the handles because they may cause the stroller to tip.

3. Check the seat belt to make sure it is strong and durable, fits snugly around the child and can be easily fastened and unfastened. Use the seat belt each time you place the baby in the stroller.

4. Make sure the brake is convenient to operate and actually locks the wheels. Brakes on two wheels provide an extra measure of safety.

Safety tips

1. When folding or unfolding a stroller, keep the child away from it. Children's fingers have been cut off by folding mechanisms.

2. Always secure the seat belt.

3. Never leave a child alone in a stroller.

4. A stroller is not a toy. Don't allow children to use one as a plaything.

5. Babies can slip feet first through a leg opening and become caught by the head between the seat and the handrest bar.
   - Never leave a child unattended in a stroller, especially if the seat's backrest is in the flat "carriage" position.
   - Be aware that infants only a few weeks old can creep or move when asleep in a stroller.

CHILD CAR SEATS

All states have child passenger restraint laws. Stringent federal standards apply to all child safety restraint systems. All systems sold in stores must meet stringent requirements. There have been several recalls of well-regarded seats and you should be certain that there is not a recall for the seat you are purchasing.

Your local library has sources that can supply this information.

Types of child car seats

In addition to car's safety belts, there are four auto child restraint systems to consider:

1. Infant seats (birth to about 9-12 months). An infant safety seat cradles the child in a semi-reclining position facing the rear of the car, and anchors to the car with the vehicle's safety belt. The child faces the rear so the back can absorb crash forces. By the time the infant can no longer comfortably face the rear, the chest and hips will bear the forward facing position. Do not use these restraint systems after the baby weighs 20 pounds.

2. Toddler seats (children who can sit up without support—about 20-43 pounds). Use the seat with the child facing forward. Most have a 5-point harness to protect the child's upper body.

3. Convertible seats (birth to about 4 years). Convertible seats recline and face rearward for infants and can be changed to the front-facing, nonreclining position for toddlers. Convertible seats save money because only one seat is needed as the child grows. It is critical to follow the manufacturer's instructions when changing to the toddler position. This is so important that extra care must be taken to retain the instructions. The seats are heavier and are harder to move than infant-only and toddler-only seats.

4. Booster seats (older children who weigh at least 30 pounds). These seats raise children so they can see out car windows. They have no back and use the car's lap belts, which fit across the hips and pelvic area. Boosters with a harness must be used with that harness as directed. Models with a shield should always use the shield along with the car's lap belts. Booster seats can be used until the child weighs about 60 pounds (7-8 years old).

5. Others. The 5-point restraint system has a good reputation. It holds the child at the shoulders, hips and with a crotch strap between the legs. A few use a shield instead of a harness. Some models have a bar-shield, a thick, padded bar that replaces the lap portion of a five-point harness. Still others are the T-Shield design in which a high chest shield, similar to a bicycle seat, restrains the child's chest and abdomen. Use all models exactly as directed.

Use. When there is no safety seat, any child who can sit up should use a seat belt. If the shoulder harness falls across the neck, use only the lap belt fastened snugly and low across the child's hips. The best place for a child who is too small for a shoulder harness is fastened in a seatbelt in the rear seat. Don't use automatic safety belts that move into place when the doors close or shoulder-only automatic belts for children.

Problems in use. Every state requires children to buckle up or be in safety seats when riding in automobiles. The laws seldom mention proper use. However, if seats are not used correctly they will not work. Some believe that the incorrect use of child safety seats has reached epidemic proportions. The problems fall into two main areas: incorrect seat installation and incorrect use of the seat's restraining system. Jack Gillis, author of the *1993 Car Book* offers these suggestions:

1. The safest place for the seat is in the center of the back seat.

2. Regularly check the seat belt for a tight, secure fit.

3. Always use a locking clip with passive belt systems in the front seat.

4. On long trips, stop every two hours or so to let the children stretch, as they must remain fastened in seats while in the car.

5. Set a good example for the child. Fasten your own safety belt every time you get in the car.

6. Don't leave sharp or heavy objects loose in the car and put groceries in the trunk. In a crash they can fly about and hit someone.

7. Dress the baby in a legged suit, instead of gowns or buntings, to allow the harness to fasten properly.

8. Be sure all doors are locked and teach children not to play with door handles or locks.

9. Do not give lollipops or ice cream on a stick to children while driving. A bump or swerve could jam the stick into the child's throat.

SCHOOL TIME

When the time comes for a youngster to leave home to go to a preschool or school, a new chapter in safety is opened. Some children walk to school, while others ride buses, and still others ride in the family car or a car pool.

Take a walk. Before the first day of class, choose a safe route for your child. Pick the most direct route, with the fewest street crossings. Next, walk the route with the child so it becomes familiar. Finally, tell your child to take the familiar route every day.

Child's viewpoint. Children aged 5 to 9 have a greater chance of being hit by a vehicle, because they dart out into traffic. Small children are especially at risk for these reasons:

1. Young children think that if they can see the driver, the driver can see them.

2. They think cars can stop instantly.

3. They cannot tell where all sounds come from.

4. Few children can judge how fast traffic is moving.

5. Small children have one-third the field of vision adults have.

6. Children may not recognize danger or react to it.

7. Very young children see cars as friendly, living creatures.

Parents. Teach children street safety when they first begin to walk outdoors. They learn from you when you take them walking. Set a good example.

1. Stop at the edge of the curb or edge of the road. Never run into the street.

2. Listen and look for traffic to the left, the right and to the left again. For younger children, teach looking "this way" and "that way."

3. Don't cross the street until it is clear. Keep looking until you've crossed the street.

4. Teach older children to:
   • Use sidewalks.
   • Walk on the left, facing traffic, where there are no sidewalks.
   • Wear bright clothes that can be seen at night. Use reflective tape on clothes.

5. Start children for school early enough so they don't have to hurry.

6. At bus stops, wait on the grass or sidewalk, not in the street.

7. Never run into the street to recover papers or other objects.

8. When crossing the street, make sure drivers see you and are stopped.

9. Instead of carrying school supplies in your hands, use a backpack or tote bag.

10. Brief children on what to do if the bus is late.

11. For children who may miss the school bus home, parents should:
    • See that children always carry telephone money so they can call.
    • Arrange a safe meeting pickup spot at or near school.

Older children. While children ages 5 through 14 are only 15 percent of the population, they are involved in 30 percent of pedestrian accidents. Their exposure is especially high at the start of the school year for several reasons:

1. There is more exposure to traffic in walking or riding a bike to school, or at bus stops.
2. Children are more excitable and unpredictable at the start of the school year.
3. Children have little traffic experience.
4. Motorists may not be as alert for children because they have not encountered them on the streets during the summer months.

Here comes the bus. More than 22 million children ride school buses each morning. With the safety of so many at stake, these age-old warnings are worth repeating to your children:

1. Remain seated and keep the aisles clear.
2. Do not throw objects.
3. Do not shout or distract the driver.
4. Keep your head inside the bus.
5. Exit after the bus stops completely.

Parents. Parents bear the burden of preparing children for traffic safety.

1. Teach and show children the rules of the road for autos, bicycles and people.
2. Teach children that parked cars are like curbs. They should never step out from behind or between parked cars. But if they must, they should look as carefully as they would from a curb.
3. Don't allow children to play in a driveway near the street, and preferably not in driveways at all.
4. Pick play areas that do not readily access streets.

Drivers. Drivers should remember that youngsters behave differently than adults. They are unpredictable and their side vision is not as good as adults' side vision. They cannot be expected to hear a particular car approaching because of other street noise. Children are usually in a hurry to get places and tend to move suddenly without thought as to danger.

1. Slow down when driving around schools and residential areas.
2. Watch for children—they may not be watching for you.
3. Obey the school bus stop laws.
4. Clear fogged windows before starting out in the morning.
5. Obey all traffic signs and symbols.
6. When turning, look left-right-left for approaching autos, and then look again for pedestrians.

Bicycles

1. Children need to wear helmets every time they ride bikes.
2. Children should follow the rules of the road that apply to all vehicles.
3. Teach children not to ride their bikes at night. Night riding is 20 times as risky as day riding. When night riding can't be avoided, be sure your child wears reflective clothing and always uses a bike light.
4. Don't allow a child under age 8 to ride a bike to school.
5. Choose a safe route, which may not be the same as a safe walking route. Young cyclists should avoid streets with a steady flow of fast-moving traffic.
6. See to it that your child's school has safe areas for bikers, away from cars and people.

Kids and cars

1. At school, pick up children at a safe spot, away from crowds of cars.
2. Make sure children get out of the car on the sidewalk closest to the school in order to avoid crossing the street. Also,

children should always get in and out of the car on the curb side.

3. Use seat belts and remove loose or heavy objects in the car that could cause injury if you stop suddenly.

SUMMARY

The first two chapters of this book are a foundation for the remaining chapters. To recognize the hazards of toys and outdoor activities, it is important to understand the skills and abilities of children of all ages. We paved the way also by discussing the various types of hazards, mechanical, electrical and thermal, and testing. The overview of three main hazards—suffocation, choking and falls—also applies to the entire book.

BIBLIOGRAPHY

"A Lesson in Back-to-School Safety," *Aide*, San Antonio, TX: USAA, pp. 10-11.

"Child's Play," Seattle, WA: Children's Hospital and Medical Center, 1988, pp. 12, 15, 18, 21, 24, 27.

"Child Safety in Your Automobile," (pamphlet), Washington, DC: National Highway Traffic Safety Administration.

"Electrically Operated Toys and Children's Articles," *Product Safety Fact Sheet No. 61*, U.S. Consumer Product Safety Commission, September 1985.

1993 Car Book, Gillis, Jack, New York, NY: Harper's Perennial, 1993.

"Infants Choke on Plastic Decals From Baby Walkers and Other Products," *Consumer Product Safety Alert*, U.S. Consumer Product Safety Commission, May 1990.

"Infants Can Die When Their Heads Become Trapped in Strollers," *Consumer Product Safety Alert*. U.S. Consumer Product Safety Commission, May 1992.

"Prevent Infant Choking and Suffocation," *Community Safety and Health*, National Safety Council, pp. 3-4, May/June 1991.

"Ride'em Safely," Pamphlet, Chicago, IL: National Safety Council, 1988.

"Some Crib Cornerposts May Be Dangerous," *Consumer Product Safety Alert*, Safe Kids, Washington, DC: The National Safe Kids Campaign, U.S. Consumer Product Safety Commission, August 1991.

"The Silent and Invading Trap," Stephenson, Elliot O., *Building Standards*, January February, 1989, March April, 1989, p. 27.

The TMA Guide to Toys and Play. New York, NY: Toy Manufacturers of America, October 1990.

"Think Toy Safety," U.S. *Consumer Product Safety Commission*, October 1988. Thomas, John B.

"Safety Tips for School-Bound Students," *Better Homes and Gardens*, September 1991, p. 42.

Toy Industry Fact Book—1992-1993 Ed. New York, NY: Toy Manufacturers of America, 1992.

"Toys," *Product Safety Fact Sheet, No. 47*, U.S. Consumer Product Safety Commission, August 1986.

"Which Toy for Which Child, Ages Birth Through Five," *A Consumer's Guide for Selecting Suitable Toys*, U.S. Consumer Product Safety Commission, 1988.

"Which Toy for Which Child, Ages Six Through Twelve," *A Consumer's Guide for Selecting Suitable Toys*, U.S. Consumer Product Safety Commission, 1988.

RECREATION AND SPORTS

The subject of recreation and sports safety is a challenge to cover. Many activities fall under this broad category and the safety and health hazards of many leisure time activities are not well-researched.

In keeping with the purpose of *Home Safety Desk Reference*, this section of the book focuses on activities that take place in or near the home and yard. Included are activities in which safety can be directly influenced, such as bicycling, sledding and skating, with emphasis on the young player and sports fan.

CHAPTER 3

RECREATION AND SPORTS

Developing a high degree of skill in a sport or with a recreational device may involve quite a bit of time. Years of study may back up the expert ball player, bicyclist or toboggan user. Here, in a few pages, are the highlights of the hazards and the safe operation of play and sports equipment used closer to home. It is not enough wisdom to build expertise, but it is enough to put you on the road to safer and more enjoyable recreation.

Teaching children the safe use of toys and recreational gear is a shared duty of the home and the school. The manufacturer, distributor and seller also have responsibilities.

Teaching about all potential hazards should start in the home, well before entering school. Although home safety training should begin very early, the young child receives toys before he or she can understand safety teachings. This means that playthings should be carefully chosen.

Two reasons for the tremendous growth in recreation activities are the great increase in leisure time and a higher standard of living. While recreation has many benefits, many activities are dangerous enough to require more safety attention than we tend to give. Safety in choice, use and maintenance of equipment takes on new importance in the effort to curb the trend toward more accidents. Even a few simple precautions can help prevent recreational mishaps. A basic rule for recreation and sports is to take part only in those activities that are within your emotional and physical capabilities.

CHILDREN AND ORGANIZED SPORTS

Home-based sports are not usually organized sports. But because of the growth of organized sports for young people, a few words of caution are necessary. During the past 25 years there has been an explosion in different types of injuries suffered by young athletes, often in the so-called "safe sports," such as swimming, distance running and dance. The CPSC reports that 4 million children receive emergency room treatment for sports injuries every year. They estimate that family doctors treat another 8 million.

Today, many of the injuries seen in children are like those suffered by their active parents. Stress fractures, tendinitis and bursitis, once confined to professional athletes, are now "Little League elbow," "swimmer's shoulder" and "gymnast's back." Knee injuries in children, once nearly unheard of, are now common in clinics.

The whole nature of children's sports has changed. Organized sports have replaced free play and the sandlot sports. About 20 million boys and girls take part in nonschool recreational and competitive sports. Organized sports have brought on overuse injuries caused by repetitive trauma to the body tissues and constant overarm throwing. The sources are baseball, pounding of the feet in dancing and distance running and the flexing and extension of the back in gymnastics and dance. Children in organized sports often overtrain and play when hurt. Kids may conceal sore elbows or aching knees because they don't want to look like sissies.

Sports injuries are serious. Growing children tend toward overuse injuries because of the softness of their growing bones, and the relative tightness of their ligaments, tendons and muscles during growth spurts. Because overuse injuries grow slowly and insidiously, unlike sprains and fractures, which happen suddenly, they often go undetected. Unknown or unreported damage can be permanent, and perhaps even lead to problems in later life, such as arthritis.

What should you do? The quality of volunteer coaches should be upgraded. As sandlot play has moved to organized sports, we have not responded by training the coaches who lead our children in running, lifting weights and swimming. Training errors by well-intended coaches lead to most overuse injuries. Volunteer coaches should receive training in first aid, playing techniques and injury prevention. Parents should ensure, whenever possible, that coaches receive the training they need and insist that coaches be certified through an organized sports program. Although three programs now exist, certification is not required. More information on certification can be found in the book by Jenkins and Micheli in the bibliography.

Eye protection. Both children and adults should use eye protection in certain sports to avoid injuries such as black eyes, inflammation and irritation. Unfortunately, sometimes vanity overcomes common sense when it comes to eye protection.

Does eye protection pay? In Canada, when face shields became mandatory for junior hockey, eye injuries dropped by 95 percent.

Activities in which eye protection is important include racquet sports, hockey, baseball, basketball, wrestling and boxing. Swimming and track and field sports tend to be lower risk. Many other sports fall between these extremes. Use care to select the right type of glasses, goggles or face shields.

Many experts suggest goggles and shields of super strong polycarbonate.

Sports eye guards come in a variety of shapes and sizes. Regular eye guards cost $20 to $30. Guards with prescription lenses are more expensive. For more information on sports and eye safety contact the American Academy of Ophthalmology, 855 Beach Street, San Francisco, CA, 94109-1336.

SPORTS: EXTREME TEMPERATURES

Anyone who spends much time outdoors knows that exposure to extreme temperatures is very hazardous. You should know how to recognize:

1. Hypothermia: a critical drop in the body's temperature.
2. Hyperthermia: a critical rise in the body's core temperature.

You should also know the basic first aid for each.

Hypothermia. Hypothermia causes as many as half of all water fatalities by reducing the ability to swim or stay afloat. Hypothermia occurs when the body loses heat faster than it can produce it. Although the body loses heat 25 times faster in cold water than in cold air, both are deadly. Because it can occur in any water less than 70°F, even in the summer, larger lakes can be a hazard.

The first sign of hypothermia is feeling cold. Shivering and loss of coordination follows. As body temperature drops, mental dullness and apathy appears. This can lead to a coma. In the water, exercise does not slow heat loss. You can increase survival time if you assume the H.E.L.P. position: Place arms to the side with wrists crossed over the chest and head out of the water as much as possible. This slows heat loss from the head and neck, the sides and the groin.

First aid for hypothermia begins with stopping the body's heat loss. Replace wet clothes with dry clothes and blankets, and seek shelter. Give the victim warm drinks, but not coffee or alcohol. If the person loses consciousness, a trained person should begin rescue breathing or CPR, and get medical aid quickly.

Hypothermia is insidious. By the time victims recognize the signs, they may not be able to help themselves. Because of this, it is important that adults supervise children playing outdoors in very cold weather. Children will often insist they are not cold so they can stay and take part in group activities. Older persons seem to have less sensitivity to the cold and may not recognize the early signs of hypothermia.

Children in the cold

1. Dress children in layers to maintain body temperature. Some fabrics are better than others. Wool is the warmest material, but it also retains moisture and feels cold next to the skin.
2. The American Academy of Pediatrics suggests that children wear the newer high-tech, synthetic fabrics next to the skin when outside on cold days. Layer wool on top of these fabrics.
3. Do not allow children to play outdoors when the wind-chill is as cold as -20°F.
4. Children get cold faster than adults. Adults should monitor them carefully as they may be too busy playing to want to go inside.
5. Don't allow children to take part in unsupervised winter sports.
6. Snowmobiling is not for children younger than 16 years of age.

Hyperthermia. The first stage of hyperthermia is heat exhaustion and excessive sweating. The skin may be pale or flushed without being warm. Dizziness, nausea, confusion and a weak rapid pulse may also appear. The corrective action is to get out of direct sunshine and raise the legs a few inches. Cool victims with water and fanning. Loosen the person's clothes. If the victim is alert, he or she may sip water.

Untreated heat exhaustion may lead to a heat stroke, a serious and sometimes deadly condition. With heat exhaustion, victims stop sweating. Skin becomes hot and dry and may appear mottled or red. The victim may be disoriented, lose consciousness or have chills, nausea and dizziness. Heat stroke is life-threatening. Move the victim to a cool, shaded area and cool the skin with water, while massaging the extremities and torso. Check the person's temperature every 10 minutes. Seizures will occur near 102°F. until the condition passes. If the person loses consciousness, give rescue breathing or CPR and call for medical help as soon as possible.

Children may dissipate heat more quickly, but this can lead to rapid dehydration. A child can become quite dehydrated without showing signs of being thirsty, so be sure children have plenty to drink.

Sunburn. You can hardly take part in outdoor recreation without tempting sunburn. Too often the proud mark of the outdoor person is a deep tan. This is not as true today as in the past, as men and women now recognize that avoiding the sun helps avoid premature skin aging and skin cancer.

Avoiding sunburn, usually brought on with first exposures to the sun, is not easy. How your skin reacts to initial exposure to the sun depends partly on the type of skin you have. Reactions range from "always burns" to "never burns." Whatever your skin type, sunscreen is advisable.

Practice safe sun

1. Wear sunscreen, even when in the sun for short periods of time.
2. Sun lotion needs to be applied and should dry before sun exposure. It may need to reapplied at intervals, certainly after being in the water.
3. Avoid the peak sun exposure in the middle of the day.

4. Know your sunscreens. There is a different type for water sports, for example. Read the sunscreen labels carefully.

5. Remember that you can burn on cloudy days as well as sunny days. Ultraviolet rays that go deep into the skin can be reflected by water, sand and snow.

6. A T-shirt or scarf that is a loose weave is not much protection from the sun. Hold it up to the light to see how much light comes through.

7. Children get more sun than adults, so:
   - Teach children to regularly apply sunscreen, just as you teach them to brush their teeth.
   - If children are going to be outdoors at school, pack sunscreen in their school packs.
   - Keep infants under 6 months out of the sun and away from sunscreen.
   - Limit children's time in the sun and avoid the peak sun hours.
   - Dress children for sun protection.
   - Use a special sunscreen meant for children.

FIREWORKS

Fireworks, for all their patriotic associations, are a very serious safety hazard, particularly for children. Deaths, blindings, amputations and severe burns all too often result from fireworks at Fourth of July celebrations.

- A 40-year-old man lost a foot after a friend threw a "silver salute" at him and yelled. The victim stepped back onto the firecracker.

- A 12-year-old's hand was partially amputated after he lit the fuse of an M-100, tried to extinguish it with his fingers and then could not get rid of the firecracker before it exploded.

- An 8-year-old girl received second and third degree burns to her leg when a sparkler she was holding ignited her dress.

- A 14-year-old boy was seriously injured while mixing chemicals for making explosives in his family's home. The chemicals, from a mail-order firm, exploded unexpectedly, destroying much of the home.

To help prevent mishaps like these, the Federal Hazardous Substances Act prohibits the sale of the most dangerous types of fireworks, as well as the mail-order kits to build them. Those prohibited include cherry bombs, aerial bombs, M-80 salutes and large firecrackers. Firecrackers cannot contain more than 50 milligrams of powder, and fuses must burn between 3 and 6 seconds. However, illegal fireworks are still a problem and you must realize that what is for sale is not necessarily legal or safe. And, while many victims treated in emergency rooms are injured by illegal fireworks, most injuries result from legal fireworks.

Use. Fireworks should be used only with extreme caution. Used carelessly, they can cause painful, possibly severe injuries. To help use fireworks more safely, consider these recommendations:

1. Before using fireworks, be certain they are permitted in your area. Permission and prohibition of most fireworks is on a state-to-state basis. Only two states (in 1990, Hawaii and Nevada) have no fireworks laws except at county level. Fireworks are banned in 13 states. A few states allow only sparklers.

2. The sparkler, thought by many as the ideal "safe" firework for the young, burns at a very high temperature and can easily ignite clothing. Do not allow younger children to play with fireworks anytime. They cannot appreciate the danger involved and cannot act correctly in case of an emergency. Always have an adult present when using fireworks.

3. If you let older children use fireworks, be sure they use them only under close

supervision. Do not allow any running or horseplay while they are in use.

4. Before using any fireworks, read and follow all warnings printed on the label.

5. Light fireworks outdoors in a clear area, away from houses, dry leaves or grass and flammable materials.

6. Light one firework at a time.

7. Keep a bucket of water nearby for emergencies and for pouring on fireworks that don't ignite.

8. Do not try to relight or handle malfunctioning fireworks. Douse and soak them with water and throw them away.

9. Be sure people are out of range before lighting fireworks.

10. Never light fireworks in a container, especially a glass or metal container.

11. Keep unused fireworks away from firing area.

12. Store fireworks in a cool, dry place. Check special instructions for storing.

13. Parents should supervise the ordering and use of mail-order "make your own" fireworks kits to be sure they do not contain chemicals or paper tubes to make firecrackers. These are illegal parts of fireworks kits, which can produce dangerous explosives.

HALLOWEEN SAFETY

That same Halloween costume that transforms your little angel into a little devil can turn trick-or-treating into a nightmare. Costumes are dangerous if the child cannot see or be seen. In addition, there's the danger of tampered candy and other "tricks" played by pranksters as your children wander the streets of your neighborhood in the dark. You can help your child have a safer Halloween by taking a few precautions:

Trick-or-treat safety tips

1. Warn children not to eat any of their treats before they get home. When you child returns, sift through the bag of treats and discard unwrapped or rewrapped candy. Cut up fruit to make sure nothing is hidden inside.

2. Look for costumes, masks, wigs and beards labeled "flame resistant." This does not mean they won't catch fire, only that they will resist flame and extinguish quicker if taken from the flame. Avoid big, baggy or billowy clothes that will more easily come in contact with candles or other fire sources.

3. Many parents do not allow their children to trick-or-treat after dark. If your children do venture out after sunset, dress them in light-colored costumes or put reflective tape on all sides of a dark costume. Give each child a flashlight, with new batteries, to carry.

4. Check that your child's costume is short enough to prevent tripping and falling. The costume should allow good ventilation and movement. Make sure the costume won't tangle in shrubbery or get caught in doors.

5. Tie hats and scarves securely to keep them from slipping over children's eyes.

6. Make sure beards, hats, veils and wigs don't obstruct the child's vision.

7. Paint your child's face rather than covering it with a mask which might restrict breathing or hinder vision. Makeup is safer and more comfortable for the child.

8. Have your children wear sensible shoes. High heel shoes may cause falls. Sneakers or loafer are a better choice.

9. Don't allow children to carry swords, daggers, arrows or other sharp objects, unless they are made of soft flexible material.

10. Smaller children should always be accompanied by an adult or older, responsible child. Children under 10 should never trick-or-treat alone.

11. Children should use the sidewalk instead of the street and they should

walk, not run, from house to house. They should be warned against running out from between parked cars or across yards where ornaments, clotheslines or furniture present dangers.

12. Children should always cross streets at crosswalks or well-lighted intersections.

13. Children should only go to homes where outside lights are on as a sign of welcome. Children should not enter homes or apartments, unless accompanied by an adult.

14. Review the safety rules for trick-or-treating with your children before they leave the house. Encourage them to travel in groups and only in familiar areas. Set a precise curfew.

15. If the child is under 12, attach the child's name, address, and phone number in an easy-to-find place on the costume, but do not display the information openly.

16. Protect other children as your own. Parents will appreciate your concern for their children's safety.

   - Light the path to your door and remove any obstacles along the way.
   - Remove any candle-lit jack-o'-lanterns from landings and doorsteps where costumes could brush against the flames.
   - Consider giving stickers, favors and other noncandy treats.

BICYCLES

In some years, bicycles have been at the top of the Hazard Index List, which lists the 100 consumer products that cause the most numerous and severe injuries. Bicycles are involved in about 600,000 injuries per year. For example:

- Karen applied her hand brakes and lost control of her bicycle. She went down an embankment into a creek and fractured her shoulder.

- As Jimmy was riding his bicycle downhill, the front wheel of his bicycle suddenly became loose and twisted. Jimmy lost control and crashed, fracturing his knee.

- Bob was riding a bike without a chain guard when his foot was caught between pedal and chain. He fell, suffering a concussion and skull fracture.

- Pat was riding her bicycle uphill when one foot slipped off the pedal. She fell on the hard pavement and fractured her arm.

- Michele was riding her bike alongside a friend's. As her friend moved his bike to the right, the two front wheels locked together, causing Michele to fall. She suffered a concussion and fractured a wrist.

Accident patterns

1. Loss of control. This occurs because of trouble braking; riding too large a bike; riding double on banana seats, rear fenders, handlebars or the horizontal top tube on a man's bike; stunting and striking a rut, bump or obstacle.

2. Mechanical and structural problems. These include brake failure; wobbling or disengagement of the wheel or steering mechanism; problems in shifting gears; chain slippage; pedals falling off and spoke breakage.

3. Entanglement of a person's feet, hands or clothing in the bicycle.

4. Feet slipping from pedals.

5. Collision with a car or another bicycle.

Selection of bicycles

1. If you buy an unassembled bicycle, it is your responsibility to follow all assembly and adjustment instructions exactly as set forth in the owner's manual. If it is bought assembled, it is still your responsibility to make sure it is properly assembled and adjusted.

2. If you're buying a bicycle for a child, choose one that fits today, not one the child will grow into later. The child

should be able to straddle the top horizontal bar with both feet on the ground.

3. A bicycle should suit the rider's ability and type of riding done.

4. Buy reflectors that make the bike visible at night from front, back and sides.

5. Tape retro-reflective trim to the fenders, handlebars, chain guards and wheel sidewalls to make the bicycle instantly recognizable in the dark.

6. Attach a headlight and tail light.

7. Check hand and foot brakes for fast, easy stops without jamming or instability. Most young children do not have the strength to use hand brakes, so test your child's "squeeze" ability before buying.

8. Avoid slippery, plastic pedals. Look instead for rubber-treaded pedals, or metal clips with serrated rat trap edges or with firmly attached toe clips.

9. Don't buy a bicycle with sharp points and edges, especially along fenders, or with protruding bolts that could scrape or tear clothing.

10. Don't buy a bicycle with gear controls (or other protruding attachments) mounted on the top tube.

11. Make certain the toe on the pedal cannot contact the front wheel when turning.

12. If you expect to use a bicycle for stunting and jumping, buy a bicycle designed for that purpose.

Use of bicycles

1. Observe all traffic laws and signals, just as automobile drivers do. Give hand signals at least 100 feet before turning or stopping and also while waiting to turn, unless your hand is needed to control the bicycle. Ride on the right, look back and yield to traffic coming from behind before turning left at intersections.

2. Don't ride double or attempt stunts.

3. Ride near the curb, but not so close that your pedal will catch on a curb.

Watch for car doors opening or for cars pulling into traffic. It is the law to ride on the right-hand-side of the road in all states. Don't bob in and around cars and drains.

4. Ride in single file.

5. Choose routes that do not go through busy intersections and heavy or high-speed traffic.

6. Walk—don't ride—your bicycle across busy intersections and left-turn corners.

7. Avoid riding in wet weather. Tires will slide more easily on a damp surface. When wet, hand brakes will require a longer distance to stop.

8. Adults should avoid riding bicycles at night and children should never ride bicycles at night. If you must ride at night, avoid heavy traffic and narrow roadways where the posted speed is over 35 mph. Use an adequate headlight and taillight for nighttime riding. For more visibility, apply retro-reflective trim to clothing or wear reflective vests or jackets. You can also strap front-back flash lights on the legs and arms.

9. Avoid loose clothing or long coats that can catch in pedals or wheels. Do not let a coat or other clothing hang down and cover the rear reflector. Use leg clips or bands to keep pants legs from tangling in the chains. Wear bright, easily visible clothing.

10. Do not wear anything that restricts your hearing or vision.

11. Do not attach anything to your bicycle that will hinder your vision or control.

12. While riding, don't hold on to anything, or attach your bicycle to any truck, car or any vehicle in order for it to pull you along.

13. Avoid crossing raised drain grates. Try to avoid drain grates, gravel or sand, wet leaves, soft road edges, pot holes or runts and uneven paving.

14. Cross railroad tracks at right angles.

15. Keep both hands on the handlebar.

16. Do not use a bicycle designed for general transportation and recreational use for stunts and jumps.

17. Wear a helmet that meets ANSI or Snell standards. There will be a sticker that identifies this on the helmet.

18. Always be courteous to pedestrians.
    - Give pedestrians the right of way.
    - Make a sound loud enough to alert them if you want to pass.
    - Don't ride too close to them.
    - Do not park your bicycle where it may be in someone's way.

19. Do not allow younger children (under 9 or so) to ride beyond local paths, sidewalks and driveways until they can show that they can ride well and observe bicycle rules of the road.

20. Ride predictably in a straight line and signal before turning.

Maintenance

1. Safe riding requires regular maintenance. An experienced repair person should do complicated work.

2. Cover sharp points and edges with heavy, waterproof tape.

3. Replace protruding bolts with shorter bolts, or add crowned nuts or other protective devices to prevent catching on bolts.

4. Align (or "true") wobbly wheels for better control. Adjust spokes.

5. Replace missing, damaged or worn parts; such as chain guards, chain links, spokes, screws and bolts, handlebar grips.

6. Tighten and adjust loose parts.

7. Inflate tires to the proper pressure.

8. Tighten spokes to prevent wobble. If they can be moved sideways more than one spoke thickness, they need to be tightened.

9. Lightly oil and clean moving parts.

Inspect brakes regularly and adjust when they are not working normally.

Caliper brakes need adjustment regularly. Never allow anything (oil, grease, wax) on wheel rims or caliper brakes. Use hot water and soap to wash these parts. Wipe wheel rims dry before riding. Make sure caliper brakes do not rub on tires. Keep bicycles indoors when not in use. Moisture can rust and weaken metal parts.

Bicycle regulations. During the 1970s, a flurry of legislative activity brought new bicycle safety standards. Some major provisions are:

1. Sharp edges and protrusions of certain sizes. Some exposed protrusions, such as control cable ends, must have protective caps. This should help reduce the large number of cuts and punctures that occur in bicycle accidents.

2. Good brakes. Braking requirements depend upon the speed of each bicycle. Bicycles capable of speeds of 15 miles per hour (many of these bicycles have hand brakes) must be able to stop in 15 feet at 15 miles per hour. Those bicycles capable of only slower speeds (many of these have foot brakes) must be able to stop in 15 feet at 10 miles per hour. Sidewalk bicycles with a seat height of 22 inches (with the seat at its lowest position) must have foot brakes. Small bicycles with a seat height less than 22 inches, and without brakes, must be labeled with the words "No Brakes" and cannot have a free-wheeling coasting feature.

3. The handlebar and stem must not break when subject to certain tests. The handlebar must allow comfortable and safe control of the bicycle. Handlebars must be symmetrically located and no more than 16 inches above the seat surface.

4. Single-gear ratio bicycles must have chain guards meeting specific requirements. Guards are not required where the chain can be pedaled in reverse. *Derailleurs*, the mechanisms that produce gear shifting in multi-sprocket bicycles,

must have guards to keep the drive chain from interfering with the wheel rotation because of improper adjustments or damage to the derailleur.

5. The tire must not blow off the wheel when the tire is inflated to 110 percent of maximum recommended pressure. (Tubular sew-up tires, nonpneumatic tires and nonmolded wire-on tires are exempt from this requirement.) There must be no missing or loose spokes. The wheels must be aligned, "trued," so that there is at least 1/16-inch clearance between the tire and the fork or any part of the bicycle frame. This clearance helps assure good caliper brake performance. The hubs must lock securely to the bicycle frame. The front hub must have a safety device that will hold the wheel in place if the front axle nuts loosen. These requirements should reduce injuries due to wheel separations.

6. The front fork and frame must meet certain strength requirements. The seat must attach firmly to the seat post tube so that it will not move or break under normal riding conditions, and it must not have any part or support more than 5 inches above the seat surface. This allows a rider to dismount by swinging a leg over the seat and rear wheel.

7. Treads must be an integral part of the pedal, unless the pedals are for use only with toe clips (toe clips must be attached to these). Ground and toe clearances for pedals are specified.

8. The drive train must pass a strength test so that it won't break under normal use.

9. All bicycles, except sidewalk bicycles, must have reflectors on the front, back, pedals and sides. The bicycle may have either reflectorized tires or reflectors mounted on the wheel spokes. These give the motorist a unique pattern of reflective devices, and help distinctively identify a bicycle from any angle.

10. Easy assembly and labeling. Each bicycle must have an instruction manual attached to the frame, or within the packaged unit. If not fully assembled, the bicycle must have instructions listing the tools needed for proper assembly and adjustment, and showing the correct leg-length measurements of the rider. Instructions should allow an average person to assemble the bicycle. Bicycles must have labels showing that they comply with the regulations. They must also be permanently marked or labeled to identify the manufacturer, or private labeler, and date coded, so that the month and year of manufacture can be found.

Other requirements. All bicycles, other than sidewalk bicycles, must pass a road test that simulates a bicycle ridden over a rough road. This test should expose potential problems with the bicycle. Sidewalk bicycles must pass certain strength tests, but do not require a road test.

HELMETS

Bicycle riding is one of the four leading causes of the 3 million head injuries reported each year. Fewer than one in ten bicyclists wear helmets. About one-third of the bicycle-related deaths (600 per year) involve school-age children under the age of 14. About one-third of the injuries—causing three out of four of the deaths—are to the head and the face. Thousands of the injured suffer brain damage.

Some of these deaths and injuries would have been prevented by wearing helmets. By mid-1993, only five states required children under 14 to wear helmets when bicycling, but more are expected to follow.

A bicycle helmet should be snug, but comfortable on the rider's head. Some helmets come with several different thicknesses of internal padding to custom fit the helmet to the user.

The purpose of the helmet is to absorb the energy of an impact to minimize or prevent a head injury. Crushable, expanded polystyrene foam generally is used for this. Many helmets also have a hard outer shell to protect the head. For a helmet to protect during impact, it must have a chin strap and buckle that stays fastened. No combination of twisting or pulling should remove the helmet from the head or loosen the buckle on the strap. Children should be taught to always wear the helmet with the chin strap firmly buckled.

When buying a helmet, carefully examine the helmet and instructions. You should buy only helmets that meet voluntary standards of an approved organization. Buy helmets that meet or exceed the standards of the Snell Memorial Foundation or American National Standards Institute (ANSI). A sticker on the helmet will verify approval by one of those two organizations. A good helmet costs $35 or more. Some people will spend more than that for a bicycle lock. For children who have difficulty affording good helmets, some schools have programs that allow them to be sold for as little as $13, although $20 is closer to normal. (They would retail for $40 to $90.) Some programs provide low-income family members with helmets free.

Prevention of head injuries

Wearing a helmet is the best way to prevent a head injury. People have many reasons for not using helmets. None of them hold up under examination. It is critical that children wear helmets and, since they follow the lead of adults, important that adults set an example by wearing helmets. Any child or adults should wear a helmet when:

1. Riding a motorcycle. Wearing a helmet reduces the risk of head injuries in motorcyclists and the risk of head injury death.
2. Riding a bicycle. Bicyclists are at greater risk than motorcyclists, partly because they tend to land on the head more often. Helmets can prevent 85 percent of the head injuries of bicyclists.
3. Other high-risk activities, including football, rock climbing, boxing and construction work. Also follow these recommendations:
   - Use seat belts and restraint seats on motorcycles and bicycles.
   - Keep infants and young children from unguarded windows.
   - Don't leave youngsters alone in highchairs, strollers, buggies or walkers.
   - Supervise children playing with projectile type toys such as BB guns and archery sets.
   - Pay close attention when using nailing machines and power staples.
   - Use only ladders in good condition that match the task.

Older persons should see that their environment is as safe as possible from hazards that cause slips and falls. See the checklist for older persons in the Appendix.

TRICYCLES

While related and similar to bicycles, tricycles (trikes) present special construction and user problems for the age group using them. Tricycle injuries are common in hospital emergency rooms. Look at these examples:

- Joy and her brother were racing when she turned her tricycle sharply. She was flipped up and over the tricycle and onto the sidewalk, fracturing her collarbone.
- Marsha's father was pushing her tricycle from the rear when her foot was caught in the spokes of the tricycle. Her left ankle was fractured.

Accident patterns

1. Poor construction or design. This includes breakage while in use, sharp edges or points.

2. Instability, which causes a tricycle to tip over.

3. Striking obstacles and colliding with other tricycles.

4. Entanglement in the tricycle's moving parts.

5. Inability to stop the tricycle. Usually because tricycles do not have brakes.

Selection of tricycles

1. Match the size of your child to the size of the tricycle. If a child is too large for the tricycle, the trike will be unstable. If the child is too small, it may be hard to control.

2. Look for a trike with stops that keep the handlebars from being turned too far, too fast. Otherwise, the trike can be turned so fast that it will overturn.

3. Low-slung tricycles with seats close to the ground are more stable.

4. Avoid tricycles with sharp edges on or along fenders, axles and fender nuts. Trikes with fenders pose a threat of scrapes and cuts, and of rusting, which can lead to infections.

5. Consider carefully trikes with deep U-shaped handlebars. Children can catch body parts in the handlebars, as well as between the handlebars and trike body.

6. Select trikes with seats curved at the rear, not at right angles, in case the child falls or is pushed off backwards. Seats should not extend beyond the back axle so the trike breaks the shock in case of a backward fall.

7. Avoid tricycles with spokes that can cause injury to fingers and feet. Spokes that are far apart are better, but still a hazard.

8. Look for pedals and hand grips with rough surfaces to prevent the child's hands and feet from slipping.

Use of tricycles

Teach children safe riding habits, then monitor them frequently.

1. Caution your child against riding double. Carrying a passenger on a tricycle greatly reduces its stability.

2. Teach your child that riding down hills is dangerous. A tricycle that picks up too much speed becomes impossible to stop.

3. Teach your child to avoid sharp turns, to make all turns at low speed and not to ride down steps or over curbs.

4. Advise your child to keep hands and feet away from moving spokes.

Maintenance of tricycles

1. Keep the tricycle in good condition. Check often for missing or damaged pedals and hand grips, loose handlebars and seats, broken parts and other defects.

2. Cover any sharp edges and protrusions with heavy, waterproof tape.

3. Don't leave tricycles outdoors overnight. Moisture can cause rust and weaken metal parts.

EXERCISE BICYCLES

Each year Americans buy 3 million exercise bikes, making them the most widely sold piece of exercise equipment. A survey by *Consumer Reports* magazine revealed that 42 percent of their readers own an exercise bicycle. Exercise bikes have their advantages:

1. You can stay fit, even when bad weather prohibits outdoor activity.

2. You can exercise in the privacy of your home—anytime.

3. There is no risk of injury from cars, potholes and dogs.

4. You can stop when tired and not have to make the return trip home.

5. You can easily maintain a desired pace and thus a better workout.

All exercise bikes make possible sustained aerobic exercise in one of two ways: single-action and dual-action.

On single-action bikes, you pump your legs and turn a flywheel linked to the pedals. Resistance to the pumping comes from a strap around the outside of the flywheel or a set of caliper brake pads. The tighter the strap or pads, the more resistance to pumping and the more intense the workout.

Dual-action bikes link the handlebars to the pedals, which in turn attach to a fan. The faster you pedal and pump the handles, the more air resistance you work against. Some of these bikes add a strap to the fan so you can adjust the resistance. Other variations provide resistance, sometimes separately, to the upper and lower body.

Hazards

1. Handlebar uprights hit the knees when pumping.
2. Seats have sharp edges on bottoms that can chafe thighs when wearing shorts.
3. Seat posts that are not secure permit too much shaking.
4. Seat posts held in place by clamps allow the seat to slip if not tightened enough.
5. Some seats are held on posts by pins that can work loose, which allows the seats to drop.
6. Toe straps do not come with the machine. Straps are sometimes available.
7. Some flywheel straps are not protected from sweating. If they become wet they may change their friction suddenly.
8. Some bikes come with pulse monitors, which are not always reliable gauges of heart rate.
9. Some exercise bikes permit a child to poke a finger into the flywheel or chain mechanism. There were 1,200 amputations of children's fingers through contact with exercise bikes from 1985 through 1989.
10. Children may use a bike without supervision and get hurt.
11. Problems in moving the bike can lead to injury.
12. Pedal-seat relationship may place the rider's knees in front of pedals, an improper alignment.

Buying exercise bicycles

1. The bike should feel solid. The frame should not flex and wiggle when you pedal.
2. Pedaling should be smooth.
3. The seat should be padded.
4. The flywheel, if there is one, should be massive enough to simulate the momentum of an outdoor bike.
5. Look for a coaster mechanism that lets you stop pedaling without bringing the fan or flywheel to a halt.
6. The pedals need straps to keep your feet from slipping and allow you to apply force on the upstroke.
7. The seat, handlebars and resistance level should be easy to adjust.
8. Handlebars should be adjustable to the "drop-bar" position used by road cyclists.
9. Make certain the highest and lowest seat positions allow proper use of pedals, whether the user is tall or short.
10. Check that the monitor is easy to use and understand.
11. Make certain a child cannot poke a finger into the wheel or chain mechanism.
12. Look for rollers or wheels that allow the bike to be moved easily.
13. Persons with back problems may want to consider a recumbent model of exercise bicycle.

Note: Nothing takes the place of trying out the exercise bicycle before buying. Consider the points raised above under both the "Hazards" and "Buying" headings.

MOPEDS AND MOTORBIKES

Two-wheeled, powered motor vehicles fall into three classifications: moped, motorbike and motorcycle. All-terrain-vehicles (ATVs) may be either three- or four-wheeled with large flotation tires. Following some general safety information, this section primarily addresses moped safety, although much of it applies to motorbikes also.

1. Mopeds have less than 50 cc of power and can be crank-pedaled if necessary. The rider may not need a license, although the vehicle may have to be licensed.
2. A motorbike has more than 50 cc of power, but less than 15 horsepower. The driver and bike need a license.
3. A motorcycle usually has more than 15 horsepower.

Children on mopeds and motorbikes face a dangerous dilemma. These vehicles cannot be driven legally on streets, highways, freeways, sidewalks or parking lots. However, acceptable riding locations, such as yards or open fields, often have uneven or bumpy terrain that can cause a bike to bounce or throw its rider.

The following explains how to avoid the four most common causes of moped and motorbike injuries: mechanical and structural problems, poor riding conditions, contact with vehicle parts and rider misuse.

Mechanical and structural problems

- Dick tried to stop his moped when another boy rode toward him, but his hand brakes failed to work. They collided and Dick fell, hitting his head and pinning his right arm and leg under the bike. He suffered a slight cerebral hemorrhage and a sprained right arm.

This accident illustrates brake failure. Other mechanical and structural problems include throttles that stick, instability, chain breakage, poorly located exhaust pipes and loose, missing or broken parts.

To avert accidents due to mechanical and structural problems:

1. Look for a moped or motorbike with larger wheels. Those with smaller wheels are more unstable.
2. Check for durable, sturdy construction.
3. Look for exhaust pipes that point rearward, away from the legs of drivers. A hot exhaust pipe, if directed toward the side or upward, could burn the driver's leg or damage clothing.
4. Brakes should be easy to use and easy to reach.
5. Hand brakes alone are not enough for children. Buy a bike with foot brakes, or hand and foot combinations.
6. The rider should be able to reach all controls easily without undue effort.
7. After buying a moped or motorbike, do not modify its design.

Periodic maintenance is essential:

1. Lubricate and clean moving parts.
2. Tighten parts, such as levers, handlebar clamps, nuts and bolts.
3. Have a qualified mechanic adjust brakes, wheel bearings, throttle, chain tensions and other components.
4. Check fuel hoses (if any) for leaks.
5. Replace lost or broken parts, particularly chain links and guards.

Poor riding conditions

- Ralph, 9 years old, and his younger sister were riding double on a motorbike. The bike was traveling fast when they ran over loose gravel, which caused the bike to go out of control. They both fell off the bike. Ralph suffered a concussion while his sister received contusions and abrasions to her head and hands.

Riding over uneven terrain or hitting a bump, hole or other ground hazard, can cause a driver to be thrown from the bike and suffer serious injury. Wet grass and pavement and loose gravel can cause a moped or motorbike to skid out of control.

1. Before buying a bike for children, parents should consider where the bike can be ridden legally. If no off-street sites with smooth terrain are available, don't buy the bike.
2. Don't ride in the rain.
3. Avoid riding on wet pavement, gravel or grass, especially going up or down a grade.
4. Beware of fence wire or cables that cannot be seen when stretched in open fields and backyards. They can strangle a driver or overturn a minibike.

Contact with parts

- Micky was riding a motorbike when his left pants leg caught in the chain drive and sprocket mechanism. He suffered puncture wounds on his leg.

Chain sprocket mechanisms can catch clothing, toes and fingers and cause painful injuries, even amputations. Moped and motorbike drivers also can be lacerated on sharp edges and loose or protruding parts, such as on kickstands or pedals.

1. Check the bike for sharp edges by carefully running your hand along fenders and other metal parts. On an older-model bike, cover sharp edges with heavy, waterproof tape.
2. Buy a bike with chain guards and don't remove them.

Rider misuse

- On a dare, Jeff tried to jump his moped over a plank on a cement block. As he left the jump, he lost control of the moped and was knocked unconscious when he hit the ground. He was in the hospital for 11 days with a fractured rib, ruptured spleen and internal hemorrhaging.

Children may try maneuvers beyond their skill, such as "wheelies," with the front wheel up in the air, or jumps that professional motorcyclists might perform. Riding double is also unsafe behavior that can throw a moped or motorbike off balance.

1. Parents should warn children of the dangers of "stunting" and riding double, and supervise children when possible.
2. Don't ride in the dark. You can't see bumps, holes and other obstacles. Even a light on the moped is not enough.
3. Certain acceleration problems result from inexperience with the bike. Riders have mistaken the gas throttle for the hand brake and have speeded up and thrown themselves off balance.
4. Before riding a new bike, drivers should read the driver's manual carefully to learn the placement of the controls and take safety precautions. Since children may not read instructions, parents must take extra care to teach them proper use of the bike.
5. Before letting friends ride for the first time, make sure they know where the braking and acceleration controls are.

Additional hints

1. Be careful when filling the gas tank. Either fill it before riding or turn off the motor and wait until it cools. Don't fill the tank near a utility room (a pilot light from the water heater can cause an explosion of gas vapors) or near any other ignition source.
2. When riding, wear protective clothing, such as long pants, sturdy shoes and a heavy duty helmet marked Department of Transportation (DOT) Approved.

ROLLER SKATES

Many children and young teens learn new skills on roller skates, ice skates and skateboards. But hard falls go with these learning experiences. These cases illustrate this often serious and painful activity:

- Jim was roller-skating when another skater close in front of him stopped abruptly. Jim ran into the other skater, fell and fractured his right wrist.
- The original wheels and mounting had broken on his skateboard, so 12-year-old

Jon repaired and modified the skateboard. Unfortunately, the wood screws came off and Jon fell and fractured his left hand.

- Bruce's ice skates struck a rut in the ice. He fell and crashed into the wooden boards on the side of the rink, fracturing his right leg.

IN-LINE ROLLER SKATES

In-line roller skating has exploded in popularity. However it has proven to be very hazardous if skaters do not wear helmets and other protective equipment, or do not learn to skate and stop properly. There are a whole new set of considerations for safe in-line skating. The International In-line Skating Association (800-FOR-IISA) publishes an in-line skater's magazine and serves as a resource for instruction, books, videos and guidelines. Most places that sell in-line skates can provide guidelines for learning more about the sport. Meanwhile, these four steps will help ensure injury-free fun:

1. Wear a helmet, elbow pads, knee pads and gloves.
2. Learn to stop safely.
3. Skate on smooth, paved surfaces without any traffic.
4. Avoid skating at night.

SKATEBOARDS

As the use of skateboards increases, so do the problems and hazards associated with skateboards. Hospitals treat nearly 100,000 skateboard injuries each year, and 70 percent of these injuries are to children under 15 years of age. One-third of the injuries happen to those who have been skating less than a week, and these accidents are mostly due to falls.

Skateboarding requires good balance and body control, yet many young riders do not yet have the necessary balance and reaction needed for safe operation.

Contusions, abrasions and fractures are the most common skateboard injuries. Lack of protective equipment, poor board maintenance, poor riding surfaces and not enough practice are major factors in injuries.

Selection of skates or skateboards

1. Buy skates that fit well. Choose skates that fit the child's present foot size, not a pair they can grow into. Avoid hand-me-downs that don't fit.
2. Carefully run your hand over metal parts (Do not do this with ice skate blades.) to check for sharp edges and points that can cut in the event of a fall.
3. Skateboards need to "wobble" to maneuver corners, but too much causes instability. Choose a sturdy skateboard with only enough "play" to turn corners well.

Use of skates or skateboards

1. Skateboard riders under 13 years of age may lack the muscle coordination to maintain balance, and enough maturity to judge what types of maneuvers to attempt on the skateboard.
2. Learn basic skating and skateboard maneuvers well before trying more complicated or "trick" maneuvers.
3. Check the skating surface carefully before and while skating. For street skating or skateboard riding, avoid uneven or broken cement, branches and rocks in the skating path. On outdoor ice rinks and ponds, look for patches of grass, rocks, ruts and thin ice.
4. Warn children against roller-skating or using a skateboard in the street or on crowded sidewalks, or ice-skating on outdoor ponds that are not solidly frozen. Obey "No Skating" signs on ponds.
5. Learn how to fall to reduce the chances of serious injury. Try to break your fall with your hands and avoid hitting the flat of your back or your head. Try to

roll into fleshy parts of the body, such as buttocks, upper legs and shoulders. It will help if you can learn to relax, rather than go stiff, when falling.

6. Take off roller skates before crossing streets.

7. Wearing safety equipment, such as protective knee and elbow pads, is a good idea when skating. This may help prevent more serious injuries. Other equipment can include wrist braces, helmets and mouth guards. The latter may prevent knocking out or breaking teeth. Wearing helmets while skating, especially on skateboards, is necessary. Special padded clothing and accessories are good for skateboarders.

8. Beginning ice skaters with weak ankles may want to tape their ankles, until they are stronger, to prevent falls.

ICE SKATES

Whether you ice-skate on indoor rinks or outside, the preparations are the same:

1. Select skates that fit snugly so you do not wobble when you walk. A pair that fits well will often be smaller than your street shoes.

2. Prepare for the buying decision by renting skates first. When buying, it pays to buy good skates (about $80). Cheaper ones will not provide the needed ankle support.

3. Beginning ice skaters can benefit from lessons, but it is possible to learn on your own.

4. Falls are inevitable, so learn to relax and reduce your chances of serious injury. Recover and stand up quickly.

5. Never skate outdoors alone. Make sure the ice is thin enough (at least 4 inches thick) and note any warning signs that are posted.

Maintenance

1. Keep skates in good repair. Don't skate on wheels or blades that need repair.

2. Keep parts tightened. Replace broken straps of strap-on roller skates at once.

Accident patterns for skates or skateboards

1. Skating too close. Other skaters can stop quickly in front of you or skate across your path and cause accidents.

2. Product structural problems. These include improper changes and repairs, excessive wobbly skateboards that tip over easily or wheels falling off loose axles.

3. Poor skating or skateboarding surface. Environmental hazards such as cracked or uneven cement sidewalks, tree branches, rocks or other debris can cause tripping or skidding. Ice skaters can encounter ruts in the ice or grass and gravel on outdoor rinks.

4. Other causes of accidents involve the "human factor":
   - Inexperience with the skates or skateboard or with "trick skating."
   - Horseplay and pushing.
   - Lack of attention.
   - Misuse, such as going up and down steps wearing skates.
   - Roller skating or riding a skateboard in traffic.

SWIMMING POOLS

About 300 people drown each year in home swimming pools. One recent study found that 75 percent of the drowning and submersion accidents, for children under the age of 5, happened to children between 12 and 15 months of age. This group is at the highest risk of drowning and deserves our concern. Here are examples of typical swimming pool accidents:

- After a long walk on a hot day, 10-year-old Jimmy eagerly ran to the back yard for a swim in the pool. He fell on the smooth deck which was slippery, because there was water on it. Jimmy's arm was broken in the fall.

- Mr. Carr dove from the side of his pool into 4 feet of water. He hit the bottom with his hands and head, suffering lacerations and bruises.
- Susan, 7, always envied her neighbor's backyard swimming pool. One Sunday while they were gone, she climbed the 5-foot fence surrounding the pool. Susan didn't know how to swim very well, and drowned when she got into deep water.

Accident patterns

1. Accidents to children can happen in familiar settings during short lapses in supervision.
2. Falling on slippery walkways, diving boards or ladders is a common problem. Reduce it with the use of nonslip cement or similar materials.
3. Striking the bottom or sides of the pool when the water is too shallow. People are also injured when they hit water pipes, ladders or other objects in the pool.
4. Drowning can happen when swimming alone or without adult supervision. Inadequate fences contribute to this problem because children can get into a pool without the owner's knowledge.
5. Shock hazards are usually due to faulty wiring.
6. Dangerous explosions can result from excess pressure in the filter tank.

Pool construction

1. Use nonslip materials on the deck surrounding your pool and on diving boards and ladders. The use of these materials may cause water to collect on the deck and, if the deck is not regularly cleaned, moss will begin to grow.
2. Avoid sudden drops in depth when building a pool. Show safe diving areas with a different color on the pool bottom. Paint numbers on the edge of the pool to show water depth at various points.
3. Make all water pipes flush with the walls and bottom of the pool.
4. Have all electrical systems installed to recognized safety standards by a licensed electrician.
5. Provide enough lighting so people can see at night. Install underwater lighting if the pool is used at night. Underwater lighting circuits should be protected by GFIs (ground fault circuit interrupters). While electrical codes provide for this, older pools or spas may not have it.
6. Ladders need handrails on both sides (the diameter of the handrail should be small enough for a child's firm grip), and there should be at least one ladder for each end of the pool.
7. The steps of the ladder should be at least 3 inches deep and made of nonslippery material.
8. There should be a fence around all four sides of the pool to keep children out when there is no supervision. Do not provide direct access to the pool from a house or patio door. Toddlers, in particular, can wander out and fall into the pool. Place tables and chairs well away from the pool fence so they cannot be used to climb over the fence.
9. The barrier should be at least 4 feet high and difficult to climb. If a chain-link fence is used, no part of the diamond-shaped openings should be more than 1¾ inches. Vertical slats should be less than 4 inches apart.
10. Gates that provide access to the pool should be self-closing and secured with a lock. The gate latching mechanism should be out of the reach of children.
11. Check local ordinances for safe pool construction requirements.
12. Doors that exit to the pool should have alarms so that those inside are warned

that someone has gone into the pool area.

13. Seconds count in preventing death or brain damage. Know CPR and begin resuscitation immediately, even in the water. A poolside telephone showing emergency numbers will enable you to summon help after starting CPR.

14. Keep rescue equipment by the poolside.

15. Government experts believe that warning signs about diving and supervising children would prevent many drownings. Check the CPSC for release #91-106 for samples.

Use of swimming pools

1. Always have competent adult supervision while the pool is in use. Flotation devices cannot be relied on to protect children. Baby sitters and caretakers should always be given instructions on potential hazards to young children in and around the pool.

2. Never swim alone. Swim with a buddy.

3. Don't use diving boards in pools that are not deep enough. (The often recommended depth of 8½ feet may not be deep enough. The safe depth depends on the style of diving and the skill of the diver.) Don't permit diving into above-ground pools. Before diving, always wade into water first to check the depth.

4. When diving, go straight off the end of the board. Don't dive from the side of the pool, but enter the water feet first.

5. Dive with your hands in front of you and steer up immediately upon entering the water to avoid hitting the bottom or sides of the pool.

6. Never put a slide in the shallow end of the pool. A person entering the water head-first from the slide can hit the bottom and be seriously injured. The sitting-down, legs-first position is the safest way to use a slide.

7. Improper use of pool slides presents the same dangers as improper diving techniques. Never slide down head first. Slide down feet first only.

8. Place a safety float line where the bottom slope begins to deepen (at the 5-foot level).

9. Keep essential rescue and first aid equipment ready at the pool.

10. Don't swim after drinking, eating or taking drugs and other medications.

11. Keep all electrical appliances, such as radios, away from the pool because of the potential shock hazard they represent.

12. Don't show off by swimming long distances under water.

13. Learn to swim well.

14. Keep toys away from the pool area because a child playing with the toys could accidentally fall in the water.

15. No running, pushing or dunking around swimming areas.

16. No glass or bottles near swimming or wading areas.

17. Yell for help only when you really need it.

18. Remove steps from above-ground pools when pool are not in use.

Maintenance of swimming pools

1. Keep the fence in good repair. Don't put anything outside the fence that will enable a child to climb over the fence.

2. Check the electrical equipment regularly to see that it meets local codes.

WATER PLAY AREAS

Water play areas for younger children pose some special problems, especially if they do not fit into the swimming pool category. Here are a few guidelines:

1. Whether it is a natural or artificial area, care is needed to keep the area from becoming a breeding ground for insects and a health menace.

2. Most water play areas, public or private, must conform to health regulations.

3. Water play areas should not have hidden spaces. All areas should be visible to allow proper supervision.

4. Spray and water collecting areas need a nonslip surface, such as asphalt.

5. Water play areas should not have sudden changes in water depth, to prevent falls into deeper water.

6. Drains, streams, water spouts and hydrants should not create strong suction effects or water jet forces.

7. Toys and play equipment used around the water play area should be made of sturdy plastic. Don't allow glass in the area.

8. Inspect water play areas where there has been standing water for more than 24 hours. Check for glass, trash, animal excrement and other foreign material.

9. Don't allow children to play in hot tubs, spas or saunas.

10. Do not permit electrical wires or unprotected electrical equipment to be located over or in the play area.

11. Keep pool equipment and chemical storage rooms locked and ventilated.

TRAMPOLINES

The many trampoline injuries that are treated each year indicate that trampolines are not toys. They are gym equipment that can be dangerous if not equipped, maintained and used safely. This section covers the use of trampolines in amateur settings.

There is seldom room for a good trampoline inside a house. If there is to be room for jumping, the trampoline is set up outdoors and subject to wear and tear from the elements. This outside display also makes them an attractive nuisance to neighborhood children.

- Mike, 12 years old, was jumping on a trampoline with a friend. He lost his balance when his friend stumbled, and Mike hit his head on the trampoline's metal frame. Although frame pads were provided, they were not in place at the time of the accident. He required 7 stitches for a laceration of the scalp.

- Leo, 13, fractured his ankle when dismounting from a trampoline by doing a handspring from the bed (the jumping surface) to the ground.

- Mark, 11, landed on the exposed metal frame of a trampoline when he tried to execute a back flip with no spotters. He died of head injuries in a hospital several hours later.

- Ellen, 6, sat on the corner of the frame of a trampoline while acting as a spotter. She lost her balance, fell backwards to the ground and sustained simple and compound fractures of her arm.

Selection and placement

1. Trampolines should have frame pads. These pads should be made of a firm, yet flexible, resilient material and should be wide enough to cover the frame and the hooks of all the springs.

2. If there is a covering over the springs between the frame pad and jumping bed, it should be of a color that contrasts with that of the bed.

3. Set up the trampoline on a level surface.

4. Use trampolines only in well-lighted areas. If you intend to use the trampoline outdoors at night, set up enough outdoor lighting that the entire trampoline is evenly lighted.

5. Safe jumping requires a minimum ceiling height of 24 feet as measured from floor to ceiling. Gyms with high ceilings can handle indoor jumping, but most homes cannot.

6. Inspect your trampoline carefully and check the condition of all parts after each use. These conditions suggest potential hazards:

   - Punctures or holes worn in the bed.
   - Deterioration in stitching of the bed.

- A sagging bed.
- Ruptured springs.
- Missing or insecurely attached frame pads.
- A bent or broken frame.
- Sharp protrusions on the frame or suspension system.

Use of trampolines

1. You should be able to do the basic bounces, drops and body positions before attempting any tricks or stunts.
2. Control your bounce by flexing your knees slightly when you contact the trampoline bed. Flex them more to stop bouncing.
3. Good supervision is vital to safe trampoline use. The supervision required varies with the skill of the user and the difficulty of the jumps.
4. Spotters are essential for all novice or beginning jumpers, as well as for advanced jumpers building new skills. Spotters stand on the ground around the frame and watch the person who is jumping. There should be a spotter at each side of the trampoline. Spotters should know how they can help prevent injuries. Their task involves:
   - Making sure the jumper stays in the middle of the trampoline bed. They tell the jumper to move back to the middle if he or she starts to "travel" or move to the outer parts of the bed.
   - Telling the jumper to "break bounce" or bend the knees and drop immediately to the bed of the trampoline if the jumper appears to lose control or is off balance.
   - Gently pushing the jumper back to the center of the bed if he or she comes too close to the springs.
5. Don't talk to spotters or onlookers unless it is necessary. Spotters must concentrate on your jumping.

6. Avoid bouncing too high. Keep your bounces low until you can control your bounce and consistently land in the center of the trampoline.
7. If you feel nervous about jumping or executing a stunt, don't do it! Being tense makes it harder to control your bounces and keep your balance.
8. Consider a trick thoroughly before starting it. Changing your mind in mid-air is dangerous.
9. Allow only one person at a time on the trampoline.
10. A "spotting" or "twisting" belt can greatly increase your safety when attempting new tricks. More often found in a gym than a home, this jumper-worn device attaches to several ropes by an overhead pole or rig and controls a jumper's movements. The ropes are controlled by spotters who should be expert in their use. The spotters can stop you in the middle of a trick if you lose control and can lower you gently to the trampoline bed. The belt is no guarantee that injury will not occur, but it is safer than doing the activity without a belt.
11. Keep jumping periods short, particularly when you are a beginner. Don't jump when you are tired.
12. Don't use the trampoline while you are under the influence of alcohol or drugs.
13. Wear socks, pants and a shirt while jumping to avoid mat burns.
14. Climb, don't jump off the trampoline.
15. When supervised use of the trampoline is over, lock or secure the trampoline to prevent unauthorized and unattended use.

FIREARMS SAFETY

In this book, there is no attempt to cover the legal or regulatory aspects of buying, keeping or using a firearm. For our purpose, we assume that the firearm was bought legally and is legal to own and use.

Firearm safety generally falls into two categories: keeping the firearm in the home and using it in the field or woods. Here, we've divided firearms into two types, shoulder guns and handguns. We'll concentrate on handguns because they are more likely to be kept at home.

Handguns. One in four households contains a handgun, and 70 percent of these are meant for home security. Some research, however, shows that handgun owners are much more likely to shoot themselves or family members than intruders. The fact that most handguns are kept for security means the owner wants them ready for use. They are likely to be loaded and stored without safety measures such as locks. Generally, handguns are either semi-automatic or revolvers.

Semi-automatic. Semi-automatics have a magazine and are operated by grasping a slide and pulling it back. The slide will lock, allowing the chamber and the magazine to be inspected and to remove the magazine.

Revolver. A revolver has a cylindrical shaped magazine, called a cylinder. This holds the cartridges and can often, but not always, swing out for easy inspection, unloading or loading. Revolvers without a swing-out magazine require extra care to be certain they are empty. Remove cartridges by shaking or using a small ejector rod located alongside the barrel.

General safety rules. There are three basic rules for safe gun handling according to the National Rifle Association (NRA). Follow these rules, which apply to rifles and revolvers:

1. Always point the gun in a safe direction. This is the primary rule in gun safety. This means that the gun should be pointed in such a direction that it will not cause injury or damage if it goes off. The key to following this rule is to always control where the muzzle or front end of the barrel points. Common sense dictates the safest direction, depending on the circumstances.

2. Always keep your finger off the trigger until ready to shoot. When holding a gun, people have a natural tendency to place their finger on the trigger. Don't do it! Rest your finger on the trigger guard or along the side of the gun. Until you are ready to fire, do not touch the trigger.

3. Do not load the gun until ready to use. Whenever you pick up a gun, first open the action and look into the rear of the gun's barrel. This is the chamber and should be clear of ammunition. (If the gun has a magazine, remove it before opening the action and make sure it is empty.) If you do not know how to open the action, leave the gun alone and get help from someone who does.

When using or storing a gun. Follow these NRA rules:

1. Be sure the gun is safe to operate. Just like other tools, guns need regular maintenance. Regular cleaning and proper storage are a part of the gun's general upkeep. If there is any question about a gun being able to function, a gunsmith should look at it.

2. Know how to use the gun safely. Before handling a gun, learn how it operates. Know its basic parts, how to safely open and close the action and remove any ammunition from the gun or magazine. Remember, a gun's mechanical device is never foolproof. Nothing can replace safe gun handling.

3. Use only the correct ammunition for your gun. Only BBs, pellets, cartridges or shells designed for a gun can be fired safely in that gun. Most guns have the ammunition type stamped on the barrel. Ammunition can be identified by information printed on the box and sometimes on the cartridge. Do not shoot the gun unless you know you have the proper ammunition.

4. Know your target. Identify your target beyond any doubt. Equally important, be aware of the area beyond your target. This means noting your proposed area of fire before you shoot. Never fire in a direction in which there are people. Think first. Shoot second.

5. Wear eye and ear protection. Guns are loud and the noise can cause hearing damage. They can also emit debris and hot gas that could cause eye injury. For these reasons, wear safety glasses and ear protectors.

6. Do not use alcohol, or any other substance that impairs normal physical or bodily functions, before or while handling or shooting guns.

7. Store guns so they are not accessible to unauthorized persons. Consider carefully when you decide where and how you intend to store guns. Safe and secure storage means that you deny untrained persons (especially children) access to or use of your guns.

Many people do not know that BB guns, especially high-velocity guns, can cause death. BB guns are dangerous up to 350 yards and can kill a person. High velocity BB guns, with muzzle speeds higher than 350 feet per second, increase this risk. Do not let children under 14 use high-velocity BB or pellet guns. They are not toys. Never aim these guns at another person.

Cleaning. The first step in cleaning a gun is to make sure the gun is not loaded. There should not be any ammunition in the cleaning area. The "action" should be open during cleaning.

1. Regular cleaning is important. Clean your gun following each use and before using it after it has been in storage for a lengthy period of time.

ARTS AND CRAFTS

The CPSC has a mandatory labeling standard for arts and crafts products that have chronic, long-term health hazards. These products include solvents, spray paints, silk-screen inks, adhesive and others marketed for use in the visual or graphic arts.

Public law requires safe use of arts and crafts materials. The law establishes guidelines for determining if arts and crafts materials present chronic, long-term health hazards and adopts a voluntary standard—ASTM D-4236-88. Many want the guidelines to be mandatory and the CPSC announced in 1993 that it would codify the standard. The standard requires labels for all arts and crafts materials that might present a chronic hazard. Among other requirements, the labels must provide:

1. A warning statement of the hazard.
2. Identification of the hazardous ingredients.
3. Guidelines for safe use.

A label might have this statement:

WARNING! HARMFUL IF SWALLOWED, MAY PRODUCE BIRTH DEFECTS.
Contains lead.
When using, do not eat, drink or smoke.
Wash hands immediately after use.
Should not be used by pregnant women.
Keep out of reach of children.
Conforms to **ASTM D-4236.**
(Name, address, and telephone number of Manufacturer or importer.)

The labeling for chronic hazard is in addition to labeling for acute hazards, such as flammability or irritation, which is required by another act. While only hazardous art materials must have safety labeling, all art materials will have the statement: "Conforms to ASTM D-4236" or a similar statement.

Do not buy potentially hazardous arts and crafts materials for children under 12. Children under that age are not likely to follow instructions on labels. Do not use any materials that have lead or metal

Home Safety Desk Reference

pigments, fumes or powders. If you cannot find arts and crafts materials without the warning label, consider these substitutes:

Instead of	Use
Rubber cement	Water-based adhesive
Chalk that creates dust	Crayons
Commercial dyes	Vegetable dyes
Permanent markers	Water-based markers
Powdered paints	Liquid paints
Epoxy instant glues	Water-based glues
Clay in dry form	Clay in wet form

Look for the label that says: "Conforms to ASTM D-4236" or a similar statement. Labels must also address the flammability or irritability of the substance and provide guidelines for its safe use. A toxicologist must evaluate products every five years.

Although products with a seal from The Arts and Crafts Materials Institute, Inc., should be nontoxic, you should not allow children under 12 to use potentially hazardous arts or crafts materials. Good substitutes for any hazardous substances, such as those listed above, are available for use by children under 12 years of age.

SAFETY RECAP

1. Pursue only recreation and sports you are mentally and physically prepared to handle.

2. Teaching the hazards of sports and recreation should start in the home.

3. The hazards of organized sports for children is increasingly similar to the hazards and injuries of adult participants.

4. Coaches and managers of organized sports need special training to coach and manage safely.

5. Proper protective equipment is a key to safety in recreation and sports.

6. Hypothermia and hyperthermia are two great dangers of outdoor sports. Know how to recognize, treat and avoid both.

7. Proper use of recreational and sports equipment helps assure safety.

8. Three rules of gun safety will prevent most accidents:
   - Always point the gun in a safe direction.
   - Keep your finger off the trigger until ready to shoot.
   - Never load the gun until ready to use it.

9. Most moped and motorbike accidents can be prevented by using good equipment in good condition, having good road conditions and using the equipment properly.

10. Use outdoor equipment outdoors only.

11. Prevent most home swimming pool accidents by protecting pools from unauthorized use and always supervising children in pools.

12. Every sports and recreation activity requires protective equipment, proper training and proper use of equipment.

BIBLIOGRAPHY

"Always Supervise Children, Safety Commission Warns," *Consumer Product Safety Alert*, Consumer Product Safety Commission, May 1987.

"BB Guns Can Kill," *Consumer Product Safety Alert*, U.S. Consumer Product Commission, May 1990.

"10 Tips on Choosing Trikes That Are Safe for Trikes," Bowler, Jan, *Child Care Information Exchange*, Redmond, WA: Child Care Information Exchange, June 1989, p. 14.

"Blade Runners," Brown, Jo, *Pacific Northwest*, Seattle, WA: April 1993, pp. 35-36.

Caring for Our Children, Elk Grove Village, IL: American Academy of Pediatrics, 1992, p. 172.

"Children and Pools," U.S. Consumer Product Safety Commission, 1990.

"CPSC Declares New Art and Craft Label Standard," *Product Safety Up-To-Date*, Chicago, IL: National Safety Council, January/February 1991, p. 4.

"CPSC Issues Halloween Safety Tips," *Consumer Product Safety Alert*, U.S. Consumer Product Safety Commission, October 1986.

"CPSC Promotes Safety Labeling for Art and Craft Materials," *Consumer Product Safety Alert*, Washington, DC: Consumer Product Safety Commission, July 1990.

"CPSC Urges Bicyclist to Wear Helmets," *Consumer Product Safety Alert*, U.S. Consumer Product Safety Commission, August 1989.

"CPSC Warns of Illegal Fireworks," *Consumer Product Safety Alert*, U.S. Consumer Product Safety Commission, June 1983.

"Oregon Nurse Joins Growing Cause," Crum, William C., *Seattle Times*, Local News, Sunday, July 11, 1993.

"Dive Into Water Safety," *Family Safety and Health*, Chicago, IL: National Safety Council, Summer 1933, p. 14.

"Come Home to Traditional Winter Sports," Eden, Amber, *Family Safety*. Chicago, IL: National Safety Council, Winter 1992-1993, pp. 11-13.

"Equipment Makes Winter Sports Safer," *Product Safety Up-To-Date*, Chicago, IL: National Safety Council, January/February 1991, Vol. 19, No. 1, p. 2.

"Exercise Bicycles," *Consumer Reports*," November 1990, pp. 746-751.

Child Care Safety and Health Management, Ferry, Ted, Des Plaines, IL: American Society of Safety Engineers, 1993.

"Fireworks," *Product Safety Fact Sheet*, U.S. Consumer Product Safety Commission, May 1990.

"Halloween Safety," *Product Safety Fact Sheet*, U.S. Consumer Product Safety Commission, September 1987.

"Head Injuries Require Quick, Skilled Care," *FDA Consumer*, Washington, DC: Food and Drug Administration, GPO, September 1990, pp. 9-13.

"Health and Safety," *Aide*, San Antonio: USAA, p. 24.

"How to Make Your Workouts Safer," *Vitality*, Dallas, TX: Vitality, Inc., August 1991, p. 20.

Huffy Bicycles Owner's Manual, USA: Huffy Corporation, January 1990.

"Fitness Matters," Legwold, Gary, *Better Homes and Gardens*, September 1991, p. 80.

"Line Up Protective Gear This Spring," *Family Safety and Health*, Chicago, IL: National Safety Council, p. 3.

"Children and Sports," Micheli, Lyle J., *Newsweek*, October 29, 1990, p. 12.

"Myths That May Make You Drown," *Community Safety & Health*, Chicago, IL: National Safety Council, July/August 1991, p. 4.

"Prevent Finger Amputations to Children From Exercise Bikes," *Consumer Product Safety Alert*, August 1990.

"Recognize Illness Caused by Extreme Temperature," *Community Safety and Health*, Chicago, IL: National Safety Council, January/February, 1991, p. 4.

"Roller Skating and Ice Skates," *Product Safety Fact Sheet*, U.S. Consumer Product Safety Commission, September 1979.

"Safety Commission Warns About Hazards With In-Line Roller Skates," *Consumer Product Safety Alert*, U.S. Consumer Product Safety Commission, August 1991.

"Safety is the Key," *Aide*, April 1991, pp. 20-21.

"Skateboards," *Product Safety Fact Sheet*, U.S. Consumer Product Safety Commission, March 1988.

Making Art Safely, Spandorfer, Merle, Deborah Curtiss and Jack Snyder, New

York, NY: Van Nostrand Reinhold, 1992. (Not yet in stock).

"Don't Use Your Head; Use Your Helmet," Thurber, Sarah, *Family Safety and Health*, Chicago, IL: National Safety Council, Summer 1933, pp. 26-27.

"Will Handguns Keep You Safe?" Tritsch, Shane, *Safety and Health*, Chicago, IL: National Safety Council, August 1933, pp. 68-70.

"VitaSafe." *Vitality*, Dallas, TX: August 1991, p. 30.

"Wear Helmets To Prevent Sports-Related Head Injuries," *Consumer Product Safety Alert*, U.S. Consumer Product Safety Commission, April 1990.

THE HAZARDOUS HOME

The chapters in this section cover two areas of hazards in the home: the hidden hazards, from asbestos and radon to insecticides; and highly visible consumer product hazards, from blenders, to curling irons and humidifiers.

Both are dangerous to us for what we don't see—dangerous invisible or hidden processes and common appliances, whose familiarity often breeds carelessness.

CHAPTER 4

HIDDEN HAZARDS AND HOUSEHOLD PRODUCTS

Environmentalists will find much of interest here in the discussions of vinyl chloride, fluorocarbons, aerosols, pesticides and insecticides. Note that current environmental information is soon obsolete as researchers uncover new dangers, as activists adopt new causes and as new consumer products appear.

AEROSOL CANS

About 5,000 people per year receive emergency room treatment for aerosol associated injuries. Billions of aerosol cans are made in the U.S. each year. These pressurized cans dispense pesticides, paints, hair sprays, medications and many other household products.

- Wilma discarded an empty can of insect repellent in a waste-paper fire. The can exploded and a piece of flying metal pierced her jugular vein. She died 15 minutes later.
- Jimmy, 8, used a hammer and nail to puncture an old can of spray paint. The can exploded hurling pieces of metal into his face and upper chest, cutting him severely.
- Laurie was smoking while she used an aerosol can of hair spray. Her cigarette ignited the spray and she received severe burns that permanently disfigured her face.
- Stuart was spray-painting a bookcase in his basement. There was no ventilation and the fumes accumulated to such a level that he became dizzy and

collapsed. When his wife found him, he was dead.
- Ken, 6, found a can of insect spray and accidentally sprayed it into his face. He was severely burned by the chemical.

Accident patterns. These cases listed depict these mishap patterns:

1. Explosions caused by high temperatures. Throwing an aerosol can into a fire or storing it near a radiator or in the sun can cause it to explode.
2. Explosions caused by puncturing. Even if you think a can is empty, there can be enough pressure to cause it to explode if punctured.
3. Flammability of contents or propellants. Some propellants, such as propane, are highly flammable, and many of the "usable contents" are also flammable. Some sprays will burn like a blowtorch when lit by matches or other flame sources.
4. Toxicity of contents or propellants. Propellants (such as vinyl chloride) can be toxic if used in unventilated rooms and large amounts are inhaled. Some people who inhaled aerosols have suffered dizziness, lack of coordination, nausea, headache or blurred vision, while others have died. Aerosol sprays can also cause heart trouble, skin problems, breathing problems and are linked to cancer.

5. Chemical burns. These are often caused by children who misdirect the spray.

Use of aerosol cans

1. Read the instructions and warning statements before using.
2. Be sure there is plenty of fresh air when you spray indoors, because of the toxicity of the contents and propellant.
3. Don't smoke while spraying because many aerosols are flammable.
4. Don't use sprays near heaters, gas stoves or other flame or heat sources.
5. Keep your body well covered and wash exposed areas after spraying. This is very important with insecticide sprays.
6. Stop spraying at the first sign of dizziness, nausea, headache, blurred vision or skin irritation. Seek fresh air at once and call a doctor if the symptoms persist or are severe.
7. Don't use aerosols around food. The spray can contaminate the food.
8. Teach children about the hazards of aerosols—explosions and flammability.

Storage of aerosol cans

1. Keep aerosol containers in a cool location. Some aerosols can explode at 120°F or higher.
2. Do not expose aerosols to direct sunlight radiators, stoves or other heat sources. Don't leave aerosols in your car where temperatures can reach high levels on hot days.
3. Keep all aerosols out of the reach of children.

Disposal of aerosol cans

1. Dispose of aerosols with other nonburnable trash.
2. Do not puncture aerosol containers. There are some devices on the market that claim to be safe for puncturing aerosol cans, but the directions for using them are complicated and dangerous if not followed carefully.

3. Do not throw "empty" aerosols in incinerators or trash compactors. They may still contain propellants that can build up pressure, causing the cans to explode.

Tire inflators. Aerosol tire inflators, made to help stranded motorists inflate flat tires, are compressed gas and sealant in cans. Some inflators use highly flammable gases as propellants and are dangerous to both the person using the can and the person who later deflates the tire. Most, but not all, cans have good labels. Some labels indicate the inflator in not flammable, but this may not be true. Some manufacturers have switched to chlorofluorocarbon propellants, considered to be less of an environmental hazard. They are safe around a flame, but still harmful to the earth's ozone layer.

ASBESTOS

Asbestos is a mineral fiber used to insulate and retard fire. It is more often found in older buildings, in insulation, shingles, mill board and floor tiles. The manufacturers of asbestos products voluntarily limit its use in several banned products. In 1989 the EPA announced a phased-in ban of most asbestos products, capping in 1996.

Handling asbestos products. Not all products containing asbestos are dangerous. If in doubt, hire an asbestos contractor or obtain proper training before taking any action. Higher concentrations of asbestos result when you cut and sand asbestos materials. Improper removal also releases asbestos fibers into the air. Even if you have training, don't make minor repairs on surfaces that are larger than your hand.

Questions for an asbestos contractor. To judge the skill and experience of an asbestos contractor, ask:

1. Are you certified? (Ask to see the certificate.)
2. Do you and your workers have training?
3. Do you have experience removing asbestos from buildings?
4. Will you provide references of people for whom you have worked to remove asbestos?
5. Will you provide a list of places where you have removed asbestos?
6. Will you use the wet method (water and wetting agent) now required by the EPA?
7. Will you use polyethylene plastic barriers to contain dust?
8. Will you use a high-efficiency particulate air (HEPA) filter vacuum cleaner?
9. Will your workers wear approved respirators?
10. Will you properly dispose of the asbestos and leave the site free of asbestos dust and debris?
11. Will you provide copies of air monitoring test results and, upon completion, test results to show all surfaces are within EPA limits?
12. Will you provide copies of disposal manifests?
13. Will you provide a written contract specifying these procedures?

Monitoring the asbestos contractor. Make sure the asbestos contractor follows these procedures:

1. Seals off the work area from the rest of the building and closes off the heating/air conditioning and electricity in work areas.
2. Clearly marks off the work site as a hazard area and does not permit non-workers to enter.
3. Workers wear approved respirators and other protective clothing. All personal protective equipment should be disposed of or removed from the site, along with asbestos material, immediately after use.

4. Thoroughly mists (spraying, not dripping) the asbestos material to keep fibers from blowing and for easier cleanup.
5. Cutting or drilling asbestos material is done outside or in special containment room.
6. Asbestos material is be removed in pieces as large as possible, to help contain fibers.
7. Asbestos debris removed goes into sealed, leak-proof, properly labeled plastic bags and is disposed of in a proper landfill.
8. On completion of the job and removal of the material, the contractor thoroughly cleans the area with wet mops, wet rags or sponges. Repeats the process a second time and then takes surface and air tests.

Health effects. Soft, easily crumbled, asbestos-containing material has the greatest potential to create health risks. The most dangerous asbestos fibers are too small to be seen. Asbestos fibers in the air present a health hazard. After they are inhaled they can remain in the lungs and can cause several kinds of cancer and asbestosis (lung scarring). Either can be fatal. Symptoms do not appear for many years after the exposure. Indirect contact through clothing and job equipment can endanger family members.

Reduce building exposure

1. If you think you have an asbestos problem, get help from an expert.
2. Do not cut, rip or sand asbestos-containing materials, including asbestos-containing vinyl floor tiles.
3. When replacing floor tiles, handle them as little as possible. Leave undamaged materials alone.
4. When you must remove or clean up asbestos, use a professionally trained contractor. This applies to:
   - Asbestos insulation.
   - Certain older textured paint.

- Some ceiling material (it usually looks crumbly).
- Older stove insulation.
- Some roofing, shingles and siding.
- Furnace door gaskets.
- Insulation on pipes.
- Some appliances.

5. While not proven specifically, scientific evidence (EPA) suggests smoking and asbestos exposure together can be a greater cancer risk than either one alone.

CANNING

Can defects. More than 1,500 food products are canned, making up more than 12 percent of grocery sales. Canning foods is an old process that is safe under the right conditions. Some products canned well over 100 years ago have been safe when opened, although they've lost a bit of color and flavor.

Food-spoiling bacteria, yeasts and molds are naturally present in foods. Foods are kept from spoiling by controlling their moisture, acid, nutrient content and temperature. The canning process controls these to preserve and store them indefinitely. Today, using the proper process, products can be canned in glass jars, paperboard and plastic containers. New processes and containers continually make canning safer and more convenient.

A critical element in canning is sealing products in airtight containers, using a vacuum process. The loss of vacuum is seen in cans with bulging ends. If the seal is not airtight, bacteria can enter the can, grow and contaminate the product.

How to recognize can defects. Following are guidelines to help recognize defects in cans. Look for:

Metal cans
1. An obvious opening underneath the double seam on the top or bottom of a can.
2. A can with bulging ends.
3. A fracture in the double seam.
4. A pinhole or puncture in the body of the can.
5. An unwelded portion of the side seam.
6. A leak from anywhere in the can.

Plastic cans
1. Any opening or nonbonding in the seal.
2. A break in the plastic.
3. A fractured lid.
4. A swollen package.

Paperboard cans
1. A patch in the seal where bonding or adhesive is missing.
2. A slash or slice in the package.
3. A leak in a corner of the package.
4. A swollen package.

Glass jars
1. A pop-top that does not pop when opened (showing loss of vacuum).
2. A damaged seal.
3. A crack in the glass of a jar.

Flexible pouches
1. A break in the adhesive across the width of the seal.
2. A slash or break in the package.
3. A leak at a manufactured notch used for easy opening.
4. A swollen package.

Home canning safety

To avoid injury or illness, as well as the loss of time and money, from spoiled food, the home canner should check for faulty equipment, use canning equipment carefully and follow proven canning procedures.

- Mrs. McGuire had just taken seven jars of home-canned prunes out of her pressure cooker and was carrying them on a rack when one of the jars exploded, separating the lid and part of the jar rim from the rest of the jar. Scalding hot prunes and juice flew into her face, causing second and third degree burns.

Injury causes. The above case shows one example of injury caused by home canning. Others are:

1. Exploding, cracking or imploding (bursting inward) jars, often caused by jar lids that are too tight to allow escape of steam during the hot pack process, defects in the glass and sudden changes of temperature.
2. Splashing scalding water by careless handling or tipping of canning boilers.
3. Inattentive or careless use of peelers, grinders and juicers during food preparation can cause cuts and bruises.

Illness. Food-borne illness from home canning ranges from mild to severe and sometimes results in death. Illness may result from:

1. Canning lids and jars that fail to seal properly, causing contamination and spoilage.
2. Failure to follow complete, correct food preparation and canning procedures.

Selecting canning equipment

1. Examine canning lids for nicks, irregular surfaces, dents and rust. Avoid any imperfect lids that will prevent proper sealing.
2. Check jars for cracks, chips or bubbles before buying or using.
3. Carefully run your fingers around the mouths of jars to test for uneven edges.
4. Buy lids and jars that come with clear, detailed instructions. Even experienced canners should read instructions carefully before using any brand, especially an unfamiliar one. Different procedures may be used for proper sealing.

Canning the food

1. Follow instructions in canning bulletins and those on canning equipment.

The U.S. Department of Agriculture (USDA) offers guidelines.

2. Use only lids, seals and jars made for home canning.
3. Do not reuse sealing lids. Buy new sealing rings and lids.
4. If you move to a different part of the country, adjust cooking time for altitude. The USDA offers guidelines for this.
5. Use grinders and other food appliances with care.
6. Make sure canning boilers are stable before boiling the water. Avoid splashing scalding water during processing and when taking hot jars from the boiling water bath.
7. Don't pour cold water over hot canning jars or set hot jars on cold surfaces.
8. Test the seal according to instructions. If many lids fail to seal even after you have followed correct canning procedures, try another brand of lids and reprocess the food.

Maintaining equipment and storing canned goods

1. Clean the weighted gage on a pressure cooker now and then.
2. Check pressure cooker gauge before and during canning season.
3. Clean the petcock and safety valve openings of your canner by drawing a string or narrow strip of cloth through them. Clean them before and during the canning season for safe operation.
4. Store canned goods in a cool, dry place, away from heat sources such as hot water pipes or sunlight, and away from moisture that can rust lids.

Food contamination. Defective seals or incorrect canning may cause leaks and allow contamination. Generally, you will see obvious signs of spoiled food: mold, leaks, bulging lids, discoloration or bad odors. Do not taste such food. Destroy it and discard it out of the reach of children and pets.

Another more serious type of food poisoning, botulism, occurs when certain spores are present in vegetables and other foods. If not cooked long enough and at high enough temperatures, these spores can produce virulent toxins, regardless of the seals. Botulism *cannot* be seen or smelled. To destroy botulism spores and keep the deadly toxin from forming, thoroughly wash raw fruits and vegetables and follow proper canning procedures. Then, to be absolutely safe, boil all home-canned goods for 10 to 20 minutes before eating, to destroy any toxins that may be present.

CARBON MONOXIDE

Hundred of people die each year from carbon monoxide poisoning. Thousands more suffer dizziness, nausea and confusion as a result of carbon monoxide. You can't see, taste or smell carbon monoxide, but it kills.

- Because it was cold, the Taylor family rolled the car windows up tight as they drove through the mountains. When they stopped to take a break, the mother found that her two young sons in the back seat were dead. Carbon monoxide poisoning had leaked in from the engine exhaust.

- Surprised by rain during a cookout, Nancy carried her hibachi grill into a tool shed where she continued cooking. She was dead when her husband came to look for her.

- On a cold winter morning, all four members of the Jones family were found dead. The unvented liquefied petroleum gas space heater, which they used to heat their small three-bedroom house, was still hot. It had been left on all night. With no ventilation in the tightly closed house, the carbon monoxide accumulated to a fatal concentration.

Accident patterns. The above cases are examples of these accident patterns:

1. Lack of ventilation in the car. Carbon monoxide gas in the auto exhaust can leak into the car and slowly overcome passengers. It can also kill passengers if the car is running in a garage.
2. Using a charcoal grill inside. Many people use charcoal grills for cooking or heating inside their houses, camping trailers or mobile homes. High levels of carbon monoxide are released by burning charcoal.
3. Unvented space heaters. Unvented fuel-burning appliances, including gas ranges, can produce deadly levels of carbon monoxide.
4. Heating equipment. Carbon monoxide can leak from loose or cracked vent pipes and heat exchangers.

Avoiding carbon monoxide

Carbon monoxide results when fuels burn incompletely, as almost all fuels do to some extent. When there is a good supply of fresh air and the fuel burns properly, there is little danger of carbon monoxide poisoning. But running an internal combustion engine or a poorly adjusted fuel-burning appliance in a closed area without fresh air can be fatal.

At home

All these suggestions also apply to mobile homes, particularly smaller ones that may have less ventilation.

1. Home fuel-burning equipment should be inspected yearly by an expert to keep it working efficiently and properly vented.
2. Fuel-burning heaters used to warm the house should be vented to the outside. If you must use an unvented heater, be sure to leave a window open at least one inch. Turn off unvented heaters at night.
3. Do not use a gas range or oven to heat a room.
4. Never use a charcoal grill or hibachi inside, unless it is in a well-ventilated area.

5. Burning charcoal, whether it is glowing red or turning to gray ashes, gives off large amounts of carbon monoxide.

In the car

1. Always leave all garage windows and doors open if you run an auto engine, or any other internal combustion engine, inside a garage. If you have an attached garage, be sure the fumes do not vent into the house. Avoid running an engine inside for a lengthy period of time.
2. Have your muffler and tail pipes checked regularly. Carbon monoxide can leak into the car from a faulty exhaust system.
3. Open your car windows when the car is stopped with the motor running for any period of time.

Signs of carbon monoxide poisoning

1. Mild cases produce sleepiness, headache, dizziness, blurred vision, irritability and an inability to concentrate.
2. Severe cases cause nausea, vomiting, shortness of breath, convulsions, unconsciousness and death.

   First aid. Get plenty of fresh air and see a doctor immediately.

CARBONATED DRINKS

Bottles of carbonated drinks may be more dangerous than those with noncarbonated beverages because of the internal pressure that may burst the bottle. Internal pressure also may lead to the propulsion of a twist-off cap when opening the bottle. You may have noticed that bottles are thinner now, although the strength is thought to be the same or better.

Each year more than 23,000 persons suffer injuries from soft drink bottles serious enough to require emergency room treatment.

- Jane had just placed a bottle of carbonated soda in her grocery cart when it exploded and cut her face.

- Gary removed an unopened bottle of carbonated soda from the shelf and was turning the twist-off cap when the cap blew off the bottle and struck his eye. He suffered a hemorrhage of the eye.

Accident patterns

1. Explosion of bottles. Reports suggest that some bottles explode spontaneously without being handled, or after normal handling, and that some explode after being jostled or dropped. Explosions can cause glass fragments to travel at great speed and distance.
2. Propulsion of bottle caps. Victims were opening bottles when the caps flew off. Such flying caps may occur because of internal pressure and may fly with great force.
3. Breakage resulting from impact. The victim falls while holding a bottle or drops a bottle.
4. Accident contact with already broken glass. There is more danger of breakage and injury with nonreturnable bottles that often have thinner glass than returnable bottles. Injury reports indicate that carbonated beverage bottles larger than 16 oz. are involved in more accidents than smaller bottles.

Selection

1. Don't buy bottles in wet or damaged cartons.
2. Know that beverages in bottles larger than 16 oz. may have higher injury risks.
3. For easy handling, some beverage bottles come with a plastic protective covering over the bottle.

Use and storage

1. Don't jostle or hit bottles against one another when you carry or store them.
2. Open bottles with the cap pointed away from your face and body.

3. Before drinking, look for broken glass on the mouth of the bottle and inside.

4. Store bottles in a cool place.

5. Store bottles on the floor or on the lowest shelves to reduce the hazard if a bottle falls or explodes.

Housekeeping. If a glass bottle does break, be sure to pick up pieces of broken glass. If bottles break indoors, avoid contact with the broken glass by heeding these cleanup hints:

1. Use a broom and dustpan, cardboard or heavy paper to pick up pieces of broken glass.

2. To pick up smaller pieces of broken glass, use several thicknesses of wet paper towels or tissues.

3. Never use your hands to press down trash in a garbage can. You could cut yourself on pieces of discarded glass.

CHILD ENTRAPMENT

Since 1980, there have been reports of more than 80 suffocation deaths of children who crawled inside latch-type freezers, clothes dryers, combination washer-dryers or old-style, latch-type refrigerators. The children often were playing hide-and-seek. In most of the cases, when the door slammed shut, the tight fitting gasket on the appliances shut off air to the child and prevented screams from being heard. Ice boxes in campers parked outside the home have also caused suffocation deaths.

Recommendations. The most effective way to childproof old-style refrigerators and other unused appliances is to remove the door completely. Many cities will not permit an old refrigerator to be stored otherwise. If the door cannot be detached, remove the latch. Keep children away from old-style refrigerators, freezers, washers and dryers. Lock the door to your utility room and warn children not to play inside these appliances. If a child is missing, check these appliances immediately.

DRAIN CLEANERS

When a drain is sluggish or clogged and mechanical efforts to clear it fail, many consumers use a chemical drain cleaner. Although most of these products are quick and effective, you should use them with caution. Remember that the effectiveness of these cleaners is due to the highly corrosive chemicals they contain. The chemicals make drain cleaners among the most hazardous of products that are normally used around the house.

The corrosive chemicals in drain cleaners react in water to dissolve fat blockages quickly and to attack and destroy other accumulated waste in the drain. But what works so effectively in a drain will cause harm when in contact with the skin or in the eyes. And the damage can be even more severe if the drain cleaner is swallowed. Extensive and repeated surgery is often needed to correct the destruction done when a corrosive is swallowed, if it can be corrected. Improper first aid treatment, such as making the victim vomit, can further increase the injury.

- A 15-month-old boy suffered permanent scarring of his esophagus after swallowing a small quantity of caustic drain cleaner, which was left under the kitchen sink.

- A 34-year-old man received burns on his arm after using a caustic drain cleaner to unclog a bathroom sink. Fifteen minutes after applying the chemical, he ran water into the sink, but the remaining drain cleaner splashed on his arm.

Not all drain cleaners are corrosive. For example, one aerosol drain cleaner contains a halogenated hydrocarbon under pressure. When the gas releases into a drain, the force dislodges the blockage in the pipe. While such a product may not have the extreme hazards of a corrosive drain cleaner, it—like any other aerosol—must still be used with caution.

Purchase of drain cleaners

1. Before buying any type of drain cleaner, see if a plunger or a flexible wire snake will clear the blockage.
2. Household substances containing more than small amounts of the chemicals commonly used with corrosive drain cleaners must be packaged in child-resistant containers. For the benefit of the elderly and handicapped, however, one size of many of these products can be sold without safety packaging. (Liquid drain cleaners with more than a small amount of these chemicals are banned if not sold in a safety package.) It is very important to buy a child-resistant package if small children live in or visit your home.
3. A granular drain cleaner is slightly less hazardous than a liquid. If it spills, a granular cleaner may be brushed off dry skin before damage results. When the skin is wet or the product is liquid, tissue destruction can start immediately.
4. Flexible plastic containers can increase the chance of an injury. If the container is grabbed suddenly, as it might be if it began to fall, the force of the grip could shoot a stream of corrosive liquid from the container.

Use of drain cleaners

1. Read the product's entire label before each use and follow the instructions exactly. Do not use more of the product than is recommended or improvise on the instructions any other way. Never use an aerosol drain cleaner if there is corrosive drain cleaner already in the drain.
2. Be sure that children are out of the area before using any drain cleaner.
3. Protect the skin and eyes as much as possible when using a corrosive. At the very least, wear rubber gloves. Keep the face as far away from the chemical as possible. Use wrap-around plastic goggles to protect the eyes. Such goggles are a good investment, since there are many other household jobs for which they can be used.

Storage and disposal

1. Ideally, do not store corrosive drain cleaners in the home at all. Instead, use and discard them. Drain cleaners are seldom needed and it is not worth the risk to keep such a hazard in the home.
2. If you must keep a drain cleaner, put it in a dry storage area that can be locked and is out of the reach of children. Be aware, however, that storage above eye level can be hazardous. If the container tips as it is removed from the shelf, chemical may spill in the eyes or on the skin.
3. Before you discard a drain cleaner, empty the container and rinse it. Before placing it in the trash, be sure that the cap is on and the safety closure is secure, if it is a child-resistant container. There can be enough residue inside the container's cap to cause serious injury. If possible, discard the container in an outside trash can.

First aid treatment for drain cleaners

If swallowed:

1. Don't try to make the victim vomit. This increases the severity of the injury.
2. Immediately, give large amounts of water or milk to dilute the chemical and call a doctor or hospital emergency room.

If splashed or lodged in the eye:

1. Rinse the eye with running water for 10 to 15 minutes.
2. Call a doctor or hospital emergency room.

If spilled on the skin:

1. Wash with running water for 10 to 15 minutes.
2. Call a doctor or hospital emergency room.

Remember that, by law, drain cleaner labels must carry emergency first aid instructions. It may be your closest source of information in case of an accident.

FAST FOOD

In this chapter, fast food is defined as those foods that you buy at fast food outlets to be eaten either at those locations or at home. Although they are not confined to fast food, recent E.Coli outbreaks at several locations have focused attention on this subject. The guidelines for avoiding E.Coli in fast food also apply to food prepared at home.

E.Coli. In 1992-93, reports of contaminated, undercooked meat and sick children caused panic in parts of the U.S. The attention and concern was overdue, as sloppy cooking practices and under-staffed health departments had become common.

Technically, the deadly bacterium known as E.Coli is called E.Coli 0157:H7. E.Coli contamination of food, particularly meat, is not a new problem. It has always been in meat. We have always known how to prevent it: Wash your hands thoroughly before handling food and cook meat well. Unfortunately, there has been an unexplained increase in E.Coli.

Precautions. Not all the sources and causes of E.Coli are known, at least not to everyone's satisfaction. As this is written, one troublesome and still unsolved outbreak concerns food handling at the salad bar of a fast food restaurant. And, at the time of this book's final draft, an E.Coli outbreak in Oregon was being blamed on contaminated mayonnaise. It was unclear to the state health department how the mayonnaise was contaminated by the bacteria E.Coli, which is normally associated with meat.

Most E.Coli comes from infected cattle. The E.Coli is in the cattles' fecal matter, some of which comes in contact with meat during the slaughterhouse process. Because E.Coli cannot be seen, all beef should be treated as contaminated and should be cooked well. E.Coli turns up less often in other meats.

1. Cook hamburger until the inside pink center is gone. To be certain, break it open when it is served.
2. Wash hands thoroughly after using the bathroom. E.Coli can be passed on by failing to wash hands properly after using the bathroom, then touching food.
3. Be especially careful to wash hands frequently in childcare settings. Clean hands thoroughly after changing diapers.
4. Treat all meat as if it is contaminated and cook it thoroughly.

Take-out food. Take-out food, or more accurately, "bring-in" food, presents several hazards to the consumer. Over 60 percent of supermarkets now have delis with salad bars and prepared foods. Safety experts are not as concerned about the deli food as they are with the way consumers handle it. The delis meet health care standards, but you may not.

If you buy a carton of cold food, take it to a hot car and then run a few errands before eating it, the food can be warm enough for bacteria to grow rapidly. Plastic and cardboard containers do not provide good insulation. When you buy prepared foods, you should take them home and serve them at once. Refrigerate the leftovers immediately after the meal. Throw out any food that has been unrefrigerated more than an hour or two.

Cooking on time. Cook or heat foods when you are ready to eat them. The *Wellness Letter* of the University of California suggests:

1. Cook foods as close to serving time as possible.
2. When you boil vegetables, use as little water as possible.
3. Cook vegetables whole and unpeeled when possible.
4. Never soak fruits and vegetables.
5. Don't leave cooked food standing at room temperature.

FLAMMABLE LIQUIDS

We hear about flammable and combustible liquids, but seldom understand the difference. Flammable liquids are the more dangerous of the two, because they have a flash point below 100°F, while combustibles ignite at over 100°F. (The flash point is where a liquid gives off enough vapors to ignite.)

Each year, 26,000 people require emergency room treatment for injuries involving flammable liquids. These often involve gasoline, and most burns result from fire or explosion. Most of us don't realize how easily flammable liquids can burn. The heavier-than-air vapors can flow invisibly along the floor or ground and be lit by a flame or spark from a good distance. Here are some examples of common mishaps.

- Bill threw some additional denatured alcohol into the charcoal fire after it was lit. The vapors ignited, the flames traveled up to the can, and it exploded. Bill was sprayed with flaming liquid, which ignited his clothing. He suffered burns over 60 percent of his body and spent 111 days in the hospital.

- Carolyn was using gasoline to remove paint, which had spilled on the floor of her small utility room. The burner of the hot water heater came on and ignited the gasoline vapors, causing the room to explode in flames. Carolyn suffered burns on her face, hands and legs and spent weeks in the hospital.

- Marty, 4, took the kerosene can out of the closet and opened it. His mother found him just as he was sipping the kerosene. She took him to the hospital immediately. He suffered mild kerosene poisoning, but recovered quickly.

LEAD IN WATER

Drinking water is seldom a major source of lead exposure. More often, any exposure comes from household plumbing and fixtures. In 1986, Congress banned the use of lead solder greater than 2 percent lead and restricted the lead content of pipes and other plumbing fixtures. Since then, the Environmental Protection Agency has set stricter standards for lead and copper in drinking water. A continuing nationwide monitoring effort will determine if more measures are needed.

Drinking water. Drinking water should be tested at least once a year for bacteriological quality and no less than once in three years for chemical quality. Testing should meet the standards of the National Sanitation Foundation. New standards for lead in bottled water were proposed in January of 1993. Following are ways to reduce exposure:

1. Have your drinking water tested for lead.
2. Do not use drinking water systems that contain lead solder.
3. Water systems with interior or other service piping, or joints with lead or other toxic materials have special requirements:
   - Test the water for lead at the start of operation and at least every two years.
   - Samples of water should be first in the draw after at least a six-hour lapse in use.

MATCHES AND LIGHTERS

Each year about 8,700 people receive emergency room treatment for injuries with matches, 2,000 for injuries with lighters and 4,400 for injuries with lighter fluid. Children under 11 and elderly people suffer the most severe burns.

- Lynn, 2, was playing with matches alone in the living room. She dropped a flaming match on her dress, which ignited and caused fatal burns over 70 percent of her body.

- Mr. Vickers struck a match against the striking surface of a matchbook cover and a burning fragment flew off and hit him in the eye. He was treated for burns around his eye.

- While lying in bed, an 86-year-old man attempted to light his pipe and dropped a burning match onto his pajamas, which ignited. He died in the resulting fire.

- A young woman spilled lighter fluid on her hands and blouse while refilling a lighter. When she lit the lighter, the fluid ignited and caused severe burns on her hands, arms and chest.

Accident patterns

1. Children playing with matches and cigarette lighters. This is most common for children under 11 years of age. Some children under the age of 2 are able to operate cigarette lighters, which fascinate children because they are colorful, fit easily into a small hand, emit sparks and produce a flame. Further, they come in many shapes attractive to children and may look like toys: small autos, jeeps, motorcycles, cameras and ice-cream cones.

2. Product failures. Sparks, fragmentation and flaring can be caused by non-uniform application of ignition compounds to the match tips. Some lighters have unexpectedly high flame heights or spit drops of flaming fuel.

3. Use of matches by the elderly. The elderly may not be physically able to light

a match safely or to put out a fire, particularly a clothing fire.

4. Spilling lighter fluid. Most people aren't aware of the hazards of lighter fluid. Fluid that overflows onto your hand or clothing, or leaks through a crack in a defective lighter can ignite from a spark or flame from the lighter.

5. Smoking is the most common activity associated with match and lighter accidents for people over 16 years of age. Difficult and awkward activities, such as lighting an oven, also figure in these accidents.

Friction matches. Other hazards include old-fashioned, friction matches, which ignite when rubbed against any rough surface. They may ignite the entire matchbook because of the exposed match heads or trouble in closing the matchbook. Some match hazards can be eliminated:

1. Covers can be made to enclose the matches more effectively.

2. The staple holding the match cover to the base of the match cluster can be inserted so that it doesn't interfere with striking the match.

3. The striker strip can be placed on the back rather than on the front of the cover.

4. Ignition compounds can be applied to match tips more uniformly.

5. The afterglow (after a match flame extinguishes) can be reduced to no more than 3 seconds.

Purchase of matches and lighters

1. Look for matchbooks with the striking surface on the back, not the front of the cover; or look for matchbooks that open at the top, not at the bottom.

2. Buy safety matches, which require a striker strip, instead of friction matches, which can be ignited by rubbing against any rough surface.

3. Look for matches with plain covers that will be less attractive to children.

4. Look for lighters that are easy to fill and self-extinguishing. Lighters with large flames or containers attractive to children are potentially more dangerous than plain, small pocket lighters.

Use of matches and lighters

1. Always close a matchbook cover or box before striking a match. Hold a match or lighter away from your face while striking.

2. Concentrate on what you're doing when you light a match or lighter. Don't try to light a match or lighter while driving, using tools or doing something that distracts you.

3. Wait for the match to cool before discarding it.

4. Be sure the lighter flame is out before putting the lighter away.

5. Teach children the dangers of playing with fire. Show them the proper, safe way to light matches: hold at arm's length and strike away from yourself. Be aware that a child often seeks an isolated area to play with matches or lighters, which—in the event of a fire—may make it difficult for the child to get help.

6. Be aware that elderly people with poor coordination may drop lighted matches or lighters. This can occur in bed while an elderly person is alone.

7. Do not use matches or lighters near flammable liquids, particularly gasoline.

8. When refilling a lighter, clean up any spilled fuel before using the lighter.

9. Fill butane or gas-fueled lighters outside or in a well-ventilated area so flammable vapors can disperse quickly.

10. Keep matches and lighters out of reach of children. Never allow a child to play with a lighter. Be careful about how you use lighters when small children are present.

11. Do not store matches or lighters near flammable liquids, rags or papers.

12. Keep only one matchbook at a time in a pocket to avoid ignition from the contact of the matches in one book with the friction strip of another.

MEDICATION SENSE

In *Home Safety Desk Reference*, no attempt is made to prescribe medical treatment of any kind, for any purpose. Only your doctor can do that with any real meaning or authority. Follow your doctor's or pharmacist's directions. (The Food and Drug Administration found that 55 percent of all patients don't take their medicine as directed.)

Following are some common sense guidelines for consumers of all ages:

Undesirable food and drug interactions. You may have wondered why the doctor or pharmacist tells you to take some drugs on an empty stomach, others before meals and some after meals. The reason is that food and drugs affect each other in the system. Some combinations make some drugs ineffective and others downright dangerous. Three examples:

1. Calcium in milk impairs absorption of the medicine tetracycline.

2. Some medication, especially if taken over a long period of time, will compromise vitamins and minerals.

3. Long-term use of diuretics can reduce the potassium in the body.

Preventing undesirable interactions

1. Follow the orders of your doctor or pharmacist about when to take drugs and what foods or beverages to avoid while taking medication.

2. Ask the doctor or pharmacist how drugs will react with your favorite foods. Be sure to tell your doctor about any unusual symptoms that develop after eating certain foods.

3. Read the labels on over-the-counter remedies, as well as the inserts that come with prescription drugs.

4. Do not take alcohol with prescription drugs or over-the-counter medication. The combination of alcohol and many drugs produces drowsiness.

5. Soda, acidic fruit or vegetable juice can result in excess acidity. This causes some drugs to dissolve quickly in the stomach instead of in the intestines, where they are properly absorbed into the bloodstream.

6. Don't store medicine in the refrigerator unless the pharmacist advises it.

What is in the medicine cabinet? Clean out your medicine cabinet. Discard medicines that are out of date or those that you no longer need, that you can't identify, or that have been around for a long time. Medication that has been kept for about three years probably has deteriorated to the point that it is no longer effective. Discarded medication should be flushed or washed down the drain. Don't throw it away where children or animals might find it.

Expiration dates of medicines are important, particularly for the young and old. Codeine, a common medicine for children, does not age well. The drug evaporates and becomes much stronger and can make a child dizzy and disoriented. Always check the label for the expiration date and to confirm you have the correct medicine. Another medicine that is commonly prescribed, especially to children, is tetracycline. Outdated, it can cause kidney damage.

Just because a drug is over-the-counter (OTC), as opposed to prescription, doesn't mean it is harmless. If it is combined with another drug and taken incorrectly, you could become more ill. Be sure to tell your doctor about any OTC drugs you take, so he or she can advise against detrimental drug interactions.

You do need to keep some medicines on hand. These are staples:

1. Aspirin and/or acetaminophen for fever, headache or minor pains.

2. Antacid for stomach upset.

3. Adhesive tape and bandages for minor cuts.

4. Hydrogen peroxide for cleansing wounds.

5. Sodium bicarbonate for soaking and soothing.

6. Liquid acetaminophen for pain and fever in small children, especially those under 12 years of age.

7. Syrup of ipecac to induce vomiting, especially in small children.

Feeling better? If you are taking a prescription drug, take it until the prescription is finished, unless the directions say otherwise. When taking prescription drugs, you may soon feel better, but may not be cured of the illness for which the medicine was prescribed. Don't think the lack of symptoms is the end of the problem. Finish the prescription.

Over-the-counter medication is a different matter. When you feel better, stop taking the medicine. Treat over-the-counter medicines as hazardous, and particularly be aware of what medicines are combined. Never take them with alcohol.

If you travel abroad, know that U.S. manufactured drugs may not be labeled the same as they are in the U.S., especially in developing countries. One result is that foreign doctors may not be able to properly prescribe U.S. drugs that have dangerous side effects.

Even when drugs are labeled to U.S. standards, the information needed for a foreign doctor to prescribe them properly may be lacking. This results from lengthy and complex labels, which are partly liability-driven.

NITROGEN DIOXIDE

The cooking of food creates unwanted vapors and other airborne substances, such as grease. Both gas and electric burners cause indoor pollution through the burning of airborne particles, such as dust. In addition, cooking with gas creates a unique problem. Burning gas gives off significant indoor air pollution. Most importantly, this includes: nitrogen dioxide, carbon monoxide and, to a lesser extent, nitrous oxide, aldehydes (including formaldehyde) and particulates. All of these can cause several ailments. Emissions are greatest from poorly adjusted burners.

Studies have linked nitrogen dioxide to a greater risk of infectious respiratory disorders. The studies indicate greater susceptibility to nose, throat and breathing irritations. Those who have respiratory diseases are most susceptible.

OVEN CLEANERS

Of those who receive emergency room treatment for injuries from oven cleaners, the most common injuries are chemical burns to the face and hands.

- A woman poured boiling water into a can of oven cleaner, according to the directions on the can. As she carried the can from the table to the oven, it spilled, burning her hand and producing large quantities of ammonia gas, which gave her a choking cough.

- A 2-year-old boy opened a bottle of liquid oven cleaner, which was stored under the sink. He spilled some on his legs and then inadvertently rubbed some of the cleaner on his face. He suffered chemical burns on his legs and face.

- A woman held a spray can of oven cleaner backward and when she pushed the nozzle it sprayed into her face. Although she flushed her skin with water immediately, she received burns on her face and in one eye.

Associated hazards. These examples represent the following hazards of oven cleaners:

1. Chemical burns and inhalation of fumes. Some oven cleaners rely on a reaction between a chemical and boiling water to produce ammonia gas that cleans the oven. The gas can be so strong that it causes extreme discomfort if the product is not used as directed, and the hot liquid can burn skin. Some oven cleaners use sodium or potassium hydroxide, caustic chemicals that can burn you. Oven cleaners, like other poisonous household substances, are hazardous to children if they drink them or spill them on their skin.

2. Misdirected spraying of oven cleaner. Most aerosol oven cleaners use ammonia or a caustic substance that is hazardous if sprayed onto your skin or into your eyes. Adults and children can misdirect the spray of an aerosol can. (Also see *Aerosols* in the previous chapter.)

Many oven cleaners must be highly caustic to do an effective job of cleaning greases and other foods in an oven. You should understand the hazards of caustic substances and safe ways to use these products. Some cleaners work better with a hot oven surface, but the heat may allow hazardous fumes to expand more quickly than if the oven was at room temperature.

Oven cleaners that contain more than 2 percent sodium or potassium hydroxide (caustic substances) must be packaged in child-resistant containers. However, some children can open the safety containers, so it is important to store them out of children's reach.

Selection of oven cleaners

1. Know the different types of oven cleaners. Some contain ammonium chloride and use boiling water to produce the ammonia gas that cleans the oven. Others contain sodium or potassium

hydroxide (caustic substances) and are used directly on the oven surfaces. Some are liquids, while others are aerosols. You may be able to use one type more safely than others.

2. Most oven cleaners require safety or child-resistant packaging. However, some oven cleaners do not require safety packaging. If the label says that the oven cleaner contains sodium and/or potassium hydroxide (lye), be sure that the product you buy is in a safety package to help protect children.

Use of oven cleaners

1. Read and follow the directions before each use. In addition:

   • Wear protective gloves for your hands and goggles for your eyes.

   • Open windows and be sure that children and other family members are not in the room.

   • If your oven cleaner requires boiling water, place the can in the oven before adding boiling water so you won't be overcome by ammonia fumes.

2. If the fumes began to irritate you, close the oven door, leave the room and seek fresh air.

3. Read the label for information about antidotes. For most oven cleaners the label recommends:

   • If the chemical is swallowed, drink diluted vinegar, lemon juice or grapefruit juice, followed by milk or egg white beaten in water.

   • If the cleaner is spilled or sprayed on skin or into eyes, flush with water immediately.

   • Seek medical help.

Storage of oven cleaners

1. Keep oven cleaners, like other poisonous household substances, locked away from children.

2. Don't keep oven cleaners under the sink or in other accessible places.

3. Keep aerosol oven cleaners away from heat sources, such as furnaces or water heaters.

PAINT REMOVERS

Many products are available to remove paint. They work in one of three ways: with chemicals, with heat or with mechanical force.

1. Chemical strippers soften and dissolve the old finish so it can be scraped.

2. Heat guns emit air at over 800°F and make the paint bubble and blister so it can be scraped. Heat guns resemble hair dryers.

3. Mechanical stripping is done with tools such as files, rasps and sanding devices. The disadvantage of this process is that it leaves marks on smooth finishes.

In this section, we focus on the first method, chemical strippers. Some strippers use methylene chloride, a chemical widely linked to cancer. However, some newer strippers do not. Many strippers contain volatile solvents, including wood alcohol, acetone and toluene. Although they are cheaper than less toxic types, they leave a sticky film that you may need to remove with mineral spirits. Most chemical strippers are highly flammable and their vapors can cause headaches and even nerve damage after lengthy exposure.

Methylene chloride, which can dissolve many tough finishes and is not flammable, gives off fumes that can lead to irregular heartbeat, heart attack or kidney disease. It is a known carcinogen, based on animal tests. It can be sold if it has a warning label.

Any solvent-based paint remover is dangerous to use, even if a window is open. Neoprene gloves and goggles are needed and a respirator is very desirable.

Newer chemical strippers, based on nonvolatile substances, are nearly odor-free, safer to breathe and easier on the skin. Once the paint softens and is scraped off, cleanup is easier. Light scrubbing with a brush, sponge, or cloth will clear away the residue. These new strippers are slow and may have to sit overnight. In addition, most take several hours, even overnight, to dry. They also are more expensive.

PESTS AND PESTICIDES

The simplest way to rid your home or apartment of mice or roaches is to use pesticides. Pests include anything from termites, fleas and rodents, to algae in your swimming pool. Pesticides include insecticides, herbicides, fungicides, rodenticides, disinfectants and plant growth regulators. To prevent infestations of pests:

1. Remove water sources. All pests need water to survive. Fix leaky plumbing and do not let water collect anywhere in your home. Do not put water in trays under your plants if you have cockroaches.
2. Remove food sources. This may require you to avoid leaving your pet's food out for long periods and to close garbage cans tightly.
3. Remove or destroy pest shelters. Caulk cracks and crevices to control cockroaches. Remove piles of wood around your home to avoid drawing termites. Remove and destroy diseased plants, tree prunings and fallen fruit.
4. Remove breeding sites. The presence of pet manure attracts flies. Litter encourages rodents, and standing water provides a breeding place for mosquitoes.
5. Use preventive cultural practices such as careful selection of disease-resistant seed or plant varieties.

Nonchemical controls. Preventive steps such as those above will reduce your chances of infestation. If you already have an infestation, there are alternatives besides chemical control. One or a combination of alternatives may be used, depending on the pest and where the pest lives. Nonchemical approaches work, but take more time. They include biological and mechanical treatments.

1. Biological treatments. Includes predators such as purple martins, praying mantises, lady bugs, parasites and pathogens, such as bacteria, viruses and other microorganisms.
2. Mechanical treatments. Includes controlling weeds, hand-picking weeds from turf and pests from plants, trapping rodents and some insects and screening living space to limit fly and mosquito access.

Chemical control. If you must use chemicals to control pests, if possible use the services of a professional. If you do it yourself, be sure you know what you're doing. The most common types of home-use pesticide formulations include:

1. Solutions with an active ingredient and one or more additives.
2. Aerosols that control one or more active ingredients and a solvent, and are ready to use.
3. Dusts that contain active ingredients and are ready for use.
4. Granulars like dusts, but with larger and heavier particles.
5. Baits, mixed with food or other substances to attract the pest.
6. Wetable powders, which are dry, finely ground and generally mixed with water for spray application.

Most chemical controls are poisonous. If these poisonous products are not used or stored safely, they are a serious hazard for children and pets.

- An 8½-month-old girl who had been suffering from a cough for a few weeks died five days after her room was sprayed by an exterminator.

- A 4-year-old girl was poisoned after eating a small quantity of rodent-killer, left under the kitchen sink.

Precautions. Every year, about 10,000 children receive emergency room treatment after being poisoned by pesticides or similar products. Many of these mishaps can be prevented by following a few simple steps.

1. Many people store these pesticides where they can reach them quickly. A favorite storage place is beneath the kitchen sink, which is within reach of children. Keep these products out of children's reach and in locked storage when not in use.

2. Always read warning labels. The labels tell the seriousness of the products' dangers and list all hazardous ingredients. If your child is poisoned, the first thing a doctor must know is the name of the substance involved. The label will tell you what immediate first aid you can give. Look for one of these words on the label:

   - "Danger" means highly poisonous.
   - "Warning" means moderately hazardous.
   - "Caution" means least hazardous.

3. Don't use a "restricted use" pesticide unless you have formal training to do it.

4. Remember that a less toxic product may do the job as well as a highly toxic product.

5. Do not spread pesticides where children or pets can touch them.

6. Do not spray pesticides near small children or pets. Never spray them on playpens, cribs or toys.

7. Cover all food and cooking and eating utensils before spraying.

8. Pesticides used in farming are usually much more powerful than the household varieties. It is very important to keep these poisons locked up when not in use and to use them only with great caution.

9. Wear protective clothing if the label advises it.

10. If you must mix or dilute a pesticide, do it outdoors in a well-ventilated area.

11. If a spill occurs, clean it up promptly.

12. Apply surface sprays to smaller areas. Don't spray entire floors, walls or ceilings.

13. When applying spray, cover fishponds and bowls and avoid spraying near wells.

14. Don't smoke when applying pesticides. You could transfer pesticides from hand to mouth.

15. Never transfer pesticides to another container not intended for them.

16. Shower and shampoo thoroughly after using a pesticide product.

Child-resistant packaging. Many household pesticides are in child-resistant packages and can greatly reduce accidents if used properly. Be sure to:

1. Buy pesticides in safety packaging when you can, and store them in the packaging.

2. When using child-resistant packaging, close the containers tightly after each use, using the safety feature.

3. Remember that most children cannot open poison-prevention packaging, but some can. Safety closures will help, but they can't do the whole job. Even pesticides in child-resistant packages should be locked away from children.

First aid

1. When you realize a pesticide poisoning is occurring, before calling for emergency help, be sure the victim is not further exposed to the poison.

2. Drag an unconscious person into fresh air.

3. Take care not to be poisoned yourself. You may have to put on protective

clothing or breathing equipment to avoid being the second victim.

4. First aid is the first medical step in treating a pesticide poisoning. After the initial first aid, call for medical emergency help *immediately*.

5. Bring or send the product container with its label to the doctor's office or emergency room. Keep the container out of the passenger space of the vehicle. Sometimes the label will include a telephone number to call more information.

6. Use the NPTN (National Pesticide Telecommunications Network) as a resource. Operators, on call 24 hours a day, provide information about pesticides, and recognizing and responding to pesticide poisonings. They also answer questions about animal poisonings. At publication date, the toll-free telephone number was 1-800-858-7378.

PLASTIC BAGS

Unacceptable numbers of children still suffocate with plastic bags. They are mostly children younger than 1 year of age. Plastic dry-cleaning, garbage or trash bags are usually involved. Plastic bags can block the nose and mouth and prevent breathing. Most dry-cleaning bags, and some other plastic bags, bear a voluntary warning label such as:

"Warning: To avoid danger of suffocation, keep this plastic bag away from babies and children. Do not use this bag in cribs, beds, carriages or playpens. The plastic bag could block nose and mouth and prevent breathing. This bag is not a toy." Although these warnings are on the outside of boxes filled with plastic bags, usually they do not appear on individual bags purchased for home use.

Never allow children to sleep or play near plastic bags. Following are examples of cases in which children have suffocated with plastic bags:

- A child pulled a plastic dry-cleaning bag over his face while lying on an adult bed.

- A plastic garbage bag (filled with clothes) fell over the face and mouth while the child was on an adult bed.

- A child crawled into a plastic garbage bag.

- A child rolled off a mattress onto a plastic bag filled with clothes.

- A child slept on a mattress that was covered by a plastic bag.

POISONOUS SUBSTANCES

It's attractive, perhaps brightly colored. Or maybe it looks like food. It's within reach. And, it's poison.

- An 18-month-old boy died after drinking floor cleaner containing petroleum distillates.

- An 8-year-old grabbed a bottle of liniment that he thought was cough syrup and drank it down.

- A 1-year-old girl spent nine days in the hospital after swallowing charcoal lighter fluid from a can left in the yard after a family picnic.

Poison proofing your home. Each year household substances poison thousands of children and adults. Furniture polishes, lighter fluid and turpentine are only a few of the many potentially dangerous products commonly found in the home. Perhaps most surprising is the high percentage of home poisonings from medicines. Yet we can prevent most household poisonings if adults take proper precautions. Here are a few suggestions to help you poison-proof your home:

1. No matter how attractive a hazardous product may be, children are not usually poisoned by something they can't reach. Therefore, one key to poison prevention in the home is to keep all

medicines and other hazardous products locked up when not in use.

2. Don't depend on close supervision. One cannot watch a child every minute and children can move very quickly.

3. Always read the warning labels on hazardous products. They will tell you the seriousness of the danger and list all hazardous ingredients. If your child is accidentally poisoned, the first thing a doctor needs to know is the name of the poison. The label will also tell you what immediate first aid to give.

4. Keep all hazardous products in their original containers. Never store them in cups, soda bottles or other containers that normally contain food or drink.

5. Avoid taking medicine in a child's presence. Children imitate adults, particularly their parents.

6. Call medicine by its proper name. Never suggest that medicine is candy.

7. When giving medicines to children, give only the proper dosage. Don't think that because a little medicine gives relief, that more will do an even better job.

8. Promptly dispose of prescription drugs. Pour them out once the illness for which they were prescribed is over.

9. Do not store other hazardous products with medicines that are to be taken internally. There are many look-alike containers on the market. You or your child could make a tragic mistake.

10. Be careful when using a hazardous product. Keep it out of childrens' reach. If you are interrupted while using the product, carry it with you.

11. Be sure to keep a product in its safety packaging.

12. Check with your spouse or baby sitter before giving a child medicine to prevent double doses.

13. Keep a 1-ounce bottle of *ipecac* on hand in case you have to induce vomiting. Don't use it unless a poison control center advises it. You'll find syrup of ipecac at your local pharmacy.

14. Remember that poison prevention packaging is only an additional safeguard. Safety closures help, but cannot do the whole job of protecting your children. Most children cannot open poison-prevention packages, but some can.

15. Never give or take medicine prescribed for someone else.

16. Don't read medication labels or take medication in dim light. Keep a daily record of medications you are taking, including over-the-counter drugs.

17. Ask your doctor or pharmacist about any possible side effects, how to store medication and any food or beverages that should be avoided while on the medication.

18. Separate foods and household products. Cleaning fluids, lye, soap powders, detergents, insecticides and other everyday household products should be stored away from food and medications to avoid mistaken identity, a frequent cause of death.

19. Always try to buy household substances in child-resistant containers and insist on safety packaging for prescription medicines.

Quick response to accidental poisoning

1. Separate the victim from the poison.
   - If the substance is a medicine, don't give anything by mouth until you receive advice.
   - If the substance is a solid, such as pills or mothballs, remove it from the mouth using a clean, wet washcloth wrapped around your finger.
   - If the substance is a gas, provide fresh air at once.
   - For other substances, unless the victim is having convulsions, give water immediately to dilute the substance.

2. Quickly evaluate the victim's condition and administer life-saving action:

- Maintain an open airway.
- Give artificial ventilation or, if you're trained, CPR.
- Manage shock by keeping victim warm and still.
- Don't attempt emergency procedures in which you are not trained.

3. Call your local poison control center, family physician or emergency room. Don't treat the victim without professional advice. The treatment instruction on product labels may not apply in your case.

4. Take the container, if any, to the phone with you and be ready to answer these questions:

- What substance was taken?
- What symptoms does the victim have?
- How old is the victim and how much does he/she weigh?
- How long ago was the substance taken?
- Does the victim have any health problems and is he or she taking any medication?
- Where are you located and what is your phone number?

POISON CARE

In any year, one in 100 children under the age of 5 will accidentally ingest something poisonous. Because young children eat and drink almost anything, including poisons, you should make an extra effort to keep all liquids and solids out of their hands.

Child-resistant containers. All consumers, whether they have children of their own or not, should obtain their prescriptions in child-resistant containers, based on findings of the Poison Control Centers. Thirty-one percent of the medications involved in accidental ingestions among children did not belong to the child's immediate family. These medicines were among the most potent found in the study.

Just before the accident, the medicine was stored where it was easy to take, which made it readily accessible to children. Kitchen tables, counters and cabinets are some common places of storage.

Household chemicals. In addition to medications, many other products that are dangerous, especially to children, are kept around the house and garage. Some other potentially harmful chemicals are:

- Automotive products, including engine fluids and auto cleaners.
- Petroleum products.
- Paints and varnishes.
- Charcoal starter.
- Paint thinner.
- Glues.
- Lye.
- Rodent and insect poisons.
- Pesticides and herbicides.

It is vitally important to keep these products away from children. Only one teaspoon of windshield wiper solvent or antifreeze can kill an adult. These products often have delayed symptoms, so the person who ingests these items may not realize he or she is poisoned.

Workshop and garage products should be stored in a locked cabinet. Know, however, that some of the vapors that escape from these products are dangerous. Always use them in a well-ventilated area. When discarding containers, make sure they are not within easy reach, such as the top of a garbage can.

POISON PACKAGING

Until recently, the main effort to reduce the number of household poisonings focused on educational efforts and labeling of hazardous products. While warning labels prevent many accidents, small children (the group most often poisoned) cannot read. Continued fatal and injurious ingestions led to poison prevention packaging.

The enabling legislation provides that hazardous or potentially hazardous household products may have to be in child-resistant containers that most children under 5 years of age cannot open. It may also be forbidden to package these products in a manner that is unnecessarily attractive to children.

There may be more requirements, such as forbidding reuse of the container and/or restricting the flow of liquid products.

Safety closures. The ideal safety closure is one that a young child cannot open, but which the average adult can open easily. Knowing that some aged or handicapped adults cannot open such a container, the product may be packaged in one noncomplying size. It must, however, carry a warning that it is not for households with children. In the case of prescription drugs, the noncomplying package is available only on request of the prescribing physician or customer.

Have you wondered how a safety closure design is tested? A group of 200 children and 100 adults is selected to determine how easily a certain design may be opened. The children are given five minutes to try to open the container. If they cannot, they receive a silent demonstration of the how the device works. They then have another five minutes to open it. For a safety closure to pass this test, 85 percent of the children must fail to open the lid before the demonstration and 80 percent must fail to open it after the demonstration.

Adults receive a five-minute period to open the safety closure—90 percent of them must be able to open the container after reading the instructions for opening it. Other tests are used, but these are the most common.

Products now regulated. The products that must be in child-resistant containers (not including products in pressured spray containers, except for aerosol sodium in powder form, other than those for pediatric use) include:

1. Aspirin-containing products to be taken by mouth.
2. Furniture polishes that contain 10 percent or more petroleum distillates.
3. Liquids containing more than 5 percent of methyl salicylate (oil of wintergreen).
4. Oral products with any controlled substance such as certain depressants and stimulants.
5. Dry household substances with 10 percent or more of sodium and/or potassium hydroxide (lye), and all other household substances containing 2 percent or more of sodium and/or potassium hydroxide.
6. Liquid household substances containing 10 percent or more (by weight) of turpentine.
7. Prepackaged liquid kindling and/or illuminating preparations, such as fuel for cigarette lighters, charcoal, camping equipment, torches and decorative or functional lanterns, which contain 10 percent or more (by weight) of petroleum distillates.
8. Liquid household substances containing 4 percent or more (by weight) of methyl alcohol methanol.
9. Household substances containing 10 percent or more (by weight) of sulfuric acid (but not wet-cell storage batteries).
10. Oral prescription drugs unless specifically exempted.
11. Household liquids containing 10 percent or more of ethylene glycol.
12. Noninjectable animal and human drugs providing ion for therapeutic or prophylactic purposes that contain a total amount of ion equivalent to 250 mg in a single package (except for animal feeds used to give drugs.)
13. Iron medications (sometimes called ferrous sulfate, ferrous gluconate or ferrous fumarate). Even a small amount, either alone or in combination with vitamins, can be deadly to a small child.

14. Dietary supplements that contain 250 mg or more of elements, except for those preparations in which ion is present solely as colorant.

15. Solvents for paint or other similar surface-coating materials that contain 10 percent or more (by weight) of benzine, toluene, xylene, petroleum distillates or any combination thereof.

16. Acetaminophen (aspirin substitutes). Preparation for human use with more than one gram in one package. (There may be exceptions by the time you read this.)

17. Methylene chloride products must be labeled with a warning that they may be a possible cancer hazard. At least some, but not all, products in these categories contain methylene chloride:

   - Paint strippers.
   - Adhesive removers.
   - Spray shoe polish.
   - Adhesives and glues.
   - Paint thinners.
   - Glass frosting and artificial snow.
   - Water repellents.
   - Wood stains and varnishes.
   - Spray paints.
   - Cleaning fluids and degreasers.
   - Aerosol spray paint for autos.
   - Automobile spray primers.

Precautions to reduce exposure by breathing methylene chloride include: Using paint strippers and other products containing this chemical outdoors; if the product must be used indoors, even in a garage, opening all windows and doors and using a fan to exhaust the air outside during application and drying; and knowing that respirators may not protect against methylene chloride vapors.

Alternatives for the older and handicapped consumer. Certain hazardous products must be sold in safety packaging that most children, 5 years or younger, could not open. Because the packaging must also allow access for most of the adults who use it, the package is a compromise. For some adults—the very old and those with handicaps, such as arthritis—the law allows two ways to obtain easy-open packaging.

- One size of the product can be marketed in easy-open packaging, with the proper label, if the same product is available in child-resistant packaging.
- If the package is small, the prescribing physician or the consumer can request prescription medicine in ordinary packaging, without safety features.

POTPOURRI POTS

Simmering potpourri pots, which give off pleasant scents, are everywhere, especially during the holidays. Each year, there have been about 130 incidents of flare-ups of potpourri units, when the small candle used to simmer the potpourri ignites soot, wax or candle debris. This causes flames to flare up around the side of the simmering unit. The use of small candles contained in metal cups can also generate excess heat, causing the unit to flare-up or ignite.

Potpourri units come in many designs. Two common characteristics are:

1. A base in which a small, warmer candle is lit.

2. A bowl or ladle, supported by the base, in which water and potpourri are simmered to give off a pleasant scent.

Guidelines

1. The bowl that contains water and spices should always contain water when in use.

2. Clean the outside of the unit before or after every use. Don't allow soot to accumulate above or around the candle flame. Keep the wick clean of debris and candle wick material.

3. When replacing a candle, use the proper size and type candle to avoid excessive soot buildup.

4. Avoid using the candle in a metal cup.

5. Place the unit in a clear and open area, free from drafts or flammable materials.

6. Never leave a potpourri unit (or any burning candle) unattended.

7. If the unit should flare up, smother the flames with a wet cloth. Do not throw water on the flame.

RADON

Radon, a colorless, odorless, naturally occurring gas, is everywhere at low levels. When trapped in buildings, it becomes a concern. The most common radon source is uranium in soil and rocks. As the uranium decomposes, it releases radon. It enters through dirt floors, cracks in concrete walls and floors, floor drains and sumps. In some areas of the country, it can enter buildings through well water. In rare cases, radon enters through building supplies, such as rocks, that can trap gases. Radon can be found only with radon detectors.

Health effects of radon. Lung cancer is the only known health effect (1990) associated with radon. An estimated 3.6 to 14 percent of the cancer deaths in the U.S. *may* be linked to radon. The risk has not been proven to everyones' satisfaction.

Measuring radon. Two types of detectors measure radon levels in small buildings. One is a charcoal canister ($10 to $25 per canister), which is exposed for two to seven days. The other is an alpha track detector ($20 to $50 per detector), which is exposed for a month to a year. Alpha types must go to a lab for analysis. Look for a test kit with an EPA or state approval on the package.

Radon is measured in *picocuries*. Test results are given in the form of exposure of pCi/L (picocuries per liter of air). An acceptable level in the home is 4 pCi/L, roughly the same risk run by a two-pack-a-day smoker. A result of over 4 pCi/L is above average. If radon is detected at levels from 4 pCi/L to 20 pCi/L, you should monitor it and, within a few years or sooner, talk to the toxic substances branch of the health department about it.

You can hire a company to do radon tests for you or you can do the testing yourself with easy-to-use, inexpensive ($20 to $25) detection kits. In some areas, an agency provides free or subsidized radon measuring. The state radiation protection office also can advise you on radon measurement and equipment.

Reducing exposure to radon. Once you know the level of radon exposure, there are steps you can take to reduce the risk. The higher the radon level, the quicker you should act. Other factors to consider are:

1. If anyone smokes in your home, it appears to increase risks of radon exposure.

2. There are no studies to determine the sensitivity of children to radon. Some evidence indicates they may be more sensitive to radon.

3. Radon is concentrated more on the lower levels of buildings. The risk of radon exposure is greater in the basement than upstairs.

4. Filter radon-contaminated well water through granulated-activated charcoal.

5. Keep an under-building crawl space well-ventilated. Ventilate air that contains radon from the building by bringing fresh air in through ventilation systems. Make certain fresh air inlets are not blocked out of ventilation systems.

6. Remove the source of the radon, probably by working with a radon contractor. There is a radon office in every state, usually in the health department. The radon office will furnish information to help you reduce radon exposure.

Scam warning. Because of the high visibility given radon hazards by the

Environmental Protection Agency (EPA) and professional writers and advocates, the field is fertile for less-than-ethical radon cleanup promotions. It is difficult to pin down radon abatement schemes. State attorney generals, better business groups and chambers of commerce cannot document radon cleanup scams as yet, but expect them to surface.

Radon experts have been adamant in expecting "radon cleanup scams." A March 1993 publicity release from the EPA on radon in classrooms may accelerate this expectation. The release claims that 15,000 schools have radon over the agency's "action level" of 4 pCi/L. The problem is that this "level of action" is a suspect base that many reputable scientists do not accept.

1. Beware if anyone offers to test your home for radon and offers immediate test results. Testing takes time and so does getting test results.

2. If someone says they use a Gieger counter, be wary. Geiger counters cannot give the radon level in your building.

3. Be wary if you are asked to buy equipment that either filters or electrostatically removes particles from the air. The EPA does not endorse this equipment, nor has it found it effective in reducing health risks associated with radon.

Choosing a radon reduction contractor. Most homes or places of business can take significant and inexpensive steps to reduce radon levels. If you think you need a professional contractor, select one carefully, for high-level radon removal is expensive.

1. Most state and local entities require that solicitors, including door-to-door solicitors, have a license to do business. Check with the local business license office to confirm that your prospective contractor has a license for this work.

2. Many state radon protection offices will offer a list of contractors doing radon mitigation work. They will not likely endorse any particular one.

3. Some states require contractors to complete certification programs for radon measurement and mitigation.

4. The Environmental Protection Agency has a voluntary Radon Measurement Proficiency Program, which allows laboratories and businesses to demonstrate their ability in measuring indoor radon. Contact your state radon protection office for the listing of contractors.

5. Find out how long your prospective contractor has been in business. Although radon detecting is a new field, the contractor should have some experience.

6. Get a second estimate for the work from another contractor.

7. Get an estimate and guarantees in writing. This should include follow-up testing after the job is complete.

VINYL CHLORIDE

Vinyl chloride is a monomer or molecule that is used as the propellant in many aerosols, including hair sprays, insecticides and spray paints. In its polymeric (combination of molecules) state, vinyl chloride is known as polyvinyl chloride (PVC). In that form, it is a plastic used for shampoo and detergent containers, water pipes and plastic upholstery on furniture. In laboratory tests, vinyl chloride has been linked to a rare form of liver cancer. It also has been linked to liver cancer in some workers who process the chemical. Various federal agencies have taken action in response to the hazards of vinyl chloride and PVC:

1. Consumer Product Safety Commission—use in aerosol products.

2. Food and Drug Administration—recalled those products using it as a propellant.

3. Occupational Safety and Health Administration—limited worker exposure.

4. Treasury Department—liquor bottles.

SAFETY RECAP

1. Be alert for glass in bottles, or broken or chipped tops on bottles.
2. Beware of toxic cleaners and keep them away from children. Some household equipment (drains, ovens, etc.) rely on poisonous cleaners to keep them operating properly. The use of these cleaners requires special precautions in storage, use, cleanup and first aid.
3. Keep matches and lighters away from children.
4. Plastic bags and covers are a hazard to children of all ages.
5. Some hazards are invisible or hidden.
6. Aerosols, so common in everyday living, pose many safety and health hazards.
7. Don't handle asbestos. Even if it is in safe form, working with it can make it dangerous.
8. Beware the silent killer, carbon monoxide.
9. Although E.Coli sources have not been identified completely, it is essential that you cook meat thoroughly and use different utensils for meats, fruits and vegetables.
10. When purchasing fast food, keep it hot or cold, as it is bought, and eat it as soon as possible.
11. The vapors of flammable fluids are more dangerous than the liquid.
12. Keep lead out of your water and paint.
13. Everything except food is dangerous in one way or another for children. If you do not want children to have them, keep products out of their reach.
14. Know first aid and the common procedures for poisoning situations.
15. The most dangerous cabinet in the house is the medicine cabinet.

BIBLIOGRAPHY

"Big Fires Start Small," *Newsletter*, International Child Safety Center, National Safety Town Center, 1990.

"The Canning Process," Blumenthal, Dale, *The Canning Process*, Washington, DC: Food and Drug Administration, GPO, pp. 14-18.

"Children Still Suffocating with Plastic Bags," *Consumer Product Safety Alert*, U.S. Consumer Product Safety Commission, March 1990.

Citizen's Guide to Pesticides, U.S. Consumer Product Safety Commission, September, 1989.

Community Safety and Health, Chicago, IL: National Safety Council, November/December 1992, p. 6.

"CPSC Urges Caution With Consumer Products Containing Methylene Chloride," *Consumer Product Safety Alert*, U.S. Consumer Product Safety Commission, September 1987.

"CPSC Warns About Child Entrapment in Household Appliances and Picnic Coolers," *Consumer Product Safety Alert*, U.S. Consumer Product Safety Commission, December 1988.

"CPSC Warns About Hazards of Do-it-Yourself Removal of Lead Based Paints," *Consumer Product Safety Alert*, U.S. Consumer Product Safety Commission, February 1989.

"Danger—Children and Lighters," *Consumer Product Safety Alert*, U.S. Consumer Product Safety Commission, June 1987.

"Drug Labels in Foreign Countries Could Mean Deadly Interpretation," *Product Safety Update*, Itasca, IL: National Safety Council, September/October 1993, p. 3.

"The Right Way to Take Medicine," Feldman, Debbie L. and Mick Hans, *Family Safety and Health*, Itasca, IL: National Safety Council, Fall 1993, pp. 6-8.

"Flammable Liquids," *Product Safety Fact Sheet*, U.S. Consumer Product Safety Commission, September 1980.

"Food, Glorious Food," *Community Safety and Health*, Itasca, IL: National Safety Council, July/August 1992, pp. 2-3.

The Smart Kitchen, Goldbeck, David, Woodstock, NY: Ceres Press, 1989, pp. 61-62.

"Hidden Hazards in Some Aerosol Tire Inflators," *Consumer Reports*, October 1990, p. 643.

"Home Canning of Fruits and Vegetables," USDA Home and Garden Bulletin No. 8, U.S. Department of Agriculture.

"Living Lead Free," Edmonds, WA: City of Edmonds.

"Locked Up Poisons Prevent Tragedy," U.S. Consumer Product Safety Commission, January 1987.

"Mixing Food and Drugs," *Aide*, April 1991, pp. 22-23.

"Paint Removers: New Products Eliminate Old Hazards," *Consumer Reports*, May 1991, pp. 340-341.

"Pest Control," Ernst Hardware, 1990.

"Poison Prevention Packaging," *Product Safety Fact Sheet*, U.S. Consumer Product Safety Commission, September 1980.

"Prevent Poisoning and Death With Iron-Containing Medicine," *Consumer Product Safety Alert*, Consumer Product Safety Commission, February 1992.

Preventing Accidental Poisonings, Chicago, IL: National Safety Council, 1987.

"Save a Child: Use Child-Resistant Containers," *Consumer Product Safety Alert*, U.S. Consumer Product Safety Commission, 1987.

"Use Potpourri Pots Safely," *Consumer Product Safety Alert*, U.S. Consumer Product Safety Commission, November 1989.

"Warning—Children and Lighters Do Not Mix," *Consumer Product Safety Alert*, U.S. Consumer Product Safety Commission, April 1988.

"What You Should Know About Lead-Based Paint in Your Home," *Consumer Product Safety Alert*, U.S. Consumer Product Safety Commission, September 1990.

CHAPTER 5

HEATING

The time to check your heating system is before the cold season arrives. Give special attention to fuel-burning systems, to prevent fire, burns and carbon-monoxide poisonings.

Carbon monoxide (CO) is colorless, odorless and very toxic. CO can escape from faulty furnaces or room heaters through faulty or cracked vents. It also can be trapped inside homes by blocked flues.

The presence of CO can be determined only by special detectors or by its symptoms, which are just like flu symptoms: dizziness, nausea, headaches, vomiting and confusion. In 1992, home CO detectors became an important and modestly priced addition to CO prevention. Be certain that your CO detector has a UL label.

Heating system inspections should be done by qualified service technicians. Any inspection should include home furnace components, including thermostats, vents, flues and flue connectors. Chimney inspections are especially important after furnaces are converted to gas.

BASEBOARD HEATERS

Many people do not realize how hot electric baseboard heaters can get, and each year these products cause many injuries. As in accidents with space heaters, the most severe injuries are burns.

- Three-year-old Richard reached through the metal shield on an electric baseboard heater and touched the hot electric cell. The coil and even the shield were so hot that Richard was severely burned on his hand and lower arm.

- Beverly smelled smoke from the vicinity of the sofa, which was pushed against the electric baseboard heater in the wall. When she moved the sofa away she saw that the fabric was charring and beginning to smoke.

Accident patterns

The above accidents are typical of these accident patterns linked with electric baseboard heaters:

1. Children reach into the heater and touch the hot coil or other hot surfaces.
2. Drapes, bedding, rugs and furniture ignite when too close to heaters.
3. Short circuits caused by:
   - Burning through the insulation of nearby appliance cords.
   - Combustion of dust, dirt and other debris gathered around the baseboard.
4. Cuts caused by sharp edges on unguarded metal fins around the heating elements.

Safer use. Baseboard heaters may be safer than portable space heaters because people cannot trip over them and because they do not have open flames. However, electric baseboard heaters can start fires and cause burns. Here are some suggestions for safer use of electric baseboard heaters:

1. Keep drapes, bedding, shag rugs, toys, furniture and other combustible objects away from the heaters.
2. Keep all electric cords away from heaters to prevent short circuits caused by burning through the insulation.

3. Clean the heater often to remove dust, dirt and other debris that could ignite.

4. Teach children that the coil and even the metal shield can be hot enough to burn them.

5. Don't let infants crawl or play near electric baseboard heaters.

FIREPLACES AND CHIMNEYS

Each year, fireplaces are involved in 25,000 home fires. The most common causes are:

1. Creosote, a black tar-like deposit that builds up on the inside of the chimneys and ignites. Sometimes it is soft and sticky and other times it is hard, depending on the temperature. When hot enough to burn, it burns furiously. Mostly the fire stays within the chimney, but sometimes the heat from the chimney fire ignites nearby materials.

2. Poor construction or installation of a factory-built fireplace can cause heat from the fireplace or chimney to ignite nearby materials.

3. Soot also causes problems. It narrows the opening of the fire flue, affecting the draft. It also provides a surface for creosote to adhere. Both soot and creosote may cause a foul odor to come from the fireplace.

4. Sparks from an unscreened fireplace land on nearby flammable material.

5. Vapors from flammable liquids used to kindle a fire ignite explosively, or flammable liquids spilled on clothing ignite.

6. Carbon monoxide poisoning can occur if the fireplace is not properly vented, even if there is no fire.

Use of fireplaces

1. Make sure the fireplace is ready to be used as a fireplace, not just for decoration. It must meet all building codes. If it is factory-built, it must be installed to the manufacturer's instructions. Have it inspected by a fireplace contractor to meet all linings and clearances.

2. Have a professional chimney sweep inspect your fireplace for damage and creosote buildup before each heating season. If you use glass doors or have an insert, inspect for creosote buildup monthly during the heating season.

3. Don't use gasoline, charcoal lighter fluid or other highly flammable liquids to kindle or rekindle a fire. The flammable vapors can explode.

4. Never use or store flammable liquids near a fire. Vapors can travel the length of a room.

5. Always keep the damper opened properly while the wood is burning or smoldering.

6. Burn only one artificial log at a time. Because of the sawdust and wax content, using more than one log produces too much heat for some fireplaces to withstand. Follow the directions on the wrapper.

7. Always use a screen that covers the opening around the fireplace completely, to keep sparks from flying. Don't put combustible items, such as rugs, furniture or newspaper near a fireplace.

8. Be very careful when wearing loose-fitting clothing near a fireplace and keep children away from the fire.

9. Always open the damper before lighting the fire and keep it open until the ashes are cool. Check fireplaces every year to see that the damper operates properly.

10. Keep your fireplace clean of heavy accumulations of ashes. Use only metal containers when taking hot ashes from a fireplace. Be sure they cool fully before disposing of them.

11. Make sure the fire is out completely before leaving the house or going to bed.

12. Use chimney guards to keep small animals and bird nests out of chimneys.

13. Do not burn coal, charcoal or any type of polystyrene in a fireplace. Their combustion can create a dangerous amount of carbon monoxide.

14. Keep fuel for the fireplace—kindling, newspapers, firewood—stacked at least 3 feet from the hearth.

15. Keep a fire extinguisher nearby. An ABC type is the best all-around type.

FURNACES

In any year, 6,000 to 7,000 people receive emergency room treatment for injuries linked to central furnaces. Another 1,600 receive treatment for floor furnace mishaps.

- A 2-year-old boy crawled into the hot grate of a floor furnace. He received second and third degree burns to his hands and legs.

- A woman stuffed a towel into the intake vent for her furnace because the air made her utility room cold. This took the oxygen the furnace needed to burn the fuel, and produced large amounts of carbon monoxide. She was found dead from carbon monoxide poisoning.

- While trying to light the pilot light in his furnace, a man ignited the gas accumulated in the combustion chamber. His shirt caught fire and he received burns over 50 percent of his body.

Accident patterns

1. Contact with hot metal grates and other hot surfaces. Children can crawl into or push each other against hot furnace grates. Adults can also fall and be burned by hot surfaces.

2. Carbon monoxide poisoning. All fuel-burning appliances need air to burn the fuel properly. If an oil, gas, coal or wood furnace is "starved" of its intake air, it works inefficiently and produces large amounts of carbon monoxide. In addition, if the exhaust pipes are clogged or cracked, carbon monoxide can leak into your home.

3. Ignition of accumulated fuel vapors. Trying to light a pilot light or do maintenance can be hazardous if you are not familiar with the furnace. Also, accumulated vapors can ignite and cause a fire.

Hazardous operation. To save energy, many people insulate their homes and close all drafts and air leaks. This is hazardous if it blocks air intake vents. In some older homes, furnaces need a drafty door or window to get enough air to burn the fuel properly. Have your furnace checked regularly by a service company to make sure it gets enough air to burn the fuel safely.

Selection of furnaces

1. Be sure that the furnace has a safety pilot that automatically stops the fuel flow when the pilot light goes out.

2. Have the furnace installed to local codes. These usually give the air-intake and exhaust needs for safe use of the furnace.

Use of furnaces

1. Cover metal grates with metal screens that prevent children—and adults—from touching hot surfaces.

2. If you insulate your house or try to block air drafts around doors and windows, be sure you don't cut off air needed for the furnace to burn fuel properly. Have a service company check for this. Generally, you need 1 square inch of intake air piping for every 5000 BTUs/hour of heat from the furnace. If the furnace doesn't get enough air to burn fuel fully, it produces large amounts of carbon monoxide, which can leak and be fatal.

3. Keep flammable liquids (such as gasoline) away from furnaces. The furnace pilot light can ignite their vapors. Keep flammable liquids in tightly capped

safety cans in a shed outside, away from any flame or heat sources.

4. Do not try to light a pilot light unless you are familiar with the furnace and proper techniques. If the pilot light goes out or if the furnace needs adjustment, call a service company or the gas company.

Maintenance

1. Have your furnace checked at least once every year. Do it before the heating season to be sure that there is enough intake air and that the exhaust system works properly.

2. Have flues checked to be sure they are not blocked by debris. This could allow fumes to enter the house.

3. Because furnace filters keep dust from circulating through the house, they get very dirty. When dirty, they restrict air flow, which makes the furnace less efficient. Some filters can be cleaned with soap and water, while others need to be replaced.

4. Fan blades, usually located behind the filter, also become dirty and less efficient. Soap and water usually will clean the blades. The fan motor and bearings need periodic lubrication.

SPACE HEATERS

Each year, 5,000 people receive emergency room treatment for injuries associated with oil, gas, kerosene and electric space heaters, and wood and coal burning heating stoves.

- Jenny, 4, was standing close to the gas space heater to keep warm. Her dress was ignited by the open flame and she suffered severe burns over 70 percent of her body.

- Mr. Bloom turned on the gas for his space heater and lit a match to light the heater. The accumulated gas exploded and Mr. Bloom died from the resulting burns.

- An unvented space heater was left on all night and produced enough carbon monoxide to asphyxiate a family of three.

- Karen was running in the living room when she tripped and fell against the electric space heater in the center of the room. She was seriously burned.

- Richard received a serious electrical shock when, just after taking a shower, he turned on the electric space heater in his bathroom.

- Mr. Johnson tried to build up a smoldering fire in his heating stove by squirting gasoline on it. The vapors from the gasoline caught fire and traveled up the gasoline stream to the can, which ignited. Mr. Johnson was seriously burned.

Accident patterns

1. By contact. Contact with the flame, heating element or hot surface areas can ignite clothing and cause severe burns. Falling against or touching the outside surface can cause severe burn injuries.

2. Explosion of accumulated gas. This often happens when trying to light the burner.

3. Carbon monoxide poisoning. An unvented space heater or one that is not properly adjusted and dirty can produce deadly amounts of carbon monoxide. Incomplete burning of solid fuel in a heating stove also produces carbon monoxide.

4. Electric shock. This often results when a person who is wet touches the controls.

5. Using flammable liquids to stoke the fire. The flammable vapors can ignite and cause an explosion. Using these liquids in the same room with a heater or stove can create the same hazard.

Most space heaters involved in accidents are gas space heaters, but electric heaters can also cause burns and electrical shocks.

Using the wrong fuels—such as charcoal lighter fluid in a stove or kerosene in an oil heater—creates special hazards of carbon monoxide and overheating. Following are suggestions for the selection, safe use and maintenance of space heaters and heating stoves.

Selection of space heaters

1. Buy a properly vented heater or stove. Old-fashioned or second-hand heaters and stoves may be cracked, poorly adjusted or improperly vented, producing deadly amounts of carbon monoxide.

2. When buying a new, unvented gas space heater, look for a label that states, "This heater is equipped with a pilot light safety system designed to turn off the heater if not enough fresh air is available." New heaters have this system, which is called an oxygen depletion system (ODS) device.

3. Unvented heaters are banned in some communities because they are more likely to produce carbon monoxide than vented heaters.

4. Buy a space heater or a stove with an effective guard around the flames or heating coil, to keep children, pets and clothing away from the heat source.

5. If you buy an electric space heater, be sure it has an automatic switch that cuts off electric power if the heater tips over.

Use of space heaters

1. If you must use an unvented space heater or heating stove, keep a window partly open. Plenty of oxygen is needed for good combustion, and the fresh air helps keep carbon monoxide from building.

2. Use the proper fuel for each heating device:

   - Don't use coal in a wood-burning stove. It can overheat.

   - Don't use flammable liquid on a wood or coal fire. It can cause an explosion.

   - Don't use charcoal or styrofoam in a heating stove. These fuels produce deadly amounts of carbon monoxide.

3. Keep children away from space heaters and stoves, because they can be burned simply by touching the hot surfaces.

4. Keep at least three-foot clearances in all directions around space heaters or stoves. Don't put a heater near drapes, furniture or other flammable materials, or near areas people routinely walk.

5. Maintain proper ventilation and rate of burning. Keep the fire at moderate heat, neither too cool or too hot. If the fire is too cool, it may permit flammable gases and residues to gather, which can explode when reheated by adding more coal or wood.

6. Always use a screen around a stove or space heater with open flames.

7. Keep the damper open when the fuel is burning. This provides better burning and prevents the accumulation of explosive gases.

8. Learn how to light a gas space heater. If you smell gas, turn off all controls and open a window or door. Don't turn on the gas until your match is ready. Don't allow time for gas to gather. If you don't light the heater on the first try, allow enough time for the gas to dissipate before trying again.

9. Never use flammable liquids around a space heater or heating stove. Vapors can flow from one part of the room to another and ignite from the open flame.

10. Never leave an unvented space heater or stove on overnight. Carbon monoxide may accumulate and overcome you while you sleep, causing death.

11. Do not use an extension cord for an electric heater, unless it is a heavy-duty cord. Have an electrician check

the wiring if you plan to use a heater with higher than usual wattage. If you must use an extension cord, make sure it is a heavy duty cord rated at least as high as the cord on the heater.

12. Never place an electric heater near a bathtub, shower or sink. Avoid using a portable heater in a bathroom. Never touch an electric heater when you are wet.

13. Place a metal sheet under a coal or a wood-burning stove to protect the floor from live coals or burning wood and from overheating.

14. Do not use the heater as a dryer by placing clothing over it to dry. Do not use it to thaw pipes.

15. Be aware that using space heaters or heating stoves in mobile homes can be more hazardous, because they are smaller than most houses and may have less ventilation, more closely in- stalled electrical appliances and more combustible construction.

Maintenance of space heaters

1. Inspect gas, kerosene and oil space heaters regularly to ensure that they are properly adjusted and clean.

2. Inspect heating stoves regularly to in- sure that all linings and chimneys are intact, and that the stove is properly adjusted and clean.

3. Check stoves for cracks or faulty legs and hinges.

4. Replace loose or missing guards on all heating stoves.

5. Keep all electrical wiring in electric space heaters in good working order.

6. Be sure that all ashes are thoroughly cool before you dispose of them.

Oil and kerosene space heaters

1. Never use gasoline. Even a small amount can cause fire. Only use kero- sene the dealer can certify is 1-K kero- sene. All clear kerosene is not alike. A blue container labeled "kerosene" is the recognized color for storing 1-K kero- sene. A red container signifies gaso- line. Store 1-K fuel and gasoline apart. Gasoline inadvertently placed in a kero- sene container can cause a destructive flare-up.

2. Do not allow children to use or refuel a kerosene heater.

3. Be aware that some people are more susceptible to the gases given off by kerosene heaters and other unvented sources. Particularly at risk are those with asthma, respiratory diseases or heart diseases.

4. Do not use a kerosene heater in a small, tightly closed room. There must be enough fresh air. In a tightly sealed home or room, open a window slightly and open the doors to other rooms for better circulation.

5. Set the wick height to the manufac- turer's guidelines. If the room becomes too hot, turn off the heater or open a window.

6. Do not leave an operating heater unat- tended. Do not operate the heater while people are sleeping or confined to bed.

7. Do not attempt to move or refuel the heater while it is running or still hot.

8. Never fill a heater with cold oil. When the oil warms it could spill and flare.

9. Never use a kerosene heater where flammable vapors, such as gasoline, solvents or paint thinners, are present. Don't use heaters in areas such as grain elevators, where combustible dusts are likely to be present.

Selection of space heaters

1. Select a heater that is the right size for the heating task.

2. Look for a heater that is tested and approved by a nationally recognized testing firm.

Caution

1. Never use a cooking stove as a heater. Don't leave open the oven door more than a few minutes at a time because an oven can produce large quantities of poisonous gas.
2. Keep at least one dry-powder, ABC-type fire extinguisher in the home.
3. Keep areas around heat sources free of paper and trash.
4. Have a fire-escape plan that all members of the household know and can follow in case of emergency.

In case of fire

1. If your clothes catch fire, don't run! Drop down at once and roll to smother the flames. Teach your children how to react to fire.
2. If a flare-up or uncontrolled flaming occurs, do not try to move or carry the heater. If the heater has a manual shut-off valve, use the switch to turn off the heater.
3. Do not attempt to put out a kerosene heater fire with water or blankets. In most cases, it is best to call the fire department immediately.

COAL-, WOOD-BURNING STOVES

Many consumers turned to wood-burning and coal-burning stoves as a way to avoid high heating bills. Unfortunately, often they are not aware of the importance of proper installation, use and maintenance to the safety of their homes. The result is a dramatic increase in fires and burns involving wood and coal burning stoves. These case histories are examples of the trend:

- Mr. Jackson decided to vent his new stove to an existing brick chimney. The connector pipe between the stove and the chimney was installed through the wall, too close to the wood paneling. The hot pipe caused a fire, which gutted the family's house.

- When Earl installed a new wood stove and metal, factory-built chimney, he neglected to insure the necessary clearance at the point where the chimney projected into the attic. One day, after he started a hot fire, the attic joists caught fire, causing extensive structural damage.

- Mrs. Watson neglected to have the chimney, attached to her air-tight stove, cleaned. Creosote deposits, which accumulated in the chimney, eventually caught fire when the stove was fired. Heat from the chimney fire ignited nearby wood joists, and the resulting fire left Mrs. Watson homeless.

- Before retiring one night, an elderly woman placed firewood behind her wood stove for use the following morning. During the night the firewood ignited, resulting in a fire that caused her death.

Causes of accidental fire and injury

1. Failure to keep proper clearance between nearby combustible materials and the stove. The stove should be kept at least 3 feet from walls, ceiling and furnishings, unless instructions say otherwise. Do not pass a single-wall chimney through a combustible wall without using special protective methods as found in the manufacturer's instructions, building codes and fire codes.
2. Failure to keep the chimney and chimney pipe clear of creosote. Creosote is a black, tarry or flaky substance that becomes a fire hazard when it builds up on the inside the chimney wall. During the burning season, your chimney should be inspected monthly for these deposits.
3. Contact with flame or hot surface area.
4. Using flammable liquids to start or stoke a fire. Liquids, such as gasoline, may ignite explosively and start a fire or ignite clothing.

5. Carbon monoxide poisoning. Usually carbon monoxide is vented up the flue. If the flue becomes blocked or does not draw properly, the gases can enter the living area. If the flue is connected according to local building codes, there should not be a problem.

Selection

1. Before you buy, ask your local building inspector or fire department for any requirements of heating stoves. They are constantly updated, so be sure to get the latest information.
2. Consider the environmental aspects of wood-burning or coal-burning stoves. Nearly all communities where wood- or coal-burning stoves are common have passed laws that permit only certain types. Many stoves approved by testing agencies will not meet local requirements. Even then, local regulations may preclude using your new stove, sometimes for several days at a time.
3. Pick a stove tested by a nationally recognized testing agency.
4. Be aware that older stoves may have cracks that can allow deadly quantities of carbon monoxide to escape.
5. Other rules may apply to stoves for mobile homes. Check with your local building inspector.
6. Consider the area you plan to heat when deciding what size stove to purchase.

Installation

1. The stove should be installed by a qualified person. If you must do it yourself, first check with your local building code office or fire marshal. Also, carefully read the manufacturer's instructions.
2. Some local governments require a permit to install a wood burning stove and must inspect it for safety.

3. To prevent overheating, place the stove on a suitable floor protector. Local codes and manufacturer's instructions provide the best guidance.
4. Place the stove at least 36 inches from walls unless advised otherwise.
5. Don't place a stove near drapes, furniture or other flammable materials.
6. Don't use a pipe labeled "vent" as a chimney, because it can get very hot. Use instead an all-masonry chimney or a factory-built chimney certified as a "residential" type.
7. Don't pass a chimney connector through a combustible wall without proper protection and clearance.

Use of coal-, wood-burning stoves

1. Keep a window open slightly when using a wood burning stove, to provide enough air for proper burning.
2. Keep kindling, drapes, newspapers and other flammable materials away from the stove.
3. Use the proper fuel:
   - Prevent overheating. Don't use coal, charcoal, plastic or paper in a wood-burning stove.
   - To prevent explosions, don't use flammable liquids on a wood or coal fire.
   - To avoid carbon monoxide and other poisonous gases, don't use fuels not meant for the wood- or coal-burning stoves.
4. Keep children away from the stove.
5. Keep the stove door closed or use a metal screen while the fire burns, to keep sparks from flying.
6. Keep fire at a moderate heat for best results and safety.
7. A glowing red stove is dangerous. Cool the stove quickly by closing the stove's dampers. If that does not cool the stove fast enough, put a few shovelfuls of ashes on the fire.

8. Use chimney guards to prevent squirrels and birds from building nests in the chimney.

9. Don't dispose of paper, plastic or trash by burning them in the stove.

10. Don't hang clothes near the stove to dry, because they can catch fire.

Maintenance

1. Have your chimney inspected before the heating season and check it twice a month during the season. Check for soot and blockage, and clean when necessary.

2. Check to see that chimney linings, and the chimney itself, are intact.

3. Check stoves for cracks, faulty legs and hinges.

4. Replace loose or missing guards and defective parts of the stove and chimney.

5. Don't transfer hot ashes from the stove to a cardboard container. Hot ashes may be "live" for up to 24 hours and can cause delayed fires. Use metal containers to discard ashes when cool.

Effects of wood smoke. There is some concern about the effect of wood smoke on humans. In Washington, where wood stoves and fireplaces are common, there has been much research on the subject. The State Department of Ecology offers this:

The particles in wood smoke are too small to be filtered by the nose and upper respiratory system, so they end up deep in the lungs. Poisonous and cancer-causing chemicals often enter the lungs by adhering to such particles.

These tiny particles are emitted in neighborhoods, both indoors and out, where people spend most of their time. The particulate matter in wood smoke from chimneys is so small that it is not stopped by closed doors and windows, and often seeps into neighbors' houses. Even more smoke can be released inside homes that heat with wood.

Wood smoke exposure causes a decrease in lung function and in the severity of existing lung disease, with more smoke concentration or exposure time. It also aggravates heart conditions. The presence of respiratory illness in children has been shown to increase with exposure to wood smoke. Long-term exposure may lead to emphysema, chronic bronchitis, arteriosclerosis and nasal, throat, blood and lymph system cancers.

WATER HEATERS

The gas water heater is easy to forget. Once installed, it sits unnoticed and ignored for years, until it must be replaced. However, there are some very serious hazards associated with gas water heaters. Each year, perhaps 1,200 people receive emergency room treatment for injuries received from gas water heaters. Many of these accidents happened because the water heater was forgotten.

- A 62-year-old man was cleaning the floor of his basement with gasoline. The vapors were ignited by the pilot light of a water heater in the next room. He spent 13 days in the hospital with second and third degree burns.

- A 53-year-old man turned off all the gas in his home in order to attempt to repair his own heating equipment. When he attempted to relight the pilot light of the water heater after completing the job, accumulated gas exploded.

Operation. The typical gas water heater is a metal tank lined inside with glass-like enamel to protect the inner metal surface from corrosive agents in the water. Normally, however, there are some small areas of metal left unprotected. So, added protection comes from a long magnesium rod (the anode) inside the tank, which the corrosives will attack instead of the tank itself. Over a period of years, the anode is gradually eaten away and must be replaced.

Cold water enters from the top of the tank through the dip tube. This is a pipe of metal or plastic that extends into the tank and discharges the water near the bottom to be heated. This prevents the incoming cold water from mixing with heated water near the top of the tank.

The water is heated by a gas burner at the bottom of the tank and by the hot gases flowing up the central flue. A metal baffle in the flue slows the flow of these gases.

Safety features. To control the temperature of the water, an automatic thermostat turns the burner on and off. This keeps the water temperature from rising above a set point. There is also a safety relief valve that takes over if the thermostat fails.

An added feature on most late-model water heaters is a cut-off device, which shuts off the gas if the pilot light goes out or if the water temperature rises too high. Voluntary industry standards require these safety features on all water heaters.

Purchase and installation

The capacity and style of the water heater you will buy depend on your household needs and where you locate the heater. To be sure that the water heater meets safety standards, look for the symbol of approval of the American Gas Association.

Only an experienced plumber should install a water heater. Don't try to do it yourself. If installed incorrectly, the heater, at best, may simply not work properly. But there is also a chance that it could result in gas leakage and an explosion.

You also must have a temperature- and pressure-relief valve or valves installed. The type is specified by local ordinance. Replace the valve if it becomes defective. Never plug a leaking valve. Any time you replace a water heater, replace the valve.

When installing the water heater, test to be sure that the temperature of your hot water corresponds to the thermostat setting. The service person can adjust the thermostat for you.

Another safety device you may want is a thermostat tempering (mixing) valve on the water to the tub, shower and sink. This mixes cold water with the hot and moderates the water temperature at these points to prevent scalding injuries. This device is good for households with small children.

Use of water heaters

Some of the most serious accidents involving gas and water heaters occur when a flammable liquid, such as gasoline or vapors, flow along the floor. The heavier-than-air vapors of gasoline can flow the entire length of a basement or garage and be ignited explosively by the water heater's pilot light or burner.

1. Never, under any circumstances, use a flammable liquid near a gas water heater or any other open flame.

2. Never store flammable products—including paint products—near the water heater.

3. Warn children not to play with or around the water heater. The metal surface of the heater can get quite hot, and the heater may have sharp metal edges.

4. Follow all directions carefully when attempting to relight a pilot light.

Maintenance. Periodic maintenance of the water heater is an often ignored necessity. Be sure that the safety devices are working properly, that no significant deterioration has occurred and that the burner and vents function properly. Clogged burners and vents, for instance, may cause carbon monoxide poisoning. Only an expert should attempt this maintenance.

SAFETY RECAP

1. Carbon-monoxide gas is an invisible and silent killer associated with heating equipment.

2. Hot heating surfaces cause nearby materials to catch fire or cause burns when touched.

3. Gas appliances have two main hazards: gas fumes and ignition of gas or gasoline fumes.

BIBLIOGRAPHY

"A Home Fire-Prevention Checklist," *Aide*, San Antonio, TX: USAA, October 1991, p. 19.

"Coal and Wood Burning Stoves," *Product Safety Fact Sheet*, U.S. Consumer Product Safety Commission, November 1984.

"Electric Baseboard Heaters." *Product Safety Fact Sheet*, U.S. Consumer Product Safety Commission, February, 1980.

"Fireplaces," *Product Safety Fact Sheet*, U.S. Consumer Product Safety Commission, July 1987.

"Fireplaces Need Extra Care," *Community Safety & Health*, Chicago, IL: National Safety Council, July/August 1992, p. 5.

"Electric Space Heaters," *Product Safety Fact Sheet*, U.S. Consumer Product Safety Commission, November 1984.

"Health Effects of Wood Smoke," Olympia, WA: Washington Department of Ecology, 1992, p. 8.

"Heating With Wood," Washington, DC: U.S. Department of Energy, Superintendent of Documents, May 1980, 20 pages.

"Kerosene Heaters," *Product Safety Fact Sheet*, U.S. Consumer Product Safety Commission, September 1985.

"Safety Tips," pamphlet, Nashville, TN: National Kerosene Association, 1991.

"Space Heaters," *Product Safety Fact Sheet*, U.S. Product Safety Commission, September 1985.

"What You Should Know About Kerosene Heaters," U.S. Consumer Product Safety Commission, August 1987.

"What You Should Know About Space Heaters," U.S. Consumer Product Safety Commission, September 1987.

"Inspecting Your Home Heating System Before Winter Could Save Your Life," CPSC Release 93-016. November 1992.

CHAPTER 6

MAJOR APPLIANCES

AUTOMATIC WASHERS

1. Never use flammable liquids in or near a washer.

2. Hand wash and air dry any fabric that has solvents on it, before placing in the washer.

3. Don't store detergent near the washer where children can reach it.

4. Do not pour chlorine bleach into wash water with ammonia or acids such as vinegar. Harmful fumes can result.

5. Never put your hands into a spinning washer.

6. Don't let young children play with or operate a washer or dryer.

COMPUTERS

Home computers are commonplace and most consumers are familiar with them, whether through school, business or home use. For the most part, computers are not sources for common household hazards that threaten injury or health. Nevertheless, the use of computers is so common that their care needs to be emphasized, if for no other reason than to properly maintain an expensive consumer product.

Typical uses for the home computer, beyond the home office, fall into four categories: educational, home management, personal and entertainment.

Eyestrain. Naturally, there are some eyestrain hazards from watching a small screen (monitor) for long periods. This can be reduced with a treated glass on the screen or a mesh that cuts glare. Some monitors can be tilted or swiveled to reduce or eliminate glare. A clean monitor screen does the most to reduce eyestrain so it should be cleaned often. Do not use window cleaner because it creates a wax film, which attracts dust and yellows the screen.

Computer virus. A computer virus can damage your software or wipe out data, but does not endanger your health.

Power supply problems. Surges in the power supply, caused by electrical storms, can damage computers. Following are some protective guidelines:

1. Use three-wire electrical outlets for your computer system. This is important for:
   - Safety (a 3-wire plug grounds the equipment).
   - Avoiding errors in data caused by electrical noise on the wires when refrigerators or other electric appliances cut in.
   - Preventing interference in TVs and radios that your computer system might cause. If you do get interference, turn off your computer to see if the interference stops.

2. Plug your computer into a surge protector, a device that prevents hardware damage or loss of data from electrical surges.

3. In electrical storms, unplug your computer from the outlet and the modem from the phone line.

4. If the power goes off when you are working on the computer, turn it off. Otherwise a very large voltage spike, called a transient, could damage your computer when the power returns.

Normal precautions. In many ways, the computer and its peripherals are like any major appliance and most of the same precautions apply. It is not a toy, so children should not play with it without supervision. Powered by electricity, it may shock and electrocute the same as a TV or radio. If precariously balanced, it can injure someone when falling.

The radiation health hazards associated with closeness to TV screens are possible, but, based on research, not fully accepted. Research continues and both positive and negative results have been found.

Eyestrain problems, which were discussed earlier, are valid. The possibility of back strain and carpal tunnel effects from keyboard use are real also. Both can be eased, if not prevented, by proper design of work stations and support equipment, such as adjustable monitor bases, and ergonomically proper furniture.

DISHWASHERS

1. Let the washer cool for at least 30 minutes before reaching into the area below the bottom rack.
2. Never try to use a dishwasher that is not working properly.
3. Do not sit, stand on or abuse a dishwasher door, racks or controls.
4. When you discard a dishwasher, remove the door, block it open or chain it shut to keep children from crawling inside.

DRYERS

Most injuries linked with dryers are cuts and bruises from falling against the dryer. There are more serious injuries, however, from child entrapment, fires and poisonous gases. Both gas and electric clothes dryers can present shock and fire hazards. Many older clothes dryers can entrap children and cause death as the dryer begins operating when the door closes.

- Mike, 4, climbed into his grandmother's old dryer and pulled the door closed. The dryer began operating immediately. The heat and reduced oxygen level caused his death.

- Marilyn put a load of clothes into the dryer and set the timer for 70 minutes. She had not emptied the lint trap for several cycles, and the collected lint ignited, causing the clothes to ignite.

- A gas dryer was vented into a chimney. There were several turns in the vent piping and some of the connections were loose. As the dryer was being operated, the poisonous gases produced by the burning gas began to leak into the laundry room, causing the woman in the room to suffocate.

Accident patterns

1. Child entrapment. Some dryers may start as soon as the door is closed. In contrast, most newer dryers have safety buttons on the control panel to push *after* closing the door, in order to start the dryer. Even with these safety devices, however, children can climb inside dryers and become trapped because they panic or cannot push open doors.

2. Fires. Failure to clean the lint trap can permit lint to collect and, if heated enough, ignite.

3. Poisonous gases. Gas produces carbon monoxide and other poisonous gases when it burns. If gas dryers are not well vented to the outside, these gases can accumulate, and result in a fatal lack of oxygen in the body. Faulty vent piping, piping with obstructions or piping with several turns in it, can permit lint to block the exhaust pipes, allowing carbon monoxide to accumulate. Exhaust can also cause leaks to develop and let poisonous gases into the laundry room or other rooms in the house.

4. Electric shock. If dryers are not properly grounded (for example, by use of three-prong plugs and outlets), a current leak or short circuit in the dryer can give an electric shock. This risk increases in the laundry room, where plumbing is often nearby. Electric current can conduct through you much easier if you are wet or touching a water pipe.

5. Anti-static compounds. The use of anti-static compounds in dryers has added fire hazards. These compounds reduce static electricity on drying clothes, but spraying them on electric coils in dryers can cause overheating and start fires.

Selection of dryers

1. Be sure that the dryer you buy has a safety start button on the control panel that must be pushed after closing the door in order to start the dryer. This reduces the risk of trapping a child in an operating dryer.

2. Purchase a dryer with a door that opens easily from the inside so a child who climbs inside can get out. Avoid dryers with doors that can only be opened by an outside latch.

3. If you are buying a gas dryer, buy one with an electric ignition system. This removes the need for a pilot light and so avoids the problems and risks of lighting a pilot light.

4. If you are buying an electric dryer, be sure that your house wiring can carry the required current. Consult an electrician for expert advice. You may have to install another circuit and wiring.

Use of dryers

1. If you use anti-static compounds when you dry clothes, do not spray the substance directly on or near the electric coils in the dryer. This can cause the dryer to overheat and start a fire.

2. Vent all dryers directly to the outside and not to a chimney. Avoid turns in the piping. They can permit lint to block them and allow poisonous gases to leak.

3. Do not overload a dryer. Heavy, wet laundry can impede the motion of the drum and cause overheating.

4. Follow directions for drying various types of clothing to preserve their quality and safety features:

   • For synthetic, permanent press fabrics, extremely hot drying can cause shrinking and melting. Use moderate heat.

   • For flame-retardant, treated fabrics (such as children's sleepwear), extremely hot drying can reduce the effectiveness of the flame-retardant treatment. Use moderate heat.

5. Electric dryers

   • Be sure that both gas and electric dryers are grounded by three-prong plugs and properly grounded outlets, or other means. Have an electrician check this to be sure.

   • If you ever sense even a small electric shock when you touch the dryer, have it checked by a competent electrician before using. Current leaking into a dryer can give a serious electric shock, especially if you are wet or standing on a wet floor.

6. Gas dryers. If you have an older gas dryer with a pilot light, remember that the gas is highly flammable. Have a match ready before you turn on the gas so that you can light the pilot light immediately.

7. Do not dry items that have been used with kerosene, gasoline, spot removers, turpentine, alcohol, household or other chemical cleaners, because the flammable liquid could ignite. Hand-wash and air dry such items before placing in a washer or dryer.

8. Do not dry anything in the dryer for which the manufacturer instructs "dry away from heat." These fabrics should be dried in a well-ventilated room or outdoors.

9. Turn off a gas dryer's gas valve before going on vacation.

Maintenance of dryers

1. Keep the lint trap clean. Remove lint before every load of laundry. Do not let lint and dust to accumulate around a dryer.

2. Check for leaks in the vent piping and have them repaired at once. Do not turn any electric switches on or off if you smell gas from a gas dryer. Call the gas company for service. Operating the switches could ignite the gas.

3. If the dryer is not drying as quickly as it once did, check for blockage of the dryer vent. With the dryer running, check the outside air vent to make sure exhaust air is escaping normally. If it is not, look inside both ends of the duct and remove any lint.

4. Check the exhaust duct more often if you have a plastic, flexible duct. This duct traps more lint than ducting without ridges.

5. If there are signs that the dryer is hotter than normal, the dryer's temperature control thermostat may need servicing.

6. Make sure the dryer is level. If not, the rotation of the drum could cause the dryer to move and put undue stress on electrical and gas connections.

7. Don't use flammable liquids in or near a dryer.

MICROWAVE OVENS

Microwave ovens are almost as common as kitchen ranges or refrigerators. They range from small (counter-top models are typically 15 inches wide and 12 inches deep) to large (23 inches wide and 17 inches deep). They are most frequently used to heat leftovers, followed by heating beverages, frozen entrees and snacks, as well as for defrosting.

Most microwaves work in the same way. A tube sends a beam of high-frequency radio waves into the oven's interior and disperses the beam throughout the oven and, in turn, heats the food. Microwaves pass easily through glass, plastic and wood, but water, sugar and fat molecules absorb the energy. The microwaves vibrate rapidly and heat up the food from the energy of the vibration. The walls and glass doors do not pass the microwaves and thus protect the user.

Hazards. The hazard foremost in the minds of most consumers is the amount of radiation that might be leaked by a microwave. Nobody knows for certain what constitutes a safe level of microwave leakage. Research reports vary from no injuries blamed on the ovens, to the Consumer Product Safety Commission estimate of many microwave injuries from radiation, to those who claim several recorded injuries per year.

Purchasing microwave ovens

1. Look for a lock-out device to keep small children from using the microwave.

2. Inspect the instruction manual and be certain it is easy to read and use. There should be a quick-reference instruction card so you don't have to go through the instruction manual for normal cooking instructions.

3. Look for an angled plug, so the oven can be mounted close to the outlet.

4. The display should show the power level in use.

5. Look for an end-of-cycle visual signal. A beeper that sounds when cooked food is left inside is an added safety feature.

6. Be certain the keypad will be easily readable in the proposed location. Look for size and contrast of numbers. Bright

colored numbers with high contrast are favored.

7. A well-lighted interior is desirable. Be certain the interior light is consumer replaceable.

8. Beware of sharp, exposed corners or rough, exposed edges.

9. Look for smooth surfaces and rounded edges for easy cleaning. A removable glass tray is helpful.

Microwave problems and use

Most of the radiation worries that dogged earlier microwave models are no longer concerns in newer model microwave ovens. Today, most problems are not related to the microwave ovens themselves:

1. Never use a microwave oven that was dropped or has seriously overheated at any time. Either incident may cause a door to warp or become misaligned, keeping it from closing tightly.

2. Microwaves don't cook evenly without a fair amount of turning and stirring, so it is easy to undercook parts of a product. Pork and chicken must be cooked evenly to kill parasites. To overcome this problem, follow instructions closely. Cook stuffing separately.

3. Don't heat baby food in jars, since they may explode. If you must use the microwave, spoon the food into a shallow container to heat, and stir afterward to equalize heat. Finally, taste it to make sure it is not too hot for the baby.

4. Popcorn tends to have more uncooked kernels when microwave-popped and there is a chance the paper bag can be scorched or even ignited.

5. Beware of brown-and-crisp packaging and dual-oven trays used to package microwave foods. Regulations on these are forthcoming. The heating process may cause chemical leakage from the packing into the food.

6. Use plastic wrap with care. Some plastics leach chemicals, and the wrap can melt if it touches hot food. You can prevent

risks by poking holes in the wrap and keeping it from touching the food.

7. Do not use the microwave oven—with or without the Micro-Dome—for canning. The uneven heating tendency of microwave ovens can allow food to be contaminated with deadly botulism toxins.

8. Don't deep-fat fry. Microwaves do not let you control the temperature of the oil, which can splatter or boil over even when not overheated.

9. Let steam escape from covered dishes. A tight seal can allow steam to build up and cause burns when it is removed.

10. Don't heat baby bottles. The liquids inside can become very hot, even when the bottle feels only warm. The Shriner's Burn Institute reports many burns and scalds to children from heated formula. Also, a buildup of steam in the bottle liner can cause the formula to explode over the baby and the feeder when the bottle is shaken. Another problem is the "eruption" phenomenon. When heating clear liquids in glass, ceramic or smooth plastic containers, the liquid can become extremely hot, although not boiling. It can then erupt violently when moved or stirred or when something is added to it (for example a spoon of instant coffee).

11. Heat susceptors are metallized plastic strips in wrapping, which become very hot (500°F) and, in turn, heat the contents of the wrapper. There is some concern that at such high heat, very small quantities of plastic and adhesive parts are released into the food. This can happen, but current research fails to show that there are any harmful releases.

12. Train children in basic microwave use. Be certain they know how to use the microwave before they use it without supervision. Many burn cases indicate that young children use the microwave, both alone and with supervision.

13. Do not turn on the oven when it is empty.

14. Do not use the oven when anything is touching the top or sides.

15. Canning jars cannot be sterilized in a microwave.

Microwave cooking safety. Reports of food poisoning from microwave-cooked meat, poultry and fish are not uncommon. Since microwaves often cook food unevenly, bacteria flourishes in underdone spots. To be certain food cooks evenly, and that its surfaces stay warm, follow these guidelines:

1. Cook food long enough, cook it covered and, during cooking, move it with a turntable or by stirring by hand. Let food stand covered after cooking, so the heat can spread and the cooking finish.

2. If you use the microwave to defrost meat, do it just before cooking it.

3. Never partially cook food. If combining microwave cooking with roasting, broiling or grilling, transfer microwave foods to conventional heat quickly.

4. Use a temperature probe or meat thermometer to verify the food has reached a safe temperature. Check temperature in several places, avoiding fat and bone. It should reach 160°F for red meat, 180°F for poultry and 170°F for pork.

5. Make allowances for oven wattage variations. Ovens vary in power and operating efficiency. Make certain that food is done, with a meat thermometer and visual inspection. Juices should run clear; meat should not be pink.

6. Bone large pieces of meat before cooking. Bone shields the meat around it from thorough cooking.

7. Don't stuff chicken or turkey if you want to cook it in the microwave.

8. Check your microwave manual or cookbook for standing times for meat after it has cooked in the microwave. (Letting food stand covered after cooking allows the heat to spread and cooking to finish.)

9. Reheat food until hot and steamy, not just pleasantly warm.

10. Arrange food items evenly in a covered dish, and add a little liquid. Under the cover, steam helps kill bacteria and ensure uniform heating. Use a glass cover or plastic wrap, but do not let the plastic touch the food.

11. Sample foods intended for young children before allowing them to eat them.

12. Watch out for foods unevenly heated. Stir foods to spread the heat evenly. The jelly filling in a pastry may be scalding, while the pastry is only lukewarm.

13. When directed to cover food with plastic, you must vent it. Cover with plastic, then pull back a corner. Do not slit the cover, or steam may escape under pressure through the slit.

14. If food is not labeled "microwavable," do not microwave it.

15. Do not hardboil eggs in the microwave. They can explode, possibly with enough force to blow off the door.

16. To poach eggs in a microwave, pierce the yoke before cooking.

17. Pierce potatoes and apples several times with a fork before microwaving.

18. To avoid steam burns, after heating foods in bags or containers, let the food and container cool on the counter to allow vapor pressure to decrease.

19. Salty foods tend to stay cooler and are not easily penetrated by microwaves. Sometimes salted food is not heated enough to kill certain bacteria, resulting in food poisoning. Cook or reheat salted foods to a high enough interior temperature to kill bacteria. Simply warming is not good enough. Consider using a temperature probe.

20. Use a potholder to remove any container from the microwave.

RANGES

Each year, more than 100,000 kitchen fires involve fixed cooking appliances. These fires result in 300 deaths and nearly 6,000 injuries. Emergency rooms treat another 25,000 burn or shock injuries not related to fires each year. Seniors and the very young often have mishaps with gas and electric ranges. Although electric and gas ranges/ovens differ greatly in operation, the hazards are similar.

- Selma was wearing a housecoat with loose-fitting sleeves. She reached across the front burners of her gas stove to stir something in a pot on the back burner. One of the front burners was on and her garment ignited. Fortunately she was able to smother the fire by dropping to the floor and rolling. She received painful burns, but they were confined to her arms.

- Tommy, 3, climbed onto an electric range to reach a cookie jar stored in the cabinet directly above. In the process of climbing onto the range, he inadvertently turned the control knob to the high temperature setting. The burner heated up while he was sitting on top of the range and his pants ignited.

- Joan was using contact cement to secure the paper in her kitchen cabinets. Even though the burners in her gas range were off, the pilot light was on. After a period of time, the flammable vapors from the cement accumulated to a concentration that was ignited by the pilot light. The room suddenly was engulfed in flames and Joan was burned seriously.

- Bob, 60, turned on his gas stove and then lit a match to light the oven. He dropped the first match and had to light a second. By that time, enough gas had accumulated to cause an explosion. Bob was burned severely.

Accident patterns

1. Leaning against the stove. Many range accidents involve people leaning with their back to the range. Victims are often wearing loose-fitting garments or shirts that are not tucked in.

2. Reaching over or across the range. A burner can easily ignite a dangling sleeve or a towel used to move a pot.

3. Climbing on or around the range. This is a special hazard for young children. An electric burner coil can reach a temperature of more than 1,000°F and can ignite fabric that contacts it, even if the range is off already.

4. Flammable vapor fires. Flammable vapors from contact cement, kerosene and gasoline can be ignited by a pilot light or burner and cause the whole room to erupt in flames.

5. Natural gas explosions. If the oven has no pilot light, or if the pilot light goes out, gas can gather and ignite from a match or other source.

6. Ranges without a pilot light. Some people do not know how to light such ranges.

7. Ovens without a pilot light. Some ranges have a pilot light for the burners, but not for the oven. This is dangerous if the oven is not lighted quickly after turning on the gas.

8. Unattended grease pans. If a pan of grease is left unattended on a burner, the grease may burst into flames. It can spill and ignite garments if carried to the sink.

9. Fabrics hanging over burners. Curtains and dishtowels hanging over the burner can ignite and cause a fire. Be aware of this while out of the kitchen.

Purchase of ranges

1. Knobs on ranges should be difficult for children to reach and turn on. They should require going through lower temperatures before reaching the high setting.

2. Controls should be placed to eliminate the need to reach over the burners in order to turn the range on or off.

3. Buy an electric range with signal lamps that warn when a burner is on.

4. Buy a gas range with pilot lights for the burner and for the oven.

5. Free-standing kitchen ranges and improperly installed built-ins may tilt forward easily when too much pressure is applied to an open oven door. This can be done by placing heavy pans on the door or by a small child sitting on the door. Be certain the range will not tip easily under these conditions. If a built-in, be sure it is installed properly.

Use of ranges

1. Do not wear loose-fitting clothing when you use a kitchen range. Loose sleeves are easily ignited by electric and gas burners.

2. Use potholders, not towels or paper tissue, to move pans on the range. The burners can easily ignite towels and tissues.

3. Keep children away from kitchen ranges. Don't store cookies or other items above the range or in a place that will entice children to climb on or near the range.

4. Keep curtains and towels away from the range. A wind can blow fabric onto the burners and start a fire.

5. Don't lean your back against the range while it is on. Don't lean against it for any purpose.

6. Don't use the oven for storage (crackers, cereal, oven cleaner or anything else). These materials could ignite and start a fire.

7. Use the proper size burner for each pot. Don't put a small pot on a large burner, because the exposed part of the burner could ignite your clothing. (A larger burner doesn't make the pan heat any faster and it wastes energy.)

8. Flat-top electric ranges (which have no visible burners) make it difficult to tell which burner is on. You should not use the surface as a counter before it has cooled adequately.

9. In general, don't use the top of the range as a storage area. Paper and cloth can catch fire and plastic can melt or ignite. Glass pans and casseroles can explode when overheated by a burner that was left on unknowingly.

10. Learn the correct way to light a gas range. If you smell gas, turn off all controls and open a window or door. Call your gas company immediately.

11. If the oven has no pilot light, don't turn on the gas until you have a match lighted. Don't give the gas time to accumulate.

12. In gas ovens, turn off the pilot light when you use oven cleaner, because the spray could be ignited by the flame.

13. Never use flammable liquids around a gas range. Pilot lights are often forgotten and they can easily ignite flammable vapors that flow from one part of the room to another.

14. With a gas range, keep all air vents open so the gas gets enough oxygen to burn properly. Don't cover air vents with cloth, carpeting or anything that will "starve" the gas when it burns.

15. Keep children out of the kitchen when you use the range. They may fall against the hot surface and be burned, or they may climb on the top burners and ignite clothing.

16. Don't use the oven or the top burners to heat the room. This can cause a fire and may damage your range thermostat.

17. Use the proper utensils: sturdy pots and pans with tight handles. Avoid the following:
    - Plastic utensils, which can melt, and glass, which can break.
    - Pots with loose handles.
    - Pots that are too heavy to move easily when filled with food.

- Pots that are too small for deep fat frying because spilled grease can ignite and cause a fire.

18. Turn handles to the side or back of the range to reduce the risk of hitting the handles and spilling the hot contents on yourself or your children.

19. Be aware that electric coils can be hot enough to ignite clothing, potholders or paper, even if the coils are not red. On some ranges/ovens and at some heat settings, it's difficult to tell if an electric burner is on. Always check controls to make sure the heating elements are off when you stop cooking.

20. If you cannot stay in the kitchen when preparing food, check the kitchen often to make certain that food does not catch fire.

21. Do not place excessive weight on open oven doors because it could tip over the range.

22. If you have a grease fire in a pan:
    - Turn off the burner.
    - Cover the pan with a lid.

    Some people recommend throwing baking soda on a grease fire, but this can splash the grease and spread the fire. If you want a fire extinguisher for grease fires, be sure you get a dry-chemical fire extinguisher. The easiest and quickest thing to do is to cover the pan to smother the fire.

23. If you have a grease fire in the oven, close the oven door and turn off the heat.

Maintenance of ranges

1. If you smell gas when using the range or oven, turn off all controls and extinguish any open flame. Open a window to ventilate the room. Have your gas company check immediately for any suspected gas leaks.

2. Keep pilot lights lighted. If you're not sure how to light one, don't take a chance. Call your gas company for help.

3. Always check electric ranges to be sure they're off. Unlike gas ranges which may have visible flames, many electric ranges give no signal that they are on.

4. Check your kitchen occasionally to look for possible hazards, such as curtains or dishtowels hanging over the burners, or cookies (which attract children) stored over the range.

5. Clean up grease deposits around the burners. They can ignite.

6. Never use flammable liquids, such as gasoline, paint thinner or kerosene, around the gas range. The pilot light can ignite the vapors.

7. If the gas flame is yellow, the burner is not adjusted properly. Call a service technician or refer to the owner's manual to adjust the burner.

8. If the gas range/oven connects to a gas supply line with a corrugated metal connection, do not move the range for cleaning. The connectors will not take repeated bending.

9. Do not use ammonia-based cleaners near brass flexible connectors.

10. Move your smoke detector away from the kitchen, so steam from cooking does not set it off.

If you have a fire

1. Turn off the burner, if possible.

2. If you have a flaming pan, cover it with a metal lid larger than the pan. Do not attempt to move the pan until the fire is out and the pan is cool.

3. If you have a cooking fire in the oven, close the oven door and turn off the control to the oven. The fire should go out by itself.

4. You should have a fire extinguisher for household use. For kitchen use, you will need one that will douse grease fires. The best type is a dry-powder fire extinguisher. Your fire department can advise you.

5. If your clothing catches fire, don't run! Drop down immediately and roll to smother the flames. Teach your children to do this.

6. If you receive burns from flames or from a hot pan or burner, cool the burn in cold water. Do not apply butter, grease or ointments. Seek medical attention, because even a small burn can become serious if not treated.

REFRIGERATORS

Every refrigerator made after October 1956 must have a way to open the door from the inside. This law was necessary because of the rising number of deaths of children caught inside old refrigerators with latches that could be opened only from the outside.

Precautions. Some old refrigerators are still in use or have been thrown out recently, and children become trapped in them. If you have or know of a refrigerator or freezer that is not being used, follow these safeguards:

1. Completely remove the door. This can be done quickly and easily with a screwdriver, and you can replace the door if you want to use the appliance again. Some communities have laws that require doors to be removed from unused refrigerators.

2. Chain and padlock the door. An ordinary chain and padlock, wrapped tightly around the refrigerator, will keep the door closed. But this is not as effective as removing the door.

3. Remove the latch. Some latches can be removed and replaced with a wooden block screwed flush to the inner door surface, which prevents the door from being closed. When you want to use the door again, simply remove the wooden block and replace the latch.

4. If you find a discarded refrigerator, make sure you take one of the above measures to make it safe.

5. Teach your children the hazards of entrapment in refrigerators, ice boxes or freezers.

HAIR ENTRAPMENT IN SPA DRAINS

There have been several reports of accidents, and at least four deaths, in which people's hair was sucked into the drain fittings of spas, hot tubs or whirlpool baths and their heads were held under water. The suction from drain outlets is strong enough to trap hair or body parts, and cause drowning. Most accidents with drain outlets involve people with hair that is shoulder length or longer.

Hair entrapment occurs when a bather's hair becomes entangled in a suction-fitting drain cover, as the water and hair are drawn powerfully through the drain. In several incidents, children were playing a "hold your breath the longest" game, leaning forward in the water, which enabled their long hair to be sucked into the drains.

Precautions

1. There is a voluntary standard for drain covers that should help reduce hair entrapment. Ask your dealer about drain covers that meet this standard.

2. Keep long hair away from the suction fitting drain cover. Wear a bathing cap or pin up hair.

3. Never allow a child to play in a way that permits the child's hair to come near the drain cover. Always supervise children around a spa, hot tub, whirlpool bathtub, wading pool or swimming pool.

4. If a drain cover is missing or broken, shut down the spa until the drain cover is replaced.

TELEVISION

Estimates indicate there may be 10,000 television fires each year, some of which result in injuries and deaths. Electrical shock is not uncommon.

- Mr. North had turned his portable color TV off when the TV began to smoke. He quickly pulled the plug from the wall socket and called the fire department, which arrived in time to extinguish the fire before it ignited other materials in the room.

- Michael kept his TV in a corner of the room very close to the wall and the radiator. He piled newspapers on top of the TV and some of them covered the air vents in the back of the cabinet. One night, the set began to smoke and then burst into flames, destroying everything in the room before the fire was extinguished,

- Gail reached into the back of the TV set to touch a malfunctioning tube. She contacted a wire that was carrying current and received a painful electrical shock.

- Sherry, 12, was electrocuted when she touched the antenna of the TV set she was watching as she bathed. The TV was on a stool near the bathtub.

- A schoolteacher asked two young children (ages 7 and 12) to move an audiovisual cart, with a TV on the top shelf, to another room. One child was pulling and one was pushing the cart. The cart overturned when it hit a child's foot and fell on the child in front, seriously injuring her.

Accident patterns. The above cases represent some of the major accident patterns associated with TV sets:

1. Electrical problems within the TV set. These hazards are reduced in later model TV sets that follow newer safety guidelines. However there is still a chance of fire or shock.
2. Covering the ventilation openings. This happens when the TV set is placed too close to the wall, radiator or piece of furniture. Excessive heat can build up within the TV cabinet and start a fire.
3. Electrical shock. Shocks can occur when people contact TV parts that carry hazardous voltage.
4. Liquid spillage. This happens when liquids (such as water) spill into the TV cabinet. This can cause a short circuit and start a fire.
5. Moving audiovisual carts. These carts, approximately 50 inches high, can tip over easily over when being moved from one location to another. Children have been killed, and many injured, when the equipment they were moving fell on them.

Purchase of TVs

1. Be aware that the "instant-on" feature is suspect in some TV fires. If you do not desire this feature, don't buy a TV set with it, or buy one with an "instant-on defeat switch," which can be switched to the off position.
2. Be aware that many TV-related fires involve portable color TVs with plastic cabinets.

Use of TVs

1. Follow all operating instructions and safety precautions that come with your TV. Operate your TV set only from a power source designated in the instructions.
2. Always turn the TV off when leaving the room for more than a short period of time. Never leave a TV on when leaving the house.
3. When going on vacation, unplug the TV from the wall outlet and disconnect the external antenna lead-in wire at the TV set. This prevents a possible TV fire hazard from lightning and electrical power-line surges. You should not routinely unplug the TV from the wall outlet after each viewing session, because this can cause the stranded

wires within the cord to break and develop a fire hazard.

4. Warn children never to drop or push objects into the TV cabinet. They could contact parts carrying hazardous voltage and receive electrical shocks.

5. Don't cover the ventilation openings in the TV set with cloth or papers, or by placing the set close to a wall or furniture. This can cause the heat inside the TV cabinet to build up and cause a fire.

   - Never block the bottom ventilation slots in a portable TV by setting it on a bed, sofa, rug, etc.
   - Never place the TV set or its power cord near or over a radiator, heat register, heat lamp, etc.
   - Never place a TV set in a built-in enclosure unless proper ventilation is provided.

6. Don't put containers of water or other liquids on the TV cabinet. These can spill and cause short circuits, which can cause fire and shock hazards.

7. Never clean the face of the picture tube while the TV is on because excess liquid may drain inside causing a fire or shock hazard.

8. If you own a set with "instant-on" and your set does not have a defeat switch, you should use a wall outlet that regulates current to the TV. To avoid electrical stress on the wall switch, turn the wall switch on before turning the TV on, and turn the TV off before turning off the wall switch.

9. Never expose the TV set to rain or water. If the TV becomes damp or wet, pull the plug and have the set checked by a technician before further use. Rain or excessive moisture—even as a result of long exposure on a porch— may cause electrical shorts, which can result in fire or shock hazards.

10. Your TV set has either a polarized alternating line current plug or a three-wire plug with a third (grounding) pin. If the plug doesn't fit into the power outlet, have your electrician replace your old outlet. DO NOT defeat the safety purpose of the type of plug on your set.

   - Polarized alternating current line plug. A plug having one blade wider than the other. This plug fits into the power outlet only one way. If you cannot insert the plug into the outlet, try reversing the plug.
   - Three-wire grounding type plug. This plug has a third (grounding) pin and will fit into only a grounding type power outlet.

11. Never operate a TV set in a tilted position. It is designed to operate on a flat, horizontal surface.

12. Do not allow anything to rest on, or roll over, the power cord and do not place the TV set where the power cord is subject to traffic or abuse. This may result in a shock or fire hazard.

13. Do not place a TV set on an unstable cart, stand or table. Use only a cart recommended for use with the set. Don't try to roll a TV on a cart with small casters across thresholds or deep-pile carpets.

14. For added protection of the TV set during a lightning storm, unplug it from the wall outlet and disconnect the antenna. This will prevent possible shock and fire hazards from lightning storms or power line surges.

15. Never add accessories to a TV set that have not been designed for this purpose. Such additions may result in a shock hazard.

16. Do not let children move a TV or audiovisual cart.

17. Do not allow anyone to step or ride on a TV or audiovisual cart when it is being moved.

Maintenance of TVs

1. If very loud or continuous snapping or popping noises are made by the TV set, unplug the set and consult your dealer or service technician.

2. Have your service technician verify that replacement parts have the same characteristics as the original parts.

3. If your TV power cord has been subjected to many flexings due to plugging and unplugging from the wall outlet, have the cord checked by a service technician to see if it requires replacement.

4. Periodically clean the ventilation slots with the plastic crevice device on your vacuum cleaner.

5. Turn off the TV set before cleaning the face of the picture tube. Use a slightly damp (not wet) cloth. Do not use an aerosol directly on the picture tube since it may over-spray and cause electrical shock.

6. Removal of the back cover of the TV set or defeat of a power line interlock may expose you to very high voltage and other hazards. Observe all cautionary labels and warnings.

7. If the TV set has been dropped or the cabinet damaged, fire or shock hazard may exist. Unplug it and have it checked by a service technician before use.

8. When a TV set reaches the end of its useful life, improper disposal could result in a picture tube implosion. Ask a service technician for instructions.

If a fire starts

1. Pull the plug at once to disconnect the electrical circuit.

2. Go to a neighbor's house and call the fire department.

3. If you have a dry-chemical fire extinguisher, attempt to put out the fire. However, do not use water to extinguish the fire, because you could receive an electrical shock.

WRINGER WASHERS

The main hazards of the wringer washer are the power-driven rollers held together under pressure, which can catch fingers, hair or clothing and draw them into the wringer. Most victims of these kind of accidents are young children.

Children are naturally curious and the wringer washer in operation is fascinating. If children investigate and catch their fingers between the moving rollers, they usually cannot help themselves. Many children do not know about the safety devices of the machine. Those who have learned to use them may panic and forget or may not be able to reach them. Since a child's arm is often no longer than folded heavy clothes, the machine may continue to draw the arm in until it hits an obstruction (an extended thumb, elbow or the armpit). Even though its upward movement stops, the rollers may continue to grind away at the skin until help arrives.

• A 3-year-old boy died after he was drawn into the rollers of a wringer washing machine up to his armpit, and the sweater he was wearing tightened around his neck.

• The fingers of a 28-month-old boy had to be amputated after their blood supply was cut off when the boy's hand was caught between the rollers of a wringer washer.

Safety devices. Safety features on wringer washers have improved in recent years, but many old machines are still in use. A safety device on most wringer washers is a mechanism that when pushed, releases roller pressure. On older machines this often is a button on the operator side. Later models have release bars that run the length of the washers. These devices are better and require less pressure to operate.

The safety device may not be much help to children. A young child may not be able to reach it or be strong enough to operate it. Its main fault is that it takes positive action to activate it and a child is often too terrified to act rationally.

Much more effective is a safety control that stops the rollers with a backward pull by an object between the rollers.

Since the natural instinct of a person is to pull back when caught, this control can be very effective in preventing serious injury. Once the rollers have stopped, the release bar can be used to remove the pressure. Another improvement is this device combined with a simultaneous release of the pressure.

An equally good control on some models is a foot pedal that must be depressed for the wringer to operate. When pressure on the pedal is released, the wringer stops.

Safe use of the wringer washer

1. A person using a wringer washer should always be alert. Don't use the washer when tired, and don't do anything else at the same time.
2. Keep children away from the washer while it is in use. Any child old enough to understand should be taught the danger of the machine. Be sure that older children who operate the machine know how to work the safety devices.
3. Don't wear loose clothing that may catch in the rollers. If your hair is long, wear it up while using the washer.
4. Test safety devices before each washing to be sure they work correctly.
5. Keep the floor dry around the machine.
6. Disconnect the cord and release the wringer any time you leave the machine or are cleaning it.

In case of accident. If your child catches a hand in the rollers, stop the rollers, then release the pressure. Do not try to pull the hand out against the motion of the rollers. This will only increase the chances of serious injury.

Always have the injury checked by a physician immediately. Do not think that the injury is minor because there is no visible damage. The full seriousness of such an injury usually will not become apparent for 24 hours or more. Any delay in treatment can cause complications and permanent damage.

SAFETY RECAP

1. Don't use flammable liquids near automatic washers or any other flame source because of the possibility of the fumes igniting.
2. Flammable liquid fumes can travel long distances (even across a garage) to reach a washer, dryers or heater.
3. Electric shock is a possible hazard with nearly any major appliance. Don't repair appliances while they are plugged in.
4. Child entrapment is possible with dryers, refrigerators and some washers.
5. Take care to avoid burns from pans, plates and food heated in microwave ovens. Radiation is seldom a problem with modern microwave ovens.
6. Stay clear of range and counter-top cooking surfaces. Most accidents happen when the body or clothing contact hot surfaces or flames.
7. Know how to handle kitchen fires and know when to evacuate the house and call the fire department.
8. The best defense against harm from a wringer washer is to buy one that will stop or reverse when backward pressure is applied.

BIBLIOGRAPHY

"Clothes Dryers," *Product Safety Fact Sheet*, U.S. Consumer Product Safety Commission, December 1982.

Community Safety and Health, Chicago: National Safety Council, March/April, 1991, pp. 5-6.

"Consumers Should Know," Washington, DC: Electronic Industries Association, 1990.

"Four Children Drown and More Are Injured From Hair Entrapment in Drain Covers for Spas, Hot Tubs, and Whirlpool Bathtubs," *Consumer Product Safety Alert*, U.S. Consumer Product Safety Alert, June 1988.

The Smart Kitchen, Goldbeck, David, Woodstock, NY: Ceres Press, 1988, pp. 67-70, 72-73.

"Are Microwave Ovens Safe, Hillyer, Linda, *PCC Sound Consumer, No. 210*, Seattle: September 1990, pp. 1, 12-13

"Large Microwave Ovens," *Consumer Reports*, November 1990, pp. 733-737.

"Overheated Clothes Dryers Can Cause Fires," *Consumer Product Safety Alert*, U.S. Consumer Product Safety Commission, September 1990.

"Ranges and Ovens," *Consumer Safety Fact Sheet*, U.S. Consumer Product Safety Commission, March 1987.

"Safety Points You Should Know About Your Television, Revision 1," Washington, DC: Consumer Electronics Group, Electronic Industries Association.

"Television Safety: A Guide for Consumers," Washington, DC, Electronic Industries Association, 1986.

"TV Fire and Shock Hazards," *Product Safety Fact Sheet*, U.S. Consumer Product Safety Commission, 1980.

"Warning: Tip-Over Hazard," *Consumer Product Safety Alert*, U.S. Consumer Product Safety Commission, February 1987.

CHAPTER 7

MINOR APPLIANCES

ANTENNAS

There have been many reports of electrocutions that occurred when metal antennas—radio, television and citizens' band radio—touched overhead power lines. Typically, a person is holding a metal antenna for installation or removal when electric circuit flows from the power line through the conductive metal to the victim. The following example illustrates how such an accident occurs:

- Don climbed up a metal ladder to his roof, carrying a TV antenna he was going to install. As he reached the top of the ladder, a strong wind blew the top of the antenna into the power line leading into the house and Don was electrocuted.

Power line hazards. Most residential power lines carry more than 2,000 volts A.C. to transformers in housing areas. Then wires carry electricity from transformers to houses at 240 or 120 volts, powerful enough to kill. High-voltage electric power lines are often mistaken for low-voltage telephone lines, since both are strung on poles. Power lines are usually 18 to 25 feet above ground in residential areas. Since the power and telephone wires may be hard to tell apart, avoid touching *any* wires that go above or into your house. High-voltage power lines or the lines from the transformer into the house can shock a grounded person if he or she touches the wires with a metal object.

Most high-voltage wires are not insulated. Besides, weathering and years of use can cause any insulation to degrade, peel or crack, which lessens or eliminates protection against shock.

Antenna mounting. An outside antenna should not be near any overhead power lines. When placing an outside antenna system, use extreme care to keep it from touching power lines, as contact with them might be fatal. If you are unfamiliar with this kind of work, use a professional installer. Even if you are experienced, seek professional help and equipment if the length of the antenna and mast exceeds 30 feet, or the distance between the site and the nearest overhead power lines is less than twice the length of the antenna and its mast. If you do the work yourself, observe these rules:

1. Work only in good weather. Thunderstorms, rain, moderate to heavy winds and damp or icy ground can create serious hazards.

2. Follow the manufacturer's instructions for assembling the antenna and support mast.

3. Be sure the antenna system is grounded so as to provide some protection against voltage surges and built up static charges. Section 810 of the National Electric Code gives all information on proper grounding of all parts of the system.

4. Use No. 10 AWG copper wire, No. 8 AWG aluminum or No. 17 AWG copper-clad steel or bronze wire for both mast and lead-in.

5. Secure the lead-in wire from antenna-to-antenna discharge unit and mast ground wires with stand-off insulators, spaced 4 to 6 feet apart.

6. Mount the antenna discharge unit as close as possible to where the lead-in enters the house.

7. Use large enough jumper wire: 6 AWG copper when using a separate antenna-grounding electrode.

8. If the antenna should fall, let go and stay clear. Don't touch the antenna until you know that no part of it is touching an overhead wire.

Increased hazards. These conditions increase the likelihood of electrocution:

1. Moisture. Wet or sweaty feet and hands decrease the body's resistance to current. For better insulation against shock, wear rubber boots or rubber-soled shoes when working around power lines.

2. Metal. Touching a grounded metal ladder or gutter while holding an antenna against a power line turns the body into an excellent path for electrical current. The current can then flow from the power line to the antenna, through the body, through the metal ladder or gutter and finally to the ground. Metal ladders 20 to 30 feet high can easily touch overhead power lines and make a path for the electricity to flow through the person on the ladder. Use wooden or fiberglass ladders if working around electrical wires.

3. Wind. The wind can blow an antenna into a nearby power line. Don't install or remove antennas in moderate or heavy winds.

Emergency first aid for shock. It is best to work with another person when installing or removing antennas. If your partner receives a shock, don't touch him or her, since the person's body could conduct the electricity to you. Instead, try to pry or pull the person away from the source of electricity with a length of dry wood, rope, a blanket or another nonmetallic object.

If breathing has stopped, do mouth-to-mouth resuscitation until the doctor or ambulance arrives and you are relieved. If the heart has stopped, closed chest cardiac massage must also be done. When the ambulance is called, it should be reported that an electric shock has occurred. The ambulance can then bring an extensive care or cardiac care mobile unit with a heart defibrillator, as well as trained personnel.

BLENDERS

Listed here are typical cases of injuries from electric blenders, mixers, meat grinders, choppers and slicers:

- Gloria was blending a thick soup when the blender jar came loose from the base. When she grabbed the jar to keep it from falling, it separated from the collar, exposing the rotating blades attached to the motor drive. Her hand was struck by the blades, and she suffered severe cuts to her hand.

- Joanne was stirring a cake mix in her mixer when the blades jammed. She started to push the beaters around but accidentally turned on the motor. Her thumb was caught in the whirling beater. She suffered a contusion and lacerations of the thumb.

- Max was chopping potatoes in his blender. The potatoes at the bottom became slushy, and the blades could not reach those at the top. Max poked his fingers into the blender to push down the food when his fingers met the blades. The tip of one finger was amputated.

Accident patterns. Contact with blades, beaters or cutting edges is the major cause of accidents with blenders, mixers, grinders, choppers and slicers. The preceding cases illustrate the most frequent accident patterns:

1. Product defects, such as when a blender jar unscrews in the same direction a blade rotates. This lets the jar loosen

while in operation and the user grabs for it.

2. Malfunction, such as when the beaters jam or won't insert properly into a mixer and the user attempts to correct the problem.

3. Misuse, such as when the user puts his or her fingers into or near moving blades or when children play with appliances.

Purchase of blenders

1. Look for electric appliances with sturdy construction.

2. Check to see that the appliance stands firmly and level without danger of tipping.

3. When buying a blender, look for one in which the jar screws to the collar in the same direction that the blades rotate.

4. Look for a blender with the blades contained within the jar.

Use of blenders

1. Read the instructions for proper use, care, cleaning and maintenance.

2. Always insert the beater into the mixer before plugging it in.

3. Do not adjust parts or stick utensils into mixers, blenders or grinders while the motor is on or the power cord is plugged in.

4. Make sure all parts connect tightly before operating. For example, see that the jar screws tightly into the base of the blender and that the beaters click into place on mixers.

5. Keep fingers and hands away from the blades of operating appliances *always*.

6. Avoid handling the appliance with wet hands or when standing on a wet or damp floor.

7. Disconnect appliances by grasping the plug, not the cord. Remove the plug from the wall outlet first, then from the appliance, if it is a detachable cord.

8. Don't run cords near ovens or other hot objects.

9. Unplug the appliance when not in use to lessen the danger of fire, electric shock and injury from moving parts.

10. Warn children that these appliances can injure them.

Maintenance of blenders

1. Disconnect electrical appliances before oiling or cleaning.

2. Keep parts clean, particularly of food that can rust or clog up the mechanism.

3. Immediately replace worn cords and plugs.

CARBON MONOXIDE DETECTORS

Carbon monoxide (CO) is a colorless, odorless, invisible gas that kills many people each year. It is produced when any fuel does not burn completely. Carbon monoxide can leak from faulty fuel-fired furnaces or heaters and can be trapped indoors by faulty flues or blocked chimneys.

The first line of defense is to make sure that all fuel-burning appliances work properly. Properly working carbon monoxide detectors can provide an early warning, before the deadly gas builds to a dangerous level. Exposure to a low concentration of CO over several hours can be as dangerous as exposure to a high level for a few minutes. The new detectors can detect both conditions. At this writing, a detector costs less than $100, but the price should drop. The CPSC believes CO detectors are as important to home safety as smoke detectors.

CHRISTMAS LIGHTS AND DECORATIONS

Christmas light sets are a safety concern. Defective light sets present fire and shock hazards. Following is a simple inspection process to detect common defects in new and older light sets.

Inspection procedure. Before using a light set, take the lights out of the box and, with the lights unplugged:

1. Check for cracked or broken sockets. A damaged socket will not effectively insulate a person from electric shock. Do not use sets with cracked or broken sockets.

2. Check the plug or connector for loose or missing plastic inserts. These inserts are used to plug in more strings of lights. If loose or missing, they can expose bare metal conductors. Be safe. Do not use light sets with loose or missing inserts.

3. Push the prongs on the connector against a hard surface to simulate plugging in the set, or plug the connector into a disconnected extension cord five times. The prongs should remain fixed, neither becoming loose nor causing an insert to push out from the end. If the prongs or the insert move, do not use the set.

4. Spread the wires where they enter the bulb sockets and connectors. Check for exposed bare wires, where insulation may have pulled back. To avoid shock hazards, do not use a light set with exposed bare wire.

5. With the bulb in place, check between the bulb holder and socket for exposed hair-like wires. These wires may be improperly trimmed filament wires, which are a contact between the bulb and the socket. Exposed, they are a shock hazard. Remove the bulb and trim the wires so they are not exposed outside of the socket. When reinserting, make sure the bulb leads touch the contacts inside the socket. To avoid shock hazards, do not use light sets with exposed filament wires.

6. When inserting and removing the bulb and its holder from the socket, the contact in the socket should not slide out of the socket. To avoid a shock hazard, do not remove the bulb and its holder when the set is plugged in. Also, do not use a set if the contacts are not fixed in the recessed part of the socket.

7. Before beginning to decorate, place the light set on a nonflammable surface and leave it plugged in for 10 to 15 minutes. Check it for smoking and melting.

Use of Christmas lights

1. Never attach lights to metal trees. Sharp metal edges may cut the cord insulation, or the metal needles may touch an electrically charged part.

2. Careful handling during unpacking, decorating and repacking reduces the chance of hazardous damage.

3. Do not overload extension cords or light strings. Do not connect more than 200 midget lights through one string or cord. Do not connect more than 50 larger lamps together through one string or cord. Do not connect large lamp sets to miniature light sets.

4. Do not use any light set unless it is specifically labeled for that purpose.

5. Do not use indoor lights for outdoor purposes.

6. Keep "bubbling" lights away from children. These lights, with their bright colors and bubbling movement, can tempt curious children to break the candle-shaped glass, which can cut, and attempt to drink the liquid, which contains a hazardous chemical.

7. Remove outdoor lights as soon as the season is over. They are not made for prolonged exposure to the elements.

8. Be sure all lights are off when you leave the house or go to bed. Unplug lights from the wall outlet.

9. Always disconnect any electrical appliance by grasping the plug, not the cord.

Defective light sets. If you recently purchased a defective light set, report it to the Office of Product Defect Identification, Consumer Product Safety Commission, Washington, DC 20207. They will want to know the nature of the problem, the name and model number of the light set, the name of the manufacturer or distributor (preferably from the box) and the place of purchase.

Spray snow

Artificial snow sprays can irritate the lungs if inhaled. To avoid injury, read container labels and follow the directions carefully.

Candles

1. Never use lighted candles on a tree or near evergreens.
2. Always use nonflammable holders.
3. Keep candles away from other decorations and wrapping paper.
4. Place candles where they cannot be knocked down or blown over.

Trimmings

1. Use only noncombustible or flame-resistant materials.
2. Wear gloves while decorating with spun glass (angel hair) to avoid irritation to eyes and skin.
3. Choose tinsel or artificial plastic icicles or nonleaded materials. Leaded materials are hazardous if ingested by children.
4. Avoid decorations that may break easily or have sharp edges.
5. Never use ornaments that could be mistaken for food.
6. Mistletoe and holly berries may be poisonous if more than a few are swallowed. Keep out of the reach of children.

Fire salts

Use care with fire salts, which produce colored flames when thrown on wood fires. They contain heavy metals that can cause intense gastrointestinal irritation or vomiting if eaten. Keep away from children.

COOKWARE

With new cookware—sometimes made of new materials or coverings—come questions of safety. For example:

1. Do scratches on a nonstick coated pan mean that you've scraped a toxic material into food?
2. Does aluminum from pots and pans leach into food and cause health problems?
3. Should you take precautions when cooking with copper-clad pans?
4. Do glazed crock pots contain dangerous amounts of lead?

Regulating these products to ensure the user's safety is the job of the Food and Drug Administration (FDA), but only after safety concerns are raised. Until that time it is "Let the buyer beware." The FDA looks at safety concerns about cookware on a case-by-case basis. Courtesy of the FDA, here is a review of materials used in popular cookware today.

Aluminum. More than half the cookware in use today is aluminum. Most is coated with nonstick finishes or treated by a process that alters and hardens the metal structure. Research on the hazards of aluminum cookware is continuous and much of it is done by scientists from respected organizations.

Most research shows that some amount of aluminum enters the body through food prepared in aluminum cookware, however the harm it does is very much in question. Aluminum is in many places around us and it is likely we take in more aluminum through antacid tablets or aspirin than through a meal prepared in aluminum cookware.

Aluminum cookware manufacturers agree that storing highly acidic or salty foods, such as tomato sauce, sauerkraut or rhubarb, may cause more aluminum than usual to leach into those foods and enter the body. Some acidic foods left in aluminum cookware cause the aluminum to pit on the surface.

In 1986, the FDA reported that the agency "has no information at this time that the normal dietary intake of aluminum whether from naturally occurring levels in food, the use of aluminum cookware, or from aluminum food additives of drugs, is harmful."

Anodized aluminum. One reason aluminum is popular for cooking is because it is an excellent heat conductor. Manufacturers have developed a method to treat aluminum so that it retains its heat conductivity. The process, called anodization, hardens the metal, making it more scratch-resistant. Food barely sticks to the hard, smooth surface of this product, making it easy to clean. One firm claims that its sealing process prevents leaching of aluminum into food. Anodized aluminum doesn't react to acidic foods, so this type of cookware is a good choice for tomato, wine, rhubarb and lemon juices.

Nonstick coatings. Before anodized aluminum, the nonstick coating Teflon (trademarked), was most often used on cookware. Teflon is made of tough, nonporous material called perfluorocarbon resin that permits cooking without using fats. It was used first in fry pans, but now nearly all cookware comes with this nonstick finish.

Because nonstick finishes can be scratched by sharp or rough-edged kitchen tools, manufacturers recommend using plastic or wooden utensils. You should not use abrasive scouring pads or cleansers on these finishes. If bits of the coating do chip off and enter the food, they will pass through the body with little change or effect.

When heated for a long time at high temperatures, the nonstick coating does decompose, but the toxicity of the fumes is less than that of ordinary cooking oil. Several types of tests have measured the various fumes and particles that might come from nonstick coatings and have not found any real dangers.

New, nonstick coatings are continually appearing on the market. Most of them are tougher, more heat and scratch resistant and extremely durable.

Stainless steel. Consumers who don't buy aluminum cookware usually buy stainless steel. Buyers like its attractive finish that won't corrode or tarnish permanently, and its tough, nonporous surface is resistant to wear. Stainless steel contains at least 11 percent chromium, which makes it "stainless" all the way through.

Because stainless steel does not conduct heat evenly, stainless steel cookware often has copper or aluminum bottoms. Although there are no known hazards from this, manufacturers warn against allowing acidic or salty foods to remain in the container for long periods.

Copper. Copper is an excellent conductor of heat, especially good for rangetop cooking and items that need precise temperature control. Copper cookware, however, contains tin or stainless steel linings. The FDA cautions against using unlined copper for general cooking. The reason is that some foods easily dissolve the metal in large enough quantities to cause nausea, vomiting and diarrhea.

Cast iron. Cast iron is the all-time classic cookware and has been with us for 3,000 years. It is strong, inexpensive and an even conductor of heat for frying, browning and baking foods. Cast iron products are a source of an important nutrient, because the unglazed iron gives off twice as much iron as glazed.

Cast iron utensils require different treatment than other utensils. To prevent rust damage, the inside of cast iron cookware should be coated with unsalted cooking oil frequently. Do not wash it with strong detergent or scour. Wipe it dry immediately after rinsing.

Ceramic and enameled cookware. Enamel-coated iron and steel cookware is a colorful and practical addition for the cook's collection. Enamel-coated cookware is safe to cook with, according to the FDA. Because of the high-firing temperatures, lead is not used.

Lead is used, however, in some glazes for slow-cooking pots (crock pots). But again, tests showed no significant leaching into foods from using these pots.

Dishes and cookware. The levels of lead (1993) in food and drink are the lowest in history, 90 percent lower than 12 years earlier. Concern remains about lead leaching into food from ceramic ware, especially ceramic mugs. FDA scientists found that about 80 percent of adult exposure to lead from food comes from frequent use of mugs for hot beverages.

Imported dishware may be improperly fired and may release toxic levels of lead into food. U.S. government standards prevent marketing dishes with lead in their glaze. Older cookware, other than pottery, does contain lead. Following are ways to reduce exposure:

1. Use dishes that have smooth, hard-glazed surfaces, which are free from cracks or chips.
2. Check imported dishes for the required certificate of compliance with U.S. standards.
3. Before using imported dishware or pottery, have it tested for lead or other heavy metals by the local health authority.
4. Do not feed babies from lead crystal bottles.
5. Do not store acidic foods, such as fruit juices, in ceramic containers.

Excessive amounts of cadmium were found in some imported cookware, which is not allowed in the U.S. The problem was mainly with the red, yellow and orange pigments in the interiors of the cookware.

Choose the cookware that best suits your purposes. If you give it proper care and follow manufacturer's directions, you should not expect health problems.

Cookware summary

1. In aluminum cookware, acidic or salty foods, such as tomato sauce, sauerkraut or rhubarb, may cause more aluminum than usual to leach from the cookware, but the amount is usually insignificant.
2. Some acidic foods left in aluminum cookware will cause the aluminum to pit.
3. Food barely sticks on the hard smooth surface of anodized aluminum, which makes it easy to clean. A sealing process may prevent leaching of aluminum into food.
4. Anodized aluminum doesn't react to acidic foods, so these pans are top choices for tomato, wine, rhubarb and lemon juices.
5. Because nonstick finishes can be scratched by sharp or rough-edged kitchen tools, use plastic or wooden utensils. Do not use abrasive scouring pads or cleansers on these finishes.
6. When heated for a long time at high temperatures, nonstick coatings decompose, but the toxicity of the fumes is less than that of cooking oil. Tests measuring fumes and particles that might be given off nonstick coatings have not found any significant dangers.
7. Because stainless steel does not conduct heat evenly, this cookware often has copper or aluminum bottoms. Although there are no known hazards, you should not allow acidic or salty foods to remain in these containers for long.
8. Copper is an excellent conductor of heat, especially good for range-top cooking and precise temperature control. Copper cookware is lined with tin or stainless steel.

9. The FDA cautions against using unlined copper for general cooking, because some foods easily dissolve the metal in enough quantity to cause nausea, vomiting and diarrhea.

10. Cast iron utensils require different treatment than other utensils. Prevent rust damage by coating the inside of cast iron cookware with unsalted cooking oil. Do not wash with strong detergent or scour. Wipe dry immediately after rinsing.

11. Cookware made of enamel on steel and iron is safe to cook with, according to the FDA.

12. Lead is used in some glazes for slow-cooking pots (crock pots). Tests showed no significant leaching into foods.

13. Never let any cookware boil dry, but do not remove it until it has cooled. If aluminum cookware is allowed to boil dry, separation or melting may occur.

COUNTER-TOP COOKING

Injuries from portable electric appliances are similar to injuries from traditional pots and pans. However two inherent features add to the hazards of cooking with counter-top appliances: electric cords and heating units.

Each year, emergency room treatments result from injuries involving the following electrical, counter-top cooking appliances: coffeepots, teapots, kettles, grills, broilers, corn poppers, toasters, deep-fat fryers, fry pans and skillets, griddles and waffle irons. Following are the hazards associated with these products, as well as suggestions for safer selection, use and maintenance.

Electrical problems

- A corn popper that had been left plugged in, overheated and caught fire. The flames spread throughout the apartment killing a 21-year-old woman.

- The toaster in the Jackson household was placed on a radiator. The toaster's heating element was broken and the wires came in contact with the metal frame of the toaster, causing a short-circuit, which electrified the radiator. Linda, 16 months, touched the metal radiator under the toaster and was electrocuted.

In addition to mild electric shocks, fires and electrocutions can be caused by:

1. A defective or worn heating element.

2. A short circuit in the appliance or the electrical outlet circuit.

3. Overloading the circuits (items that produce heat usually have high wattage).

4. A combination of these causes when the appliance is connected.

5. A metal utensil touching the heating element, such as when a knife is placed in a toaster to free a slice of bread. (Never do this.)

Safety features. Look for these safety features when selecting counter-top appliances:

1. An on-off switch so you need not rely solely on unplugging the appliance to turn it off.

2. A thermostat that shuts off the heating element of appliances if they cook dry.

3. Three-prong grounded plugs on appliances to help prevent shocks. If the appliance does not have the three-prong plug, ask the salesperson if it is double-insulated for protection against shocks.

4. If the toaster has a UL (Underwriters' Laboratories) seal, it will also have a two-pole switch in the electrical system to reduce the shock hazard if a metal utensil contacts the heating wires.

5. Because cuts from sharp metal edges, sharp points and broken glass on countertop appliances are a danger, check appliances and their lids and spouts for sharp and rough edges.

Promoting safety

1. Don't leave portable appliances plugged in unless they are in actual use, even if they are turned off.
2. Don't overload electrical circuits. Be certain to use the proper ampere fuses in fuse boxes. Don't plug two heat-producing appliances into the same circuit because these high-wattage appliances could blow fuses or start a fire.
3. Unplug electrical appliances before filling with water.
4. Keep floors and countertops around electrical appliances dry.
5. Never insert a metal object near the heating element of an appliance that is plugged in. Always unplug before probing, then probe carefully.
6. Don't heat sugary-topped pastries in a toaster. The sugar can ooze, clog the toaster and cause a fire, or may become hot enough to burn your hand when you remove the pastries.

Maintenance

Keep appliances in good working order with periodic checks and maintenance.

1. Immediately replace any frayed electrical cords or damaged plugs.
2. Follow the manufacturer's instructions for cleaning. Don't immerse the appliance for cleaning unless the instructions clearly state that it is safe.
3. Immediately repair, or have repaired, appliances that are damaged or give electrical shocks. If appliances cannot be repaired, dispose of them immediately.

Electrical cord hazards

• Susan, 2, was in her high chair, next to the kitchen counter where a percolator was plugged in. As Susan pulled on the appliance cord, the percolator fell on her, spilling boiling coffee over her left arm and side.

Children are the leading victims of mishaps associated with electrical cords and appliances. They may either pull, or become entangled in, long, dangling cords or overturn appliances, spilling the contents on themselves.

Unfortunately, it is common for children to overturn coffeepots. Most accidents happen in situations such as these examples:

1. The cord is plugged into an outlet above a counter or table and the electric cord hangs below the surface.
2. The pot is located some distance from the outlet and the cord extends across that distance.
3. An outlet is located below the counter level, allowing the cord to be pulled by passersby or when a cabinet opens.

Buying portable appliances

1. Buy appliances with cords only long enough to reach the closest top-of-the-counter wall outlet. Short cords (2 to 3 feet long) are preferable.
2. Plug in appliances above counter or table level.
3. Never let an appliance cord dangle from a counter or table, especially when children are in the area. If the cord is long, place the excess length out of the way on the counter or table top.
4. Don't place high chairs near appliances or their cords.
5. Don't use extension cords on appliances. Neither the long cord nor the extra outlets are safe in the kitchen. If an extension cord must be used to plug in an appliance outside the kitchen, make sure the extension cord has the same wattage and ampere rating as the appliance. General lightweight cords are not adequate.

Burns from the surface

• Mary had difficulty opening the door of her counter-top broiler because it stuck when heated. As she was trying to open the door, the plastic cover on the handle

139

came off, exposing the hot metal underneath and burning her arm.

Plastic handles and temperature-selection dials also can become hot enough to burn someone who touches them. In some appliances, the heating elements may become exposed to the touch during use. They should be covered or guarded.

1. Teach children to respect the dangers of appliances.
2. Keep appliances out of reach of small children.
3. Don't use slippery kitchen rugs or mats that could cause you to fall against a hot appliance.
4. Look for handles that protrude far enough from the appliance to prevent burns when picking it up.
5. Keep handles from protruding over the edge of the stove where children can reach them.
6. Periodically check appliances (when they are disconnected and cold) to be sure that handles are securely attached.

Cooking hazards

- Doris was frying chicken in her deep-fat fryer when the shortening ignited and started to burn the curtains. She threw water on the fire, but it caused the shortening to splatter on her.

Grease can splatter or ignite under very hot temperatures. When cooking with grease, it is best to cover the appliance with a lid or wire mesh screen to prevent splatter. To prevent grease ignition, don't heat the pan any hotter than needed to cook the food. If the grease is smoking, it's too hot. Lower food gently into hot oil to prevent splashing. Avoid adding wet or cold food, which will produce a much bigger splash.

Keep cooking utensils away from flammable objects and use nonflammable curtains in the kitchen. If fire occurs, DON'T THROW WATER! First, turn off and un-

plug the appliance. Then put out the fire by:

1. Sliding a lid or other nonflammable cover over the appliance.
2. Using a dry chemical extinguisher.
3. Carefully tossing a handful of baking soda (not baking powder) on the fire (not recommended by some experts).

FIRE EXTINGUISHERS

Fire extinguishers are classified to correspond to the type of fire they will put out. The type of extinguisher is prominently displayed on it.

1. Class A fires, which contain ordinary combustibles, such as wood, paper, some plastics and textiles, require a quenching, cooling effect.
2. Class B fires, which involve flammable liquids and gas fires (oil, gasoline, paint and grease), require excluding oxygen or interrupting flames.
3. Class C fires involve electrical wiring and equipment in which the conductivity of the extinguishing agent is important. For example, electrical current might travel back over a water stream.
4. There also are Class D fires. They involve fires in combustible metals, such as magnesium, powdered aluminum, zinc, etc., and seldom occur in the home.

Some extinguishers are multipurpose and will put out all three types of fires, so they may be classified as ABC.

Extinguishers also are classified as water, dry chemical, foam, carbon dioxide and Halon (liquid when expelled). All types, except carbon dioxide, work on Class A fires, but their use on other classes of fires is restrictive.

Four questions about an extinguisher must be answered:

1. Is it the right type?
   - Class A extinguishers contain water and are found in home and office areas. They are intended to put out

fires that leave ash, such as wood, cloth, paper and rubbish. Water extinguishers do not work well on grease or electrical fires. They can cause grease fires to splatter and spread. If used on electrical fires they present a shock hazard to the user.

- Class B extinguishers are intended for flammable liquids, such as oil, gasoline, paint and grease. They are usually the best extinguisher for a kitchen fire on the stove.
- Class C extinguishers put out fires caused by electrical equipment and wiring.
- Extinguishers are sometimes combined, such as Class BC for both grease and electrical fires. Some dry-chemical extinguishers are multipurpose, identified as Class ABC, which will put out all three types of fires. Still other extinguishers have special uses, but normally have little use in the home.

2. Do all residents know where the extinguisher is located? The best extinguisher is no good if it cannot be found quickly. Caregivers need to be reminded of the locations, types and uses of fire extinguishers. The location should be highly visible.

3. Do all residents know the limits of the extinguisher? Portable extinguishers carry from 1 to 30 pounds of extinguishing agent. The most common size is 5 pounds.

4. Do all residents know how to use the extinguishers? Most smaller fire extinguishers must be handled properly before their contents are gone. It is not practical to demonstrate the extinguisher and then expect to use the rest of the contents in an emergency. After an extinguisher's seal is broken, replace or refill it. Fire departments in most communities will demonstrate the proper use of various extinguishers.

Proper use of extinguishers. When circumstances permit, first turn off the fuel supply to the fire, whether it be natural gas, propane or electricity. The National Fire Protection Association (NFPA) urges you to remember PASS if you face a blaze. It provides practical guidance and is easy to remember.

1. **Pull** the pin or, with some units, **Press** the puncture lever to release the lock latch.

2. **Aim** low. Point the unit's nozzle at the base of the fire.

3. **Squeeze** the handle to release the contents.

4. **Sweep** from side to side. Aim the extinguisher at the base of the fire and sweep back and forth until the fire is out. Don't turn your back on the fire until you know it is out.

Using a fire extinguisher should only be one step in dealing with a fire. Someone should call the fire department and evacuate residents while the extinguisher is being used. Once the heat starts to build and the fire is no longer under control, get out of the building and let firefighters handle the situation.

Using the wrong extinguisher can be dangerous. For example, using a Class A extinguisher on a grease fire may cause that Class B fire to spread. Too small an extinguisher may not control a fire. Keep on hand the largest extinguisher that members of your family can easily handle, probably one that holds at least 5 pounds of extinguisher material.

The best type of extinguisher for home use is probably ABC, but good protection usually requires several. To be effective, extinguishers must be available, in sight and easy to use. Do not place them over likely fire sources, such as a kitchen range. Use your fire extinguisher only if:

1. You've called the fire department.

2. Everyone is out of the house.

3. The fire is small and confined.

4. You can fight the fire with an exit at your back.
5. Your extinguisher works and you know how to use it.
6. You know when to quit and get out.

FONDUE POTS

Although fondue cooking is a fun way to prepare a meal, it can be hazardous.

- Bob took a pot of nearly boiling cooking oil from the stove to carry to the fondue stand at the dinner table. The charred and loosened pot handle turned in his hands and the scalding oil spilled over his arms and lower body, causing painful second and third degree burns.

- Nora, 4, was attracted by the flame from the liquid alcohol container under the fondue pot. She reached for it and spilled the flaming alcohol on the table cloth and her clothing. Nora received serious burns over 50 percent of her body.

Accident patterns

1. Spattering or spilled hot oil. When oil used in meat fondue starts to boil and steam, it can spatter or burst into flames. Hot oil can be spilled when moving the pot from the stove to the table. Many fondue pots have unstable, three-legged bases. Handles may get so hot that pots cannot be carried without dropping them, and sometimes the handles loosen or fall off.

2. Clothing ignition. The open flames or the alcohol burner under the pot can easily ignite frilly dresses or floppy sleeves.

3. Ignition of the fuel. Denatured alcohol is a common fuel used to heat fondue pots. Even if the flame appears to be out, it can still be hot enough to ignite alcohol used to refuel the heating unit. Other fuels include solid alcohol and electricity. The solid alcohol does not spill, but its flame can ignite clothing

just as easily as a liquid alcohol flame. Electricity is probably the safest source of heat because it doesn't need to be re-fueled and has no open flame. However, it requires a nearby outlet and a cord. Children can grab or trip over the cord and spill the fondue on themselves.

Selection of fondue pots

1. Buy a fondue pot with securely fastened, heat-resistant, flameproof handles. Pot handles that are charred or loosened can cause scalding liquid to spill. Buy a pot with a handle on each side.

2. Be sure that both the pot and its stand have broad bases for more stability.

3. Buy a pot that slopes inward at the top and is as deep as possible.

4. You should know that liquid alcohol burners can spill flaming alcohol and ignite clothing. Solid alcohol is safer because it can't spill. Electricity is even safer because it has no open flame.

Use of fondue pots

1. When cooking, place a tray under your fondue pot to catch any spillage and to provide insulation for the table surface.

2. Be sure that the flame is out and that the burner has cooled for about 15 minutes before refilling a liquid alcohol burner. Alcohol burns with an almost invisible blue flame. The burner you think is empty may still be burning. Its heated vapors could ignite the fuel used to refill the burner, and burning fuel could be spilled on you.

3. Never hold a burner in your hand to light it. Instead, carefully wipe the outside after filling and place it in the stand before lighting it.

4. Keep an electric fondue pot as close to the outlet as possible so that the cord won't be tripped over, spilling the hot fondue. (This applies to any countertop appliance, including frying pans.)

5. Carefully watch heating oil. Smoking oil is too hot and should be taken from the heat quickly and carefully.

6. When cooking meat, reduce spattering by adding a teaspoon of salt to 3 cups of oil and blotting the meat dry before adding it to the pot.

7. Ignore recipes that tell you the oil is ready when it bubbles. The oil smokes or blazes before that. Test the oil with a piece of meat to see if it is hot enough.

8. Don't use ceramic (pottery) pots for meat fondue. They are not meant to withstand high temperatures.

9. You should know about the hazards of *flambé* cooking, often used with fondues. This style of cooking uses brandy or other liqueurs of high alcohol content, which are set ablaze to appeal to your eyes and nose.

10. In *flambé* cooking, use only alcohol suitable for food consumption. This include brandies and other liqueurs. Heat the sauce slightly before igniting it, to insure a quick, easy ignition. Don't add more liqueur after heating has started or after the sauce ignites, because the heated vapors can ignite and cause the liqueur container to explode.

GARBAGE DISPOSALS

Sink-mounted garbage disposals are efficient and almost maintenance-free. Garbage goes into the hopper of a disposal and the disposal is then turned on. A motor drives a flywheel, impeller and cutters, which pulverize the garbage into tiny bits by throwing the garbage against a shredder device. The tiny bits are then flushed down the drain/sewer pipe with water from the kitchen sink. The main hazards are obvious:

1. The combination of water and electricity requires care to prevent electrical shock, particularly if working on the disposal.

2. The rotating flywheel, impeller and cutters are dangerous if you try to retrieve an object that has fallen into the hopper. A child's hand, and that of most adults, can easily reach into the hopper and be badly mangled. Be quick to turn off the power if something does fall into the hopper.

3. Debris put into the hopper can, under some circumstances, be thrown back out of the hopper into the eyes.

Do-it-yourselfers are usually able to fix disposals, once the problem is identified. Disposal repairs are concentrated in five areas; (a) stuck grinding wheel (b) water leakage (c) slow drainage (d) noise and (e) inability to start.

Purchase of disposals

Before buying a new disposal, check your local plumbing codes or laws. Some communities forbid garbage disposals because they discharge garbage into the sewer system, overloading it if it is marginal. Disposals are not recommended for use with septic tanks, but a reputable plumber may provide advice about this.

Maintenance and safe use

1. Never reach into the garbage disposal until the power is off. The best plan is to turn off the power at the main electric service to the house before reaching into the disposal. It is too easy for the power to be turned on accidentally from the wall switch, which you might not be aware of when working on the disposal.

2. Never, never, under any circumstances, put your hand down into the hopper of the disposal. Use tongs, pliers or even a coat hanger to retrieve ungrindable debris.

3. When you operate the disposal, use plenty of water. Water cleans the working parts and keeps them in working order.

4. Load the disposal hopper lightly. Don't overload garbage into the hopper and expect the disposal to handle it. Do several smaller loads instead of one big load.

5. Never, under any circumstances, put metal, glass, stoneware or other hard objects, including bones, into the disposal. Disposals may claim to grind bones, but they are best disposed of in garbage bags.

6. Never use drain cleaners in disposals.

HAIR DRYERS AND CURLING IRONS

There are many hair drying and styling devices on the market. Most common are: the hand-held, dryer/styler with brush and comb attachments; the salon-type dryer with hard plastic hood; and the bonnet-type dryer with a soft plastic bonnet connected to the heating element by an air hose.

Each year, about 1,000 people receive treatment in hospital emergency rooms for injuries from hair dryers. Only a few years ago, you were almost certain to be electrocuted if your blower-dryer fell into the water; an average of 17 people each year died that way. A 1987 law changed that. Blow dryers made after that time switch off when they fall into water. Dryers made since 1991 have the added protection of a safety plug that shuts off the current whether the dryer is switched on or not.

- Barbara used a bonnet-type dryer after bathing, without first getting dressed. She fell asleep while the appliance was on. She was treated for second degree burns on her back from the hot dryer hose.

- Rick, 12, fell asleep while using his mother's hair dryer. The dryer overheated and shorted out four hours later. The dryer's plastic case melted, spilled onto the blanket and mattress on which Rick was sleeping. Both the blankets

and the mattress caught fire. The boy's parents extinguished the flames, but Rick was treated for first and second-degree burns.

- A 23-year-old man was electrocuted when a hair dryer that was plugged in fell into the bathtub while he was bathing.

- A dryer that was plugged in, although switched off, short-circuited where the dryer joins the cord. There were no injuries, although the burning dryer scorched the bathroom vanity where it lay.

- A youngster received a severe shock when she grabbed the hair dryer with her wet hand.

Major hazards. The preceding are examples of the following major hazards with hair dryers.

1. Burns. These can be caused by skin contact with hot parts of the dryer, particularly on dryer/stylers on which there are metal parts that become very hot and can cause serious contact burns, or on bonnet-type dryers on which air hoses become very hot and can burn bare skin.

2. Electric shock. Shocks from hair dryers are common because they are often used in the bathroom where water in bathtubs and sinks is an electrocution hazard. Many shocks occur when hand-held dryers fall into bathtubs or sinks. Plugging in or turning on a hair dryer with wet hands can result in shock. When wiring is faulty, especially exposed wiring, even careful handling can cause a shock. Many hair dryers made before 1987 do not meet 1987 voluntary standards and are electrocution risks if they fall in water, even when the dryer is off.

3. Overheating. This can occur if the air intake vents of the dryer are covered by clothing, a towel, lint, hands or hair, or if the thermostat fails. This is a serious fire hazard if the dryer does

not have an automatic cut-off device that turns off the heating element when the dryer gets too hot.

4. Some injuries happen when hair is caught or sucked into a dryer. This is particularly a problem with mini-dryers, small, lightweight models made for travel.

Selection of hair appliances

1. Make sure that the dryer has a cut-off device that turns off the dryer if it starts to overheat. These devices are either heat-activated switches that turn on the dryers again when they cool, or fuses that blow when the dryers overheat. The fuse must be replaced before the dryer is used again.

2. When buying a salon-type dryer, make sure the hood will accommodate the head and rollers easily. To avoid neck strain, be sure the angle of the hood is comfortable.

3. Make sure the dryer/styler you buy can be held easily, without covering the air intake vents with your hand.

4. Look for dryer/stylers without exposed metal strips close to where the hot air is released. These can come in contact with skin and cause burns.

Use of hair appliances

1. Read and follow all manufacturer instructions. Keep instruction booklets and other information for future reference.

2. Keep air intake vents clear of towels, clothing, lint, hair or other obstructions.

3. Do not use a hair dryer when you are sleepy. Falling asleep while using a hair dryer is dangerous.

4. When using a hand-held dryer, dry hair at the back of the head carefully to avoid burning the nape of the neck.

5. When using a bonnet-type dryer, wear clothing or a towel that covers the back of the neck and the back. This protects against burns from the dryer's hot air hose.

6. Never use hair dryers while in the bathtub, and never immerse them in water. It is best not to use hair dryers in the bathroom.

7. If a hair dryer accidentally drops into water while plugged in, be sure to unplug it before touching the dryer. If a hair dryer falls into the water, it should not be used again unless reworked by the manufacturer. Some will not even work unless first returned to the manufacturer.

8. Do not dip the brush or comb end of a dryer/styler into water in order to dampen the hair. The water could run back into the element and cause an electrical shock.

9. Do not poke hairpins or any wires through the grill work over the heating element of any kind of hair dryer. This could cause a shock.

10. Never set down a dryer/styler while it is on. The vibration of the motor could cause the dryer to fall off a table or other surface and injure feet or legs.

Storage of hair appliances

1. Keep hair dryers out of the reach of small children.

2. Do not store hair dryers in the bathroom or other places where they might get wet.

Curling irons. Each year, over a three-year period, children under 5 years of age suffered 6,400 curling iron burns severe enough for emergency room treatment. This accounts for about 60 percent of curling iron burns. Teenagers and adults should never leave curling irons where young children can reach them.

Eye injuries are also associated with curling irons. This injury happens when the hot iron is touched to the eye accidentally. With ever-increasing temperatures available in hair curling irons, this may be a growing problem.

HUMIDIFIERS—ROOM

The main problems with room humidifiers are the hazards of electrical shock and bacteria and fungus growth.

Electrical shock. There is an added danger anytime electricity and water are near each other. This is a common problem with many household products, such as pressure washers, trouble lights, extension cords and others listed in the appendix on electricity. See one of these listings in this book for more complete coverage of electrical hazards.

Bacteria and fungus growth. Room humidifiers have tanks of water and electrically operated devices to release water into the room in the form of mist. Bacteria and fungus grow in the humidifier tank and may be released when the unit is on. Tap water has more organisms and more minerals than distilled or demineralized water.

Disconnect the humidifier from the electrical outlet before cleaning or filling. Use distilled or demineralized water in your humidifier. Do not allow scum and scale to form. Change the water daily. Empty the tank before you fill it. Use a brush or other scrubber to clean the tank. Follow manufacturers' suggested cleaning methods. If you use chlorine bleach, disinfectants or other cleaning products, rinse the tank well to avoid breathing harmful chemicals.

IRONS

The household iron is a very dangerous appliance. It is scorching hot, heavy and pointed for penetration. It is filled with scalding water, throws off hot steam, often stands on a shaky base, carries an electrical charge and is easily reached by a long dangling cord. We need irons and cannot eliminate them, but we can control

their use. More than 6,000 people receive emergency room treatment every year for injuries associated with irons.

- A 4-year-old boy tripped over the electric cord of the iron his mother was using. The iron fell on the boy and severely burned his arm.
- Margaret set the iron down hurriedly. It tipped over and spilled scalding water on her, burning her hands and arms.

Iron hazards. The preceding cases depict the following hazards associated with irons:

1. Pulling or tripping on the cord. Irons, like other electrical appliances, have cords that can trip you or your children. This can cause the hot iron to fall and cause a burn. Because irons are used in exposed traffic areas, unlike other appliances that are permanently placed on counters or against walls, their electric cords are more accessible to children.

2. Knocking over the iron. Some irons have unstable resting bases, and a slight push will tip them. If they do tip over, you or your child can be burned by hot water or by the hot face of the iron itself.

Other iron hazards:

1. A child climbing on a chair and touching the hot iron.

2. Being hit by the iron if a child pulls it off the ironing board.

3. Electric shock that can occur if any water spills on areas that carry electric current.

Many people leave their irons to cool on counters, with the cords in reach of children. Even after several minutes of cooling, an iron can still be hot enough to burn or scald with hot water. Also, if an iron is pulled down or falls, it is heavy enough to cause serious cuts and bruises.

Another situation that can lead to a mishap occurs when a left-handed person uses an iron with a cord mean to fit right-handed people. Unless the cord can be moved to the other side of the iron, it can get in the way and lead to an injury. An iron with the cord in the middle can be used by those either right- or left-handed.

Selection of irons

1. Buy an iron with a cord that works for left- or right-handed users, such as an iron with a cord permanently centered at the rear of the handle.

2. Choose an iron with a wide resting base that will not tip over easily when it sits in the upright position. Some irons have stands that allow you to safely place the irons on their face while cooling.

3. If buying a steam iron, choose one with a large water opening so that it will be easy to fill. Irons with small or obstructed openings can permit water to spill on electrical parts of the iron.

Use of irons

1. Read all instructions about a new iron before using it.

2. Use the iron only as it is intended to be used.

3. Do not operate an iron with a damaged cord.

4. Do not immerse the iron in water.

5. Do not allow the cord to touch any hot surfaces.

6. When not ironing, always unplug the iron and place it out of reach of children, even if you leave it for only a few minutes. A child can trip over the cord or pull on the cord, causing the hot iron to fall.

7. Disconnect the iron from an electrical outlet when filling it with water, emptying the water or when it is not in use. Use caution when turning a steam iron upside down; there may be hot water in the reservoir.

8. Use a sturdy ironing board, and place the board as close as possible to a wall and the outlet where the iron plugs in. This reduces the risk of tripping over the cord or causing the ironing board to fall.

9. Use the proper temperature setting for your fabrics. Synthetic fabrics will scorch or melt if the temperature is too high. Many fabrics will ignite if the iron is in contact with them for a few minutes.

10. When filling a steam iron with water, unplug it to prevent an electrical shock if water spills on live electrical parts of the iron.

11. Use demineralized or distilled water in a steam iron because normal tap water may leave mineral deposits that can clog steam and vent openings. (Some irons are self-cleaning and advertise that tap water is acceptable.)

12. When you finish ironing, coil the cord and put the iron up to cool. *Do not leave the iron within reach of children* because they can pull the cord and bring the iron down on themselves.

13. Most irons use 1,200 watts. Do not use an iron on the same circuit as another high-wattage appliance.

14. An iron should not be used with an extension cord. If it must be, use an extension cord rated at 10-amperes.

15. Do not mix child play areas and ironing activities.

Maintenance of irons

1. If the cord is frayed, repair it or replace it immediately.

2. If water in a steam iron leaks, either repair or replace the iron. Leaking water could cause scalds or contact electric components and give a fatal electrical shock.

Storage of irons

1. Be sure to empty the water and cool the iron before you put it away. A hot iron or escaping steam could damage materials next to the iron.

2. Coil the cord so that it does not kink and so that it is out of the reach of children who might pull the iron down on themselves.

For more information about safe use of irons, see the section on cords and outlets.

KNIVES

Most people treated in hospitals for kitchen knife injuries had cuts on fingers, hands and arms. These injuries could have been avoided.

- Ann unsuccessfully tried to split a frozen bagel with a 5-inch knife. Becoming frustrated, she tried to force the bagel apart, but instead brought the knife down on her finger. She severed an artery and damaged a nerve, which required surgery and several months to heal.

- Margaret reached into a sink full of dirty dishes. Her hand struck a butcher knife at the bottom of the sink and she received a laceration of the knuckles, for which she received three stitches.

- John was slicing roast beef, holding the meat in one hand and the knife in the other. As he cut through the meat toward his hand, the knife slipped and cut his thumb. He received 10 stitches in a hospital emergency room.

Accident patterns

1. Improper usage. Many accidents happen when cutting toward, instead of away, from fingers, or because the knife is directed up, instead of down toward the cutting board. Other injuries happen because the wrong kind of knife is used, or because the knife is used to cut frozen food or some other object for which most kitchen knives are not suitable.

2. Improper storage. Unless knives are in a select place known to all family members, serious injuries can result from reaching into a drawer, box, dish drainer or sink and unexpectedly hitting a sharp point.

3. Distraction and haste. Mishaps can occur when using a knife and talking or becoming distracted. Also, using a knife when in a hurry increases the chances of injury.

Selection of knives

1. Learn the types of kitchen knives available before buying and be sure to buy the size and style knife needed for your cutting work.

2. Check to see that the knife you buy is sturdy:

   - The tang of the knife is the part of the blade that extends into the handle and to which the handle fastens. It should be at least one-third the length of the handle. A good knife has a tang that extends the full length of the handle.

   - Check to see that the knife has a handle riveted to the blade in at least two places.

   - Buy a knife that feels comfortable in your hand. The balance of the weight of a small paring knife should be in the handle, but the balance of the weight of larger knives should be in the blade.

3. Serrated knives are good for cutting bread, cake, meat and other foods that may tear easily. Be aware that they cannot be resharpened without losing their serrations.

Use of knives

1. Cooking experts advise that cutting safety starts with a sharp knife. A dull

knife requires more pressure, increasing the chances of a slip.

2. Always use a cutting board. Tables and countertops are often very smooth and can allow the food being cut to slip. Hold the food firmly with one hand, or with a fork, and angle the knife downward toward the cutting board and away from your fingers.

3. Use the correct knife for the job.

4. Don't use a knife for purposes it is not intended, such as chopping ice or opening cans.

5. Even if you are in a hurry, take your time while chopping or slicing food.

6. Using a knife is a task that requires your full attention. Keep your eyes on the knife you are using throughout your task.

7. Never permit roughhousing in areas where knives are being used.

8. When handing someone a knife, extend the handle for the person to grasp, and turn the cutting edge away from your hand so you won't be cut.

9. Do not allow young children to use knives. Teach older children to use knives properly.

10. Do not attempt to catch falling knives.

Maintenance of knives

1. Wash, dry and put away kitchen knives right after use. Don't keep knives in the sink where they can injure an unsuspecting person.

2. Keep knives sharpened. Dull knives are inefficient and can cause the user to become impatient and so less cautious.

3. Let everyone in the family know when you sharpen your knives or have them professionally sharpened. If you are unaware that a knife has been sharpened, you can misjudge how much pressure to use while cutting and can cut a finger before realizing what happened.

Storage of knives

1. If possible, keep knives in a special rack or block where the blades won't hit each other. This keeps the knives sharp longer and reduces the chances of cutting a finger on a carelessly stored knife.

2. If you do not have a knife rack or block, keep kitchen knives in a partitioned drawer with the blade ends away from the front of the drawer.

3. Do not store large knives in the same drawer as flatware. The best drawer for the storage of knives is one that is not often opened for reasons other than getting a knife.

4. Store knives out of the reach of small children.

NIGHT LIGHTS

Fires can start when flammable materials touch a night light. Injuries and deaths happen when night lights are so close to beds that fallen pillows or blankets can touch the hot bulbs of the night lights and start fires. To reduce the chance of fire:

1. Locate night lights away from beds where the bulb might touch flammable material.

2. Look for night lights that bear the mark of a recognized testing laboratory.

3. Consider using night lights that have cooler, mini-neon bulbs instead of 4-watt or 7-watt bulbs.

PRESSURE COOKERS

Pressure cookers permit water to boil at a higher temperature, cooking food very quickly. However, the high pressure and temperature can be dangerous. Most injuries from pressure cookers that require hospital emergency room treatment are related to steam. Accidents happen with 4-quart and 6-quart pressure cookers, as well as large pressure cookers used in canning fruits and vegetables. The normal operating pressure for most pressure cookers is about 15 pounds per square inch. At that pressure, the pressure regulator begins to vent excess steam.

- Carolyn removed the pressure gauge on the pressure cooker and let the steam rush out. Thinking that the pressure inside must be down, she began to open the cooker. Although it was difficult to push the handles apart (indicating there was still pressure inside), Carolyn opened the pressure cooker. The remaining steam escaped and caused second degree burns on her face and arms.

- After only 3 or 4 minutes of cooking, Alan decided to add more water to the pressure cooker. The gauge showed a few pounds-per-square-inch, but he didn't think this level was dangerous. When he opened the pressure cooler, the steam caused serious burns to his face and arms.

Accident patterns

1. Forcing open the pressure cooker. If it opens before it has cooled and thoroughly depressurized, the steam can pour out and burn.

2. Opening the pressure cooker when it registers low pressure. This can often happens when trying to add more ingredients shortly after the pressure cooker is pressurized. Even a small amount of pressure can be hazardous.

3. Not reading instructions. Many serious injuries occur because people do not read the instructions and do not know how to operate a pressure cooker properly. Parents may tell children to watch the cooker, but don't give them directions or precautions.

4. Misaligning handles. Misaligning the handles can permit the liquid to escape once the pressure builds up inside the cooker.

5. Carrying the cooker. Carrying these heavy cookers can result in spilling hot liquid. If the cooker has only one handle, the weight of the cooker and the food inside can give more weight through leverage than a person can overcome.

Selection of pressure cookers

1. Buy a pressure cooker with an emergency pressure relief device, in addition to the regular pressure relief valve.

2. Look for pressure cookers certified by an independent testing laboratory as meeting voluntary safety standards.

3. Be sure you receive an instruction manual when buying, and read it thoroughly.

4. Look for a pressure cooker with an audible pressure control or a pressure gauge that shows the precise pounds per square inch, and a visible plunger that indicates whether the cooker is still pressurized.

5. If you buy a large cooker, try to get one with handles on both sides to give you a better grip when carrying the cooker.

Use of pressure cookers

1. Do not open the pressure cooker until all internal pressure is released. If the handles are hard to push apart, this means the cooker is still pressurized.

2. Don't force the pressure cooker open. Run cold water over it to cool it and reduce the internal pressure before you open it.

3. Certain foods, such as applesauce, rhubarb, split peas, cranberries, spaghetti and cereal, can foam, sputter and clog the steam vent. It is better not to cook these foods in a pressure cooker.

4. Do not overfill the cooker (in general, not more than three-quarters full) because of the risk of clogging the vent pipe and building excess pressure.

5. When the normal operating pressure (about 15 pounds per square inch) is reached, turn the heat down so that all

the water that creates the steam does not evaporate.

6. If you have to open the pressure cooker after you have started cooking, let all pressure dissipate before opening. Even a few pounds of pressure is hazardous.

7. Carry the pressure cooker with mitts or potholders because the heat could cause you to drop the cooker and spill the contents on yourself.

Maintenance of pressure cookers

1. Keep the vent pipe clean by running hot water through it.

2. Tighten or replace any loose or charred handles.

3. Replace the gasket when it begins to crack or lose its shape.

SMOKE DETECTORS

Smoke and toxic gases cause most home fire injuries and deaths. Most fire victims die from smoke inhalation before heat or flames reach them. Smoke can overwhelm a child or adult in just minutes. A serious fire can fill a house with black smoke and soot so thick that within a few minutes you can't see your hand in front of your face. If you wake up to a fire under these circumstances you may be disoriented, even in your own home.

Time is the biggest enemy in a fire. In 30 seconds, a small flame can grow into a fire burning out of control. Your house can easily be engulfed in flames in 5 minutes.

A smoke detector provides an early warning when a fire begins and could allow you to escape safely. Since smoke spreads faster than heat, smoke detectors should give a faster warning than a heat detector. Besides saving lives, smoke detectors help reduce property loss, because fires can be detected and extinguished early in their development.

• The Lustig family was sleeping upstairs when a fire started in the kitchen. A smoke detector outside the bedroom door went off in time for the family to escape through an upstairs window. The fire was extinguished before it had spread beyond the kitchen.

Two types of smoke detectors

1. Ion chamber. This smoke detector uses a radioactive source to produce electrically charged molecules (ions) in the air. This sets up an electric current in the detector chamber. When combustion particles (smoke) enter the chamber, they attach themselves to the ions and reduce the flow of electric current and set off an alarm. In general, the ion chamber detector senses flaming fires (such as drapes ignited by a wastebasket fire) quicker than it senses smoldering fires (such as an armchair ignited by a cigarette).

2. Photoelectric. One type of photoelectric detector uses a photoelectric bulb (like an electric eye in many automatic doors) that emits a photoelectric beam of light, which sets up an electric current in the detector. When smoke obscures the light, it reduces the flow of electric current and sets off the alarm. Another type uses a light source and a light-sensitive cell inside a darkened chamber. When the smoke enters the chamber, the light strikes the smoke particles. It then scatters and reflects into the light-sensitive cell, which sets off the alarm. In general, photoelectric detectors sense smoldering fires quicker than flaming fires.

Power sources

1. Batteries. The batteries in battery-powered detectors generally last about one year. The detector starts beeping when the battery is low. It is time to replace the batteries.

2. Household electric current. A detector powered by household electric current is fine as long as it has the current to operate, but it is vulnerable to power failure. It should be connected to a

plug near the unit and fasten to the outlet with a hold-in clip.

Requirements. Smoke detectors will sense a fire only a few minutes after ignition. They will give a warning sound several minutes before the smoke accumulates to deadly levels. All levels of government now require smoke detectors in most new houses and mobile homes. You should check with local authorities about regulations in your area.

Purchase of smoke detectors

1. Buy a smoke detector that includes a full, clear account of its use, instructions for installation and information about expected life of its components (such as a photoelectric bulb or batteries). You can buy smoke detectors, often for $10 to $20.

2. Consider if you can easily do the installation yourself by following the enclosed instructions.

3. Consider the location of electrical outlets if you buy a detector that requires a power cord. You may prefer a battery-operated detector, because your house electricity could be unreliable in a fire. However, if you buy a battery-operated detector, you must be sure to replace the batteries when needed.

4. If you buy a photoelectric-operated detector, be sure that it sounds a warning when the bulb burns out. Buy extra bulbs and batteries when you buy the detector, so you will have them ready when needed.

Installation. Put a smoke detector near the ceiling in places where smoke is likely to pass as it rises, such as the tops of stairs. Ideally, smoke detectors would be placed by every bedroom, in all hallways, on each floor, in most living and working areas and in the basement. While the cost may not be unreasonable, this may be impractical. These are your priorities, local building codes permitting:

1. Place one outside each bedroom door because it is most important that you are warned of a fire when you are asleep. Local building codes may specify certain locations.

2. In a one-story house or mobile home, put a smoke detector in the hall as near to the bedroom as possible. In two-story homes, install detectors on each floor.

3. Consider putting another smoke detector at the top of the basement stairs, but away from the furnace.

4. For extra protection, consider putting a smoke detector outside each bedroom, or in the bedroom if the occupant might be tempted to smoke in bed, or if the room has electrical appliances such as heaters.

5. Avoid placing smoke detectors:

   - Near locations where combustion particles are present. This would include near stoves, ranges, furnaces, space heaters and hot water heaters.
   - In air streams passing by kitchens.
   - In damp or humid areas near baths with showers, etc.
   - In very hot or very cold, or in very dirty areas.
   - Too near fluorescent lights. Keep at least 5 feet away.

6. The best installation advice is to carefully read and follow the instructions that come with detectors.

Maintenance of smoke detectors

1. Replace batteries at least once a year, even if the warning device for weak batteries has not sounded.

2. Replace photoelectric bulbs when they burn out.

3. Test detectors monthly and when returning from a vacation or long absence.

   - For ionization units, hold a lighted candle 6 inches under it.

- For photoelectric units, extinguish the candle and let the smoke drift into the detector.
- The alarm should stop after you remove the flame or fan away the smoke.

4. Smoke detectors wired into the house circuit often have a battery backup so that they still function in case of a power failure. If you hear beeps it may be telling you that the backup battery needs replaced or the sensor circuitry is faulty. To find out, remove the cover to see if there is a battery. If you cannot find a battery or cannot remove the cover, contact your local fire department for help. If you locate a battery, simply replace it and test the unit.

5. A beeping may signal that a bulb is burned out. Check for a burned out bulb and replace it.

Caution. If the detector alarm goes off, do not open the bedroom door because accumulated smoke can kill you. Exit through the bedroom windows. Teach the members of your family how to make this exit. If you have to go out through a smoke-filled hall, stay close to the floor where the air is safer to breathe. Have the family meet at a prearranged site outside to be sure everyone is safe.

Plan on getting out. How would you escape your home in case of fire? Would your children know what to do? Do your children know how to escape from the second or third floor? Children under 5 are at greatest risk when fire strikes. They may panic and hide in closets or under furniture. They need special help to escape. Plan fire escape routes and practice them. Involve the family in your escape plan.

1. Draw a simple picture of your home.
2. Plan two ways to get out of every room.
3. Agree on an outside meeting place.

4. Decide who will take care of each child.
5. Discuss the escape plan with all family members.
6. Practice escapes. Also practice at night, which is the worst time for fires.

Flames are fascinating. Fires and flames fascinate children. Their fascination may overcome their training. Here is how to make your fire escape plan work better. Stress these points:

1. Get out fast. Seconds count. Phone from a neighbor's house, not from a burning building.
2. Crawl, or move while stooped over. Stay under the smoke, which rises.
3. Test the door before opening. If it is hot to the touch or if smoke is coming in around the edges of the door, use another escape route.
4. Once you are outside, stay out. Go to the outside meeting place. If someone is missing, tell a firefighter.

SUMMARY

Minor appliances offer major hazards in the form of electric shocks and burns from flames or hot surfaces.

SAFETY RECAP

1. Keep fingers completely away from moving parts of household appliances.
2. Turn power off before working on stubborn or broken electrical equipment.
3. Monitor electrical wiring. Defective wiring, short circuits and outlet/cord overloads cause most electrical problems with small appliances.
4. If an appliance depends on heat (fondue and potpourri pots and toasters) take care to prevent burns.
5. If an appliance works under pressure (pressure washers, pressure cookers), be alert.

6. Knives are dangerous to all ages. Use them carefully and keep them away from children.

7. In these days of cable and satellite receiver TV, avoid the hazards of installing TV antennas. If you must work on a TV antenna, the major hazards to avoid are electric shocks and falls from heights.

8. Beware of hot surfaces on appliances, such as irons.

9. Protect your home with smoke detectors. Test them regularly and keep them in good operating condition.

10. Know which fire extinguisher is best for your situation. Know how to use extinguishers and keep them ready to use.

BIBLIOGRAPHY

Accident Prevention Manual for Industrial Operations: Engineering and Technology, 9th Ed., Chicago, IL: National Safety Council, 1988, pp. 456-462.

"Antenna Electrocutions," *Product Safety Fact Sheet*, U.S. Consumer Product Safety Commission, April 1979.

"Antenna Accidents Can Kill," *Antenna Alert*, U.S. Consumer Product Safety Commission, 1982.

"Blow Dryers," *Consumer Reports*, August 1992, Vol. 57, No. 8, p. 532.

"Carbon Monoxide Detectors Can Save Lives," Consumer Product Safety *Alert*. Consumer Product Safety Commission, April 1992.

"Check on Smoke Detectors," *The Seattle Times / Seattle Post-Intelligencer*, January 6, 1991, pp. G-1, G-2

"Check Smoke Detectors," *Safety and Health*, Chicago: National Safety Council, September 1990, p. 80.

"Christmas Decorations," *Product Safety Fact Sheet*, U.S. Consumer Product Safety Commission, September 1982.

"Christmas Lights," *Product Safety Fact Sheet*, U.S. Consumer Product Safety Commission, September 1982.

Consumer Reports, 1991 Buying Guide Issue, Mount Vernon, NY: Consumers Union of the United States, Winter 1990, p. 380.

"CPSC Issues Alert About Care of Room Humidifiers," *Consumer Product Safety Alert*, U.S. Consumer Product Safety Commission, December 1988.

"Disposal Trouble," Ernst Stores, 1990.

"Hair Dryers," *Product Safety Fact Sheet*, U.S. Consumer Product Safety Commission, December 1982.

"Is That Newfangled Cookware Safe?" Blumenthal, Dale, *FDA Consumer*, Vol. 24, No. 8, U.S. Food and Drug Administration. October 1990, pp. 12-15.

"Keep Your Christmas Holiday Safe and Happy," Salem, OR: American Youth Publishers, Inc.

"Merry Christmas With Safety," U.S. Consumer Product Safety Commission, September 1985.

"Recipe For Kitchen Safety," Tritsch, Shane, *Family Safety and Health*. Chicago, IL: National Safety Council, Winter 1992-1993, pp. 6-9.

"Smoke Detectors," *Product Safety Fact Sheet*, U.S. Consumer Product Safety Commission, August 1980.

"Television Safety," Electronic Industries Association, 1986.

"Warning! Fire Hazard with Nightlights," *Consumer Product Safety Alert*, U.S. Consumer Product Safety Alert, February 1990.

"What You Should Know About Smoke Detectors," U.S. Consumer Product Safety Commission, January 1985.

"Young Children and Teens Burned By Hair Curling Irons," *Consumer Product Safety Alert*, U.S. Consumer Product Safety Commission, April 1990.

CHAPTER 8

HOME FURNISHINGS

BATHTUB AND SHOWER INJURIES

Statistics on household injuries consistently indicate that the bathroom is one of the most hazardous areas in the home. Many of the accidents that occur there are linked to bathtubs and shower stalls. Following is advice on how to avoid the four most common types of bathtub and shower accidents: falls, burns, electrocutions and drownings.

Falls in the tub or shower

- A 49-year-old woman fractured her arm when she slipped and fell back against the side of the tub.
- A 6-year-old received a concussion when she used a plastic soap dish for support while leaving the tub, and fell when the pressure on the dish loosened it from the wall.

Most bathtub and shower injuries are the result of falls on slippery surfaces. The combination of smooth nonporous surfaces and soapy water can cause serious, sometimes fatal, accidents. Though there are no sure solutions to this problem, there are procedures that can reduce the chances of injury:

1. To make your footing more secure in bathtubs or showers, use suction-cup rubber mats or rough-surfaced adhesive strips. If you're planning a new bathtub, be aware that some tubs have slip-resistant surfaces.
2. Avoid high-gloss tiles and floor surfaces in bathrooms. Be safe, instead of fashionable, and use higher friction hard surfaces or rugs.
3. Just as you would in the kitchen, quickly clean up paint, greasy or oily spills, which become hazardously slippery in the bathroom. If you hang clothes to dry in the bath, make sure they drip into the tub so they don't create puddles.
4. Most bathroom falls occur while getting in and out of the bathtub. There should be at least two grab bars securely mounted on the wall beside a bathtub, at different heights, and one in every shower stall, to help break falls. Other accessories—towel rings, towel racks, shower curtain rods—should also mount securely, as a falling person will grab at the first available support to break a fall.
5. Be sure that all tub and shower accessories are free of sharp edges. They should be made of materials that will not break when in use.
6. Use a soap holder. One built into the wall is preferred for tubs and showers. Always put soap in the dish when not in use, or it may slide underfoot.

Burns in the tub or shower

- A 1-year-old was hospitalized with second-degree burns when he accidentally turned on the hot water faucet, while using it as a support to stand on. He was in the water only 3 seconds.
- A 2-year-old died of burns received when she fell into a tub of hot running water, as her mother momentarily turned away.

The modern convenience of readily available hot water can be a serious burn hazard in the tub and shower. This is particularly true for the young, aged and handicapped, who are less able to respond quickly and effectively to an emergency. Tap water scalds cause 34 deaths and 3,800 injuries each year. Anti-scald devices can keep water temperatures below 120°F to help prevent scald burns. Set the hot water heater at 120°F to help prevent burns. (New hot water heaters are often set as high as 160°F.)

1. Never leave a baby or small child alone in a bathtub—or even in the bathroom—for any reason. They can be burned easily if they turn on hot water faucets or fall into tubs filled with hot water.

2. Always test the bath water before bathing an infant or small child.

3. Your bathtub and shower should have a faucet that mixes hot and cold water. Another way to prevent hot water burns is to control the temperature at the hot water heater or install thermostatic or pressure regulating control valves in showers.

Electrocutions

• A 53-year-old woman was electrocuted when a radio fell off the sink into the bathtub as she was bathing.

• A 37-year-old woman was electrocuted while taking a bath, when a sun lamp fell into the tub.

• An 11-year-old boy, living in an older house, stepped into the tub by holding onto a metal faucet, and was immediately electrocuted. A bad wiring connection in the wall came in contact with a water pipe that was bringing water to the tub.

While the young boy in the last example could not prevent the situation, most electrical mishaps can be prevented by avoiding using, or very carefully using, electrical equipment in the bathroom.

1. Many electrical mishaps would not happen if electrical appliances were kept out of the bathroom. Examples of such equipment are radios, hair dryers and sun lamps.

2. Never touch any electrical fixtures or appliances when you have wet hands, or while in the bathtub or standing on a damp floor.

Drownings

• A 73-year-old woman, in good health and with no history of heart problems, apparently lost consciousness and drowned in the tub while the faucet was still running.

Many bathtub drownings are senseless, particularly those involving the young. No small children need drown if their parents or other adult supervisors would follow the guidelines provided above, under "burns." Adults should not take baths or bathe without supervision if they've been drinking alcohol, are handicapped or have conditions that hinder mobility, if they are prone to seizures or are on medication that causes drowsiness.

BUNK BEDS

Each year, more than 10,000 people, most of them young children, receive emergency-room treatment for injuries associated with bunk beds.

• One night, while he was sleeping on the top bunk, 6-year-old Bill had a nightmare and tossed in his sleep. There was no guard rail on his bed, and Bill fell over the side of the bed, hitting his head on the metal edge of the lower bunk. He was knocked unconscious and required several stitches.

• As Joan began to climb the ladder to the top bunk, the ladder slipped and she fell. She cut her hands on the edges of the ladder and hit her head on the floor.

• Two young brothers were wrestling on the top bunk. One pushed the other off the mattress and he broke his wrist when he fell on the floor.

- A 4-year-old boy tried to descend from the upper unit of his bunk bed by sliding, feet first, underneath the guardrail. His body passed through the space between the mattress and the guard rail, but his head became trapped and he suffocated.

- A 4-year old child was placed in the top bunk to sleep. The bed was an extra long length, but the mattress was regular length. The child became entrapped in the space between the mattress and the headboard. Fortunately she called out and was rescued before any serious injury or fatality resulted.

Hazardous situations. These illustrations represent some of the following hazardous situations:

1. Inadequate or missing guard rails. Some guard rails are not used regularly and others don't prevent a child from falling between the rail and bed frame.

2. Sharp edges. The sharp metal and wood edges of the bed frame can cause serious cuts. Loose-fitting mattresses make this hazard worse because the edges are more easily exposed.

3. Unstable or broken ladders. Ladders can slip if they do not fasten firmly to bed frames. Ladders also can be hazardous if they have missing or loose rungs, which can make them difficult to climb. Many falls occur when, without a ladder, children climb on furniture or the bed frame itself to reach the top bunk.

4. Rough playing. Running, jumping and pushing on a bed can be dangerous. A fall from a 5-foot-high bunk bed can cause a serious injury. Serious injuries also can occur if children push each other or fall against single beds or other furniture.

5. Guard rail spacing. On some beds, the spacing between the guard rail and mattress is large enough that a young child can roll, slide or push themselves between the mattress and guard rail. This leaves the child suspended by the head and entrapped.

6. Mattress foundation becomes dislodged. Some bunk beds have cross-ties under the mattress foundation. Others include them only in the upper unit. Cross-ties can be wires, wood slats or metal strips and should be bolted or screwed to the frame to keep them in place. When mattress foundations merely rest on small side ledges, they can fall onto a child below or bunk below, if the child below kicks upward on the mattress.

Selection of bunk beds

1. Choose bunk beds that have:

   - Wood or metal with rounded edges.
   - A mattress that fits tightly to prevent exposure of metal edges.
   - A ladder that grips the bed frame firmly and does not slip when used.
   - A guard rail that does not provide open spaces (not more than 3½ inches) through which a child could fall.
   - A guard rail that can be secured into position.
   - Cross-ties to hold upper mattress foundation in place.

2. Consider buying bunk beds that can be taken down to form two single beds if you later decide you don't want the bunk bed style. This may be necessary if you have young children who cannot sleep safely on the top bunk.

3. Mattresses or foundations resting only on ledges need cross wires or other supports to help prevent dislodgment, even when beds are not stacked. If mattresses or foundations on either bunk bed rely only on side rail ledges for support, request a free wire-support kit from: Bunk Bed Kit, P.O. Box 2436, High Point, NC 27261.

Use of bunk beds

1. When possible, place bunk beds in the corner of a room so that there are walls on two sides.

2. Keep the guard rail securely in place always, no matter what the age of the child. The top of the guard rail should be at least 5 inches above the top of the mattress. There should be at least 1 inch between the top of the mattress and the bottom of the guard rail. That gap should not be more than 3½ inches. Use a thicker mattress or add boards to close any larger gaps.

3. Do not permit very young children (under 6 years of age or under 35 inches tall) to sleep in the top bunk. They have greater difficulty climbing to and from the top bunk, especially if they have to get up at night.

4. Bed end designs differ. Check openings to make sure child cannot become entrapped in bed ends or roll off.

5. Cross-ties under the mattress should fasten securely to the bed frame.

6. Consider keeping a low-wattage night light on, so that a child can see the ladder when getting up at night.

7. Instruct children how to use the ladder, not chairs or other pieces of furniture, to climb to the top bunk bed.

8. If you have enough space, use the bunk beds to form two single (twin) beds. This removes the risk of falling from the top bunk.

9. Teach children that rough play is unsafe on and around beds and other furniture.

Maintenance of bunk beds

1. Replace any loose or missing rungs on ladders.

2. Keep guard rails in good repair.

3. Cover sharp edges with heavy tape, rubber padding or towels to prevent cuts.

4. If the space between the guard rail and the bed frame is more than 3½ inches, nail or screw another rail to close the space to prevent head entrapment.

CARPETS, NEW

Hundreds of complaints associated with new carpet installation have been received by the Consumer Product Safety Commission (CPSC). Symptoms most often reported are watery eyes, runny nose, burning sensation in the eyes, nose and throat, headaches, rashes and fatigue. There may be a relationship between new carpets and health problems, although hard evidence does not exist at this writing. Meanwhile there are practical steps to take:

1. Talk to the carpet retailer or installer about the voluntary "green label" program. While not a guarantee against health problems, it indicates that the carpet has been tested and has passed emissions criteria.

2. Ask the retailer to unroll and air out the carpet in a well-ventilated area before installation.

3. Ask for low-emitting adhesives to be used for installation.

4. Make sure the installer follows industry installation standards (Residential Carpet Installation Standard CRI-105).

5. Ventilate the area with fresh air.

6. Leave the house before, and for several hours after, the installation.

7. If objectionable odors persist, contact your carpet retailer.

8. Follow the manufacturer's instructions for proper carpet maintenance.

FURNITURE TIP-OVER

Each year, several children die and thousands are injured when furniture tips over. The injuries occur when children climb onto or sit on furniture. They also happen when children try to move furniture, or open and close drawers or doors.

Children try to pull themselves up or climb on chests of drawers, TV carts, stands, tables or bookcase shelves.

In a recent 4-year period, hospital emergency rooms treated 2,000 injuries from tipped furniture. Of this group, six children under 5 years of age died. During the same period, another four children died and 2,300 were injured from tipped TV sets. About 400 of the injuries happened when the TVs were on carts, stands or tables. Another large group of injuries (580 injuries and one death each year) resulted from bookcases tipping over.

Realize that young children can be badly injured or killed when furniture tips over. Place TVs as far back as possible on lower furniture. Use angle-braces to secure furniture to the wall.

CHRISTMAS TREES

Each year, thousands of families suffer needless injuries, loss of life and property loss from accidents involving holiday decorations. We can trace many of these mishaps: From the child who swallowed pieces of a broken ornament; to the family who died after a Christmas tree caught fire. Unsafe or improperly used decorations are hazards. Many more injuries can be traced to poor selection and care of Christmas trees. To help you enjoy safe holidays, following is advice about Christmas trees:

1. If you plan to buy a natural tree, the most important factor is its freshness. The higher the moisture content, the less likely it is to dry out and become a serious fire hazard.

2. One way to ensure a fresh tree is to cut it yourself. Tree farms are within a short distance in many locations.

3. Before you buy a cut tree, check its freshness. There are several things to look for. Brittle branches and shedding needles are a sign of dryness; fresh needles won't break between the fingers. Tap the tree lightly on the ground. If many needles fall off, the tree is too dry. Don't depend on a nice, green color. Trees may be sprayed green to improve their appearances.

4. When you bring home a tree, keep it outside as long as possible, until you are ready to decorate it. Keep its base in water. When you bring it in, cut the end diagonally 1 or 2 inches above the original cut.

5. Place your tree in a sturdy, stable holder with a wide base. For more stability with a large tree, fasten it to the wall or ceiling with thin wires from at least two points.

6. Fill the holder with water until it covers the cut line and keep the water at this level while the tree is in use. Refill every day if necessary.

7. Set up your tree a good distance from any heat source. Don't rely on do-it-yourself, flame-proofing treatments, since they are nearly impossible to apply at home.

8. Dispose of the tree when the needles begin to fall in large quantities. This is a sign that it is becoming too dry.

9. Metal trees are not a fire hazard. However, they can be a serious shock hazard if electric lights are attached to the tree. Sharp metal edges may cut the cord insulation and the metal may touch an electrically charged part. In either circumstance, the whole tree will become electrically charged, and anyone touching both it and a ground object could receive a severe shock.

10. The only way to light a metal tree safely is to use colored floodlights, placed around the room. Since the floodlights become quite hot, they should be placed where children can't touch them.

11. If you buy a plastic tree, it should be made of fire-resistant material. This does not mean the tree will not burn, only that it will not catch fire easily. As with natural trees, keep it away from heat sources.

12. Buy lights, and check lights you have for safety. Look for the UL label of Underwriters' Laboratories.

13. Check your tree lights (and outdoor lights) each year before you use them. Look for frayed wires, loose connections, broken or cracked sockets and spots of exposed bare wire.

CORDS AND WALL OUTLETS

More than 4,000 injuries from extension and appliance cords are serious enough to require hospital treatment each year. Following are some typical cases:

- A four-year-old was playing with the female end of an extension cord and placed it in her mouth. Her saliva made contact with the metal parts and caused an electrical shock and a mouth burn.

- Johnny, 6, was disconnecting a record player cord from an extension cord, by using his mouth. As the connections separated, his mouth contacted the male terminals, and he suffered an electrical burn on his mouth.

- An extension cord with an exposed wire near the female end was lying behind a chair. Mike, 23 months, was trying to reach the family cat when his body touched the exposed wire. He died instantly from electrocution.

- Joan tripped over an electrical cord, which was connected to a coffee pot, causing the pot to tip over and spill hot coffee on her. She suffered first-degree burns on her leg.

Accident patterns. The cases here demonstrate some of the major accident patterns with extension cords.

1. Children put extension cord receptacles or appliance cord plugs into their mouths. Either children's lips contact the metal male prong, or saliva from their mouth causes an electrical arc in the female end. Children receive disfiguring electrical burns to the mouth. The most common are:

- Children chew or suck on the extension cord receptacle or appliance cord plug.

- It is difficult to detach an extension cord from an appliance cord, usually because the extension cord outlet doesn't fit properly. To get the cords apart, a child puts one end of the receptacle in the mouth and use both hands to pull the opposite end.

2. Short circuits are often caused by a worn cords, faulty connections or use near water. They can result in electrical burns or shocks when plugging or unplugging cords. They also can cause fabric fires when the cord is under a rug, close to floor-length drapes or near upholstered furniture.

3. Children bite the extension cord and contact a live wire.

4. Tripping over a cord. Presently, electrical contractors must follow local building codes, based on either the National Electric Code or the Uniform Building Code, which require that outlets be no more than 6 feet apart.

Suggestions for purchase. Buying extension cords and other connections will be easier after reading the Electrical Hazards section of the Appendix. The following suggestions are for the purchase and safe use of extension cords:

1. When buying an extension cord, test the receptacle to be sure the appliance plug fits tightly, but does not stick.

2. Look for extension cords with self-closing outlets to cover receptacles that are not being used or receptacles that have a single slot.

3. Cover unused extension cord receptacles with electric tape or plastic safety caps to prevent mouth contact with electric current.

4. Be sure not to expose plug prongs when the extension cord receptacle is used. Return a defective cord or throw it away.

5. Use heavy-duty extension cords for air conditioners, freezers and other high wattage appliances.

6. If an appliance is plugged into an extension cord semi-permanently, tape the plug in place to prevent children from unplugging it.

7. Instruct children not to go near plugs and outlets and not to try to unplug cords.

8. Inspect extension cords and appliance cords for fraying, exposed wires or loose plugs. Repair or dispose of these cords.

9. When buying new extension cords, buy those with No. 16 or heavier gauge wire.

10. Buy cords that indicate they've been tested by a known national testing laboratory.

11. Do not run cords under rugs. The insulation can be damaged by foot traffic and they are fire hazards. Keep electrical cords out from under feet.

Electric wall outlets are also a hazard to infants and toddlers. Most outlets are at a child's level. If children stick metal objects into empty outlets, they can receive serious burns and severe, possibly fatal, shocks.

Primary rule. The primary rule for reducing the number of accidents involving wall outlets is: *If an outlet is not in use, do not leave it exposed.*

1. To protect young children, insert plastic safety caps into unused outlets. These caps can be bought inexpensively at nearly any drug or hardware store.

2. Use rotary cap outlets that can be rotated 90 degrees to expose the slots. Many similar devices to childproof outlets are on the market. Ideally, homes with children would have wall outlets high and well away from children. However, this is annoying to adults and may not meet codes, which ordinarily place them a foot above the floor.

3. Be certain that a plug inserts fully into the outlet, with no portion of its prongs exposed.

Three-prong cords and two-prong outlets. Many appliances come with three-prong plug-in cords when only two-prong receptacles are in the house. This problem is covered in the Appendix on Electrical Hazards.

BLIND AND DRAPERY CORDS

Parents are often warned about the danger of accidental strangulations when young children become entangled in pull cords for window coverings. Window covering cords often strangle children under 5 years old.

Statistics indicate that most victims were 2 years of age or younger. Some were in cribs placed near window coverings with draw cords. Other victims were not in cribs, but were playing with the cords.

Children may find a cord hanging near the floor or they may reach the cord by climbing on furniture placed near the cord. These accidents can happen when a child is left alone in a room, even for a short period of time.

Ways to secure window cords

1. Clip the cord to itself or to the window covering with a clamping device, such as a clothespin or cord clip.

2. Wrap or tie the cord to itself.

3. Wrap the cord securely around a cleat mounted near the top of the window covering.

4. Securely install a tie-down device. This also may be useful when a longer looped cord is necessary.

Buying blinds

1. Safe cord-securing devices are found at window covering dealers.
2. When you install your own window coverings, adjust the cords to their shortest possible lengths.
3. When you order new window coverings, specify that you want short cords.

FABRICS

Each year, there are thousands of deaths and injuries from burns associated with flammable fabrics.

- A six-year-old found some matches on a coffee table in his home. He lighted one of the matches and dropped it on his shirt, which ignited. He received severe burns over 40 percent of his body and was hospitalized for six months.
- Grandpa McFee was in his basement, using gasoline to clean some paint brushes. He was smoking while he worked, and some sparks and ashes fell on one brush and ignited the flammable vapors. Some of the gasoline had spilled on his pants and the flames quickly spread to his clothing. He was burned severely and hospitalized for months.
- Several pots were heating on the gas range. Susan reached over a lighted burner to stir something in a pot on a back burner. Her long-sleeve robe ignited and the flames began to travel up her arm. Fortunately, she quickly dropped to the floor and rolled to smother the flames. She suffered burns on her arm and part of her face.
- One night, 38-year-old Roberta Smith got into bed, lit a cigarette and opened a favorite magazine. She fell asleep and dropped the lighted cigarette on the bed. The cigarette burned through the sheets and began to smolder on the mattress. Several minutes later, Roberta awakened because she was having trouble breathing. She dropped to the floor and crawled out of the room. She suffered from severe smoke inhalation.

Accident patterns with flammable fabrics

1. Playing with or using matches and lighters. Children and adults can misuse matches and lighters, although children are victims more frequently.
2. Using flammable liquids. Smoking or using any other ignition source while using flammable liquids is very dangerous. Most people don't realize that vapors from flammable liquids can travel all the way across a room and be ignited by a distant flame or heat source.
3. Using kitchen ranges. Both gas and electric ranges can ignite clothing, especially loose-fitting garments with floppy sleeves.
4. Smoking in bed. Smoking is the most common cause of fires associated with bedding, mattresses and upholstered furniture.
5. There are many other often-cited ignition sources. They include space heaters, bonfires, fireplaces and coal and wood burning stoves. The presence of clothing increases the severity of body burn.
6. Groups in most danger. Fires are most hazardous to the very young, the very old and the handicapped, because they do not know how, or do not have the physical ability, to respond in an appropriate manner.

Purchase of fabric

1. Buy flame-retardant clothing for your children. Flame-retardant sleepwear is available up through size 14, and in some other types of clothing for all sizes.
2. If you sew, buy flame-retardant fabrics to use in the garments you make.

3. Consider the following when buying any garment:

   - Tightly woven, heavy fabrics (such as denim used in jeans) ignite and burn slower than sheer, lightweight and loosely woven fabrics (such as cotton broadcloth used in shirts).
   - Napped fabric (such as cotton flannel) with air spaces between the loose fibers will ignite much faster than a smooth-surfaced material (such as denim).
   - A fluffy, high-pile fabric (such as some sweaters) will ignite and burn faster than a close-knit, low-pile fabric (such as most pants).
   - Close-fitting garments are less likely to ignite than loose-fitting garments (such as robes, housecoats, blouses, shifts and nightgowns with bell-type sleeves, ruffles and trims).

Use of fabrics

Know the hazards of ignition sources and of flammable liquids:

Kitchen ranges

1. Keep young children from climbing on top of stoves and igniting their clothing from lit burners.
2. Don't try to keep warm by leaning against a stove, because your clothing may ignite. Even an electric stove that is turned off can ignite clothing, if the stove is hot enough.
3. Don't wear loose-fitting sleeves when you reach across lit burners, because your sleeves can ignite.
4. Use a potholder instead of a towel to remove a hot pan from a lighted burner, because a towel can touch the burner, ignite and then ignite your clothing.

Cigarettes

1. Don't smoke in bed because you might fall asleep and the lighted cigarette could start a fire.
2. The elderly and handicapped are more likely to drop lighted cigarettes or ashes on their clothing. They may be unable to react to help themselves.

Matches or lighters

1. Be aware that the elderly and handicapped may often drop matches on themselves when lighting cigarettes, cigars or pipes, resulting in ignition of clothing.
2. Be aware that many people, especially the elderly and handicapped, spill lighter fluid on their clothing when refilling lighters. The fluid may ignite when the lighter is lighted, resulting in clothing ignition. Elderly and handicapped people should not use matches and lighters when alone.
3. Keep matches and lighters locked up away from children, because children often ignite their clothing while playing with matches and lighters.

Flammable liquids

1. Remember that heavier-than-air vapors from flammable liquids can travel unseen across a room and be ignited by a distant flame or heat source, such as matches, lighters, cigarettes or pilot lights from water heaters and stoves.
2. Store flammable liquids in tightly capped safety containers and keep them away from your living quarters (such as in an outdoor shed) and out of children's reach.

Flame-resistant fabrics

Flame-resistant fabrics require special care and treatment to maintain their flame-resistant qualities after washing. Care labels on all flame-resistant sleepwear identify anything that adversely affects the flame resistance. Follow the instructions carefully. There are two basic types of flame-resistant fabrics:

1. Flame-resistant fabrics that have flame-retardant chemicals added when the fibers are made. In these fabrics, flame resistance is inherent in the fiber. Examples include the modacrylics, some nylons and some polyesters. These fabrics are labeled: "Machine wash warm—use detergent—do not iron."

2. Fabrics to which flame-retardant chemicals are added by the manufacturer after the fiber is made. In these fabrics, the flame-retardant chemicals are outside each fiber. Cotton and rayon fabrics are in this category and have labels: "Machine wash warm—use phosphate detergent—or use nonphosphate heavy-duty liquid detergent." Virtually no U.S. manufacturers now add flame-retardant chemicals to sleepwear fabrics to make them resistant to fire. Instead, they rely on flame-resistant fibers or fabric construction.

Laundering tips and terms. If you don't follow the correct laundering process, the flame resistance of a fabric is lost after several washes. Follow the instructions so that clothing will stop burning when an ignition source (an open flame or hot electric coil, for example) is removed from the fabric.

1. Detergents. The instructions to use phosphate detergents may be a problem to some consumers. Some cities, counties and states have banned or limited the sale of phosphate detergents, as a result of findings that indicate phosphates may pollute waterways. (Check with your local health department to see if phosphate detergents are banned in your area.) If phosphates are banned in your area, and the label on the child's sleepwear reads "Use phosphate detergents," the best advice is to use nonphosphate heavy-duty liquid detergent.

2. Soaps. Remember that the warning "Do not use soaps" does not mean "Do not use detergents." Soaps may leave fat deposits that build up on flame-resistant fabric. Not only does this fat deposit result in loss of flame-resistant properties, it may also result in stiffness of the fabric.

3. Bleaches. For flame-retardant, treated cotton, chlorine bleach may render the flame-retardant finishes ineffective. For synthetic fabrics, chlorine bleach may be used.

4. Commercial laundering. The strong chemicals used in commercial laundries can cause the loss of flame resistance. Be sure to home launder.

5. Hard water. If hard water is prevalent in your area, you should use detergents that are at least 8.7-percent phosphate. (If you don't know about the water in your area, check with the water department.)

6. Machine wash warm. Warm water temperatures, ranging between 105° and 120°F, are safe for laundering flame-resistant sleepwear. Hot water (about 140°F) may cause shrinking and severe wrinkling of the fabric.

7. Tumble dry, low heat. To avoid fabric shrinkage and stiffness, use low heat when drying most flame-resistant sleepwear fabrics.

8. Fabric softeners. Certain fabric softeners may build up on flame-resistant fabric and cause the garment to lose its flame-resistant properties. You should use fabric softeners sparingly (once a month) with treated sleepwear.

Laundering procedures. Flame-retardant fabrics should have permanent care labels. To keep the flame-retardant qualities, always follow the care instructions. Most suggest this:

1. Use phosphate-based detergents, not soaps or nonphosphate detergents. If you live in an area where phosphates are banned, use a heavy-duty liquid laundry detergent.
2. Use warm water, not hot water.
3. Do not use chlorine bleach.

FLOORS

Most emergency-room injuries involving floors and flooring material are the result of falls.

- A 7-year-old boy slipped as he ran across a freshly waxed kitchen floor and broke his arm when he fell.
- A 35-year-old man tripped on the bowed edge of the linoleum floor covering in his kitchen and sprained his ankle.

While some floor-related injuries involve hazards not easily remedied (such as a floor that is not level), most result from preventable accidents.

Slippery floors

1. Immediately wipe or sweep up anything that is spilled on floors. This habit should be taught to children very early.
2. Wet floors are a particular problem in bathrooms, in laundry areas near the sink and in entrance ways.
3. Areas likely to be wet should have the added protection of carpeting, abrasive strips or slip-resistant mats.

Washing and waxing. Washing and waxing a floor can be very dangerous without the proper care.

1. Any time the floor is washed or waxed, block off the room until the area is completely dry.
2. When using a paste wax, be careful not to lay down an excess amount. It can make the floor quite slippery. Paste wax should be buffed thoroughly in order to harden it enough to make it safe underfoot.

3. When using a liquid self-polishing wax, it is not advisable to use the same mop or sponge for both washing and waxing the floor. It is difficult to remove all the cleaning agent no matter how well you rinse, and the residue on the applicator may make the wax smeary and slippery.

Rugs and runners. On any smooth-surfaced floor, particularly a waxed one, small rugs, runners and similar items can be treacherous. Any small rug should be anchored to the floor in some manner, such as with double-faced carpet tape.

Porch and terrace floors. Porch and terrace floors can become quite slippery when exposed to rain or snow. Use extra caution when they are wet or icy. Shovel snow off promptly and sprinkle with sand, salt or ashes.

If a terrace floor is to be painted, sand or similar abrasive materials can be added to the paint to make the paint slip-resistant. If you are building a porch or terrace, it is simple to arrange for a rough-treated surface.

Carports and garages. Carports and garage floors can be dangerous, because they may collect oil spills from automobiles. Oil on a smooth, concrete surface is extremely slippery and spills should be scrubbed thoroughly with an abrasive cleaner. A rough finish on those floors is preferable to the common smooth finish.

Tripping. Many serious accidents happen when people trip over the raised edges of linoleum, carpeting and the like, or over objects left on the floor. Ironically, a surprising number of injuries occur when people trip over improperly installed abrasive strips, mats or carpeting, which were installed to make the floor more slip-resistant. Look all around the house, inside and outside, for protrusions and objects that might cause a trip. Tack, tape or glue down carpet and tile edges.

Hammer down protruding nails. If you find an irregularity in flooring that cannot be eliminated, such as a drain or a raised doorsill, draw attention to it. Paint it a bright color, for example, to make it stand out.

Footwear. What you wear on your feet is important in avoiding falls. For example, stockings worn alone are more slippery than shoes or bare feet. Of common materials used to sole shoes, leather is the most slippery and crepe one of the least slippery. Because young children and older consumers are most susceptible to slipping accidents, it is a good idea for them to wear shoes with slip-resistant soles. Finally, and very importantly, high-heeled and platform shoes are more unstable than flat shoes. They can be a contributing factors in floor-related accidents and can make these accidents much more severe.

RECLINER CHAIRS

Young children continue to be injured, sometimes fatally, by playing on recliner chairs. Statistics reveal that victims are:

1. Between the ages of 12 months and 16 months.
2. Unsupervised.
3. Apparently climbing or playing on the leg rests of chairs while the chairs were in reclined positions.
4. Trapped when their heads enter the openings between the chair seats and the leg rests, as the weight of their bodies forced the leg rests down.

As a result of the problem, there are now voluntary guidelines that specify:

1. A device(s) will be used to reduce the size of the opening between the leg rest and seat cushion when the chair is in the reclined position.
2. All chairs will carry a caution label that reads: "Caution—Do not allow children to play on this mechanized furniture or operate the mechanism. Leg rest

folds down on closing so that a child could possibly be injured. Always leave in an upright position and keep hands and feet clear of mechanism. Only the occupant should operate it." Consumers with older chairs that may not have complied with the guidelines should take precautions to keep children from playing on the chairs.

UPHOLSTERED FURNITURE

The most serious injuries associated with upholstered furniture are burns from upholstered furniture fires. Many people die also from smoke or toxic gases generated by fire in upholstered furniture. For example:

- Larry was drinking beer while watching TV. He became drowsy and dropped a lighted cigarette between the cushion and the arm of the chair. Smoke and gas killed Larry while he slept.

Accident patterns. Some typical accident patterns in upholstered furniture fires:

1. Cigarette ignition. Data shows that cigarettes are the most common cause of fires in upholstered furniture.
2. Drinking alcohol. Many victims have drunk alcoholic beverages before a fire begins. They may be smoking when they fall asleep, and the alcohol effects keep them from awakening before they suffer burns or smoke inhalation.
3. Smoke and toxic gas. Like mattress fires, upholstered furniture fires tend to smolder for hours. Many people die from the smoke and carbon monoxide generated during that time, particularly if fires occur when they are sleeping. Many others are seriously burned if the furniture begins to flame.

Another hazard with upholstered furniture is ignition by a nearby flame or heat source, such as a space heater, heating stove or fireplace. In contrast to fires started by cigarettes, upholstered furniture fires started by these sources ignite much quicker. Polyurethane foam and other materials used to pad or cover upholstered furniture can generate deadly amounts of carbon monoxide and other gases within minutes.

The elderly and handicapped are often victims of upholstered furniture fires when they fall asleep and drop cigarettes on furniture. Their injuries are often serious if they cannot react quickly enough to save themselves once they become aware of the fire.

The Consumer Product Safety Commission has a standard for upholstered furniture that requires it to resist ignition from dropped cigarettes for a certain amount of time. This does not eliminate the problem. It simply keeps the fire from spreading as quickly and reduces the amount of smoke and toxic gases.

To prevent injuries

Placement of furniture

1. Place upholstered furniture as far as possible from all ignition sources, including stoves, space heaters, floor furnace, wall furnaces and fireplaces.
2. Examine electric cords near upholstered furniture and replace them if they are frayed or defective.

Using furniture

1. Be careful about smoking when you're sleepy, particularly when drinking alcoholic beverages or using medications.
2. Use ashtrays that are deep and have wide sides to prevent lit cigarettes from falling out. Keep ashtrays off of upholstered furniture.
3. If you drop a cigarette, retrieve it quickly and put out any sparks or ashes left on the furniture. Check thoroughly behind cushions and under furniture for ashes or sparks.

4. Put out all cigarettes in ashtrays before you go to sleep at night.
5. Remember that while watching TV, especially late at night, many people fall asleep and drop cigarettes into the furniture. Remember also that elderly and handicapped people may more easily drop cigarettes.

In case of fire. Even if you are in your bedroom while an upholstered furniture fire is smoldering in another room, the smoke and toxic gases can kill you. However, if your door is shut, the smoke and gases will not be able to reach you as quickly. A reliable smoke detector, placed outside your bedroom door to provide early warning in case of a fire, could save your life. Remember, if a fire does occur, exit through a bedroom window, not through a door, because there may be deadly quantities of smoke and gas in the hall.

SAFETY RECAP

1. Water in the home facilitates several hazards: burns, drownings and electrocution. This makes the bathroom one of the most dangerous places in the home.
2. Falls continue to be a major home hazard. This chapter covered falls involving tubs, showers, beds, carpets, electric cords and floors.
3. Fires continue to be a major home hazard. This chapter discussed electric cords and wall outlets, fabrics and upholstered furniture.

BIBLIOGRAPHY

"Bunk Beds," *Product Safety Fact Sheet*, Consumer Product Safety Commission, October 1987.

"Children's Sleepwear," *Product Safety Fact Sheet*, U.S. Consumer Product Safety Commission, August 1981.

"Christmas Decorations," *Product Safety Fact Sheet*, U.S. Consumer Product Safety Commission, September 1982.

"CPSC Warns Consumers of Bunk Bed Entrapment Hazard and Mattress Support Collapse," *Consumer Product Safety Alert*, U.S. Consumer Product Safety Commission, September 1988.

"CPSC Warns Parents Abut Child Accidents in Recliner Chairs," *Consumer Product Safety Alert*, U.S. Consumer Product Safety Commission, July 1987.

"Easy Ways to Fall-Proof Your Home," *Family Safety and Health*, Chicago: National Safety Council, Fall 1991, pp. 14-17.

"Flammable Fabrics." *Product Safety Fact Sheet*, U.S. Consumer Product Safety Commission, May 1981.

"Furniture Can Tip Over on Children," *Consumer Product Safety Alert*, U.S. Consumer Product Safety Commission, March 1990.

"Living in the Real World," Greenman, Jim, *Childcare Information Exchange*, Redman, WA: Childcare Information Exchange, December 1988, p. 17.

"Household Extension Cords Can Cause Fires," *Consumer Product Safety Alert*, U.S. Consumer Product Safety Commission, October 1990.

"Parents Warned About the Danger of Strangulation if Children Become Entangled in Window Blinds or Drapery Cords," *Consumer Product Safety Alert*, U.S. Consumer Product Safety Commission, August 1989.

"Safety at Home—Drowning," *Parents*, September 1990.

"Safety Warning—Bunk Beds," *Consumer Product Safety Alert*, U.S. Consumer Product Safety Commission, August 1989.

"Tips for Purchasing and Installing New Carpet," *Fact Sheet*. U.S. Consumer Product Safety Commission, October 1992.

"Upholstered Furniture," *Product Safety Fact Sheet*, U.S. Consumer Product Safety Commission, January 1981.

FIXING AND MAINTAINING

The chapters in this section focus on fixing and maintaining the home and its environs, including the garage, workshop, yard and garden. It is often claimed that more people are hurt in falls around the home than anywhere else. Indeed, investigation reveals that the danger is particularly high for the fix-it/maintain-it person.

CHAPTER 9

HOME FIX-UP AND MAINTENANCE

ALUMINUM WIRING

Millions of houses and mobile homes are wired with aluminum for outlets and lighting. Most communities now have standards to correct problems with earlier aluminum wiring, and new construction has standards to overcome previous problems. However, aluminum wiring still creates a potential fire hazard, especially in older homes, which develops in these steps:

1. An oxide film, which does not conduct electricity, forms on aluminum.

2. Unless the electrical connectors maintain current flow through the breaks in the oxide film, electrical resistance can build up and cause sustained overheating.

3. The overheating can lead to rapid destruction of insulating material, which can cause a fire.

Danger signals of overheating aluminum wiring

1. Usually, the switch or receptacle outlet face plate is warm to the touch.

2. The smell of overheated insulation (which smells like burning plastic) is present.

3. Lights flicker, and flickering is not traceable to any appliance or external source.

If you have any of these danger signals in your home, you should have an electrician check your electrical wiring.

NONGLASS DOORS

Accidents with nonglass doors seldom mean critical injuries, but they happen so often, they are a safety problem. Emergency room treatment for injuries with doors is common.

- A 32-year-old man was carrying a large box up the basement stairs. He had to step back when opening the door at the head of the stairs, because the door swung open over the steps. He lost his balance and fell, fracturing his arm.

- A 3-year-old girl suffered severe bruises when she was caught in a wooden, swinging door.

- A father and son received head injuries and lacerations when a garage door collapsed on them and pinned them to the ground.

Reducing door injuries is complex because while many accidents can be traced to simple human inattention, many others stem from a mix of poor planning, design and installation. Correcting such defects may be beyond the abilities of the average homeowner. Some advice on common problems with doors follows.

Poorly located doors. The location of a door can be important. One that opens into a hallway or any other frequently used area is dangerous. An unsuspecting person can be painfully injured if the door opens as they walk by.

Another poor arrangement is a door that swings open over a flight of stairs. It

170

is hazardous for a person climbing the stairs, who must step backward to open the door. Especially threatened is the person carrying something. A door should open away from the stairs if it opens over a stairway. There should be a landing at the top of the stairs on which the door swings open.

No two doors should contact each other when they open. Any door should be able to open at least halfway, and it is best if it opens completely. To correct door placement, replace a hinged door with a folding or sliding door.

Swinging doors. Swinging doors are not prudent in a home. Collisions are common, as are injuries from the door's spring-actuated back swing. They are very dangerous for small children and pets who can become wedged between the door and the frame. If it is impractical to install a hinged door in its place, replace the swinging door with a folding or sliding door.

Improperly hung doors. Any door that binds or sticks and fails to open readily and completely is a hazard. It can cause collisions and also may cause falls if a person trying to open a stubborn door loses his or her grip and balance when the door finally releases. Some chronically sticking doors can be fixed by light planing. All wooden doors should be sealed, varnished or painted to prevent excessive swelling during humid weather.

Sharp door frames and accessories. Round off the sharp edges of a door or door frame with sandpaper. The metal strike plate on the door can snag clothing and cause painful scrapes and bruises if struck accidentally. To avoid this, use large, oversize strike plates with smoothly rounded corners and lips bent back flush with the door jambs.

Door return devices. There are many different mechanisms to regulate a door closing. The safest is hydraulically operated. Those using chains or sliding devices with springs are more likely to cause injury. If the door is opened quickly, this may cause the door to rebound and strike the victim.

Door stops. Rigid, protruding door stops can cause painful ankle injuries. Flexible door stops are better. The door stop should be attached to the wall the door swings against, not the door itself. If it must be attached to the door, place it near the top.

Garage doors. Most garage doors use a counterbalancing system for easy operation and for holding the door in a fixed position. This system usually consists of springs and cable that can fail. Most likely to fail are those with a long coil spring on each side of the door, which fastens to a hook-shaped bend in the spring end. The stress on the hook may cause metal fatigue and failure. Sudden failure can result in injuries to those nearby, who may be hit by flying metal parts or crushed by the falling door.

Safety clips on the garage door counterbalance springs greatly reduce the chance of crushing a person's fingers between the hinged sections of the door as it closes. This usually happens because there is only the door handle near the bottom of the door. Rather than use the handle to close the door completely, which requires bending, a person may push on one of the section edges and risk catching the fingers.

Automatic garage doors manufactured for sale in the U.S. after Jan. 1, 1993 must comply with additional safety devices. They must have one of these devices:

1. An electric eye protection device.
2. A constant contact control button, which requires you to press it in until the door is fully open or closed.

Glass in doors. Many nonglass doors, particularly front and rear entrance doors, have glass panes or panels that can cause serious injuries. Mishaps occur when a person falls against the glass section or misjudges the strength of the glass and pushes against it. Ordinary glass panes are very fragile. They break into sharp, jagged pieces that slice deeply into the flesh and cause severe injury, permanent scarring and even death. Unless safety glass is used in the doors, use extreme caution around doors that have glass panes or panels. Never push on the panes. Keep the areas in front of the doors dry and free of throw rugs, toys or any other objects that might cause someone to slip or stumble and hit the door or panes.

Additional door hazards

1. Don't use glass, ceramic or plastic door knobs. They're hazardous when chipped or broken.
2. Clothes hooks mounted on doors should be attached above eye level. Children's hooks should be above their eye level, yet not high enough to create hazards for adults.
3. Closet doors should open easily from the inside to avoid trapping children. No closet should be able to be locked.

GLASS DOORS AND WINDOWS

Nearly 200,000 people a year receive emergency room treatment for injuries associated with glass doors and windows. Some examples follow:

- Diane was running through her family's split-level house when she smashed into the plate glass door that separates the kitchen from the den. She was looking back and did not realize the door was closed. The door shattered over Diane, severed her jugular vein and penetrated her spinal cord. She died in the hospital.
- A six-year-old was running outside to play when he tried to open the storm door by pushing on the glass part. The

glass broke on him and lacerated his stomach, causing internal bleeding.
- After her bath, Mary stood up in the tub and slipped on the soap. She grabbed at the handrail but her arm broke through the glass tub enclosure. She suffered severe lacerations on her right arm and hand.

Accident patterns

1. Walking or running into, or falling against, sliding glass doors, often because the person is unaware the door is closed.
2. Pushing on the glass portion to open or close storm doors, losing balance and falling against the glass in these doors, or opening or closing the doors against a person in the flow of traffic.
3. Slipping and falling, because of wet or soapy floors, against glass bathtub and shower enclosures.
4. Walking or running into, or pushing on, fixed glass panels, typically because the person is unaware of their presence or mistakes them for doors.
5. Falling against a window, knocking or striking the glass when opening or closing the window, hitting unmounted glass, storm windows that are in storage or broken glass in windows.

Ordinarily glass breaks easily into large and dagger-like pieces that can cut and pierce the human body. Safety glazing materials can prevent many serious injuries, because they are usually more impact-resistant and do not break into large, jagged pieces.

Some states recognize the injury hazard of ordinary glass. Their laws require safety-glazing materials in sliding glass doors, storm doors, entrance doors, fixed glass panels, bath and shower doors and enclosures in new homes, apartments and in commercial and public buildings. Tough safety standards are in effect for architectural glass.

Selecting glass doors. Install safety-glazing in sliding glass doors, fixed glass panels, storm doors, entrance doors and bathtub and shower enclosures. Since safety-glazing materials are used in replacing broken glass in these products, it is becoming less likely that you will encounter plain glass. Meanwhile, there are steps you can take to protect yourself from ordinary glass. The four types of glazing materials are:

1. Tempered glass. This type of glass is heated, then cooled in a special way that makes it stronger than ordinary glass. When broken, it crumbles into small pieces that reduce the chance of personal injury. It is the least expensive of the four types and most common in the home. It cannot be cut, and must be bought in the exact size you need.

2. Laminated glass. This clear glass is made by heating layers of ordinary glass with a resilient plastic material between them, to bond them together. It resists breaking and if it does break, the pieces generally stick to the plastic and do not scatter.

3. Wire glass. This glass has a wire mesh embedded in the body of the glass. When it breaks, the wire holds the larger pieces together. Since this wire is normally visible, this glass may not be desirable for sliding doors.

4. Rigid plastic. This glazing material is made from one or more layers of plastic heated together, sometimes with reinforcement material to make it stronger.

All safety-glazing materials have permanent labels that name the manufacturer and type of glazing material. After picking a material, see that the door is hung properly to resist shocks from slamming and minor collisions.

Before buying a storm door, check to see that it is free of sharp edges and corners, especially along the bottom edge and corners.

Using glass doors

1. Watch where you're going and don't rush when you are using a door with glass.

2. Place a piece of furniture or a tall planter is front of fixed panels to prevent collisions.

3. Place decals or colored tape on glass doors and panels to show that glass is present. Attach them at both child and adult eye levels.

4. Install safety bars at door-handle level on sliding glass doors that slide inside a fixed-glass panel. They show that the door is closed and prevent contact with the glass.

5. Place protective screens or grilles over the glass in storm doors.

6. Keep the area in front of a glass door clear of rugs, toys or other small articles that might cause a person to trip or fall.

7. Do not allow children to play or run near glass doors.

Using and storing windows

1. Don't knock or bang on windows or storm windows. Remember that they are fragile.

2. Don't leave unmounted glass doors or storm windows unprotected in storage. Store them so that children cannot easily reach them.

3. Don't push on glass when opening a window.

4. Take care not to paint your window shut. If your window sticks, try to free it with a tool rather than pushing it with your hands.

GARAGE DOOR OPENERS

Homeowners who have garage doors that do not automatically reverse should repair or replace them. Use new openers that reverse, to prevent young children from being trapped under closing garage doors. At least 50 children have been trapped and killed under automatic garage doors in the last 10 years. These children were between the ages of 2 and 14. Other children have suffered brain damage and serious injuries when closing doors touched them and did not stop and reverse direction.

To check the garage door, the opener must be taken off the door. On most openers manufactured since 1982, a quick-release device allows the opener to be detached from the door. A properly operating door is balanced. This means it will stay in place in any partially opened position. The door should not stick or bind when opened or closed. If doors do not balance, or if they bind or stick, they should be serviced by a professional.

Once the garage door works properly, homeowners can check the reversing mechanism by placing a test block (2 inches high or more) on the floor in the door's path. If the door does not reverse within two seconds on striking the block, disengage the unit until repairs are made or until a new garage door opener is installed.

Some older garage doors will stop when they strike an object, but they do not automatically reverse. These doors cannot be adjusted or repaired to make them safe enough to prevent trapping a child. Owners should check garage doors every 30´ days to be certain the system works properly. If it does not, disconnect the automatic door opener, using the owner's manual. Raise and lower the door by hand.

To childproof garage door openers, relocate the switch in the garage to as high a position as is practical, to restrict children's use. Remote control door devices should be kept locked in the car and away from children. Parents also should tell their children about the potential hazards.

HEAT GUNS

Heat guns are used to strip paint from finished surfaces. They look like hair dryers and emit air at 800°F. They make the paint blister and bubble so it can be scraped off surfaces. Using a heat gun is intense work, but it works faster than chemical strippers. Once the hot paint separates from the surface it is easily removed. Heat guns are inexpensive and use little electricity.

Heat guns may be frustrating to use. If the paint coat is very thin, it won't bubble and blister for easy removal. Heat guns don't work well on painted metal and are ineffective on clear finishes and varnish. They also can burn surfaces or operators. Children can be easily burned by the hot, metal cover of the gun. Some models do cool rapidly to ease this hazard. A less obvious hazard can occur when removing lead-based paint, since the paint dust can be thrown into the air and inhaled. You should not try to remove lead-based paint yourself. It is a job for a professional.

HEAT TAPE

Homeowners and mobile home residents who use electric heat tapes to prevent exposed water pipes from freezing should inspect the tapes for possible fire hazards. The tapes have caused several hundred home fires. Also known as pipe heating cables, heat tapes have two wires enclosed in molded plastic insulation. They emit heat as current passes through the wires, when the cables are plugged into outlets. The tapes are often used in crawl spaces and in the substructure of homes and mobile homes. They are usually energized after the first freezing temperatures. Some tapes are plugged in year-round, and thermostats turn on the tapes whenever the outdoor temperature approaches freezing.

Improper installation of heat tapes is a frequent cause of home fires. In investigated fires involving the tapes, 40 percent of the heat tapes were over-wrapped. That is, the tape was taped over itself when the user installed it around a pipe. Here is some advice about using heat tapes:

1. Inspect all heat tapes or have a licensed electrician check them for proper installation or deteriorated electrical insulation.

2. When buying new tape, know the diameter and the total length of the pipe to be protected. Manufacturers base the recommended length of their tape on this information.

3. Older tapes should be checked for cracks in the plastic insulation or bare wires. In either case, replace the tape immediately.

4. Not all heat tapes can be used with plastic pipes. Make certain you use the recommended tape for your pipes, specifically.

5. Never use heat tape over the thermal insulation on a pipe or near flammable objects.

HOME INSULATION

The use of home insulation to help reduce heating and cooling costs has focused attention on the possible hazards of insulation, as well as how to buy and install it safely.

Fires. Fires can results from improperly installed insulation. Fibrous glass and cellulose are the most common materials used in insulation. Plastic foam, rock wool, perlite, vermiculite and wood fiber board comprise a smaller portion of the market. Many building codes allow plastic foam insulations only when they are protected from potential ignition. Some use flame-retardant chemicals to make them less combustible.

1. Fibrous glass is a mineral fiber made from molten silica. It is installed by blowing it in, or it can be bought in batts or blankets, with or without vapor barriers attached to the insulation. Although fibrous glass is naturally fire-resistant, the paper vapor barriers used in some products are flammable. There may be a fire hazard where vapor barriers are left exposed.

2. Plastic foam insulation used in the home is commonly one of the following:

   • Polystyrene (used in board form).

   • Polyurethane (used in board form or sprayed in place).

   • Urea formaldehyde (UF) (generally "foamed" in place, between studs and walls). This insulation can release formaldehyde vapors into the home, causing a variety of health problems. Those with respiratory problems or allergies may suffer more.

   If you decide to buy UF you should select a reliable and experienced contractor and make sure the installer is factory-trained. Ask for written verification of this training. Also, obtain a written statement of specific corrective action the contractor will take if problems arise, including who is responsible for the removal of UF foam insulation if that should become necessary.

3. Cellulose insulation is generally made from ground-up or shredded paper, and must meet the Consumer Product Safety Commission's standard for flammability and corrosiveness. Cellulose insulation is normally treated with chemicals to make it smolder-resistant and fire-resistant. Improper treatment, however, may present a flammability hazard or cause corrosion problems.

More concerns. Adding insulation to deficient electrical systems may increase the risk of fire. Common fire-starting locations may be junction points, such as screws or wire nuts, surface mounted lights and overfused wires. It is also possible that wire surrounded by thermal insulation can operate at more than the 140°F temperature limit allowed by building codes.

Consumers may want to have their home electrical systems inspected by an electrician *before* insulating. Immediate repair should be done if there are any of the following signs:

1. Dimming or flickering lights.
2. Fuses blowing regularly or circuit breakers tripping often.
3. Electrical sparks or glowing from outlets.
4. Overheated outlets or cover plates.

Installation. Careful installation with proper clearance is necessary for *all types of insulation*. If placed too close to light fixtures and flues, even insulation that meets standards can trap heat, causing smoldering and fire. This is a job for qualified installers, but if you are doing it yourself, consider this:

1. Read the instructions on the package carefully before installing.
2. Be careful, when insulating, not to lift or pull wires. As wiring ages, electrical insulation becomes brittle, and handling can damage it.
3. Do not let insulation block attic eaves. Ventilation helps prevent moisture build-up, which lessens the insulation qualities and leads to corrosion and other deterioration of building materials.
4. A vapor barrier, used with insulation, helps prevent moisture from getting into the insulation. See your local building code official for requirements.
5. Since some fire-retardant chemicals and fibrous glass may cause skin irritation, wear protective clothing, such as long sleeves, long trousers, gloves and goggles. Wash these separately from other clothes.
6. Wear a dust mask or a single-use respirator to avoid breathing small fibers.
7. Wear a hard hat or similar head covering to avoid head injury.
8. If you must install insulation during warm weather, do it in the coolest part of the day to avoid heat exhaustion.

9. Check all light fixtures in areas being insulated and use only the correct wattage bulbs. If a label stating the bulb wattage is not on the fixture, it is probably rated for a 60 watt bulb. Bulbs with wattage that is too high may cause fixtures to overheat.
10. Be sure to use properly sized fuses or circuit breakers to avoid overheating of electrical circuits.
11. Look for a label, required for most insulation products, that states: "This product meets the amended Consumer Product Safety Commission standards for flame resistance and corrosiveness of cellulose insulation."

MOBILE HOMES

There are several potential hazards to consider with mobile homes, but the major one is fire. Some mobile homes present serious fire hazards. For example:

- On a cold, snowy day, the Roberts family put a small space heater in their mobile home living room for additional heat. The heater ignited the carpet, which, in turn, ignited the wall paneling and spread the fire to the bedroom. The occupants, who couldn't escape through one of the exit doors because it was blocked with a table, perished in the fire.

Characteristics of mobile home fires

1. Many ignition sources. In the past, most mobile homes had aluminum wiring, which is associated with fires. Another common ignition source is faulty furnaces or heaters that have misaligned flues, which can direct hot air at highly flammable paneling.
2. Rapid fire spread. This happens because of the low ceilings, narrow corridors, highly flammable, thin plywood paneling and combustible interior furnishings. Because plywood paneling is used instead of gypsum board, which is

176

usually used in houses, flames can spread quickly down the corridors.

3. Trouble getting out. This problem often arises because of blocked exits. Some mobile homes have windows of sizes that make them unable to be used for emergency exits.

High winds. Another mobile home hazard is the danger of tipping over in high winds. There are tie-downs that can hold down a mobile home and keep it from sliding sideways off its blocks, however, they must be installed before the home reaches the site.

Jurisdictions. The responsibility for the flammability of mobile homes is not clearly defined. The National Highway Traffic Safety Administration has set standards for passenger vehicle interiors, but it is unclear if those standards extend to mobile homes. The Consumer Product Safety Commission has authority to regulate consumer products used in mobile homes, including heaters, electrical fixtures and appliances. But the Commission's jurisdiction does not extend to the basic structure of the mobile home itself. The mobile home industry does have voluntary standards.

Voluntary standards
1. Fire stopping in walls and partitions.
2. Minimum flammability standards for interior finishes.
3. Two exit doors for an unobstructed means of escape.
4. At least one outside window in each bedroom, for escape.
5. At least one smoke detector outside each sleeping area.
6. No more than two LP-gas containers (45 pounds each), which must not be accessible from the inside, on the mobile home.
7. An LP-gas safety relief valve on each container.

8. Minimum strength requirements for the gas piping systems.
9. No appliance connectors through walls, floors, ceilings or partitions.
10. Oil tank vented at the bottom and not accessible from the inside.
11. All fuel-burning appliances (except ranges, ovens, light and clothes dryers) must not have their combustion systems accessible to the inside (this prevents carbon monoxide and other poisonous gases from getting into the mobile home).
12. Heat-producing appliances far enough from doors, drapes or any other combustible material to provide for safe clearance.
13. Air ducts of certain sizes and air-tight.
14. Electrical installations made according to certain standards.

This standard has been adopted by most states. The Veterans Administration and Federal Housing Administration (FHA) require it in their mobile home loan programs.

Suggestions for a safer mobile home
1. Keep all outside doors free for use as exits. In the winter, clear snow away from all outside doors, not just the one you use most often.
2. Install push-out escape windows with screens and storm windows that do not impede rapid escape. This is especially important in bedrooms.
3. Buy smoke detectors and fire extinguishers, and put a detector outside each sleeping area. All mobile homes built in recent years have smoke detectors.
4. Watch for warm switches or outlet face plates, the smell of burning plastic or flickering lights, which may signal a fire hazard with the electrical wiring. If these signals are present, seek expert advice quickly.
5. Be aware of the many appliances and fuels that can start fires in your mobile

home. Be ready to leave quickly if a fire does start.

6. Remember that unvented space heaters and fuel-burning appliances can produce deadly amounts of carbon monoxide. Keep windows open to assure enough ventilation when you use these devices.

Buying a mobile home

When you buy a mobile home, be sure that it conforms to state regulations. If your state does not have requirements for mobile homes, compare those homes that meet a voluntary standard with those that do not.

MOBILE TABLES

Mobile folding tables are singled out for attention because of their involvement in accidents with school children. The mobile table is usually found in school cafeterias and meeting rooms. However, the same tables, or smaller versions, are used in homes for games, picnics, etc.

These tables are tall and heavy and, when folded for storage, can easily tip over and fall. Often 6 feet or more, they can weigh 350 pounds. Some of the benches have seats attached and are heavier. The tables have wheels so they can be moved and unloaded in the desired location.

Most accidents happen during afterschool or nonschool activities. The table can overturn when the wheel or bottom edge hits a child's foot or when a child tries to ride on the table when it is moved. Typically, two children move the table, with one child pulling and the other pushing. The child pulling is likely to be injured or killed. To avoid injuries and deaths from the folded tables tipping over, follow these rules:

1. Do not allow children to move the folded tables.
2. Do not allow children to play with the folded tables.

3. Keep children away from the folded tables while they are being moved. Once the tables start to fall, it is difficult to stop them.

PLASTICS

Plastics are widely used today in many home applications, such as furniture stuffing and covering, carpet pads, insulation, paneling and appliances. They also are used in the interiors of cars, planes and mobile homes. Usually, plastic materials replace traditional combustible materials, such as wood, paper, wool, cotton and silk, and often replace noncombustible glass and metal. It is important to note that plastics, like traditional materials, are combustible. Once ignited, they give off heat, smoke and toxic gases.

Combustibility

Because there are more than 20 different families of plastics, it is difficult to give general combustibility characteristics to all plastics. Nonetheless, fire hazards of certain plastics include one or more of the following:

1. Rapid flame spread. Once ignited, some plastic materials burn rapidly and can spread to nearby materials.
2. Extreme heat. Some plastics generate high temperatures quickly when they ignite.
3. Large amounts of dense smoke. Some burning plastics will produce dense smoke when burned. Generally, those with flame retardants produce more smoke when forced to burn, than untreated materials.
4. Toxic gases. Like other organic materials, such as wood, paper and wool, plastics produce carbon monoxide when they burn. Some of these materials may also produce other typical toxic combustion gases, such as aldehydes and hydrogen cyanide. At times, synthetic materials produce acid gases, such as hydrogen chloride. In most cases, people die from

smoke and carbon monoxide gas before the flames reach them.

Forms. Plastics come in many forms. Polyesters, nylons and some others are often used to make fabrics. We find other plastics, such as polyurethane foams, in upholstered furniture and mattresses (when formulated as flexible), and as interior insulation (when rigid). They are also sprayed on walls and ceilings. Some restaurants have had tragic fires when their foam-covered walls caught fire and spread fire very quickly.

Polystyrene can be made in a rigid form that looks remarkably like wood and is often used for furniture and interior trim. Polyvinyl chloride (PVC) and acrylonitrile-butadiene-styrene (ABS) also can be rigid and are used in many installations, such as in plastic plumbing.

Burn characteristics. Different plastics burn differently and so require different safety considerations. Some plastics will form a char and resist burning when the heat source or flame is taken away. Some will burn quite rapidly once ignited. All will produce smoke and toxic gases, but of different kinds and to different degrees.

Retardants. Chemical retardants can be applied to plastics during manufacturing. To meet safety standards, these chemicals are becoming more widely used. However, while flame retardants make the products more difficult to ignite, materials containing flame retardants generally give off more smoke and toxic gases when they burn. This effect is true not only for plastics, but also for natural materials, such as wood, cotton and wool.

Reducing hazards

Following are ways to reduce potential hazards associated with burning plastics:

1. Plastics. Like other organic materials, plastics will burn. Some need only a small ignition source, like a match or a hot electric coil.
2. Combustible products from plastics. Plastic products and other natural materials are toxic when burning.
3. Fire prevention. Normal fire prevention steps will prevent accidental fires for combustibles found in and around the home. These steps include the use of a smoke detectors placed outside bedroom doors or at the top of stairwells to provide early warnings if fires occur.

REFUSE BINS

Because many deaths and injuries are related to refuse bins, where garbage and trash are stored before disposal, they should be used only for that purpose. Although unstable bins of more than 1 cubic yard are not available, except by renting or leasing through a refuse collection service, they continue to be a hazard.

- A 4-year-old boy was trying to climb into a 200-pound refuse container. He pulled on the slanted side and the bin fell on him. He was dead on arrival at the hospital.
- A 6-year-old girl and her playmate were swinging on the trunion bars of the 3.3 cubic yard bin located near her apartment building, when the bin tipped over onto the girls. The girl died shortly after the accident from a crushed chest and her playmate suffered a broken wrist.

Some bins are very dangerous because they are unstable. Typically used around apartment complexes, housing developments, schools, parks and stores, these heavy metal bins can tip over easily, crushing anyone playing on them or standing nearby. In addition, their heavy lids can be hazardous. The lids can be propped partially open and can fall shut, crushing fingers or entrapping children, who might be playing inside.

The unstable bins have a sloping front side. Their instability is increased by some features, including:

1. Wheels.
2. Lids that, when left open, can tilt the balance toward the slanted side.
3. Trash accumulated along the slanted side.
4. Being placed on an uneven, slanted or soft piece of ground.

Slant-sided refuse bins can be modified to make them more stable. Examples of possible modifications include:

1. Metallic extensions can be welded to the corner of the sloping front side to keep the bin from tipping over completely.
2. Moving the wheels further forward under the slanted side, to provide a wider, more stable base.

Newer bins meet standards that address instability. Meanwhile, young and old should stay away from all bins, except to place trash or garbage in them. Deposit refuse only from the side of the straight end, not along the slanted side. Parents, teachers, apartment owners and managers should instruct children:

1. Don't play in or around refuse bins.
2. Don't use them as hiding places.
3. Don't swing on the handles or top edges of the bins.

STAIRS

Each year, about 365,000 children and adults (1,000 per day) require emergency room treatment for injuries sustained on stairs, ramps and landings. Most accidents from falls take place on stairs.

- Harriet was carrying groceries up the back steps. It had snowed lightly the night before and ice had formed on the stairs. The groceries obscured her vision somewhat, and she stepped on a patch of ice and fell. She broke her left arm.

- There was only a dim light bulb at the top of the basement stairs, which were used for storage of newspapers and small boxes. John managed to step over a box, but he lost his footing and fell down the stairway, spraining both wrists and scraping his arms.

- Susan was playing in her stocking feet, running back and forth at the top of the stairway. She slipped on a small throw rug at the top of the stairs and continued to slide down three stairs to the landing. She suffered bruises and a sprained ankle.

Accident patterns

1. Weather factors and obscured vision. Ice and snow are frequent problems on outside stairs. Obscured vision, while carrying packages or laundry, is a factor in falls on stairs, both inside and outside.
2. Lighting conditions and obstacles on stairs. Poor lighting hinders vision. Boxes, toys and other objects can cause people to trip.
3. Slippery tread surfaces. This includes loose carpeting, polished hardwood, slippery footwear and running near stairs, which can lead to falls.
4. Handrails. Some falls result from loose railings. Others happen when people have their arms full and don't use the railings.
5. Stair condition. Broken steps, unstable staircases and loose concrete can cause people to fall.

Construction. Single steps are hazardous for several reasons. Often a single step is not seen and trips a person. Even when seen, it is unexpected to take one step up or down with no continuation.

1. Stairs. The run width, riser height, tread width and stairway slope all lead to the sensation of steepness on stairways.

2. The proper dimensions for interior stairs are:
   - Run width no less than 10 inches.
   - Riser height no more than 7½ inches.
   - Tread width no less than 11¼ inches.
   - Stairway slope between 30 and 35 degrees.

3. For outside stairs, the run should be wider and the risers should be lower than mentioned previously, to ease carrying heavy items.

4. Ramps. Ramps should be long enough to permit comfortable strides (at least 3 feet for one stride). The slope should be between 7 and 15 degrees.

5. Handrails. Since the accident potential is greater when going down stairs, and since most people are right-handed, single handrails should be on the right side of each descending flight of stairs. All stairs should have at least one handrail and open stairs should have railings on both sides. The space between the spindles of the handrail should not be more than the size of a child's head: about 5 inches. This prevents a child from getting caught in the handrail.

6. Landings. Flights of stairs with landings may be better than unbroken flights of stairs, because the landings may break a fall before you are seriously injured. Landings also make it easier for older people to climb, especially in flights with more than 16-inch risers. There always should be a landing (platform) at a door opening onto a flight of stairs, so you can operate the door safely and won't have an abrupt change in elevation when you step onto the stairs.

7. Slip-resistant materials. Use compressed cork, rubber treads and abrasive strips or other slip-resistant materials to cover stairs. Look for floors with a slip-resistant rating of 6 ASTM or higher.

8. Lighting. Place light switches at the top and bottom of each flight of stairs in order to light all stairs adequately. Frosted bulbs reduce glare and shadows.

9. Contrast. Don't disguise the stairs so that the edges are not highly visible. A busy pattern make it difficult to tell where the step ends. Whether carpeted or painted, the edge of the step should be distinctive.

Use of stairs

1. Wear shoes on stairs. Socks are slippery on wood and other smooth surfaces. When possible, wear corrugated-sole shoes or tennis shoes.

2. Don't carry packages in a way that blocks your vision.

3. Don't use stairs for storage and watch for toys and other objects that can cause you to trip.

4. Use the railing whenever you descend the stairs.

5. Don't climb or descend stairs from a light area to a dark area, such as an attic or basement.

6. Avoid wet or slippery stairs, indoors or out. Outside, use sand, salt or ashes on steps and try to walk on concrete with ridges, or other rougher surfaces.

7. Watch single steps. Small changes in floor level that come with one or two steps can be deceiving.

Children and stairs. Until your children are absolutely steady on the steps—at around age 3—you should block off all stairways with safety gates. Even when children do master the stairs, always keep the steps clear of objects, toys and debris. Even a single sheet of paper can be a serious hazard.

Maintenance of stairs

1. Clean off exterior stairs after every snow or heavy storm.
2. Repair broken steps, unstable staircases and loose concrete.
3. Replace any burned-out bulbs on lights that illuminate stairs.
4. Tighten any loose railings.
5. Replace worn carpets and worn rubber treads.

WATER SEALERS

There are many reports of people developing health problems after exposure to water sealers. Sometimes they have had to leave their homes because of fumes. Two people are known to have died after exposure to water sealer.

Some symptoms reported were headaches, nausea, dizziness and breathing troubles. Chemicals found in the water sealers include petroleum distillates, mineral spirits, xylene, toluene and naphtha. The label on many sealers warns against inside use.

Use solvent-based water sealers outside only, unless labels give specific instructions on how to use them safely indoors. If a solvent is labeled for indoor use, but does not advise on ventilation, open all windows and doors. Also use a fan to exhaust the air outside during application and drying.

SAFETY RECAP

1. If your home has aluminum wiring, be aware that it is acceptable, if improved to the latest codes. Make certain the changes are made.
2. Be aware of doors to avoid running into them.
3. Select strong glass doors and mark them so people realize there are glass doors in place.
4. Install a garage door opener that reverses when it encounters something on closing. Garage door openers are becoming the norm, many of them owner-installed. The best types stop and quickly reverse when they encounter something on the way down.
5. A heat gun can cause burns easily.
6. Home insulation is a hazard if the wrong kind is installed or if it is improperly installed.
7. The major hazards associated with mobile homes are the potential for fire and poisonous fumes from heating systems.
8. The primary hazard of plastics is the burning hazard presented and the poisonous fumes given off when burning.
9. Falls are a major problem with stairs. Do everything you can to make your stairs easy to use and well-lighted.

BIBLIOGRAPHY

"Household Falls: Keep Your Feet on the Ground," Abbot, Linda, *Family Safety and Health*, Itasca, IL: National Safety Council, Fall 1993, pp. 22-23.

"Children Should Not Move or Play With Mobile Folding Tables," *Consumer Product Safety Alert*, U.S. Consumer Product Safety Commission, December 1988.

"CPSC Closes in on Rules for Garage-Door Openers," *Product Safety*, Chicago, IL: National Safety Council, July/August 1992, Vol. 20, No. 4, p. 4.

"Do Not Use Indoors Any Water Sealers Intended For Outdoor Use," *Consumer Product Safety Alert*, U.S. Consumer Product Safety Commission, June 1990.

"Home Insulation Safety," *Product Safety Fact Sheet*, U.S. Consumer Product Safety Commission, July 1980.

"Non-Reversing Garage Door Openers a Hazard," *Consumer Product Safety Alert*, U.S. Consumer Product Safety Commission, October 1990.

"Pain Removers; New Products Eliminate Old Hazards," *Consumer Reports*, May 1991, p. 341.

"Refuse Bins," *Product Safety Fact Sheet*, U.S. Consumer Product Safety Commission, May 1984.

"Safety Agency Warns Consumers of Fire Hazards from Heat Tapes," *Consumer Product Safety Alert*, U.S. Consumer Product Safety Commission, October 1985.

"Safety at Home," *Parents*, September 1990, p. 112.

CHAPTER 10

GARAGE AND WORKSHOP

Before you start work or buy tools, it is important to prepare the workshop and garage environment. You need uncluttered working surfaces and nonslip floors in a well-lighted, well-ventilated workplace. You also need to be certain that paints and all appropriate implements and supplies are stored properly. This chapter provides you with the tools necessary to build safe work areas.

Workshop safety begins when you buy a tool. It pays to buy the best you can afford and buy the correct tool for the job. A well-made tool feels solid in your hand. Compare safety features on tools. Many hand tools and some electrical tools are ergonomically designed for ease of use. Electrical tools should carry the logo of a recognized testing lab, such as Underwriters Laboratories. They should feature positive off-on switches, blade guards and hand protectors.

Plan your work area so you have enough space to do a job safely. Keep work areas clean by eliminating slipping and tripping hazards and maintaining clean workbenches. Safety shoes should be worn when working in the workshop and garage.

It is a good investment of time to read owner's manuals completely and then follow the manufacturer's instructions when cleaning, lubricating and repairing tools. Smoking when you work can cause hot ashes to drop on you or get smoke in your eyes, taking your attention from the work.

BATTERIES

An estimated 6,000 people receive emergency-room treatment each year for injuries associated with wet-cell (storage) batteries and dry-cell batteries. The typical injury is a chemical burn caused by contact with battery acid.

Wet-cell batteries. The most common storage battery is in the automobile. Car batteries contain a sulfuric acid-water mix that produces highly combustible hydrogen gas. The hydrogen gas and the acid can both lead to severe injury, as in these cases.

- Henry was trying to jump-start his friend's car. While connecting the jumper cables, he unknowingly crossed the polarity by connecting a cable to the positive terminal on his battery and the other end to the negative terminal on the dead battery. As he crossed the other cable similarly, his battery exploded. He cut his hand and suffered a chemical burn to his eye from the battery acid.

- Sam was trying to jump-start his car. He connected the jumper cables to the booster battery without first removing the battery caps from his dead battery. As he was connecting the cables to the dead battery, he crossed the polarity. The battery caps flew off and battery acid splashed into his eyes, causing chemical burns.

- John took the caps off his battery to check the water level. He lighted a cigarette lighter near the holes and the battery exploded, splashing battery acid in his eyes.

- Hal was cleaning the accumulated corrosion from the terminals on his car battery with a soda solution and cleaning cloth. After he finished, he rubbed one eye before washing his hands. The acid in the corrosion caused a chemical burn in his eye.

Accident patterns. These cases illustrate the following major accident patterns linked to wet-cell (storage) batteries. Most mishaps occur when jumping, recharging or otherwise servicing batteries.

1. Batteries explode or battery caps fly off, and the battery acid splashes on the victim, causing chemical burns. This often happens when the batteries are jumped or charged, usually when connecting jumper (booster) cables to the incorrect poles. Remove battery caps before connecting the booster cables. Connect terminals of the same polarity.

   Explosions also occur when a spark from the cable connection detonates the combustible hydrogen gas in the battery. Holding a flame held near the open battery holes in order to check the water level also can cause the battery gas to explode.

2. Other contacts with battery acid include rubbing unwashed hands in the eyes or mouth after cleaning a battery. Or being splattered by battery acid when standing by an uncapped battery, while the car motor is running. Battery corrosion can fly into a person's eye when cleaning or repairing battery cables.

Makers of auto batteries must place warning labels on batteries and on boxes that hold batteries, to warn consumers of the dangers from accumulated gas and battery acid.

Keep all flames away from your car battery. Do not light matches or lighters to check the acid (fluid) level of batteries. Do not smoke when working near a battery. In addition, when you jump-start a car, carefully connect the booster cables, one at a time. Don't touch connected booster cables together. A spark from the connection could cause battery gas to explode.

First aid. If you work on your car, you should know the first aid treatment for battery acid spills on the skin or in the eyes:

1. If acid spills on the skin, wash off the skin area at once with plenty of soap and water. If a chemical burn develops, see a doctor.
2. If acid enters the eye, flood it with water and see a doctor as soon as possible. Battery acids can cause blindness.

Jump-starts

1. Do not jump a frozen battery. Before you begin, check to see if ice is in the battery water.
2. Be sure that the booster battery and the dead battery are the same voltage. Twelve-volt batteries have six caps, and six-volt batteries generally have only three caps. Most autos today have 12-volt systems.
3. Turn off accessories, such as lights, windshield wipers and radios, in both cars. Turn off the ignition in both cars.
4. Place both cars in neutral or park, and set the parking brakes. Make sure the cars don't touch each other.
5. Remove vent caps from both batteries. If the battery fluid is low, add water. Cover vent holes with a damp cloth, or if the caps are of the safety vent type, replace the vent caps before attaching the jumper cables.
6. Attach one end of the jumper cable to the booster battery's positive terminal (identified by a red color, "+," "P" or "pos"). Twist the clamps back and forth on the terminal to ensure good metal-to-metal contacts. Attach the other end of the same cable to the positive terminal of the dead battery.
7. Attach one end of the second cable to the booster battery's negative terminal (identified by a black color, "-," "N" or "neg"). Be sure the clamps do not touch the clamps of the other cable. Twist the

clamps back and forth on the negative terminal to ensure good metal-to-metal contacts.

8. Attach the other end of the same cable to the engine block of the car with the dead battery, or any other accessible metallic part attached to the engine block that is not chrome-plated, heavily rusted or covered with grease. This connection should be made as far away as possible from the dead battery so that if any sparking occurs, it will be away from the combustible gases produced by the battery.

9. Start the car with the dead battery. If it does not start quickly, then start the other car before trying again to start the car with the dead battery. Let both cars run for a few minutes. Remove the cables in exactly the reverse order from that used to connect them. Replace the vent caps.

10. Using the jumper cable requires following precise procedures. If you have doubts about how to jump a battery, ask an auto mechanic for a demonstration before you need to do it alone.

Batteries in boats. Wet-cell batteries are common in boating, and the general rules for wet-cell batteries apply. However, the confined locations of boat batteries and the proximity of gasoline fumes provides several new hazards. These hazards are important enough for you to refer to boating safety rules on refueling, battery hazards and battery care.

Dry-cell batteries. Dry-cell batteries are made from various chemicals, such as carbon-zinc, alkaline or mercury. They are used in flashlights, portable radios, battery-operated toys and other household items.

• Francis, 4, was playing with a battery-operated toy that resembled a flying saucer. As she whirled the toy, acid from the batteries escaped and splashed her, causing chemical burns on her face.

• One of the two batteries in a hand-held slide viewer exploded and tore the back off the viewer. The battery contents splattered on the wall. Because the viewer was not in use at the time, no one was injured.

Accident patterns. These cases illustrate the following accident patterns associated with dry-cell batteries. Included are suggestions for using these batteries safely.

1. Battery leakage. The chemical substance leaks out of the battery and may cause chemical burns or skin irritation. Monthly, check batteries inside flashlights and other battery-operated devices for signs of leakage or corrosion. Replace bad batteries. For seldom-used products, remove the batteries and store them separately.

2. Batteries explode. Sometimes this occurs when the polarity of a battery in a group is reversed. Always follow directions for placing batteries according to positive-negative poles. Never dispose of batteries in an incinerator or fire, since intense heat may cause batteries to explode.

There also have been cases in which children chew on batteries, and release the chemical substance on themselves. Caution children not to put batteries in their mouths. Keep loose batteries out of the reach of children. Batteries should be tightly enclosed in toys and not readily accessible to young children.

Do not try to recharge dry-cell batteries unless they are labeled as rechargeable. Recharging a nonrechargeable dry-cell battery causes a buildup of gases, if the battery has no vent. The gases may produce enough pressure to make the battery explode.

Chemical burns, household dry-cell batteries. Dry-cell batteries can cause chemical burns if they rupture and the contents are spilled on a person. Household dry-cell batteries can overheat and rupture in several ways:

1. Recharging the wrong battery or using the wrong charger. If you try to recharge a battery not intended to be recharged, the battery can overheat and rupture. *If you have a rechargeable battery, be sure to use the battery charger intended for the size and type of battery that you have.* Do not use an automobile battery charger to recharge flashlight batteries, because the batteries could rupture.

2. Mixing batteries. If you use alkaline and carbon-zinc batteries in the same appliances or if you mix old batteries with new, freshly charged ones in the same appliance, the batteries can overheat and rupture. *Always use a complete set of new batteries of the same type when replacing batteries.*

3. Putting batteries in backwards. If a battery is reversed (positive end where negative end belongs and vice versa), it can overheat and rupture. This happens when young children install batteries backward. Warn children not to take out or replace the batteries. *Parents should install batteries in household appliances and children's toys.*

Miniature (button) batteries. Electronics have progressed so much that miniature batteries, such as those found in hearing aids and watches, are common in many devices around the home. Because of their small size, they present a unique and attractive hazard to children and pets. They even can be mistaken for pills. If swallowed, they are poison and choking hazards. Following are a few rules for miniature batteries:

1. If one is missing, assume it was dropped where children or pets might find it, and locate it before they do.
2. Keep them out of the reach of children.
3. Never put them in the mouth.
4. Don't allow children to play with these or any batteries.
5. Check medication closely to be certain batteries have not mixed with pills and tablets.

TOOLS

Many people with the greatest of business and industry know-how forget what they know when they start working in home workshops. Sometimes tools are not used properly, even though it is easy to determine the correct method. Just as often, people fail to take precautions at home that they take on the job.

Using the wrong tool for a job is a common accident cause. Remember: Injury prevention is 10 percent protection and 90 percent self-education. Experience is a more painful and costly way to learn than studying and following directions.

The following are the basic steps suggested by the National Safety Council to reduce injuries with hand and portable tools:

1. Use the right fit of tool. Using a properly designed tool helps do the job better, faster and with less work. Nearly every type of hand tool has been revised to be easier to use.

   - The tool should allow you to work with your wrists straight and elbows close to the body.
   - Be certain the handles don't dig into the palm of the hand.
   - Grips should distribute force over as wide an area as possible without pressure on the sides of the finger.
   - Make sure handles with grooves for fingers fit your fingers.
   - Avoid handles that are smooth and slippery.

2. Use the right position. With most hand tools, workers must keep their arms and shoulders too high as they work. This leads to fatigue and perhaps tendonitis. While not a major problem around the home, the right position will make a big difference in your job quality and avoiding physical stress in longer jobs.

3. Select the right tool for the job. Do not permit unsafe practices, such as striking hardened faces of hand tools together (hammer to hammer, etc.), using a file as a pry, a wrench as a hammer or pliers as a wrench.

4. Keep tools in good condition. Inspect your tools for damage before using. Don't use badly worn tools until repaired. Don't use wrenches with cracked or broken jaws, screwdrivers with broken parts or handles, badly worn power cords or broken plugs and tools that have improper or removed grounding systems.

5. Use tools the proper way. Avoid using screwdrivers on objects held in the hands, pulling knives toward the body and failing to ground electrical equipment, all of which are common causes of accidents.

6. Keep tools in a safe place. Many accidents happen when tools fall from above, and when sharp tools are carried in pockets or left in tool boxes with cutting edges exposed. Carry and store tools so the blade or the point is protected.

These simple rules cover only part of the safety concerns for tools at home, but it is clear that good workplace practices should be used at home. Following are more common sense rules, which are often ignored:

1. Secure work. Use clamps or a vise to hold your work. It is safer than holding it in your hands and it frees both hands to operate the tool.

2. Don't force a tool. It will do the job better and safer working at the rate for which it was designed.

3. Maintain tools with care. Keep tools sharp and clean for better and safer performance. Follow instructions for lubricating and changing accessories.

4. Keep work areas clean. Cluttered work areas and benches invite accidents.

Hammers

In 1991, 50,000 people received emergency room treatment for injuries from hammers, the most widely used hand tool. The most frequent injury is striking the thumb or fingers (or the fingers of a partner) while hammering a nail. These accidents usually result in cuts or bruises and sometimes in broken bones. Other injuries result from accidents such as these:

- A mechanic was using a steel ball-peen hammer to drive a bolt into an axle, when a chip from the hammer flew off and hit him in the leg.

- A young boy swung his hammer back and the loose head flew off and struck his brother, who was standing nearby. His brother needed several stitches in his leg to close the wound.

- One man thought he was using the right tool, a claw hammer, to pull a nail. The nail was very long and when it came out, it flew into the air, just missing his face. He should have used a pry bar for better leverage.

Those illustrations represent the following hazards:

1. Chipping metal. Pieces of metal can chip off the head of a hammer if you strike it on its side or on any surface that is harder than the hammer head (such as a cold chisel or other very hard metal) or when you strike one hammer against another.

2. Head flying off. If the handle is cracked or if the head is loose, the head can fly off when you swing the hammer. This can injure a bystander as well.

3. Wrong tool for the job. To reduce these hazards, consider the following suggestions for selecting, using and maintaining hammers.

Selection of hammers

Choose a hammer that is the right type, size and weight for the job. A medium weight (12-ounce to 13-ounce) claw hammer is good for general purposes. Avoid fragile cast-iron hammers for anything but very light duty tasks (such as driving small nails). The hammer face should be larger than the head of the object you are striking. For example, if you are striking a half-inch cold chisel, you need a hammer with a face at least 1 inch in diameter. The hammer should feel well-balanced.

Use of hammers

1. Use a regular claw hammer for wood nails, not for masonry nails or cold chisels, because the claw hammer could chip or break when striking the heavy, hard metal.
2. Use heavier, bigger hammers (such as ball-peen or double-faced blacksmith hammers) for cold chisels, masonry walls, hardened nails and spikes. The hammer face should be larger than the chisel or other surface it strikes.
3. Strike the surface squarely, not at an angle, to prevent chipping the metal.
4. Don't strike with the side of the hammer.
5. Do not strike one hammer against another, because they could chip and send pieces flying.
6. Wear safety goggles to protect your eyes.
7. Wear heavy gloves to protect your hands.
8. Never use a hammer with a loose head or cracked handle.
9. Hold a hammer near the end of the handle for more hitting power. To start a nail, hold it in place and tap it gently

a few times until it sets firmly. Hit it squarely, straight in.

10. To avoid hammer marks on the wood or other surfaces, use a nail set or another nail to drive a nail the last 1/8 inch into the wood.
11. To remove a nail, use the claw end of the hammer. Place a small block of wood under the head of the hammer to avoid marking the wood.

Maintenance of hammers

1. Tighten loose heads, if possible.
2. Discard chipped or dented hammers.

Screwdrivers

After hammers, screwdrivers are the most commonly misused tool. They are misused for chiseling, scraping, punching, scoring and prying. You need two types of screwdrivers for household repairs: a straight blade and a Phillips head. Both come in various sizes. The blade of the screwdriver should snugly fit the slot in the screw.

1. When using a screwdriver, push against the head of the screw as you turn it.
2. It's easier to put a screw into wood if you make a hole first with a nail or drill. Rub wax or soap on the screw threads to make the screw go in easier.
3. Use the right size screwdriver for the job. Match the screwdriver blade to the pattern and size of the threaded fastener.
4. Use drivers with insulated handles on electrical work.
5. Never strike a screwdriver with a hammer unless the screwdriver has a shank extending through the handle for that purpose.
6. Wear safety goggles to protect your eyes.

Pliers

1. Use pliers to hold a nut while you turn a bolt with a screwdriver.

2. Use pliers to remove nails or brads. Pull the nail out at the same angle it was driven in. Use small blocks under the pliers if you need leverage.

3. Use pliers to bend or cut wire or to straighten a bent nail.

4. Use pliers to turn nuts. Wrap tape or cloth around the nut to avoid scratching it.

5. Use pliers with a spring return so that the tool opens automatically in use.

6. Remember when doing electrical work, that handles with cushion grips are for comfort, not insulation.

7. Wear safety goggles to protect your eyes.

POWER SAWS

Each year, power saws cause nearly 40,000 injuries serious enough to require emergency-room treatment.

- Terry was "topping" a gate post of a cedar redwood fence with his saw. He turned off the saw and held it in one hand as he lowered it. The blade continued to spin and the blade guard stayed in a retracted position. The blade hit his leg, lacerating his knee.

- Mike was ripping a board with his table saw. At least a half-inch of blade was above the stock. The blade hit a knot in the board and kicked the board out. Mike's hand was drawn across the blade, and two of his fingers were amputated.

- Barry completed his cut and turned off the table saw. He reached across the saw, but the blade continued to rotate. His thumb and two fingers were amputated.

- Jay was ripping a walnut board, using a push stick. As he completed the cut, he slipped in sawdust on the floor. His free hand hit the blade, severely lacerating his fingers.

- Larry was kneeling in wet grass, cutting fence posts. The insulation of the lead, from the "field coil" of his saw to the switch, was broken. He received a fatal electric shock.

Accident patterns. These cases indicate the major accident patterns linked with power saws.

1. Contact with the blade.
   - A blade guard either is not on the saw, was removed or is malfunctioning. The blade guard on portable circular saws can malfunction by staying retracted after completing a cut.
   - A kickback occurs when the blade jams or binds in the wood and throws the saw toward the operator (with portable circular saws), or throws the wood toward the operator (with a stationary saw). The operator's hand can also be drawn into the blade.
   - The blade keeps rotating after the power is turned off.
   - Slippery floors, sometimes from accumulated sawdust or scrap, can lead to falls.

2. Electrical shock. Saws should be double insulated or have three-prong grounded plugs. Many homes, however, don't have wall outlets to hold three-prong plugs, and proper ground connections can't be guaranteed.

Selection of power saws

1. A blade guard is necessary. Buy a saw with the guard you feel most comfortable using, and keep it on the saw always. Some types of saws, such as saber saws, cannot be designed with a guard, so be especially careful to avoid contact with the blade.

2. Ask a salesperson for anti-kickback fingers on table saws to help prevent kickbacks.

3. Test the saw to see if the blade stops *immediately* after power is turned off. (Dynamic braking is an added safety feature.)

4. Be sure to insulate your saw against shock, by double-insulation on saws or three-prong grounded plugs (if used with the proper socket or adapter).

5. A Ground Fault Circuit Interrupter in the housing circuit also prevents shocks from electrical appliances.

Using power saws

1. Read the instruction manual carefully before use.

2. Dress appropriately. Wear closed, sturdy shoes and safety glasses. Don't wear loose clothing or jewelry that may catch in moving parts.

3. Always keep the blade guard and other safety devices in place.

4. Always keep children away from the work area. Never allow them to operate power saws.

5. Use the proper socket for a three-prong plug or use a grounded adapter. Don't remove the third prong.

6. To prevent shock, don't use a saw in damp or wet areas.

7. Use rubber or other nonslip matting around the work area. Keep the floor clean.

8. Use a good strong light to illuminate the work.

9. Keep electric cords clear of cutting.

10. Keep the widest, heaviest part of a portable saw's base on the supported part of any material being cut.

11. Use a wood or sheet metal barrier as a guard on the saw blade beneath an unenclosed table.

12. Use the proper blade and install it properly.
    - Carbon-tipped blades not more than 1/2-tooth height through material.
    - Flat-ground blades, and blades with a set to the teeth, should not be more than 1-tooth height above the work.
    - Hollow-ground and planer blades go through as far as possible.

13. Use a push stick during ripping cuts with stationary saws, to keep hands away from blades.

14. Do not force the cut; the saw operates at its own speed. Forcing the wood through the saw causes the material to kick back.

15. Never let the saw run unattended.

16. Wait until the motor is off, blade stopped and saw unplugged before repairing or cleaning around the saw.

Maintenance, storing power saws

1. When repairing or replacing a three-prong grounded plug, be certain to connect the wires correctly. Otherwise, the saw may be a shock hazard. Only qualified electricians should repair plugs.

2. Store saws in high or locked places, away from children.

3. Keep the blade sharp, clean and lubricated.

4. Remove gum buildup on blades (it could cause binding) by rubbing blades with steel wool saturated with ammonia.

5. Frequently inspect and replace the carbon brushes before they wear low.

6. Inspect blades for cracks and replace promptly. A cracked blade may suggest a problem in the saw's operation.

PAINT SPRAY GUNS

Airless, paint spray guns, which offer very rapid paint application, save painters much time. But they have caused some very serious injuries to both inexperienced users and professional painters.

The airless sprayer unit expels its contents under very high pressure, much higher than that in normal compressed air spray guns. The paint sprays from the gun with enough velocity at close range to go through the skin, much like the contents of a vaccine gun. The injury is difficult to treat, as there is often little that can be done to remove the injected paint. Amputation of the injured parts often is the only treatment. Following are examples of accidents with airless paint spray guns:

- A 48-year-old man, cleaning an airless sprayer, was directing a turpentine-paint mixture into a rag, held in his hand. The high-pressure stream struck and exposed a portion of his left middle finger and the finger later had to be amputated.

- A 20-year-old professional painter, using an airless paint gun, put his finger over the nozzle of the gun and pulled the trigger in an effort to restore lost pressure. The finger had to be partially amputated.

Though mostly professional painters use these guns, anyone can rent one. Low-cost models are on the market. The equipment is sometimes modified to reduce the chance of serious injury. Several models have a nozzle guard that extends ¾ inch to 1 1/8 inches beyond the spray jet. Owners of earlier models should have received a fix kit.

Precautions. Professional and non-professional painters alike should observe these guidelines when using airless spray guns:

1. Read all guidance provided by the manufacturer. If renting the equipment, be sure instructions accompany it. Ask for a demonstration of proper use.
2. Check for a protective nozzle guard that goes beyond the gun's spray jet.
3. Never try to unclog the nozzle of a pressurized gun with the finger.
4. Shut off the pump and release the pressure in the hose before taking apart the gun.
5. The sprayer unit should have a trigger guard to prevent discharge if the gun is dropped.
6. If you are hurt while using a sprayer gun, see a doctor immediately. Be sure

to tell the doctor about the high pressure and velocity of the spray equipment, to get the proper treatment.

Ventilation. Air or airless spray guns may be used for inside painting projects. However, the room must be very well-ventilated and you must use a respirator to protect your lungs. Safety glasses are also urged.

Outside spraying. Although not a health hazard in the usual sense, the overspray is a concern with outside spraying. Overspray can float for long distances and settle on passing or parked cars, windows and porches. Some communities even have laws against outdoor spray painting, so check the codes before spray painting.

Spray outside only on a windless day and never spray around a corner or over a roof without first blocking the over spray.

ELECTRIC WORKSHOP TOOLS

Power tools are an efficient and low-cost way to build or make repairs around the home. Some of the same features that make these tools useful—sharp, rapidly moving parts and electrical current—also make them dangerous. This is especially true if they are defective, in poor repair or misused.

Records indicate that about 30,000 persons receive emergency-room treatment each year for injuries associated with these home workshop tools: drills, sanders, routers, lathes, grinders, jointers, planers, shapers, welders, soldering guns; and accessories that can be used with the tools, such as torches and work lights. Drills are the most common of these tools and cause more injuries than the other products.

Power saws account for an estimated 70,000 injuries, and chain saws for about 64,000 injuries. They are discussed in another section of this chapter.

Most injuries linked to electrical home tools are from contact with the cutting surfaces, electrocutions and shocks, fires and flying pieces of wood and other stock.

Contact with the cutting surface.
A leading cause of power tool injuries is contact with the blades, bits or other sharp turning surface on drills, sanders, routers, lathes, grinders, jointers, planers and shapers. Following are examples of these types of injuries and suggestions for avoiding them:

- John was guiding a board through a jointer when his left little finger went into the unguarded blade and was amputated.

- Bob was thinning a plywood board with a planer, when a knot in the board caught against the blade. The board kicked back and Bob's hand came in contact with the blade, which amputated the tip of his left thumb.

- As he was drilling through wrought iron, Dick exerted too much pressure on the drill. The drill bit broke and shattered. The pieces cut deeply into his hand.

- Although Mark knew he should roll up his sleeves when using power tools, he didn't. His sleeve caught in the lathe, which pulled most of the sleeve and part of his arm into the machine until his body fell forward. In this position he couldn't shut the lathe and received a contusion to his forearm.

Accident patterns

1. The tool does not have a blade guard, or the guard is malfunctioning. A broken guard spring, for instance, may prevent a guard, such as a leg-of-mutton guard, from swinging back to cover the blade. On tools such as jointers, overhead guards are safer since they have no spring to prevent covering the work. Pushing work underneath overhead guards can be difficult. The alternative leg-of-mutton guards are good only when used with a push board. Otherwise, the hands may contact the exposed blade. It is important to keep hands as far away from the cutting surface as possible.

   On portable tools, look for a "deadman" switch. This shuts off power when hand pressure is released, and stops the tool immediately after power is turned off.

2. Kickback on cutting tools exposes the hands to the blade or bit when stock is violently ejected. Kickback can be caused by cutting too deeply or quickly or cutting stock with knots, embedded nails or screws. Keep blades, bits, wheels and other attachments sharp, clean and lubricated, and cutters securely fastened in place to help prevent kickbacks and broken attachments. When feasible, move portable tools *away* from hands and body instead of toward them.

3. Blades, bits and other attachments can shatter and cut as they break, when too much pressure is placed on the tool. To avoid broken parts, don't use attachments meant for larger or smaller tools or higher tool speeds. When practical, don't start the motor when the bit or blade is in contact with the work. Finally, don't use undue pressure on the tool when in operation.

4. Tool users can be cut when repairing or carrying tools without first unplugging them, or from not following other safety precautions. Children, too, are injured when playing with tools that are left plugged in or are not stored out of their reach.

To avoid accidents involving contact with cutting surfaces:

1. Look for comfortable, securely attached handles on tools.

2. Look for an on/off switch located where it cannot be turned on accidentally.

3. Read the instruction manual thoroughly before using a new, borrowed or rented

tool, or a new model, to better understand its capabilities and hazards.

4. Dress properly. Wear sturdy shoes and safety glasses (to protect against flying particles). Don't wear loose clothing, ties or jewelry that may catch in moving parts. Roll up loose shirt sleeves.

5. To avoid falling into or dropping a portable tool, don't extend your reach.

6. Don't work when tired, rushed or anxious.

7. Keep the work area clear of loose material. To avoid slipping, use rubber or other nonslip matting on the floor around a well-lighted work area. Move electric cables and extension cords where they will not be a tripping hazard.

8. Wait until the motor is off, all parts stop and the tool is unplugged and cool before repairing, cleaning or carrying the tool.

9. When drilling in any material, wear safety glasses or goggles. Drills can stir up a lot of sawdust and flip metal shavings and chips across a room. Gloves are also a good idea when working with metal, masonry and glass.

10. Always keep children away from the work area. Never allow them to operate tools.

11. Store tools in a high or locked place away from children.

Failure to use a vise or clamps to hold work in place leads to injuries. If the hand or tool slips, or kickback occurs, the hand and fingers can be exposed to the cutting surface.

When using a drill, always lock the work in a vise, or clamp it to a table when drilling into the work, unless the work fastens to something. Do not hand-hold the work. If you try to hold it in your hand, the drill can catch on a notch or other imperfection in the material, which can cause the work to spin out of your hand.

Electrocutions and shocks

- While wearing shorts, Harvey knelt on his bare knees against the metal threshold of a tool shed as he drilled into the metal breaker box on the floor. The floor of the shed and possibly the drill were dampened by rain. As he knelt on the wet ground and drilled, Harvey was electrocuted.

- A faulty extension cord outlet on the handle of a trouble light allegedly caused a man to be electrocuted. The very flexible plastic handle on the light bent so easily that it permitted him to touch the metal conductors in the receptacle on the handle.

Electrocution and serious shocks can be caused by lack of grounding that results in electricity flowing through the tool and into the operator's body. The danger from poor grounding is bad enough, but when working in or around water, it can be fatal.

To reduce the electrocution risk, buy a tool with a three-prong grounded plug or one with double insulation. Never remove the third prong. Always plug a three-prong plug into a properly installed three-prong socket. Improperly grounded tools are every bit as dangerous as those that are not grounded.

It is safer to use wall outlets rewired to accept three-prong plugs than to use two-prong adapters. If you must use an adapter, however, the pigtail third wire must attach to the screw holding the face plate to the wall receptacle. If the screw itself is properly grounded, this should ground any leaking current.

Shock hazards are also caused by faulty or defective wiring of the tool or a frayed electrical cord or damaged plug.

To avoid electrocutions and shocks from using power tools:

- Don't use tools in damp or wet areas. Particularly, do not stand in water or on wet or damp ground.

- If a double-insulated tool runs very hot, have it tested by a qualified electrician. The insulation may be deteriorating.

- Wear special welder's gloves or heavy leather gloves as protection against mild electrical shocks, sparks and hot metal.

- Don't use metal ladders, which can conduct electricity, when making electrical repairs.

- Prevent body contact with grounded surfaces, such as pipes, radiators, ranges, refrigerators, enclosures, etc.

- Avoid using an extension cord. If you must use one, choose an extension cord of a suitable gauge or wire size for its length and with the same ampere rating as the tool. General, lightweight extension cords are not adequate.

- Keep tools and cords away from heat, oil or sharp edges that can damage electrical insulation.

- Disconnect tools by holding the plug, not by pulling on the cord.

- Disconnect tools when not in use, before servicing, when changing blades, bits, cutters, etc.

- Immediately repair any damaged tool or one that gives off minor shocks. Have electrical cables checked for breaks, loose connections and bare wires. Check that all prongs are secure.

- Never carry a tool by the cord or hose.

- Avoid accidental start-ups. Do not hold a finger on the switch button while carrying a plugged-in tool.

- Before connecting the tool to a power source, be sure that the voltage supplied is the same as that on the tool nameplate. Using a greater voltage can result in serious injury.

Fires

- Ben, 14, and his friend were repairing a minibike in Ben's garage. They cleaned a chain with gasoline, then placed the open can on a nearby workbench. As Ben was drilling the chain, he upset the gas can on his right leg. A spark from the drill ignited his gasoline-soaked clothing and severely burned his right leg and foot.

Fires can break out when sparks from power tools ignite nearby flammable liquids, such as paint, varnish, gasoline and kerosene. The best way to prevent such fires is to keep all flammable liquids away from the work area when you operate a power tool, electrical accessory or torch. Immediately after use, always close tightly such household liquids and place them out of the reach of children.

Sparks also can ignite a cloth wrapped around a hot tool. Instead of using a cloth, turn off the tool and wait until it cools.

To prevent electrical fires, don't connect a heavy-duty tool that uses 12 or 13 amperes to the same circuit on which another appliance is operating. An overloaded circuit can blow a fuse, or worse, start a fire.

Flying materials. Another cause of injuries is contact with flying particles, sawdust, wood blocks and other materials that are being cut. Hold the stock (wood, metal, etc.) with a clamp or vise and wear an eye shield or goggles to protect the eyes from fragments. The operator should always wear eye protection.

WOOD DUST

Wood dust hazards are common in woodshops and manufacturing operations. However, the small size and poor ventilation systems of home workshops, plus the growth of do-it-yourself activities, make the dangers just as real at home. The same wood dust hazards found in a large woodworking shop are found in the home workshop, so the precautions used in the woodworking industry also apply to the busy home workshop. The hazards are mainly in the concentration of dust. High dust levels are found in these operations:

- Machining operations, particularly sawing, routing and turning.
- Sanding by machine and by hand.
- Using compressed air to blow dust off furniture and other articles before spraying.

Health hazards. Too much dust of any kind is hazardous. Wood dust is no exception. It relates to these health problems:

1. Skin disorders.
2. Obstructions in the nose.
3. A type of asthma.
4. A rare type of nasal cancer.

Exposure to airborne dust may be controlled by:

- Using a process or method that reduces dust generation to a minimum.
- Providing dust-control equipment, such as local exhaust ventilation, to stop dust entering the workshop.
- Making sure to properly maintain the exhaust system.
- Using personal protective equipment, such as goggles, gloves and overalls.
- Using washing facilities with hot and cold running water.
- Using shop vacuums to remove dust from the area and from clothing and equipment.

Prevent exposure or reduce to the minimum both hardwood and softwood dust. Hardwood dust is the most hazardous of the two.

Fire and explosion. Each year, wood dust fires and explosions cause costly damage. Concentrations of small particles in the air form a mixture that explodes if ignited.

These concentrations usually occur where there is a dust extraction system. If they do, they often set off a secondary explosion of dust outside of the exhaust system.

Wood dust burns readily if ignited. Such fires are caused by poorly maintained heating units, overheated electric motors, electric sparks and sparks from other sources, such as cigarettes or open stoves. Fire and explosion opportunities can be reduced by following these guidelines:

- Keep floors free and clear from wood chips and dust, with special attention to areas around machines and on, or near, heating units.
- Regularly clean inside walls, ceilings, ledges and other surfaces of workrooms to prevent dust from accumulating. Use suitable vacuum cleaning equipment. Do not use compressed air lines. This will create dust clouds and redistribute the dust.

Safety. Wood dust on the floor can cause tripping or slipping. Vision can be reduced by airborne chips and dust generated during machining and sanding operations.

Fire extinguishers. The single, most practical type of extinguisher for the home workshop is the multipurpose type, labeled "ABC," which will handle most workshop fires.

SUMMARY

The garage and home workshop are very dangerous places. Nearly every hazard of the industrial workshop is also in your home. The familiarity of growing up with tools can breed disregard for the common hazards of rotating equipment, high pressure devices and powered rotating tools.

SAFETY RECAP

- The most common injury associated with wet-cell storage batteries is the chemical burn caused by battery acid. First aid usually involves water treatment: flood eyes or wash skin.
- Use the right tool for the job, making sure it is in good condition, as it is meant to be used.
- Secure the piece on which you are working in a vise or jig.
- The most commonly misused tools are the hammer and screwdriver.
- All power tools present hazards, especially power saws of all types.
- High pressure of any type is dangerous, even air pressure. Paint spray equipment, which can force paint into the skin (and circulation systems) is among the most dangerous.
- Don't neglect the shock, burn and fire hazards of electricity when working with power tools.

BIBLIOGRAPHY

Drill Know-How: How to Booklet, Ernst Stores.

"Electric Home Workshop Tools," *Product Safety Fact Sheet*, U.S. Consumer Product Safety Commission, December 1982.

"Follow These Guidelines to Use Tools Safely," *Community Safety and Health*, Chicago, IL: National Safety Council, July/August 1991.

Grossman, Ellie, "Easy Ways to Fall-Proof Your Home," *Family Safety and Health*, Itasca, IL: National Safety Council, Fall 1991, pp. 14-17.

"Household Batteries Can Cause Chemical Burns," *Consumer Product Safety Alert*, U.S. Consumer Product Safety Commission, June 1990.

"New Guidance for the Woodworking Industry," *Safety Manager's Newsletter*, London, England: International Institute of Risk and Safety Management, December 1990, p. 11.

"Power Tool Precautions," *Sample Issue, Your Safety News*, Oldwick, NJ: December 1990.

"The Right Tools Give Safety a Hand," Rategan, Catherine, *Safety and Health*. Chicago, IL: National Safety Council, October 1992, pp. 56-58.

Simple Home Repairs...Inside, U.S. Department of Agriculture, 1989.

SKIL Operating Guide F-353314, Chicago, IL: Skil Corporation, October 1987.

Spraying Paint, How to Booklet #34, Ernst Hardware Company, 1990.

CHAPTER 11

YARD AND GARDEN

Many yard and garden tools are so familiar that you may often overlook their dangers. This chapter focuses on the importance of using the right tools for the job and taking proper care of them.

Keep yard and garden tools clean and in good condition and keep their cutting edges sharp. Be careful not to leave tools, such as hoes, rakes, scissors, files and metal stakes, on the ground when not in use. If the tools are needed on the job, but not in use, place them with blades, forks or tines pointed downward on the ground.

Shovels, forks, spades and trowels should have smooth, properly shaped points. Your gloves should give a solid grip on tool handles.

You need a sturdy hanger for tool storage. Hang heavy and sharp-edge tools low on a wall or resting on the floor, with handles up and blades inward. Hang or place them so they are not likely to fall.

CHAIN SAWS

Gasoline or electric chain saws, often used to clear land of trees or underbrush, present a severe cutting hazard, because of their sharp, rapidly moving chains.

- Jon was pruning trees. When he finished, he released the trigger on his chain saw and drew the chain out of the branches. The chain, which was still moving, lacerated his upper arm.
- Hal rested a log on sawhorses and sawed downward with his chain saw. The saw went through the log quickly and fell onto his leg, severely cutting his knee.

- Carol was trimming the rafters of a lean-to. The chain saw kicked back as she held it overhead and her hand slipped from the handle onto the chain. One finger was amputated.
- Eric was cutting through a row of trees when his hands became tired and damp. His hands slipped off the handle and the saw turned, cutting his forearm.
- Bernard was cutting through a branch, when the rivet on his saw failed. The chain loosened and lashed at him, cutting his hand.

Contact with the chain. Contact with the chain is the main cause of serious chain saw injuries, such as those above. This often happens under these conditions:

1. The chain saw rotates after the trigger is released, and the victim inadvertently touches the moving chain.
2. The saw swings downward toward the body. This occurs most often when using the saw at or above waist level.
3. The chain on top of the bar jams or binds in the wood and throws or kicks the saw back toward the operator.
4. Loss of control occurs when sawing in a tree or on the ground.
5. Malfunction of the saw, such as chain breakage.

Other injuries

1. Cut material hits the saw which, in turn, hits the operator.
2. The saw is unintentionally turned on and cuts the operator.

3. The operator receives a shock or is electrocuted from an electric saw.

4. Excessively noisy gasoline-powered saws damages hearing.

Kickback. Kickback most often occurs when the chain saw moving around the nose of the guide bar accidentally touches another object, such as a log, branch or twig. This contact can violently throw the chain saw back toward the operator. The resultant injuries account for about 25,000 medically attended injuries to chain saw users each year. Improvements in chain saw design should reduce kickback. There also are low-kickback replacement chains made for nearly any chain saw on the market.

Selection of chain saws

1. Test the saw to see if the chain stops *immediately* after power is turned off.

2. Buy a saw no larger or longer than required for the average size of timber you will cut. Lightweight saws require less effort and cause less strain.

3. Look for guards over the sprocket and rear part of the chain.

4. Make sure the electric saw is insulated against shock, by double-insulation or three-prong grounded plugs (if used with proper three-pronged socket or adapter and tied to ground in home circuit).

5. On an electric chain saw, motor control should be through a dead-man switch that stops the chain when hand pressure is removed.

6. On gasoline-powered saws, direct the exhaust away from the operator.

7. Make certain you have a low-kickback chain on your saw.

Use of chain saws

1. Read the instruction manual carefully before use.

2. Use a lightweight hand tool to trim tree branches, not a heavy chain saw that could be cumbersome.

3. Place wood to be cut close to the ground, with the saw held parallel to the ground so it cannot swing downward toward your body after the cut.

4. Keep your legs well apart or to one side of the machine so that in case of a kickback the saw will not strike your leg.

5. Be careful the moving chain does not touch the ground. It will dull the chain.

6. Avoid touching the hot muffler.

7. Never let the saw run unattended. When a tree starts to fall, shut off the power and lay the saw on the ground at a distance from the tree.

8. Start the saw on a firm surface, such as the ground.

9. Dress appropriately. Wear closed, sturdy shoes, safety glasses and heavy trousers. You need earplugs or muffs when using a gasoline-powered saw, to prevent hearing loss. Don't wear loose clothing or jewelry that can catch in moving parts.

10. Clear away bark, stones and other debris to avoid throwback.

11. Keep the electric cord clear of cutting.

12. Keep children away from the work area at all times. Never allow children to operate saws.

Fueling chain saws

1. Fill the gasoline tank before starting a task. If you must refuel during the cut, turn off the motor and wait until the motor cools.

2. Use the mix of gasoline and oil recommended by the manufacturer.

3. Don't smoke while refueling and don't refuel in an enclosed area near a gas water heater or other flame source.

4. Wipe off any gasoline spilled on the tank or engine, before starting the engine.

5. Start the saw in a different location from where you fueled it.

6. Beware of gasoline leakage while refueling or when your saw is operating.

7. Empty the fuel tank before storing the saw for more than a few days. After long storage periods, the gas could cause starting problems.

Maintenance, storage of chain saws

1. Store saws in a high or locked place, away from children.

2. Before repairing or cleaning the saw, wait until the motor is off, chain stopped and saw unplugged.

3. Keep the chain, bar and sprocket clean and lubricated. Replace a worn chain or sprocket.

4. Keep the chain sharp. You can spot a dull chain with easy-to-cut wood.

5. Keep the chain at proper tension. Tighten all nuts, bolts and screws after each use.

6. For electric saws, inspect the electric power cord often and repair any defects.

7. For gasoline-powered saws, keep spark plugs and wire connections tight and clean.

8. A sharpened saw makes sawing easier, faster and safer. A sharp saw will shoot chips. If the saw is shooting dust, it is too dull and needs sharpening.

CHIPPER-SHREDDERS

In response to yard waste disposal restrictions, chipper-shredders that can help clean up yards are becoming popular garden/yard tools. By the nature of their operation they present many hazards.

Chipper-shredders vary in size and capacity. The smallest ones chip or shred, but rarely do both. A spinning metal blade does the work and reduces woody, reedy material on a 10:1 reduction ratio.

A growing number of hand-held blower-vacuums feature air vanes that shed leaves and other debris and send them into a collection bag. Least expensive and lightest are the electrics. Gas-powered blower-vacs cost from $80 to about $200 (1990 prices) and weigh from 6 to 11 pounds.

Their greater power means they pick up and grind debris faster and finer than electrics, but not in every case. The greatest limitations of hand-held vacs are their small vacuum openings and that most handle only leaves. Rollable vacs are faster and more versatile.

Shredder-only machines, intended mainly for leaves and other soft waste, reduce material to 1/30 of its original volume.

The next step up is the chipper-shredder (often electric powered). Typically, chipper-shredders use multiblades to do primary work, with an impeller for final work.

A full-sized residential chipper-shredder costs as much as $2,000 and uses an engine up to 8 horsepower. It hacks off pieces of wood and shred them, then forces the material through a screen. These chipper-shredders can take different-sized screens. The thicker and wetter the waste, the larger the holes in the screen should be. Some of these residential machines handle limbs up to 3 inches in diameter and reduce about 10:1.

Purchasing chipper-shredders

1. Always try a demo model first, preferably outside, to see how it really works.

2. On larger machines, make certain the shredding screen is easy to remove and replace.

3. Read the owner's manual carefully. Determine where all the controls are and what they do.

4. Before starting the machine, be certain the area is clear of people and pets.

5. Prune crooks and notches off limbs and cut vines into 18-inch lengths to avoid jams and tangles.

6. Wear goggles and gloves. Be sure your shoes give good traction. Don't wear loose clothing that can get caught in machinery.

7. Keep your head and face away from the chute and hopper.

8. Before trying to clear jammed debris, always shut off the machine, pull the spark plug wire and disengage the rotor clutch on a belt-drive machine. On a direct-drive model, be sure that the rotor has come to a complete stop before placing hands into the hopper or discharge chute.

CHAIN LINK FENCES

Most of those who receive emergency-room treatment for their injuries associated with chain link fences are between 5 and 14 years of age.

- Scott, 8, was climbing over the fence to get to his friend's house. His jacket caught on the top of the fence and he slipped and cut his arm.
- Karen, 9, was swinging in her backyard. She fell backward from the swing and struck her head on the fence, located directly behind the swing set.

Accident patterns

1. Contact with sharp edges. Falling against or contacting the sharp edges of the fence can cause injuries.
2. Contact with fences. The fence is too close to swing sets and other outdoor play equipment.

Selection of chain link fences

1. Talk to a reputable dealer about your fence needs. Consider the dealer's recommendations for height and type of fence.
2. When buying a fence for around a swimming pool, select one that is at least 4 feet high, with mesh openings of 2¼ inches or less.
3. There are specific fence requirements in many areas, so check your local municipal codes/ordinances, especially for fences around swimming pools.
4. Buy self-closing, self-latching gates if the fence is intended to keep toddlers in or out of a fenced area. The latch

should be located at the top of the gate or at least 3 feet above the ground, so small children cannot reach it.

Use of chain link fences

1. Tell your children that fence-climbing is dangerous.
2. Place backyard swing sets and climbing apparatus at least 6 feet from fences.
3. Keep fence gates securely fastened or locked, especially when the fence surrounds a swimming pool.

Maintenance of chain link fences

1. Inspect and repair your fence for damages, especially if it has become rusty.
2. Replace loose hinges or parts that may cause the gate to come apart or fall.
3. If sharp edges from screws or other fasteners are exposed, either replace them or cut them off so that they do not protrude.

GARDEN TRACTORS

Of the many injuries associated with garden tractors, the most common accident patterns correspond to the following examples:

- A 28-year-old man was driving his garden tractor across a steep hill. The garden tractor overturned and the man received several cuts and broken bones.
- A man was mowing a plot of ground with a garden tractor. He missed a strip and began to back up to go over it. He ran over his son who had been playing in the field. The boy's left foot was amputated.
- A 24-year-old man was trying to start his garden tractor. Some gas had leaked, and after the man removed a spark plug and engaged the starter, some gas sprayed on him. He received third degree burns to his legs and arms.

Accident patterns

1. Overturning. This can happen when driving over uneven terrain, steep slopes

or embankments. The rider can come in contact with the tractor when it overturns and receive serious injuries during the fall. Garden tractors may also overturn if they are used to pull heavier vehicles out of mud or from a ditch. The front of the garden tractor can rise and turn over on the victim.

2. Garden tractor running over the victim. This can occur when a garden tractor goes into reverse. The victims are often young children, who cannot be seen by the operator. Some accidents involve tractors equipped with rotary lawn mowers.

3. Ignition of flammable liquids. Using gasoline around a garden tractor can be hazardous if the gasoline spills and is ignited by sparks from any source.

4. Wrong shifting speed. Other accidents with garden tractors occur while going too fast or shifting gears. This often happens when children operate the tractor and don't control the speed, or shift gears smoothly.

Purchase of garden tractors

1. Look for garden tractors that have safety guards for all moving parts, to reduce the hazard of touching belts, chains, pulleys, gears and hot parts.

2. Buy a garden tractor that has throttle, gears and brakes that are accessible and can be operated smoothly and with minimal effort.

3. Be sure that safety instructions accompany the garden tractor and that there are warning labels on the machine itself.

Use of garden tractors

1. Read the owner's manual with attention to its recommendations, before each use of the tractor.

2. Never allow children to operate the tractor, and keep them away from the area where you are operating it.

3. Wear sturdy, rough-soled shoes and close-fitting slacks and shirts to avoid entanglements in the moving parts. Never operate a garden tractor in bare feet, sandals or sneakers.

4. Clear the area before you go over it with the garden tractor. Remove all wires, cans, rocks and sticks before you start to work.

5. Always turn off the garden tractor and wait for the moving parts to stop before you leave it.

6. Always turn off the machine and disconnect the spark plug wire when you need to adjust the machine. Turning the mower blade, for example, can cause the engine to start unexpectedly.

7. Drive up and down the slopes instead of across them for greater stability when using a garden tractor on a hill.

8. Do not attempt to use the garden tractor to tow other vehicles or to pull vehicles out of ditches or mud.

9. Never refuel a garden tractor when it is running or while the engine is hot, because gasoline can be ignited by a hot engine.

10. Start the garden tractor outdoors, not in a garage where carbon monoxide can collect.

11. Don't smoke around the garden tractor or gasoline storage cans, because gasoline fumes can ignite easily.

12. Keep children away from the machine.

Maintenance of garden tractors

1. Replace or tighten all loose or broken parts, especially blades.

2. Have the tractor serviced regularly by an expert. It may prevent serious injuries that can result from failed parts or systems.

Important note. It is impossible to cover every possible safety precaution that might involve gasoline-powered equipment.

If you plan to use a garden tractor, it's a good idea to also read the section about power mowers.

POWER HEDGE TRIMMERS

- David was cutting the hedge with an electrical hedge trimmer. He changed his left hand to the over-handle in order to reverse direction, and his left-hand ring finger came in contact with the moving blades of the trimmer.
- Terri was trimming hedges with an electric hedge trimmer. Because of the length of the extension cord, she kept the slack cord thrown over her shoulder. The cord slipped off her shoulder and as she grabbed at it to prevent it from being cut, her left index finger came in contact with the cutting blades. Her finger was amputated.

Accident patterns

1. Changing positions of the hands while the trimmer is running. If the handles are close to the cutting blades, this can be especially dangerous.
2. Moving branches out of the way. Removing the left hand from the trimmer to hold branches away from the cutting blade.
3. Cord-related accidents. People can be cut while trying to hold the cord away from the blades.
4. Dropping the trimmer. This often happens if there is a violent deflection when the blades contact fence wire, posts or heavy branches.
5. Tripping or falling. The user often attempts to catch the trimmer by the moving blades.
6. Pulling trimmer through hedge. Pulling the trimmer by the cord, through a hedge, often causes the switch to be tripped to the "on" position.
7. Picking up the trimmer by the blade.

8. Wrong extension cord. The user fails to use a three-hole extension cord with the three-hole-plugs.

Purchase of hedge trimmers

1. Buy a trimmer with cutting teeth and guards that are close together; not wide enough to put your finger between them.
2. Be sure the trimmer has two handles. The forward handle should be wide and high above the cutting blades.
3. Buy a lightweight machine that you can control easily.
4. Try to find a machine with a pressure-sensitive switch, so that it turns off when pressure is released.
5. Buy a trimmer that is double-insulated or grounded with a three-wire cord.

Rental of hedge trimmers

1. Request complete operating instructions when you rent a hedge trimmer.
2. Check for good repair and maintenance work before starting.
3. Exert special caution when using an unfamiliar power hedge trimmer.

Use of hedge trimmers

1. Read the instructions carefully before starting.
2. Use an extension cord connector that holds the trimmer cord into the socket of the extension cord so it won't come apart under tension. The connector should have a hook that allows the cord to hang on your belt, out of the way of the cutting blade.
3. Don't stand on a chair or ladder, because it can tip or move as you trim.
4. Don't hurry.
5. Keep children away from the area while you're trimming.
6. Avoid long periods of use, and cramped positions that cause fatigue.
7. Keep your hands away from the cutting blade.

8. Use a three-wire extension cord for trimmers with three-prong plugs that are properly grounded.

Maintenance of hedge trimmers

1. Never clean or adjust a plugged-in trimmer.
2. Check the cord regularly for cuts, cracks or breaks in insulation. Make repairs with electrical tape.

POWER LAWN MOWERS

- Nancy was mowing long, wet grass, and the grass began to back up at the discharge opening. She reached too far into the discharge chute as she tried to brush away a clump of grass and her fingers were struck by the blade. Nancy's finger was amputated.

- Roy was mowing grass in a hickory tree grove. A hickory nut or nut shell was thrown through the discharge chute off the mower, ricocheted off the house and hit Jim, who was standing near the house. He was blinded in the right eye.

- Mr. Coy was using a riding mower on a steep backyard terrace, when the machine started to overturn. Mr. Coy rolled over with the machine and the mower housing finally came down on his left leg, which was cut so badly it had to be amputated.

- Mr. Smith was mowing with a garden tractor. He missed a strip and began to back up to go over it. He ran over his son who was playing in the field. The boy's left foot was amputated.

- Leon and a helper were mowing with a hand power mower on a 30-degree slope, pulling the mower up the hill toward them. Robert was about a quarter of the way down the embankment when he slipped, jerking the mower toward him. His big toe was slashed open severely. He did not receive instructions nor did he read the instruction book, which advised against mowing on steep slopes. His injuries were made worse by the fact he was wearing tennis shoes.

Accident patterns. The examples above illustrate the following major accident patterns with power lawn mowers:

1. Contact with the rotating blade. This usually happens when the victim is clearing the discharge chute of grass clippings, especially wet grass. It occurs when the victim adjusts the machine without turning it off, or the machine hits an obstacle, such as a rock, and the victim's foot slips under the housing.

2. Propelled objects. Wire, rocks and twigs can be shot out either through the discharge chute or from under the housing. Many of the victims in these cases are innocent bystanders.

3. Overturning. This happens mainly with riding mowers used on steep slopes or embankments. Victims contact the blades or sustain injuries during the fall.

4. Mower running over the victim. This often occurs while driving a mower or garden tractor in reverse. The victims are usually young children who, unknown to the operator, were near the mower. Another frequent accident happens when the operator pulls the mower backward over his/her own foot.

Reel lawn mowers. Experts believe that reel lawn mowers are safer than rotary lawn mowers, mainly because their blades move slower than those of rotary mowers. A common problem with reel lawn mowers is trying to release the reel, when it is jammed by a twig or other object, without first shutting off the engine.

Because reel lawn mowers cannot cut tall grass efficiently, most consumers prefer rotary lawn mowers. Rotary lawn mower blades reach speeds of 200 miles per hour and can hurl objects 50 feet or more.

Safety standards. Safety standards for all kinds of power mowers, set in the 1980s, changed accident patterns. However, any safety device usually can be defeated and people still hurt themselves and others with power mowers. Older machines do not have some of the safeguards that are now common on newer machines.

Purchase of power mowers

If you buy a new walk-behind power lawn mower, the machine must comply with certain safety regulations:

1. An automatic brake must stop the blade in three seconds when you releases your grip on the handle-mounted control bar. You also must keep a grip on the handle-mounted control bar for the machine to keep running. In some cases, the blade will stop and the motor will keep running, but this involves more built-in safeguards.

2. There should be a rear guard to prevent hands or feet from coming in contact with the rotating blade.

3. The discharge opening should be aimed downward.

4. The machine should be easy to operate. Controls should be within easy reach and the handle should be easily adjustable. The handles should have "up stops," which prevent them from rising up when the machine hits an obstacle.

5. The engine exhaust should not be on the same side of the machine as the discharge chute. Sparks from a backfiring machine could ignite a grass fire.

6. Safety instructions should come with the mower and there should be warning labels on the machine itself.

7. You should be able to adjust the cutting height quickly.

Operator/owner/renter responsibility

1. Follow all assembly instructions when buying a new mower.

2. Correctly adjust the mower.

3. Carefully read and follow the rules for safe operation.

4. Inspect the mower.

5. Completely maintain the mower.

6. Know how to operate all standard and accessory equipment of the mower.

7. Make sure that all those who operate the mower know how to use it correctly.

8. Operate the mower only with the guards, shields and other safety items in place and working correctly.

9. Service the mower only with authorized replacement parts.

Use of power mowers

1. Check the fuel and oil before starting the engine. Do not fill the tank completely if the mower will sit in the sun, where heat will expand the fuel to overflowing.

2. Inspect the lawn for debris before starting to mow. Rake away wires, cans, rocks and twigs before you start mowing.

3. Completely maintain the mower and set the grass-cutting height.

4. Make a pre-start inspection of the mower.

5. Disengage the self-propelled mechanism or drive clutch (if provided), before starting.

6. It is best to wear safety glasses or an eye shield when operating the mower.

7. Always keep clear of the discharge chute.

8. Never attempt to adjust the wheel height or grass catcher with the mower running.

9. Do not change the engine power settings, particularly when using a grass catcher. The maximum speed of the engine has been set at the best operating speed by the factory.

10. When cutting with a walk-behind mower, always push it. Do not pull the mower. If you must back up, such as at a wall, stand well back from the mower

and make certain your feet are in the clear zone. Always keep all four wheels on the ground, including while turning.

11. Never attempt to carry small children while mowing.

12. Never leave a running mower unattended, even though it's not moving.

13. Never mow a wet lawn, because you could slip and come in contact with the rotating blade. The wet grass could clog the blades and tempt you to try to clear the machine without first turning it off.

14. Make sure the mower has stopped before leaving the operator's position.

15. Always turn off the machine *and* disconnect the spark plug wire when you need to unclog or adjust the machine. A slight rotation of the blade could start the engine.

16. Never allow young children to operate power lawn mowers. Keep them away from the areas where you are mowing. When children are old enough (12 years) to mow, see that they receive good instruction. In some areas, the Red Cross offers a free class, called "Knowing Mowing."

17. Wear sturdy shoes and close-fitting slacks. Never operate the mower in bare feet, sandals or sneakers.

18. Mow *across* any slope when using a hand mower. On a riding mower, however, you should drive *up and down* the slopes for stability.

19. When using an electric mower, be very careful not to run over the cord or entangle it in the blades.

20. Keep away from the exhaust. It takes only a couple of minutes of operation for the exhaust to become hot enough to burn a person. The exposed muffler can reach 1,200°F.

21. Wait a minute after shutting off a mower to make certain the blades have stopped.

22. Never refuel a mower when it is running or while the engine is hot. Wait about 10 minutes for the engine to cool before refueling a hot engine.

23. Start the mower outdoors, not in a garage or basement where carbon monoxide fumes can collect.

24. Stop the engine when crossing gravel drives, walks or roads.

25. If the mower starts to vibrate excessively, stop the engine and check immediately for the cause. Vibration is often a warning of trouble, such as a bent or loose blade, or loose engine mounting bolts.

26. Don't smoke around the mower, because the gasoline fumes can easily ignite.

27. Keep children away from the machines and the gasoline.

28. Mow across the lawn for better footing, never up or down. Use extreme caution when changing direction on slopes or where the ground is very rough. Do not mow slopes of over 15 degrees.

29. Mow only during daylight hours or in very good artificial light.

30. Keep any washout ports or other service openings closed during use.

31. Always take shelter in an electric storm.

Maintenance of power mowers

1. Always disconnect the spark plug before removing any grass from the mower housing.

2. Check the blade often for wear or damage, such as cracks and nicks. As a general rule, replace the blade every two years. Check the blade bolt and the engine mounting studs frequently.

3. Make sure the grass bag is empty for storage.

4. Empty or clean any grass catcher after using.

5. Lubricate according to the instruction book.

6. Replace all loose or broken parts, especially blades.

7. Keep gasoline in well-ventilated areas (away from living quarters) and in tightly capped safety cans.

8. Don't store a mower with gasoline in the tank inside a building where fumes may reach an open flame.

9. When filling a gas can, leave 2 inches of space at the top for vapor expansion. Gasoline is usually cold when taken from storage and will expand in your garage or car.

10. To reduce fire hazards, keep the mower free of leaves, twigs or grass.

Older walk-behind rotary mowers. Realize that older, walk-behind rotary mowers will seldom have the safety features to which you may be accustomed. You will need to take extra precautions, including the following:

1. If clippings jam the discharge chute, shut off the engine first. Don't attempt to clear the chute until the blade comes to a complete stop.

2. Push the mower forward. Never pull it back.

3. Adjust the blade's cutting height *before* starting the mower.

4. Shut down the engine if you must leave the operator's position.

PRESSURE WASHERS

Pressure washers, which may be used to wash motor vehicles, outdoor power equipment, porches or houses, hook up to plumbing connections and use electrical power. They pump water under high pressure through a hose, sometimes mixing the water with a cleaning solution.

- A 3-year-old boy received a fatal electrical shock when he contacted a pressure washer being used by his father.

- A 53-year-old man was electrocuted while using an electric pressure washer to wash a truck.

Since pressure washers spray water, the power cord, washer and the user are often in contact with water. This can be a fatal combination, especially if the machine is not properly grounded. It is important not to defeat a proper ground connection. You shouldn't use an adapter plug to connect the three-wire plug to a two-prong household receptacle, without grounding the adapter plug. You should have three-wire receptacles checked by a competent person to assure that they are properly wired for grounding. Even when the machine is in good mechanical condition, there are still hazards. For example, power cord connections should never lie in water.

Since 1987, pressure washers must be protected by ground fault circuit interrupters (GFCIs), however it may still be several years before the changeover is complete. Those without built-in GFCIs should be protected by a circuit breaker or a receptacle type GFCI. If they are not, portable GFCIs can be found at some retail outlets.

Precautions

1. Always plug a three-wire grounded pressure washer into a grounded receptacle.

2. If an extension cord must be used, keep the power cord connection out of any standing water, and use a heavy duty, three-wire, properly grounded type. Keep the connection as far away as possible from the object being washed and away from any runoff.

3. Never cut or splice the power cord or extension cords.

4. Wear rubber-soled footwear that gives some insulation when operating the pressure washer.

5. Never remove the grounding plug from the power cord plug.

6. Never operate the pressure washer after it has tripped the GFCI or circuit breaker without having it examined

for electrical faults by a competent person.

7. Never allow children to operate the pressure washer. Keep children at a safe distance from anyone using a pressure washer.

SNOW BLOWERS

Most snow blower injuries happen when consumers try to clear snow from the discharge chute or debris from the auger/collectors. The safety rules that follow are common sense:

1. Never put your hand in the discharge chute or near the auger/collector. Blocked auger/collectors and impellers can spring back when cleared and may cause injury, even with the engine stopped. Always use an object, such as a trowel or long stick, to clear blockages.

2. Never leave a snow blower running while unattended. Shut down the motor if you must leave the machine for any time.

3. Keep the operating area clear of people and pets. Do not aim the discharge at people, pets, automobiles, windows, etc.

4. Fill the fuel tanks of gasoline-powered machines with extreme care. Never fill a fuel tank indoors and never add fuel to a running hot engine.

5. Be aware of the power cord on electrically powered snow blowers.

6. Check the machine often if you are using the equipment sporadically over the winter season. Inspect it for loose or missing safety guards. Watch for loose nuts, bolts or fasteners.

7. Refer to the owner's manual for specific instructions on the operation, care and maintenance of the snow blower.

TILLERS

A tiller, sometimes called a cultivator, uses motorized revolving blades to churn the soil and chop weeds. The tillers discussed here are for home, yard and garden use. Even compact tillers weigh 50 to 80 pounds and have 2 to 3 horsepower motors. Lighter ones weigh as much as 30 pounds, with up to 1.6 horsepower motors.

Most models are "front tine" machines, with the tines or blades mounted on an axle or in front of it. The machine is propelled forward by digging into the dirt in front of it. The wheels on these machines are strictly to roll it to or from work areas.

Operation. Tillers are not easy for inexperienced operators to control and are somewhat harder to manage than power mowers. It takes effort to keep them digging and going straight. They tend to go too fast and get out of control. Most have a metal stake in front to keep them slow and to help measure the depth that the tines dig into the ground. While the lightweight ones are slightly easier to handle, the same problems of control exist.

Most tillers have a dead-man control, so that forward motion stops when the control is released. If there is no dead-man control, the tiller keeps trudging ahead at a quick pace, often tipping onto its side. It poses little danger to the operator who is left behind, but is a hazard to anything in its way. The same thing happens if the dead-man control locks into place.

If the locking device cannot be disabled or the tiller does not have a dead-man control, don't buy it. Some of the tillers are too difficult to control. The larger and more powerful the tiller, the larger the potential for a control problem.

Tillers, which are much faster than shovels, are great labor savers. They can do good work, but require effort, energy and control.

TRIMMERS

Weed trimmers. The flexible string weed trimmer has limited capacity. It cannot handle heavy tasks. That is a job for the brush cutter (see following). Nevertheless, the weed trimmer and edger account for nearly 5,000 emergency room treatments each year. About one-third of the injuries involve the eyes, so operators should wear goggles. Safety rules for using weed trimmers are simple:

1. Understand that trimmers can throw objects and injure eyes. Wear goggles.
2. Clear away stones, sticks and other debris before using.
3. Always unplug electric trimmers or turn off the engine on powered trimmers before adjusting or inspecting the cutting string edge of the device.

Brush cutters. While the brush cutter is somewhat similar to the flexible string weed trimmer, it has much greater potential for serious and disabling injury. The brush cutter uses a rigid cutting blade in place of the flexible plastic string line. The blade permits cutting much heavier strands of brush and small diameter saplings. However, it also can cut through a hand, arm or leg, something the flexible line trimmer will not do.

- A man was cutting brush along the bottom of a wood fence. His wife, standing nearby trimming a hedge, was severely injured when he lost control and the brush cutter swung in an arc toward his wife. The blade cut into the wife's thigh and then her left hand, nearly amputating it below the wrist.
- Two men were cutting brush. One held down a sapling with an ax while the other attempted to cut through it with a brush cutter. The blade ricocheted off the sapling and into the assistant, severely cutting his right arm.
- A man cutting brush near a chain link fence reported that the blade threw a small piece of wire from the fence into his eye.
- A man was using a brush cutter when the blade came off the end of the shaft. The blade flew off and lacerated his foot.

Precautions
1. Keep all people well away from the operator during use.
2. Before starting, make sure the blade is properly secured to the shaft. Replace damaged blades.
3. Avoid cutting close to fences or other such obstacles that could cause the brush cutter to ricochet. Clear the area of trash or hidden debris that could be thrown back at the operator or a bystander.
4. Use the proper cutting attachment for the job. Use the flexible string trimmer or hand tool for trimming near buildings, fences, etc.
5. Wear protective clothing, including safety eye goggles.

SUMMARY

The very hazardous nature of yard and garden equipment places a burden on parents for the safety of their children. Not only is careful familiarization and close supervision required, but using the equipment may be beyond the skill and knowledge of the parent. Don't buy, rent or borrow it without complete hands-on familiarization with the equipment. Know when to turn to a professional.

SAFETY RECAP

1. For the yard and garden, the hazards of power tools are magnified through larger, stronger and more powerful equipment.
2. Yard and garden tools may be used infrequently and may be rented. This calls for extra care in using the equipment properly.
3. Do not use any equipment discussed in this chapter before receiving hands-on instruction.
4. Eye protection is a must for all operating equipment mentioned in this chapter.
5. Ear protection is a requirement for most operating equipment covered in

this chapter and is desirable for all equipment.

6. Heavier, often faster-moving, equipment, causes more serious injuries, for example, amputations instead of cuts.

7. Know when to say no to using equipment because of lack of knowledge or skill.

BIBLIOGRAPHY

"Commission Issues Pressure Washer Warning," *Consumer Product Safety Alert*, U.S. Consumer Product Safety Commission, August 1987.

"CPSC Cautions Snow Thrower Users," U.S. Consumer Product Safety Commission.

"CPSC Warns of Springtime Hazards," *Seasonal Safety Alert*, U.S. Consumer Product Safety Commission, Spring 1985.

"Gasoline Sparks Ahead," *Family Safety and Health*, National Safety Council, Winter 1990-91, p. 8.

"Chipping Away," Markovich, Bob, *Home Mechanix*, Oct. 1990, pp. 75-80.

"Power Hedge Trimmers," *Product Safety Fact Sheet*, U.S. Consumer Product Safety Commission, June 1980.

"Power Lawnmowers," *Product Safety Fact Sheet*, U.S. Consumer Product Safety Commission, Spring, 1988.

"Tillers and Cultivators," *Consumer Reports*, May 1991, pp. 329-331.

"Toe Smashed in Mower Accident," *Safety Management*, October 1990, pp. 18-19.

REGULATING CONSUMER SAFETY

CHAPTER 12

REGULATING CONSUMER SAFETY

This final chapter of *Home Safety Desk Reference* provides you with new information, but also summarizes many points in the book. Most importantly, it tells you how consumer product safety regulation started and how you can take part in the ongoing process.

Background. You may see the home as a refuge from the hazards of work, the highway and the office. In reality, the home is much more dangerous.

The statistics are alarming: Each year, 30,000 accidental deaths occur in homes. And more than 4 million people receive disabling injuries in the home each year. Or, using National Safety Council figures, if 7,000 people live in your community, 140 of them will suffer home disabilities this year.

Each year, 20 million consumers are hurt in the home with 110,000 of them permanently disabled. Most of the mishaps happen to the very young and the very old.

Today home safety is much improved over what it was a few years ago. But, sorry to say, the very things that make life easier and more enjoyable—electronic equipment, polishes, cleaners, fertilizers and pesticides—often bring more hazards. Look at the new cleaning and convenience devices in every kitchen. Power tools fill our garages and basements. Better working conditions and higher standards of living provide more recreation time. However, recreation also brings hazardous products, such as minibikes, snowmobiles, skateboards and hang gliders.

As consumer products increase, so do the hazards. Home safety programs are little changed from 40 or 50 years ago, but today's home is more dangerous.

While you, as a consumer, accept risk in daily activities, you must also consider safety. It is a trade-off. Sometimes you cannot discern the product's safety. And reducing risks greatly sometimes may be prohibitively costly. The cost of safety may keep you and other consumers from buying certain products. Sometimes, though, the cost is small. It may cost nothing more—maybe even less—to make a product safer. In any case, the product is far safer when the you know the related hazards, and the correct way—the safe way—to use a product.

Protection by regulation. Consumer protection by law is not new. It started with the Sherman Antitrust Act of 1890 and grew to the Consumer Protection Act of 1972, our main legislation for consumer safety. Legislation is constantly being introduced and passed to protect consumers. This Act of 1972 brought us the badly needed Consumer Product Safety Commission (CPSC).

It is estimated that the Commission can regulate from 10,000 to 100,000 products. These are in perhaps 700 to 1,000 separate product groups. Included are everything from rubber ducks to minibikes to imports. At this writing, exports do not fall under the Consumer Product Safety Act. Foreign customers properly complain that the U.S. forces unsafe products on them.

Priorities. With so many products in use, the Commission must set priorities, which is a tough and complex task. This suggests that if a troublesome product lacks a high priority, it may not get examined. A key element in setting priorities is the National Electronic Surveillance System (NEISS). Through this computerized system, the CPSC receives daily reports from certain hospital emergency rooms about consumer product-related injuries. When a product shows up enough times to get a priority, the Commission examines it in-depth and isolates the problems. The CPSC then seeks corrective action. Other sources of information about defective products include burn centers, consumer advocates and consumers themselves.

A few years ago, consumers had to protect *themselves*. It was "Let the buyer beware." While that is changing, still, it is you, the consumer, who can do the most toward buying safer products and using them properly. Manufacturing changes help, but nothing protects an inept consumer from himself or herself. Today, there are attempts to offer safer products and to warn consumers about their hazards, but it is still up to the consumer to use products as intended, in a safe manner.

Consumer participation. Consumers now have a voice in making products safer. When you complain or report a problem, you are heard. If a product injures a consumer, the chances are good that recording the injury will lead to a safer product.

This new attitude toward consumerism comes from widespread campaigns to inform people. Government agencies have mounted expensive educational campaigns. There are many books, pamphlets and films available at little or no cost. Manufacturers themselves, quickly point out the safety benefits of their products. Consumer education has become a regular high school course in many schools, as well as in adult education.

Substantial hazards. During its first year, the CPSC received 130 defect notices on 14 million product units. Those units posed substantial risk of injury. The manufacturers, distributors and sellers of those products, cooperating with the CPSC, notified owners of the most defective products. Some of the products were fixed or repurchased.

Businesses must report to the Commission products that can create risks of injury. The manufacturers, importers, distributors and retailers must quickly inform the commission if a product doesn't meet a safety rule or creates a substantial hazard. This applies to all products that fall under the Commission's purview. Failure to do this can result in civil and criminal penalties.

The chief executive officer of the notifying company must sign and certify any information given to the Commission. This responsibility may be given to another person, but the Commission must be told in writing. The first notification must:

1. Identify the product.
2. Give the names and addresses of the manufacturer and every distributor and retailer, if known.
3. Give the nature and extent of the defect or failure to comply with a safety rule.
4. Provide the name and address of the person giving the report.

If the first notice is oral, written confirmation must be sent within 48 hours. More information to report within 48 hours, if known, includes:

1. How the information on the hazard was obtained.
2. Copies of any consumer complaints about the hazard.
3. The number, nature and severity of any injuries that relate to the hazard.
4. The number of units involved.
5. How remaining units will be discarded.

6. Any identifying marks or numbers on the potentially hazardous units.

In addition, manufacturers, importers, distributors or retailers will inform the Commission:

1. What action will be taken to correct the defect.
2. How buyers were notified.
3. Whether defective products in the hands of consumers will be refunded, replaced or repaired. The CPSC then arranges a hazard risk evaluation to see if the product defect creates a substantial injury risk.

When consumers, industry or other groups provide facts about a hazard, the CPSC field staff makes contact to gather details about it and any associated injuries. CPSC engineers and other staff members then evaluate the risk of injury with the product. If they decide there is a substantial risk of injury to the public, the CPSC sends a letter to the manufacturer, distributor or retailer. They request that the firm:

1. Evaluate the product.
2. Summarize the complaints received.
3. Estimate the number of products involved.
4. Provide details on any corrective action taken.

Standards development. The CPSC must protect the public from unreasonable risk of injury. One way it achieves this goal is to set safety standards. These standards can detail how products perform to be safe, and/or how they are labeled or include warning or guidance for safe use.

Standards begin with the CPSC deciding that a product poses "an unreasonable risk of injury" and that a mandatory standard will reduce or remove the risk. The CPSC then issues a notice that invites anyone to submit a standard or develop a standard that applies to the injury risks of that product. The CPSC may act based upon its own analysis.

The "offer" and "offerer." An offer includes a plan that ensures representative public roles in the process. The Commission evaluates the response and can either:

1. Publish an existing standard as a proposed mandatory standard.
2. Accept one or more "offers" to develop a standard. If it does not accept either option, it can propose a standard.

If the Commission accepts an offer, the offerer must develop a standard, usually 150 days after the first public notice. The next step is to offer it for public comment as a proposed standard. A standard goes into effect after:

1. Public comment.
2. Commission review.
3. Possible adoption of comments received.
4. The CPSC accepts the standard as final.

An offerer who manages the development of a safety standard needs a variety of people—technicians, industry representatives, academicians and use-oriented consumers—to help develop the standard. This takes two major forms:

1. In person, by attending meetings, serving on a standards drafting committee and other direct involvement.
2. By giving written views on the product or by commenting on the draft standard. The offerer should seek the views of all interested parties.

The roster. To help the offerer find persons to develop standards, the CPSC maintains a roster of names. The roster has background data on those willing to help develop and review product safety standards. This roster is open to offerers, who may use it to find people with certain interests, background skills or useful geographical locations. The Commission does not select people from this roster. It provides the roster solely as a service and is pleased to hear from any person who wants to be on the roster.

GENERIC HAZARDS

The CPSC usually deals with hazards of specific products, such as television sets, lawn mowers or playground equipment. It also may monitor any hazard, such as electrical shock, high surface temperatures, sharp edges or poisonous chemicals, that appears in a broad range of products.

These hazards fall into four general categories: thermal, electrical, mechanical and chemical. The CPSC also explores ways to reduce these generic hazards.

Knowing these hazards are in your home can help you prevent injuries:

1. Thermal hazards. Thermal hazards develop from fire and heat sources. Some of them are obvious, such as getting clothing too close to the flame of a gas stove or dropping a match on a nightgown. Others may not be so obvious, such as gasoline vapors igniting in a pilot light in a gas water heater. Hot cooking utensils or hot water in a bathtub can cause burns. Here are some products with thermal hazards:

   - Kitchen ranges and ovens.
   - Space heaters and radiators.
   - Fireplaces.
   - Matches and lighters.
   - Flammable fabrics.
   - Flammable liquids.
   - Countertop cooking appliances.
   - Hot water in the bathroom, kitchen or other rooms.
   - Irons.

2. Electrical hazards. Electrical fire hazards happen when circuits overload (as when a short circuit or an appliance defect lets current leak and flow through the body). The most common electrical injuries are burns and shock, both of which can have lasting, damaging body effects. Here are some products with electrical hazards:

   - Electric hair dryers, toasters, refrigerators and other appliances.
   - Electric saws, drills and other tools.
   - House wiring.
   - Extension cords and wall sockets.

3. Mechanical hazards. Mechanical hazards can develop from sharp edges, sharp points, poorly balanced products (such as some high chairs) and slippery walking surfaces. These hazards are the most common, since almost any product can cause falls or cuts. The most common injuries from mechanical hazards are cuts, bruises and broken bones. While the most frequent cause of accidental death in the U.S. is auto accidents, the second most frequent cause is falls, often from mechanical hazards in and around the home. Here are some products with mechanical hazards:

   - Power lawn mowers, power saws and other cutting machines.
   - Glass doors, walls and windows.
   - Glass bottles.
   - Ladders.
   - Stairs.
   - Children's furnishings (cribs, high chairs, infant seats).
   - Wringer washing machines.
   - Playground equipment.
   - Toys.
   - Bicycles.

4. Chemical hazards. Certain household products, such as cleaners, bleaches, flammable liquids, insecticides, drugs and paints, contain ingredients that are chemical hazards if directions are not followed. These products may be toxic if swallowed, breathed or absorbed. They may be corrosive or irritating to eyes or skin. Some of these products may be flammable or create pressure through heat or other means. Carbon monoxide from fuel-burning appliances may be a chemical hazard if used in a

room without fresh air. Here are some products with chemical hazards:

- Drugs, household cleaners, bleaches and flammable liquids.
- Insecticides and pesticides.
- Fuel-burning appliances that produce carbon monoxide.
- Aerosols.

NOISE

Often viewed as a workplace problem, noise is seldom discussed for the home consumer. One concern about home noise hazards is their cumulative effect with on-the-job noise. Although hearing loss may be temporary, it also may be permanent and irreparable. Noise is measured in decibels. In a workplace, hearing programs offer protection for decibel counts that average more than 85 decibels in an eight-hour period, or for higher counts over shorter periods. Normal phone talk ranges from 50 to 65 decibels, while heavy machinery may run 70 to 90 decibels.

Different kinds of hearing protection are available, such as ear plugs and ear muffs. There are many types of each and their effectiveness varies. Your home activity determines which is best for you. Here are four things you can do to protect your hearing:

1. Avoid high-noise areas.
2. Use hearing protection.
3. Take care of your ears.
4. Have hearing tests.

Avoid high-noise areas. Try to avoid high noise levels from loud noise at concerts and sporting events, headphones, noisy appliances and environmental noise, such as jackhammers, subways and sirens.

Protection against hearing loss. Protect your hearing by giving your ears a rest in a quiet environment. If possible, wear hearing protection when working with power tools and lawn mowers or

hunting, target shooting, boating and snowmobiling.

Hearing protectors are the best protection against this type of noise. Either ear muffs or ear plugs are easy to use, but should be appropriate for the situation. The right protection depends on:

1. The amount of protection you need.
2. What will be comfortable for you.
3. Whether your hearing protector fits over other equipment you wear, such as protection for the head, eye and breathing.

Ear plugs. Ear plugs are made of rubber or plastic and slip inside the ears to block out noise. They are fitted to your ear, and often have a string fixed to make them easy to remove.

Ear plugs work well when you turn your head often and when you work in tight places. You can wear them with almost any hairstyle, hard-hats, eye protection and respirators. They protect well against high frequencies.

Ear plugs can work loose when worn, need to be replaced periodically and are small enough to lose easily. They become dirty, cannot be used by others and should be washed each day.

Ear muffs. Ear muffs are made of plastic, have a headband and are lined with foam or other soft material to block sound. The headband can be adjusted for comfort. They seldom come loose during work, and allow you to move your head freely. Ear muffs are tricky to wear with eye, head and breathing protection.

Hearing examinations. Hearing loss may be gradual and involve small hearing loss over long periods. A hearing test can detect those small changes, if you have had a previous test to serve as a baseline.

Toys. Caps and cap guns that can cause hearing damage (those producing sound at 158 decibels or more under test conditions) are banned. Those producing sound at intermediate levels (138 decibels up to 158 decibels) must carry a warning label.

HAZARDOUS SUBSTANCES

The Federal Hazardous Substances Act stems from the Federal Hazardous Substances Labeling Act of 1960. Its first basic task was to boldly label with safety information hazardous household products.

Congress soon found that the Act—with its total reliance on labels—did not deal effectively with the hazardous substance problem. Later changes broadened the scope of the Act and recognized two facts:

1. Some products are so hazardous that no warning label can fully protect the user.
2. For some young children, labeling offers no protection. The new labeling requirements were more effective and let the agency remove products from the market that could not be dealt with by labeling.

What is a hazardous substance? There are several ways to determine that a substance is hazardous. It is hazardous if:

1. It is highly toxic or toxic; extremely flammable, flammable or combustible; corrosive; an irritant; a strong sensitizer; radioactive; or generates pressure.
2. Can cause substantial personal injury or illness.

Though these terms are in the Act itself, the regulations are more specific.

A substance that may cause substantial injury or illness through any normal or foreseeable use, and that falls into any of the following categories, is hazardous. It needs special labeling if it is for use in or around the home:

1. Toxic/highly toxic. A substance is toxic if it can cause injury or illness when ingested, inhaled or absorbed through the skin. Highly toxic substances are those proven through laboratory test-

ing to be particularly lethal. (Example: certain liquid furniture polishes are toxic.)

2. Extremely flammable, flammable or combustible. These degrees of flammability depend on the conditions under which a substance ignites or the rate at which it burns. Gasoline, for example, ignites even at subzero temperatures and thus is extremely flammable. Substances that ignite only above 150°F are not flammable or combustible by the law.
3. Corrosive substances destroy living tissue on contact through chemical action. (Certain drain cleaners are corrosive.)
4. Irritant. An irritant is a noncorrosive substance that produces inflammation of living tissue after contact. (Some laundry detergents are irritants.)
5. Strong sensitizer. There are two groups of strong sensitizers. A strong allergic sensitizer makes people very sensitive to its presence after one exposure. Thus, a person contacting a substance for the first time will show no ill effects. On a later contact (even with a small amount), the person may show a strong allergic reaction. A strong photodynamic sensitizer will make some people extremely sensitive to sunlight. The areas of sensitivity may be general or limited to the point of contact. (Formaldehyde is a strong allergic sensitizer.)
6. Generates pressure. A substance that generates pressure through heat, decomposition or any other means. (Aerosol cans.)
7. Radioactive. Any radioactive substances not regulated under the Atomic Energy Act of 1954 that are hazardous enough to need labeling.
8. Toys. Toys and other articles for children with electrical, mechanical or thermal hazards. (Examples: electrical toys with shock hazards, dolls with straight pins, toy ovens with very high temperatures.)

Regulations on hazardous substances. The Federal Hazardous Substances Act gives more protection to those who use potentially hazardous substances around their homes. The Act provides for:

1. Labels on all products that contain a hazardous substance, including data on their hazardous natures and their safe use and first aid treatment.
2. Taking from the market items that are so hazardous to the user that no label gives proper protection.

Banned hazardous substances. Any product found to be so hazardous that no warning label could protect the user may be banned from the market. Any toy or item meant for use by children that is, or contains, a hazardous substance may be banned. Exceptions are items for use by older children that by their nature may be hazardous, such as chemistry sets. These articles must have labels for safe use.

In either case, the product must have proper labels with directions for its safe use. More information on toy dangers is found in Chapter 3.

A product with a hazardous substance, which must normally carry a warning label for safe use, may be banned. Sometimes a warning label is of no help. In these cases the substance may be banned from the market. Eight of them are listed:

1. Certain flammable water-repellents that apply to interior masonry surfaces.
2. Carbon tetrachloride and mixtures that contain it.
3. Fireworks devices meant for audible effects, which contain more than two grains of powder.
4. Certain liquid drain cleaners, unless they are in child-resistant containers.
5. Products with soluble cyanide salts.
6. Any paint or similar coating substance that has more than .5 percent lead content, and any toy or other children's article bearing such paint. Artist's paints are exempt from this ban.
7. Any general-use garment that contains asbestos.
8. Self-pressurized containers for household use that contain vinyl chloride.

Misbranded hazardous substances. Any hazardous substance without the proper label, or not packaged in a proper safety container, is misbranded and cannot legally be sold.

Repurchase of banned hazardous substances. A manufacturer, distributor or retailer selling a banned hazardous product must buy it back when it is returned. To do this, every reasonable effort must be made to let the purchaser know that he/she can get a refund. When a retailer knows that a banned product was sold, customers must be notified by notices posted in the store. These include a notice that the store has sold a banned product and how customers may obtain more information. It includes a list of all banned products the store has sold and a notice telling how to get a refund. The repurchaser must pay transport expenses incurred in returning the product. The CPSC provides a list of banned products upon request.

The *manufacturer* must notify the distributor to whom the banned product was sold, as soon as it is known that it has been banned. After getting notice from the manufacturer, the *distributor* must then notify the retail dealers who sold the banned product. The *retailer* then must:

1. Display a list of "Banned Articles or Substances" with details about each product.
2. Maintain each banned article on the list for at least 120 days from the date the dealer was told that the article was banned.
3. Prominently display a notice of "Refund procedures for banned article or substance." (This tells consumers that they

can get refunds if they return banned articles to the dealer where the item was bought.)

4. Prominently display a sign telling people that the retailer sold banned articles and where they may find the list of banned products and refund procedures.

5. If the banned item was sold other than in a retail store, such as by mail order, publicize a notice of the banned article in a manner that will reach as many purchasers as reasonably possible and inform them how they may return the article for a refund.

6. Buy back the article, and give the person who purchased it the reasonable expenses incurred in returning it.

Labeling requirements. Any product that contains a hazardous substance must be properly labeled, unless exempted. This must appear on the main label panel of the product, with a statement of the hazard and instructions to read other cautionary material that must be included on the container. The remaining information must be together, prominent and apart from other wording. There is safety information for each hazard.

Hazardous substances in containers that make labeling impractical must carry the warnings on firmly attached tags. Cautionary data must be on any printed material telling how to use the product. There will no presentation that detracts from the required labeling. The labels for various hazardous substances differ, but usually are of a specific size with certain information:

1. A signal word: "Danger" on products that are extremely flammable, corrosive or highly toxic. "Warning" or "Caution" will be on other hazardous substances that bear a label.

2. The word "Poison" and the skull-and-crossbones symbol will be on highly toxic substances specifically named in the Hazardous Substances Act regulations.

3. A description of the principal hazards involved in using the product, such as "Vapor harmful" and "Flammable."

4. A statement of the measures the user should take to avoid the hazard, such as "Use only in a well-ventilated area."

5. A list of the common names of the hazardous ingredients. If there is no common name, the chemical name is used.

6. If necessary, instructions for safe handling and storage.

7. First aid instruction.

8. The name and location of the manufacturer, distributor or repacker. If it is an imported product, the name of the importer or distributor will appear.

9. The statement "Keep out of the reach of children" or its equivalent. If the product is for children the label will carry directions for the product's safe use by children. Some products must be in child-resistant safety packaging.

10. Any other information that the Commission finds necessary.

Special labeling. Some substances have special hazards such that the usual labeling will not protect the consumer. They must carry special warning notices. These items have two things in common: Their hazards are severe and they are quite common around the home. The mix of high risk and easy accessibility requires special labels.

Special labeling is required for any product with the following substances: diethylene glycol, ethylene glycol, benzine, toluene, xylene, petroleum distillates, methyl alcohol and turpentine. It also is required for charcoal briquettes.

Specific labeling also is used for certain fire extinguishers (those that produce highly toxic substances or might cause the user to receive a shock if it is used on an electrical fire) and certain very flammable contact adhesives.

Poison. When the Federal Hazardous Substances Act replaced an earlier act, it was felt that the skull and crossbones label should be kept for these substances. To remove it might suggest that the hazards are less severe. All highly toxic substances and benzene and methyl alcohol must bear this word and symbol.

Labeling exemption. Some hazardous substances need not meet all labeling needs. A few have no labeling. Others are partially exempt. Though the Commission may accept any good reason for granting an exemption, it most often gives it because the hazard is minor or the size of the package prevents full labeling. Common matches, paper products and thread, string or rope are products exempt from labeling even though they might be flammable.

COSMETICS

The Food and Drug Administration (FDA) does not require cosmetics manufacturers to prove that a product is safe. Except for color additives and a few prohibited ingredients, a manufacturer may use any raw material. Only if someone tells the FDA that the cosmetic has injured someone does it act. Only if an investigation shows that safety was not properly considered does the FDA deem the product misbranded. The FDA then may take regulatory action.

Manufacturers can avoid regulatory action by labeling their products, "Warning: The safety of this product has not been determined." If a consumer reacts adversely to a cosmetic, the manufacturer may voluntarily report it to the FDA, but only 60 to 80 percent of the firms do this.

Once again, it is "Let the buyer beware." The cautious consumer can check the label to see if the contents are something to which he or is sensitive. Another idea is to avoid keeping the product too long. For example, bacteria contamination is possible with eye mascara. It is a good idea (and less expensive than visiting an eye doctor) to discard mascara after 4 to 6 months.

Why the new consumerism? Consumerism is expensive, even if beneficial. However, a hazardous product also can be expensive. It can cause death or injury, or result in a lawsuit to the manufacturer or seller. It can force a recall of products already in the marketplace or home. A faulty product, likely to injure, can require time-consuming field repairs. Witness the common recall of automobiles. Sometimes it involves millions of cars. Hazards that everyone once took for granted are no longer accepted.

Safety has gained new respect and is being designed into products before manufacturing. The problem then, is judging when a product is safe enough and what design or uses must be changed to make it safer. The manufacturing process can be at fault.

Following are typical examples of problems with consumer products and their use:

- A missing transistor set up a potential shock hazard, forcing the recall of 52,000 color TV sets by one manufacturer.

- A doctor was doing home repairs. While repairing a door knob, lacking a vise, he held the work in his hand while trying to loosen a stubborn screw. The screwdriver slipped and plunged deep into his palm.

- A mother left her small child and his older brother for a moment to run across the street to a neighbor's home. The older child found a book of matches and suddenly the room was ablaze. The younger child died of burns.

- Electric hair dryers are often used in front of the bathroom mirror, close to a sink or tub. A young mother and 6-month-old child were bathing, when the dryer fell into the water. Mother and daughter were electrocuted.

- A woman had just lacquered her hair with hairspray. She lighted a cigarette and her hair went up in flames.

- An 8-year-old child crawled onto the kitchen stove to reach for a forbidden cookie jar and was painfully burned by a burner that was not on, but still hot.

- A housewife reached into a counter-top toaster while the other hand was touching a metal sink rim. That completed an electrical circuit and electrocuted her.

- Summer breezes fanned the curtains across the kitchen range where dinner was cooking. The breeze flipped a curtain into the flames and in a moment the kitchen was ablaze.

- A man was cleaning up the yard at his home. Trimming a tree, he sawed off a limb, which then swung around and knocked the ladder from beneath him. He was rushed to the hospital with a broken back.

- A girl and her mother were sledding together down a hill when they were stopped suddenly by soft snow. The mother was thrown clear, but the daughter's foot was caught in the steering mechanism of the sled, breaking her leg.

- A mother sat in the living room talking to a friend, while her toddler whined for attention. When the child took the friend's car keys from the end table, they thought it was cute. In a moment, there was a flash and the child screamed. The child had stuck the car key into an outlet, resulting in a slightly burned child and a terrified mother.

The new consumerism can change the home from a hazard to a haven. The home of the future can be a safer place and a more secure place for small children. The kitchen and laundry, now full of danger spots for the unwary, can be a better place to work. The workshop and yard can be less dangerous. Coming changes in sports gear, medicine and appliances promise a brighter future for all consumers. This book addresses two other aspects of consumer products, synonymous with safety:

1. Health: disease or sickness related to the product.
2. Environment: the environmental effect(s) of the product.

The new demand for safer consumer products is not a simple matter. You might think a first step would be to find out what is unsafe. But with millions of products and even more consumers, how do you determine what is unsafe? How do you decide which products should have priority for attention or change?

Proper design and building of products would solve many problems, but in an inflationary world, can the consumer pay the extra design, material and manufacturing costs? Not long ago it was found that the cost of a power lawn mower would increase by more than 50 percent if all the needed safety changes were made. Many of the changes became law and power mowers now cost about 50 percent more. The payoff is a far less hazardous product, which results in fewer injuries. A byproduct of the reengineering is a mulching mower with many environmental benefits.

SUMMARY

This chapter closes the book. It shows you how consumerism developed and who are the main government controllers of consumer safety. Focus is on the central roles of the Consumer Product Safety Commission (CPSC) in setting standards and defining certain basic policies and operations.

SAFETY RECAP

1. The home is generally more hazardous than the workplace.
2. Regulations and other government control cannot possibly protect you from all the hazards of the home.
3. Much consumer protection depends on voluntary actions by designers, manufacturers, distributors and sellers. If they choose not to act voluntarily, the safety expected by the government may not be forthcoming.
4. Consumer product hazards are: thermal, electrical, mechanical and chemical. Noise is a major hazard that falls outside those categories.
5. New and improved products also bring new hazards.
6. Labels do not protect children and are ineffective against some hazards.
7. You may return banned products to the selling dealers, distributors or manufacturers.
8. The highest value of labels may be in their value to treating physicians.
9. The signal words on labels are: "Danger," "Warning," "Caution" and "Poison."

BIBLIOGRAPHY

"Sound Sense 95M990," Chicago: National Safety Council, 12 pages, 1990.

BABY SITTER AND HOME ALONE—A PARENT'S GUIDE

It would require enough information to fill a small book to adequately prepare a baby sitter to do the job surely and safely. It is just as difficult for parents to be certain sitters know everything necessary to handle any situation that might arise. Ideally, the sitter is someone who has his or her own children and who realizes what is expected of a substitute parent.

What can you do to help your sitter be more effective and to reassure yourself about the sitter's qualifications?

The sitter should:

1. Know how to contact you or someone else in an emergency. Before leaving, give the sitter the names and phone numbers necessary to contact you or someone else for emergencies.

2. Know the layout of your home and where certain things are kept. Point out where items the sitter may need are located. This includes children's clothing and playthings.

3. Know where the emergency exits are located and what to do in case of fire. Show and tell the sitter what to do in case of fire.

4. Know how to prevent home accidents. Show the sitter potential hazards in the home, such as exposed heating elements and appliances. Make certain dangerous household products and medicines are secured away from children.

5. Know the dangers of stairs. Discuss the dangers of playing on stairs and the need to keep them clear of obstacles.

6. Keep stair gates and barriers in place and know how the locked and unlocked gates can be dangerous. Show and tell the dangers of gates and barriers, locked and unlocked.

7. Know to never leave children unattended with walkers, strollers and carriages. Explain the reasons for this and dangers involved.

8. Know the dangers of glass doors and windows. A child riding a bike or running can easily go through a glass door. Keep away from these areas: toys, scatter rugs or other articles that can cause a slip or fall.

9. Know whether or not to bathe the baby. This should not be done unless the parent specifically requests it and gives complete instructions on how to do it.

10. Know how to change diapers. Have everything needed within reach. Explain about the dangers of the baby falling while changing the diaper.

11. Know how to prevent choking and what to do if it occurs. Tell the sitter to keep small objects that can be put in the mouth away from the baby and watch the baby at all times. Be sure the sitter has the phone number for the rescue squad, in case of choking or other emergencies.

12. Know that mishaps can be prevented by looking for hazards before they cause trouble. Discuss how common things like clothing and toys can cause falls,

slips and strangulations, so preventive measures can be taken by the sitter.

13. Know how to prevent injuries by always keeping an eye on the baby, keeping doors and windows locked and other measures.

14. Know never to open the door to strangers. Tell the sitter, if someone persists, to call you to check on it.

15. Know how all the door locks work and to keep them all locked.

16. Know where the light switches are located. After dark, turn on the porch lights and close the drapes if lights are on inside.

17. Know what to do if there are accidents. In case of accident or illness, a sitter should know not to try to be a doctor or nurse, except for minor cuts or bruises. (Minor cuts are those less than ¼ inch deep.) After the minor cut is washed, the sitter should call you or grandparents, or go to a neighbor for help. The sick or hurt child may need medical care.

Where the child is:

1. Play area. Keep the child in safe areas, within sight and out of possible danger areas, such as the bath, kitchen and workshop.

2. Playpen. Know that there are strangulation dangers from toys and suffocation from blankets, mattresses or sides of mesh cribs.

3. Baby walkers. A child can tip over fairly easy and can quickly scoot to the stairs or bang into furniture.

4. High chair. Almost constant attention is required when the baby is in it, to prevent falling, tipping, sliding, etc. Don't let the child stand in it.

5. The crib. Don't allow more than 2 fingers width around the mattress, which the child could slip into. Watch out for suffocation and don't give toys the child

could strangle on or get around the neck.

Toys. Baby sitters should be particularly aware of safe and unsafe toys. Be aware of these toy dangers:

1. Small parts. Look for things small enough to be swallowed or inhaled. Be aware of toys or dolls that could break open and release small items.

2. Sharp edges. These can be found on broken plastic or glass toys and on some metal toys of poor construction.

3. Sharp points. Suspect broken toys and pins and staples in dolls and toys.

4. Loud noises. Toy caps and some guns can damage hearing. Don't allow anything noisy within one foot of baby's ear.

5. Propelled objects. This refers to projectiles, guided missiles and similar flying toys. Never allow children to play with these, or darts or arrows with sharp tips. Do not let children aim any toys at anyone.

6. Electric toys. Toys with heating elements should only be used by children over 8 years of age, and then only under adult supervision.

7. Wrong toy for wrong age. Toys that are safe for older children, like chemistry or some hobby sets, can be very dangerous in the hands of smaller children.

8. Cords and strings. Toys with long cords or pull strings can be dangerous for infants and small children. Never hang toys with long strings, cords, loops or ribbons around a baby's neck.

Outdoors with the baby sitter. Some of the baby sitter's time with your children may be spent outdoors. This presents a whole new set of hazards for children. Because the key to safe outdoor play is the parent teaching children to play safely, the sitter must assume this role in your absence. The sitter must expect hazards outdoors. This requires the sitter to be constantly alert and to supervise every moment of outdoor play. Children must be taught the proper way to climb, swing and not to overload structures and equipment. Special care is needed to keep them out of the way of other children on moving equipment, such as swings, merry-go-rounds and trapezes.

Swimming pools. Drowning is the third leading cause of accidental death in children under 5. Children are so naturally drawn to water that sitters must take precautions constantly to keep accidents from happening. It is a plus if your sitter has CPR training. If you use the same sitter regularly, insist that the sitter be trained in CPR.

Help your sitter understand these rules, and the reasons for them, if he or she will be sitting with the children near the water:

1. Fast action is needed around water. A child can leave the house and walk to the edge of a pool in seconds and can drown in only a few inches of water. It can happen in the time it takes to answer the telephone.
2. Eyes on the child all of the time is the only acceptable policy.
3. Children should be supervised and accompanied all the time, even though you have told the children not to go near the water.
4. Make sure gates to the pool are closed and locked. Keep all doors leading from the house to the pool locked with locks out of the reach of children.
5. Don't consider children "water-safe" just because he or she has had swimming lessons.
6. Don't allow children to play on the apron surrounding the pool. Keep it and the swimming or wading areas clear of glasses or bottles.
7. Don't allow children to have something in their mouths while in the water.

8. If the pool is above-ground, remove the ladder to prevent access by anyone.
9. Anytime a child is missing, check the pool, wading pool, spa or hot tub first.
10. Know the telephone numbers to call for emergency medical service (In some areas it is not 911.) and have them posted on the phone.

Poisoning situations. Parents can do the most to keep all sources of poisons and medicines out of the reach of children. Sitters need to remember a few basic points about medications and know what to do if there is a poisoning event. You and your sitter should remember the following about medications:

1. Read the label on the container carefully and instruct the sitter accordingly.
2. Never leave the child alone with medications.
3. Return the medication to its safe storage place, with the top securely fastened.
4. Do not refer to medication as candy.
5. Do not give medication in the dark.
6. Sitters should not bring anything hazardous into the house, in purses or packages the child might get into.

What to do if there is a poisoning accident:

1. Don't wait to see what effect the poison will have if you think the child has swallowed medicine or a household product. The sitter should call a Poison Control Center, doctor or hospital immediately and be ready to answer a series of questions about the child's symptoms or behavior. The sitter should not try to induce vomiting unless instructed to do so by medical personnel.
2. Instruct the sitter to call a neighbor to help care for other children in the home. Provide the sitter with a name and number for this purpose.

3. After handling the immediate emergency, the sitter should call you to explain what has happened.
4. Explain to the sitter the need to remain calm in such emergencies. A frightened or sick child will become more frightened if the sitter shows panic.

Bad weather. Prepare the sitter for bad weather emergencies. Depending on the location, different weather threats are likely. It might be tornadoes and thunderstorms, flash floods or blizzards. Following are things you should review with the sitter:

1. Tour the basement, including light switches, basement steps and emergency exits.
2. Show the sitter your emergency weather kit and what is in it.
3. Point out the circuit breaker and how to reset a breaker.
4. Leave a flashlight with strong batteries, which will be easy to locate in the dark.

In case of fire. Before the baby sitter arrives, the parent should do a few things:

1. Be certain smoke and fire detectors have batteries and are working.
2. Know that the fire extinguishers are fully charged.
3. Have a fire evacuation plan.

Review with the baby sitter:

1. The fire evacuation plan.
2. The location of fire extinguishers and what types of fire they will control.
3. When to use the fire extinguisher and when to call the fire department.

Inform the sitter. Surprisingly, parents, in a hurry to leave the house, often forget to tell sitters the address and location of the home in which they are baby-sitting. And, just as surprising, sitters often do not know. For example, if the sitter is driven to the house and dropped off, he or she may not know exactly what the location is or how to get there. How then, can the sitter explain over the telephone, in an emergency, where the child in trouble is located? Write down your address and directions to the house and provide the sitter with this important information.

Rules to cover with the baby sitter:
1. Visitors allowed.
2. Telephone use.
3. Food and drinks permitted.
4. Whether it is all right to leave the house with the children to visit a mall, go to a show, visit a friend, etc.

Rules for the children:
1. Bedtime.
2. Eating.
3. Television.
4. Leaving the house to visit.

The publication, *The Super Sitter*, which is listed in the following bibliography, has more details on baby-sitting and is an excellent reference. It is free from the Consumer Product Safety Commission. Look for addresses and telephone numbers in the appendices.

HOME ALONE

There are times when it is not possible to have a baby sitter and a child must be left alone. When children no longer need sitters, they may start staying home alone and may begin baby-sitting for others. This is a transition period when children, at a fairly young age, are home alone.

At what age can children be left alone? Children should not be considered able to be home alone before the age of 8. Maturity and home situations vary, so this cannot be a hard and fast rule. Here are some rules to discuss with children:

1. Make certain children know how to work door and window locks.
2. Instruct them to keep doors and windows locked when home alone.

3. Post a list of important contacts and phone numbers near the phone. See the form at the end of this appendix.

4. Be certain the child knows how to place a "911 call, or how to call the operator with "0":
   - Be calm.
   - Wait for the dial tone, then dial 911 or 0 for the operator.
   - Tell the emergency people exactly what is wrong.
   - Give your name, address and telephone number.
   - Don't hang up until the other person hangs up, even if you have to leave the phone.

5. Be certain, by rehearsing them, that a child knows his or her full name, address and complete phone number, including area code.

6. Tell your children never to open the door to anyone when they are home alone.

7. Teach your children how to answer the phone so they don't reveal that they are alone, such as; "My mother is busy and cannot come to the phone right now."

8. Have children check in with you or a neighbor as soon as they arrive at home.

9. Children should not wear house keys in conspicuous places, such as pinned on jackets or on strings around necks. This advertises that a child will probably be at home alone.

10. Practice your fire escape plan with your children, so they will know what to do if a fire happens when they are home alone.

BIBLIOGRAPHY

"Be the Best Baby Sitter On the Block," *Family Safety and Health*, Chicago, IL: National Safety Council, Summer 1933, p. 8.

"Home Alone," Chicago, IL: National Safety Council, 1985.

"Keep Your Children Safe," *Today's Supervisor*, Chicago: National Safety Council, March 1991, pp. 4-5.

"Five Babysitting Tips Every Parent Should Know," Luther, Amy Bernstein, *Family Safety and Health*, Chicago: National Safety Council, Spring 1981, pp. 15-16.

"Summer Safety and First Aid," *Child Care Information Exchange*, Redmond, WA: August 1984, pp. 13, 15.

The Super Sitter, U.S. Product Safety Commission, September 1989.

IMPORTANT INFORMATION FOR BABY SITTER

Name of parent(s): _____

Street address _____ City _____

Telephone #_____ Next door neighbor's name _____

Important phone numbers

Where parents will be: _____

Nearby friend or relative: _____

Grandparent's name and phone: _____

Children's doctor: _____

Fire Department: _____

Police Department: _____

Poison Control Center: _____

Hospital: _____ .

Veterinarian for pets: _____

ALL EMERGENCIES: 911

DISASTERS

Natural and manmade disasters—including floods, hurricanes, tornadoes, winter storms, earthquakes, tidal waves, nuclear power plant accidents and fires—are of great concern. Earthquakes, nuclear power mishaps and power outages usually give little warning. Other disasters, except possibly fires, usually give anywhere from a few hours to several days notice.

It is practical to prepare for those disasters you will most likely encounter. Living in the shadow of a nuclear plant or on a flood plain lends emphasis to preparations. Most of the procedures for fire disasters and emergencies are covered in earlier chapters of this book.

Home emergency planning. Know what kind of disasters could happen in your area and how to respond to them. Emergency planning is a family concern and everyone should be involved. The National Weather Service suggests having two emergency meeting spots for the family. One should be right outside the home, for an emergency such as fire, and another away from your neighborhood, if you cannot return home. An out-of-state relative or friend should be the known contact. For example, if there is an earthquake in northern California, few places in the area would be a secure communications base.

Disaster kit. It is not unusual, in case of a disaster, to be forced to evacuate your home, even your neighborhood. This calls for a disaster kit to be used when leaving home in an emergency. The evacuation kit starts with what is needed to handle either an in-house or out-of-house emergency. You want enough food and water to last at least three days, in easy-to-carry boxes or bags. Duffel bags and backpacks are ideal containers. Here is what you should have in your disaster kit:

1. One gallon of water per person per day (for at least three days).
2. Nonperishable, high-energy food, such as dried fruit.
3. One change of clothing and footwear per person.
4. A first aid kit, including prescription medicines.
5. A battery-operated radio and flashlight, basic tools and several spare batteries.
6. An extra set of car and house keys and extra cash.
7. Special items needed by infants, aged or disabled family members.

Practice your evacuation plan and recheck or refresh the supplies in your disaster kit at least twice a year.

SUDDEN DISASTERS

These are events that strike without warning. The three detailed here ordinarily give little, if any, warning: earthquakes, nuclear power plant accidents and power outages.

General guidance. There are things you can do to help you prepare for and cope with almost any type of emergency. The most basic thing to do is to remain calm. In a disaster, too many people are killed because they act without thinking or panic and do nothing.

Warning. You should be familiar with your community's warning signal, which is usually an outdoor warning system. Most use a form of loud horn or siren. The Attack Warning Signal is a wavering sound on sirens or a series of short blasts on whistles or horns.

The peacetime attention or alert signal is usually a 3- to 5-minute steady blast to signal threatening or impending emergency. For most disasters, information or advance warning comes from the radio and television. If power is lost, the citizen's band on battery radios will keep you posted during severe emergencies.

You should not use your telephone to seek information in a community emergency. Use it only to report important events, such as fires, flash floods, tornado sightings, etc.

Emergency supplies. A major disaster might interfere with your normal supplies of food, water, heat and other necessities. You should keep on hand a stock of emergency supplies that can last a few days, preferably a week. The most important supplies are water, foods that do not require cooking (canned, dried, etc.), necessary medicines, a first aid kit, blankets, a battery-powered radio and a covered container for an emergency toilet.

After the disaster. Use extreme caution in entering buildings that may be weakened. Don't take lanterns, torches, candles or lighted cigarettes into buildings, until someone assures you that there are no gas leaks or pockets. If there are gas leaks, turn off gas and electricity. Stay away from downed power lines and anything they touch. If the lines are not on, they might come on at any time.

If any of your electrical appliances are wet, first turn off the main power switch, then unplug the wet appliance. Dry it out, reconnect it and then turn on the main power switch, making sure you are not standing on or touching a wet surface.

Get rid of any food that lost its refrigeration or was covered by water. Don't use the main water supply for drinking until it is cleared by the authorities.

EARTHQUAKES

For such disasters as floods, hurricanes, winter storms, tornadoes and tidal waves, you usually have from a few minutes to hours, or even days notice. The most common of the completely unexpected disasters, and the most unpredictable, is the earthquake. You hardly feel an earthquake that is 3.5 on the Richter scale. When they hit 5.5, the damage starts to occur. Up to this point, you can protect your property fairly easily and reasonably. Most casualties result from falling objects and debris, splintering glass and fires. Following are general precautions.

Before the earthquake

1. Know the condition of your house and what needs to be done to make it safer in earthquakes. In older homes, it may be easy to make small changes that will make a big difference.

2. Avoid fire damage. Make sure a gas water heater is fastened to wall studs.

3. Put latches on cabinet doors to keep things from falling out and hitting people.

4. Be sure that heavy pictures, mirrors or lamps don't hang over beds or places where people frequently sit.

5. Anchor or brace top-heavy furniture to the walls.

6. Store hazardous chemicals where they will not spill.

7. Larger and heavier objects should be placed on lower shelves.

When an earthquake starts

1. Don't run or panic. Keep calm.

2. Stay where you are, indoors or outdoors. Most injuries occur as people enter or leave buildings.

3. If you are indoors, seek shelter in a an inside doorway or under solid furniture, such as a table or bench, or against inside walls. Stay away from glass windows and outside doors.

4. Don't use candles, matches or other open flames. Douse all fires.

5. If you are outdoors, move away from buildings and utility poles. Once in the open, stay there until the shaking stops.

6. Don't run through, or near, buildings. The biggest danger from falling debris is near outside doorways and close to outer walls.

7. If you are driving, pull off to the roadside, away from buildings, power poles and overpasses that could fall on the car.

After the earthquake

1. Check for injuries.

2. Check utility lines and appliances for damage.

3. If water pipes are damaged, shut off the supply at the main valve.

4. Be sure the sewage lines are intact before flushing toilets.

5. If electrical wiring is shorted out, shut off the current at the main meter box.

6. Check chimneys for cracks and damage.

7. Stay out of severely damaged buildings.

8. Do not heed or spread rumors.

9. Don't go sightseeing. Respond to requests in other areas only on the request of authorities or recognized relief organizations.

10. Be ready for more earthquake shocks.

Finally, all earthquakes do not cause Tsunamis (tidal waves), but expect them with large earthquakes, which have epicenters that underlie or border the ocean floor. These are nearly all in the Pacific. If you live near the shore and hear that there has been an earthquake, stand by for Tsunami warnings.

NUCLEAR POWER PLANT ACCIDENTS

Nearly 3 million Americans live within 10 miles of nuclear power plants. If you live within this distance, you should know something about nuclear power and radiation. For emergency preparedness purposes, there are 2 zones. One covers an area within a 10-mile radius of the nuclear power plant, where you could have direct exposure to radiation. The second covers a 50-mile radius of the plant, where nuclear radiation could expose you indirectly by entering the food chain through contamination of food crops, water supplies or grazing lands.

Community leaders and local governments should work together to develop protective and emergency plans. The local government should inform and advise you about what has happened and what you should do about it.

There are three ways to minimize radiation exposure to your body. They are shielding, distance and time. In a serious reactor accident, this means leaving the area or seeking proper shelter. Emergency broadcasts will direct you to the right courses of action.

Don't use the telephone. Keep the lines clear.

NOT-SO-SUDDEN DISASTERS

"Not-so-sudden" does not mean the disaster is expected or known. It only implies that you know that such a disaster is likely or in the making. In other words, you can, and should, expect the disaster and prepare for it.

HURRICANES

The hurricane season in the U.S. is generally from June through October. It brings wind, storm surge, wave action, flooding and tornadoes. If you are in the path of a hurricane, the National Weather Service suggests using your family emergency plan and minimizing your losses with the following steps.

1. Know your vulnerability. Will your house withstand the expected storm? Keeping the wind out is a major step to preventing damage.
2. Know your evacuation route ahead of time and know when it might be cut off. Expect a surge in traffic, due to others evacuating. If you are in a mobile home, always plan to evacuate.
3. Fasten down loose ends. Fasten down the lawn furniture and tie down pool equipment and the lawn mower. Fasten shutters tightly or board your windows, preferably with heavy plywood.
4. Follow tornado safety rules. If you cannot evacuate, go to an all-interior, small room on the lowest floor, as long as it is safe from flooding. The room should be windowless if possible.
5. Take care of pets. Leave them in the most secure area with food and water. They are not likely to be allowed in a shelter or hotel.
6. Care for your car. Your car should be in reasonably good shape and have a full tank of gas.
7. Before leaving, turn off all power to the house at the main switch cut-off on the outside of the house. This will decrease the chance of fire if an electric wire is exposed through storm damage.

WINTER WEATHER

The worst winter weather problems happen where and when people are least prepared for winter. Thus, the hardy farmers of North Dakota may not flinch at weather that would paralyze Florida. Winter can bring strong winds, extreme cold, ice storms and heavy snowstorms. Winter storms are killers. Heart attacks can result from shoveling snow and from accidents on icy roads. Blunt the winter storm with your disaster plan. (Much of the material in "When the Power Goes Out," which follows, is appropriate.) Keep in mind the following:

1. Have extra heating fuel supplies, since deliveries could be several days late.
2. Have an emergency heating source, such as plenty of wood for a wood stove or fireplace, or a space heater, all to be used in a well-ventilated room.
3. Close off unneeded rooms.
4. Get your car winter-ready. Have the proper emergency kit for survival and snowy roads. For cold climates, the survival kit is extensive. Use guidelines from your auto club or transportation agency.
5. Maintain your energy by eating proper foods and replacing your body fluids, but not by eating unmelted snow.
6. When you drive, dress as if you were going to leave your warm car. Wear layers of loose-fitting clothing and something for your head and face.
7. If outside for a time or taking a trip, try not to travel alone.
8. Give your home the special care it needs if you're going to be away in cold weather. Either set your furnace to minimum heat or drain all water from your pipes and turn the water off at the water main.

FLOODS

Every state in the U.S. is subject to flooding, sometimes flash floods. The intense rainfall over a short period that brings flash floods overloads the normal drainage systems. A few inches of fast-moving water moves or knocks over most things in its path. There are many things you can do to protect yourself from imminent floods.

1. Know your local flood risks and elevation above flood level.
2. Know the difference between a flood watch and a warning. A flash flood watch tells you that a flash flood is

possible. Put your disaster plan into effect. A flash flood warning means flash flooding is so certain that you should be prepared to take action in a moment.

3. Get out of the flood area. Avoid low spots and avoid already flooded areas.

4. Know that half of all flood deaths are auto-related. Do not drive on flooded roadways. If the vehicle stops, get out at once and seek higher ground.

HAIL AND LIGHTNING

Hail and lightning are thunderstorm-generated. Again, you need to realize that a watch means conditions are favorable for the event, and a warning means it is imminent or in progress. If you can hear thunder, you are in danger. Lightning can jump as far as you can hear the thunder (up to 12 miles). Take these safeguards.

1. If you are on in the water or on the beach, leave.

2. Move away from isolated tall structures, such a trees or poles.

3. Avoid metal objects, such as fences or golf clubs.

4. Don't run across an open area. It is better to make yourself as small a target as possible by rolling into a ball, dropping low in a ditch, etc.

5. Stay away from your phone unless it is cordless and well-removed from the base.

6. A surge protector will not always protect electronic equipment. Unplug it.

7. Forget about a bath/shower during a thunderstorm. Lightning strikes can travel through the pipes to you.

8. Turn off your air conditioner. A lightning strike will ruin the motor.

TORNADOES

Another act of nature associated with thunderstorms are tornadoes, violently rotating columns of air from the thunderstorm to the ground. The National Weather Service estimates that 90 percent of tornado fatalities result from flying debris. Safety measures call for staying out of the path of flying objects of any size. Even a straw, moving at 250 miles-per-hour, can pierce a brick.

1. Know your locality so that you can monitor the locations of tornadoes as they are broadcast.

2. Know the safest place in your house during a tornado. Most likely it will be an inside room with many walls between you and the outside, preferably in a basement. Get under sturdy furniture such as a table or desk. Hurry, you have only seconds.

3. Stay away from windows.

4. If in a mobile home, leave it! You are better off in a ditch.

5. Don't try to outrun a tornado in your car. They are too unpredictable in terms of speed and direction. Some experts suggest abandoning your car and getting away from it.

6. If outdoors, do anything to get as low as possible: crouch, lay low in a depression or a ditch, etc.

FIRESTORMS

Homes or vacation cabins built in wooded areas not only expose people to woodland fires, but introduce manmade hazards, such as chimneys, outdoor grills and burning trash, to the woods. Some woodland area fires are beyond individual control, but there are many precautions to take around the home. The National Fire Protection Association suggests:

1. Think flat. Since fire spreads more rapidly uphill, a level site is better.

2. Plan for easy access. Two-way roads are necessary for your evacuation and for fire fighter access to your site.

3. Say no to untreated roofs. Untreated shake or shingle roofs are a major

cause of losses. Use asphalt tile, slate, concrete shingles, etc.

4. Don't deck the slopes. Because slopes act as chimneys carrying fire and smoke upward, don't build your deck facing one.

5. Choose thick-tempered, multi-pane safety glass for windows. Non-flammable shutters and fire-resistant draperies offer added protection.

6. Cover vents with wire mesh, with openings no larger than ¼ inch. This helps prevent sparks from being drawn in.

7. Clearly post your address. Make sure fire fighters can find your address.

8. Practice fireplace safety. Store firewood well away from any structures and install a noncombustible wire mesh fire screen in your chimney.

9. Keep your yard and grounds clean. Remove weeds and litter. Check roof and eaves often and remove dried vegetation that could ignite. Keep all vegetation within 30 feet of your house well maintained, thoroughly watered and widely spaced.

10. Use fire alarms. Every home should have fire detectors and alarms.

11. Eliminate "fire-ladder" growth. Brush, shrubs and limbs can create a ladder effect for flames to climb.

12. Keep tree limbs trimmed. Make sure they don't hang over your roof. Keep vegetation next to the house under 18 inches tall. Use low growing vegetation and ground cover instead.

13. Select fire-resistant plants. They can actually create a safety zone around your house. The local fire protection group can advise you on fire-resistant plants for your area.

14. Keep up your yard work. Keep all vegetation within 30 feet of your house well-maintained, thoroughly watered and widely spaced.

WHEN THE POWER GOES OUT

Many emergencies, whether disaster-related or not, involve power outages. Here are some tested ideas to help you get through the next power outage in relative comfort, especially in cold weather.

1. Keep some basic supplies in a handy place:
   - Matches.
   - Candles.
   - Flashlight.
   - Battery-powered radio.
   - Extra batteries.
   - Manual can opener.
   - Firewood.

2. When power goes out, check to see if the outage is only within your house. If your neighbors' lights are on, check your fuse box or circuit breakers.

3. If the neighborhood lights are out, check for downed power lines and branches, flashes of light or other trouble signs. *Do not touch* and stay well away.

4. Call your public utility and then be patient. Resist the temptation to call repeatedly. Some outages take longer than others to restore.

5. Turn off the switches to furnace, stove, microwave oven, television and other appliances, to prevent a power overload that may cause a second outage.

6. Save the heat. Close windows, doors, and drapes. Insulate cracks under doors, dress warmly and use more bedclothes.

7. Save water. Fill containers if a storm threatens. Your water heater retains a supply of water for many hours.

8. Save cold. Food will be safe for at least 24 hours if freezer and refrigerator doors remain closed.

9. Listen to a battery-operated radio for the latest news about progress in restoring power.

10. When power is restored, switch on lights and appliances slowly. Turn the

furnace on and gradually return thermostats to their normal settings.

Caution with portable generators. Using portable generators can have tragic consequences, so pay careful attention to correct installation procedures and use.

If you own a generator for a recreational vehicle or cabin, you may be tempted to connect it to your home during a power outage. If the house circuits are not disconnected from public utility lines, current from the generator will travel through the electric meter to outside power lines. This is a danger that is potentially fatal to linemen working to repair lines, which they think are dead.

A generator plugged into house circuits may also overload and burn out when too many appliances are used at once, or when the power from the outside is restored. Unless the installation is engineered properly, you should plug directly into the generator only those lights and appliances that do not exceed the generator's capacity.

If you are planning the permanent installation of standby generators, you should consult your utility's customer engineer for advice on equipment, hookup procedures and load requirements.

At least two telephone numbers for your utility should be kept in a handy place; a number for regular business hours and a number for evenings, weekends and holidays.

BIBLIOGRAPHY

"Out of the Blue," Whitley, Kathi, *Aide*, San Antonio, TX: USAA, August 1993, pp. 10-18.

ELECTRICAL HAZARDS

Electricity is often taken for granted. Your home is filled with electrical products that keep you warm, cook your food, give you light and entertain you.

Each year, thousands of people receive hospital emergency-room treatment for injuries associated with electrical fires or shocks. Hundreds of people die in electrical mishaps. About 60,000 residential fires each year begin in the electrical distribution system. This type of fire results in 500 deaths and another 5,000 injuries per year.

The following brief account of electrical terms and examples will help you understand the electrical hazards of consumer products and help you recognize and handle electrical problems.

- Stuart plugged his air conditioner into the extension cord of his clock-radio and record player. One evening, while all of the appliances were running, he smelled burning plastic and saw smoke rising from the cord. When he tried to pull the plugs he burned his hand. Stuart finally shut off the power at the fuse box, but there was already extensive smoke and heat damage in the room.

- While standing in the shower, Ben reached out to change the station on his radio. He received an electrical shock and was unable to release his grasp on the radio. He died within a few seconds.

Major electrical hazards. The examples above illustrate the major hazard patterns found with electrical products.

1. Electrical fires. These can be caused by overloads on circuits that are not meant to carry the current flowing through them or poor electrical connections. A short circuit occurs when the normal current path is varied by passing through broken insulation or a bad connection to a touching conductor, thus shorting the circuit. A very hot spark or arc results, which can ignite insulation or nearby combustibles.

2. Shocks come from current flowing through the human body. A fraction of one ampere (a measure of the amount of current) can kill you. Misunderstanding often plays a part in these accidents. Many people think that when an appliance is turned to "off," there is no electricity in it. Not so. As long as an appliance is plugged into an outlet, parts of it are still "live." Cleaning a switched-off, but still plugged-in, coffee pot in the sink can be fatal.

3. Auxiliary power units (APUs). As people seek backup power for their equipment during a power failure, it is not uncommon to have APUs that automatically kick in when the power fails. These generators sense a power outage and come on-line quickly to keep essential services running. This is especially true of homes in remote locations and some apartments buildings. The problem occurs when people turn off the power at the circuit breaker or fuse box to work on the electric lines, or in an emergency, such as to fight a fire. The usually remote-located APU unknowingly comes on-line and the electrical lines are ready to shock or electrocute.

Electricity defined. Electricity can be described in the following terms:

1. Ampere: the amount of current that flows through a wire. This current can hurt or kill you.
2. Volt: the force that pushes the current along the wire. High voltage from the power plant is reduced to about 120 volts for most home circuits.
3. Ohm: the measure of resistance to the flow of current. The human body, especially when wet, has low resistance and easily conducts electric current.
4. Watt: the electrical power, or the rate of using a certain number of amperes pushed by a certain number of volts (watts = volts x amperes). Most electrical appliances list on their labels the watts and amperes they use.

To better understand, consider this example: Suppose that an electric frying pan uses 1,200 watts when it operates. Since the normal house voltage is 120 volts, then the amount of current (amperes) flowing through the pan is 10 amperes. The lethal dose of current for the human body is much less than one ampere. So, if even a small fraction of the current in the frying pan leaks and runs through your body you can receive a fatal electric shock. If the shock does not kill you immediately, it can cause convulsive heart action that may lead to death.

Consider another example: The normal wall outlet can carry 15 amperes (most fuses and circuit breakers will open the circuit if the current is more than 15 amperes). If you overload a wall outlet with a 10-ampere frying pan, a 5-ampere coffee maker, and a 4-ampere blender, there will be more than 15 amperes of current flowing through the circuit. This should blow the fuse or open the circuit breaker. However, if you have used a high-amperage fuse, the current will continue to flow. The overloaded outlet and the house wiring will heat, which can cause an electrical fire.

Grounding. Grounding is a key concept in electricity. A circuit is grounded to limit the voltage of that circuit for safety reasons. An electric appliance or tool has its exposed metal parts grounded to prevent people from receiving electrical shocks, if the insulation of the circuit operating the appliance or tool breaks down, or if the current of the appliance or tool leaks to the outside metal enclosure.

Unfortunately, the human body is a good conductor of electrical current and easily completes a circuit by letting current pass through the body and into the ground. To avoid the human body being the ground path, some electrical appliances have double insulation. Others connect to the outside metal enclosure, to ground through a third conductor in the flexible appliance cord. If there is a current leak in the normal circuit (which uses the two regular prongs in a plug), the current goes directly to the ground by the third wire. Some outlets provide for the third prong. Always use the third prong on an appliance. Do not break it off. It is safer to have wall outlets rewired to accept three-prong plugs than to use the two-plug adapters. If you must use an adapter, be sure to attach the pigtail third wire to the screw holding the face plate to the wall receptacle. If the screw itself is properly grounded (which can be determined by an electrician), this should provide a line to carry any leaking current directly to the ground. If it is not grounded, a wire from the ground to the outlet box must be installed.

Ground fault circuit interrupter. A ground fault circuit interrupter (GFI or GFCI) senses ground faults (accident electrical paths to the ground) in circuits and immediately cuts off all electrical power in the circuit. Put another way, the GFCI trips (breaks) the electrical current faster than a circuit breaker. It does it quicker than a heartbeat, thus preventing shock or electrocution. Many building codes now require one or more GFCIs in new construction. However, most existing houses do not have them. While it would be safer to have GFCIs installed, the cost can be high. A GFCI can be installed by an electrician for about $100 or less. As a standard circuit breaker replacement, one GFCI protects only one branch circuit. This means many GFCIs are needed to give your house full protection.

Priority for the installation of GFCIs would be to replace outlets where shock is likely to occur (laundry room, kitchen, bathroom, damp basement, garage and outdoor circuits). Or, GFCIs can be wired into circuits at the panel box. Priority should go to GFCIs for washer and dryer outlets.

Extension cords. Extension cords are a factor in about 50 fires every day, most of which are caused by overloading the cord. External damage to the cord and improper changes to the cord rate high as other causes of fires.

Most extension cords in the home are lamp cords, so called because they are the size commonly used by table and floor lamps. Light-duty extension cords of this size should only be used with small appliances, such as table lamps, clocks and radios. They are not meant for the rough use of vacuum cleaners or portable tools. Safety suggests the following guidelines:

1. Don't overload an extension cord by plugging too many products into it.
2. Some light-duty extension cords rated for a 10-ampere load might handle several very small appliances, but they might not safely handle one large appliance.
3. Use the right cord. For example, when using electrical lawn and garden equipment, use only a cord marked for outdoor use (which has a third safety grounding wire) unless you are using only tools labeled as "double-insulated." They require only a two-wire cord.
4. Do not buy cords that fail to list the maximum current or wattage rating.

5. Don't cut and splice cords together to create another cord. It is too dangerous to use spliced cords, because the splice is a weak link that can cause fires.

Safe use of electrical products. In addition to the GFCI, the following suggestions can help ensure safer use of electrical products:

1. Using fuses and circuit breakers.
   - If fuses blow, or the circuit breakers open, it means an overloaded or short circuit. Check to make sure you are not using a defective appliance or too many appliances on the circuit, and correct the situation.
   - Do not replace a fuse without first disconnecting or turning off the appliances and light switches in the circuit.
   - Don't use higher-amperage fuses as replacements, because the wires in the circuits can be overloaded and cause a fire.
   - Make sure that fuses and circuit breakers are well-marked on the fuse or circuit breaker box, so they can be switched off quickly.
2. Grounding.
   - Always use the third prong on plugs that have it. Check wall outlets for proper grounding. If the boxes with your two-prong outlets are grounded, you can use a two-prong adapter if you connect its third wire or metal tab to the center screw that holds the face plate to the wall outlet box. If they are not grounded, you need a wire from ground to outlet. It is better to have new three-wire conductors and three-prong wall outlets installed.
   - Keep your body from becoming part of a circuit or conducting current to the ground. Don't touch an appliance if you're wet, standing on a wet surface or if the appliance cord has broken insulation or a damaged plug.

3. Overloading wall outlets. When more plugs go into the outlet than can be handled safely, the wires get hot and can start a fire, usually inside the wall. Add more outlets if needed.

4. Misusing polarized plugs.
   - New plugs and outlets have one side wider than the other. They are called polarized plugs and help prevent electrical shock.
   - If you must push very hard to insert a plug into an outlet, check to see if the outlet is also polarized.
   - Make certain you fit the plug into the socket correctly.
   - If your wall outlets are not polarized, an expert should replace them for you, or you might use a proper adapter.

5. Using extension and appliance cords.
   - Remember that many extension cords cannot carry more than 7 amperes (840 watts) of current, so check the current rating on the cord label and don't overload it.
   - Use cords rated for at least 15 amperes for large appliances by using multi-receptacle adapters or cords.
   - Never overload a wall receptacle with too many appliances by using multi-receptacle adapters or cords.
   - Replace extension and appliance cords at the first sign of wear.
   - Do not use extension cords except on an emergency or temporary basis.
   - Never place cords along the floor in doorways. They are a tripping hazard and also may wear so that they no longer function properly.
   - Tape appliance and extension cords together when the connection is permanent.
   - Do not run extension cords near toasters, heaters or other high heat sources.

   - Don't shorten cords by wrapping them up tightly, because they can heat, dry, crack and cause a fire.
   - Don't interchange cords from different appliances.

6. Using electrical appliances outside.
   - Do not use electrical appliances, such as a rotisserie, electric lawn mower or power tool, where it can get wet or where it is raining. The water can cause a short circuit and cause fatal electric shock.

7. Making home repairs.
   - If you are not familiar with electrical work, do not attempt any repairs. Have qualified electricians rewire or install electrical equipment.
   - If you must replace a light fixture or repair an electrical appliance or outlet, first turn off the electricity at the breaker or fuse panel.
   - When making any electrical repairs, insulate yourself from becoming part of the current. Wearing dry, rubber gloves or standing on a rubber mat can prevent current from running through your body. Do not use metal ladders when making electrical repairs, because they conduct electricity.
   - When changing a light bulb, first disconnect the lamp's plug to avoid possible electric shock.

8. Watching for danger signals.
   - If you smell hot or burning plastic or notice flickering lights, have your house wiring checked immediately by a qualified electrician. You may have to rearrange your appliances so that certain high-use circuits (such as kitchen circuits) are not overloaded.
   - A "roasting" smell may mean you are using a lamp calling for too much wattage for the lamp and circuit.
   - If you smell gas from a gas range or other gas appliance, don't turn any electrical switches on or off because a spark could ignite the gas. Open

9. Reading labels.
   - Follow all directions on labels or instructions, especially on the heavy-duty extension cords or special circuits that some appliances require.
   - Remember that the UL (Under-writers Laboratories) label is not a complete guarantee of safety. It means that Underwriters Laboratories (a private testing facility) has tested samples of the product and found that they meet voluntary safety standards.
10. Dealing with current leaks.
    - If you feel even a slight shock when you touch an appliance, stop using it immediately. Unplug it and have it checked by a qualified electrician.
    - Have all broken insulation or other defects repaired immediately.
11. Using Auxiliary Power Units (APUs).
    - If the home is served by an APU, there should be a clearly labeled override control that prevents starting of the APU. A prominent sign at the control box should advise that an APU is installed and advise of the shock hazard.
12. Responding when another person is receiving an electrical shock.
    - Do not touch the person until the circuit is broken or current is cut off, because you could also receive a shock.
    - Cut off the current.
    - If you cannot cut off the circuit, use wood, heavy clothing, a broom, chair or some other insulated material to push the person away from the source of the current.
    - Begin mouth-to-mouth resuscitation immediately.
    - Call an ambulance.
13. Being prepared.
    - Have a fire extinguisher nearby. The best one for the home, and certainly the kitchen, is an extinguisher rated ABC, which can handle grease as well as electrical fires.

Need for inspection. Wiring and other electrical equipment seldom last as long as the house. Signs that your electrical system is beginning to fail are: lights dimming, fuses blowing and circuit breakers tripping. If these things happen often, it is time for an inspection of your system by a licensed electrician or your local power company. The problem may be something that could cause a fire, so the inspection should not be delayed.

Deteriorated wiring. Wiring, over the years, deteriorates and wears away, exposing the wires that carry current. Electrical appliance cords and extension cords can become damaged or overheat when placed under carpeting or furniture, or coiled during use. A check of appliance and extension cords should be part of an inspection.

Using bulbs of too high a wattage. Called over-lamping, the use of bulbs of higher wattage than recommended in light fixtures may lead to fire through overheating. If the recommended wattage is not printed on the light fixture, it is best not to use bulbs higher than 60 watts.

Over-fusing. Fuses and circuit breakers warn and protect you. When circuits are overloaded and blow a fuse or open a circuit breaker, the power is shut off to the overloaded circuit. (Overloaded means using so many appliances on a line that the combined load is greater than its capacity.)

In older homes, people tend to use higher-valued fuses than the line permits. This can cause the circuit to overheat and, instead of blowing a fuse, the lines get hot enough to catch fire. Only a trained electrician should decide what size fuses to use for circuits. Generally speaking, #12 copper wire should have a

15-ampere fuse, while #14 copper wire should have a 20-ampere fuse or circuit breaker.

Electromagnetic fields/extremely low frequency (ELF). Because of possible effects on the body, there is some concern about extremely low frequency (ELF) and magnetic fields. In December 1992, the Food and Drug Administration found that, in spite of worldwide research, no firm evidence of harm has been found. All electrical devices produce some type of electric, magnetic or electronic fields, but at many different frequencies. Research continues, but there is doubt about what to look for and what the harmful effects might be. Most research, at this writing, centers on electric blankets and video display tubes.

Most public concern about electromagnetic radiation focuses on cancer and the microwave oven. However, microwaves also are used for radar, satellite or tower-to-tower relay of telephone, telegraph and television signals and other purposes. Microwaves are part of the electromagnetic spectrum of which radio waves, ultraviolet and infrared light, x-rays and gamma rays also are a part. Common to all these forms, is the fact that they go through space as energy waves with both electric and magnetic properties; hence the name electromagnetic radiation.

Electromagnetic radiation with microwave ovens is the subject of a special section of this book. But what about other appliances? It is fair to say the research is not conclusive about the degree of hazard found by various researchers. The sum of electromagnetic radiation faced at home, work and play is a significant amount of magnetic pollution and is of concern. The hazards posed by the following separate appliances are probably of minor concern. Household appliances used all the time have varying degrees of shielding to protect the user. Here are a few findings on radiation:

1. Vacuum cleaners. Both upright and canister vacuum cleaners have small but powerful motors that project a considerable distance. A fully shielded motor might make this machine too heavy to carry.

2. Hair dryers and electric shavers. Hand-held dryers have a weaker magnetic field than dryers that blow through tubes into bonnets. Shavers and clippers have strong fields for their size, though shavers with solid state controls have much weaker fields.

3. Toasters, coffee makers, irons. Small appliances like these contain only a small resistive heating element, so their magnetic fields are smaller and weaker. The magnetic fields tend to be strongest at the sides of these objects.

4. Blenders, can openers, mixers. The motors in these appliances are small in size, but quite powerful. Their light frames do little to shield the user from the magnetic fields they produce, so the fields have an even stronger effect than that of much larger appliances.

5. Television sets. It is hard to measure the magnetic fields from a television set, due to the number of other frequencies it sends. Sets without a power transformer have been found to have almost no magnetic field.

6. Fluorescent lights. These lights use a special transformer to boost the incoming voltage. The larger the fixture and the greater the number of its light tubes, the more distance the magnetic field will cover. The field is strongest directly below the fixture.

7. Washers, dryers and dishwashers. The size of these appliances serves to shield the user from their magnetic fields. Though the motors are large and powerful, they tend to be located in the back and bottom of the machine. Magnetic fields are strongest in front of the machine as well as at floor level. The

heating element in dryers increases the size of their magnetic fields.

Prudent steps

1. Keep your video display terminal (VDT) at arms length. Stay at least 26 inches from the front of it and don't sit within three feet of the sides or back of another VDT.

2. Keep children at least three feet from color TVs, which create the same kind of fields that VDTs do.

3. Reduce the use of electric blankets, especially during pregnancy. Try turning on the blanket only to heat the bed and unplug it before getting in bed.

4. Move electric clocks, radios, answering machines and other electrical devices that stay on continuously several feet away from your head when you sleep. Or use battery-operated machines that don't emit electromagnetic fields.

5. Don't stand in front of the dishwasher or microwave oven while it's on.

6. As a very rough guideline, if you have small children or expect to become pregnant, don't buy a house within 150 feet of a local high-current line or 400 feet of a long-distance, high-tension line.

7. Measure the electromagnetic fields in your home (or prospective home). Some utilities will do this, or you can rent or buy an easy-to-operate gauss-meter.

No one ever said it was easy to be completely safe and these prudent steps illustrate the problem. A little common sense will help you decide what is prudent for your situation. Keep in mind that until more conclusive research results are in, scientists won't know whether a health problem exists.

BIBLIOGRAPHY

"A Quick Course in What They Call Prudent Avoidance," *Fortune*, December 31, 1990, p. 82.

"Extension Cords Involved in 20 House Fires Daily," *Consumer Product Safety Alert*, U.S. Consumer Product Safety Commission, May 1984."

"Focus on HAZ MAT," *Industrial Fire World*, August-September 1990, pp. 24-27.

Goldbreck, David, *The Smart Kitchen*, Ceres Press, 1989, pp. 40-43.

"Beware: 10 Electrical Hazards at Home," Mills, Richard, *Family Safety and Health*, Winter 1990-91, pp. 5-7.

"The ELF in Your Electric Blanket," *FDA Consumer*, Washington, DC: Government Printing Office, December 1992, pp. 22-25.

"The Hazards of Household Appliances," *PCC Sound Consumer, No. 210*, Seattle, September, 1990, pp. 1, 12.

"The Home Electrical System," *Product Safety Fact Sheet*, U.S. Consumer Product Safety Commission, November 1983.

FEDERAL AGENCY CONTACTS FOR CONSUMERS

Alcoholism and Drug Addiction Hotline
Treatment Center 1-800-342-4357

Alzheimer's Disease and Related Disorders Association Hotline
1-800-621-0730

American Council of the Blind Hotline
1-800-424-8669
9 a.m.-5:30 p.m.

American Diabetes Association
1-800-ADA-DISC
8:30 a.m.-5 p.m.

Asbestos Information Hotline
Asbestos Disease Association
1-800-446-6700

Asthma and Allergy Foundation
1-800-7-ASTHMA
9 a.m.-5 p.m.

Auto Defects Hotline
1-800-424-9393
8 a.m.-5 p.m., Mon.-Fri. EST

Write:
Administrator, NHTSA
400 Seventh St., SW
Washington DC 20590

Cancer Information Hotline
1-800-4-CANCER

U.S. Coast Guard Boating Safety Hotline
1-800-368-5674

Consumer Information Center Hotline
1-800-638-2772,
1-800-638-8270
Information on prescription drugs and drug interactions.

Write:
Consumer Product Safety Commission (CPSC)
Consumer Information Center
Dept. 580X, Pueblo, CO 81009

Department of Agriculture Fish, Meat and Poultry Hotline
1-800-535-4555

Dial A Hearing Screening Test
1-800-222-EARS
9 a.m.-5 p.m.

Environmental Protection Agency
1-800-438-2474

Safe Drinking Water Hotline
1-800-426-4791

Food and Drug Administration (FDA)
Responsibilities include food, drugs, cosmetics, biological products, medical devices, radiological devices and veterinary products. Consumer affairs officers respond to questions about the agency and what it regulates. Look under the Department of

Health and Human Services in the U.S. Government section of phone directory.

Consumer Inquiries Staff
301-443-3170
The staff can furnish information and is set up to help consumers track down information.

Write:
Consumers Inquiries Staff, HFE-88
Room 16-33, 5600 Fishers Lane
Rockville, MD 20857

Seafood Hotline
1-800-332-4010

For a complete list of toll-free Health Information lines
1-800-555-1212

National AIDS Hotline
1-800-342-AIDS,
1-800-344-7432 (Spanish)
8 a.m.-2 a.m.

National Child Abuse Hotline
1-800-422-4453

National Hazardous Materials Information Exchange
1-800-752-6367

National Highway Traffic Safety Administration (NHTSA)
1-800-424-9393,
1-800-424-9153
Information on vehicles, parts, supplies and child safety seats.

National Institute for Occupational Safety and Health (NIOSH)
1-800-356-4674
Information on health hazard evaluation.

National Kidney Foundation
1-800-622-9010
9 a.m.-5 p.m.

National Pesticide Telecommunications Network (NPTN)
For prompt responses and information on pesticides.
1-800-858-7378
Seeks information on adverse effects of pesticide exposure.

Write:
Pesticide Incident Responsible Officer
Field Operations Division (H-7506C)
Office of Programs, EPA
401 M St., SW
Washington, DC 20460

National Safety Council Lead Poison Hotline
1-800-532-3394

Meat and Poultry Hotline
1-800-535-4555
10 a.m.-4 p.m.

STD (Sexually Transmitted Diseases) Hotline
1-800-227-8922
8 a.m.-8 p.m.

FLAMMABILITY

The terrible losses caused by fires each year are well-known. But the losses themselves suggest that the origins and behavior of fires are not so well-understood. Although fires behave in different ways, the same three ingredients are necessary for every fire: fuel, heat and oxygen.

1. Fuel can be anything that will burn, from wood and paper to gasoline, even metals.
2. Heat is necessary for any fire and can take many forms. It might be the simple lighting of a match, the sun or some other source. Just being next to something hot like a radiator can furnish enough heat to start a fire.
3. The last ingredient needed for a fire is oxygen, the same oxygen that surrounds you in the air you breathe.

As fuel warms, it gives off vapor that reaches an ignition point and then bursts into flame. When fuel, heat and oxygen combine, a chemical reaction produces heat, flame and smoke. To prevent or stop a fire, you must either remove the fuel, lower the heat (such as with a cool water spray) or shut off the oxygen.

The ignition temperature of fuel varies greatly from the 450°F of paper, to thousands of degrees for certain metals. Flammable liquids are more dangerous because they give off vapors that can ignite at low temperatures. Liquid vapors, then, can drift to a heat source, such as a water heater. The water heater pilot light temperature of 536°F easily ignites gasoline vapors of the right mixture (they can ignite at 45°F). Nearly all heat sources produce temperatures far above that needed to ignite fuel vapors.

Depending on the heat and fuel involved, burning may start in several ways. Usually, fire begins with heat from a spark, friction, flame or a surface hot enough to ignite fuel vapors. Or it can begin with electrical current sparks. Also, there is spontaneous combustion, in which the fuel increases its own temperature in a chemical or fermenting action, such as with oily rags or damp hay.

FEDERAL LAWS

Flammability standards for fabrics. Each year there are 3,000 to 5,000 deaths and 150,000 to 250,000 injuries from flammable fabric burns. In the past several years, federal and state governments have taken steps to reduce this toll by setting flammability standards and informing the public of the hazards of flammable fabrics.

Flammable Fabrics Act

1. Passed in 1953 to regulate the manufacture of highly flammable clothing, such as brushed rayon sweaters and children's cowboy chaps.
2. Amended in 1972 to cover a wider range of clothing and interior furnishings. Responsibilities are split among different government agencies.

Consumer Product Safety Act. Passed in 1972, it created the Consumer Product Safety Commission (CPSC) with broad jurisdiction over product safety. Responsibilities under the Flammable Fabrics Act were transferred to the Commission.

The following are federal standards for the Flammable Fabrics Act:

General wearing apparel

1. Includes wearing apparel, but excludes interlining fabrics and certain hats, gloves and footwear.
2. A piece of fabric, placed in a holder at a 45-degree angle and exposed to a flame for 1 second, must not spread flame up the length of the sample in less than 3.5 seconds for smooth fabrics, or 4.0 seconds for napped fabrics.

Large carpets and rugs

1. Includes carpets with surface area greater than 24 square feet, but excludes linoleum, vinyl tile and asphalt tile.
2. Requires that 9-inch-by-9-inch samples, exposed to a burning tablet placed on the center of each sample, must not char more than 3 inches in any direction. The burning tablet simulates a lighted match dropped on the carpet.
3. All large carpets and rugs must be labeled with the letter "T" if a flame-retardant treatment has been applied. (A fiber that is inherently flame-retardant does not require a label.)

Small carpets and rugs

1. Includes carpets with surface areas less than 24 square feet, but excludes linoleum, vinyl tile and asphalt tile.
2. Uses the same burning tablet test as used for large carpets and rugs.
3. Small carpets and rugs that do not meet the standard must be labeled as follows:

Standard FF 2-70; SHOULD NOT BE USED NEAR SOURCES FLAMMABLE (Fails U.S. Department of Commerce) OF IGNITION.

---

4. Those that pass the standard must have a label with the letter "T" if a flame-retardant treatment has been

applied. Inherently flame-retardant fibers need not be labeled.

Mattresses and mattress pads

1. Includes ticking filled with a resilient material meant or promoted for sleeping upon, including mattress pads, but not pillows, box springs and upholstered furniture.
2. Requires that smooth and quilted or tufted mattress surfaces be exposed to a total of 9 burning cigarettes on the bare mattress, and that the char length on the mattress surface be not more than 2 inches in any direction from any cigarette. Two sheeted tests are also conducted with 9 burning cigarettes placed between the sheets on surfaces as described above.
3. A sampling plan provides for pre-market testing to detect noncomplying mattresses.
4. Mattresses meeting the standard do not need labels, although many manufacturers may attach a label to the mattress, stating that the mattress meets the standard.
5. Mattress pads also must pass the test. Those that have received flame-retardant treatment must carry labels with the letter "T." Care labeling is required on the treated mattress pads to inform consumers of how to protect against the loss of flame-retardant properties.

Children's sleepwear, sizes 0-6X

1. Includes any garment (sizes 0-6X) worn primarily for sleeping (such as nightgowns, pajamas, robes and sleepers) but excludes diapers and underwear. Fabrics for use in sleepwear must also meet the standard.
2. Each of five samples is hung in a cabinet and exposed to a gas flame along its bottom edge for 3 seconds. The samples cannot have an average char length of more than 7 inches; no single

sample can have a char length of 10 inches; and no single sample can have flaming material on the bottom of the cabinet 10 seconds after the ignition source is removed. This is required for both new fabrics or garments, and fabrics or garments that have has been laundered 50 times.

3. A sampling plan provides for pre-market testing of fabrics and garments.

4. The labeling requirements for children's sleepwear, sizes 0-6X, are complex and deal partly with the date of manufacture. Sleepwear made after July 29, 1973, must meet the standard. The manufacturer need not label the garment, but most manufacturers voluntarily label as follows:

> Flame Retardant Fabric. This garment meets flammability requirements of the Federal Children's Sleepwear Standard DOC-FF#-71 for sizes 0-6X.

Children's sleepwear, sizes 7-14

1. Includes any garment (sizes 7-14) worn primarily for sleeping (such as nightgowns, pajamas, robes and sleepers), but excludes underwear. Fabrics for use in sleepwear must also meet the standard.

2. Requirements are similar but slightly less stringent than for sleepwear sizes 0-6X.

3. A sampling plan will be used to test fabrics and garments.

4. All sleepwear (sizes 0-14) must bear permanent labels with instructions for proper care if the flame resistance is affected by laundering.

In addition to the Federal regulations discussed here, many states have laws concerning flammable fabrics.

Sleepwear standards ignored. At publication time, the flammability standards for children's sleepwear were so widely ignored that they had almost ceased to exist in the opinion of the American Apparel Manufacturers Association (AAMA). It claims that stores of all sizes are stocked with children's sleepwear that either completely violates the standards or closely skirts the definition of what is sleepwear.

The problem stems largely from consumers' preferences of natural fibers and the fact that untreated cotton and cotton-blend fabrics do not self-extinguish. The key is positive action by retailers, who can be pressured by consumers who insist on treated fabrics.

BIBLIOGRAPHY

"Children's Sleepwear," *Product Safety Fact Sheet*, August 1981.

"Manufacturers Seek Enforcement of Sleepwear Standards," *Product Safety Up-To-Date*, Chicago: National Safety Council, March/April 1991, Vol. 19, No. 2, pp. 1-2.

HOME ENVIRONMENT

INDOOR AIR QUALITY

In the last few years, scientific evidence has shown that air within buildings and homes can be more polluted than outdoor air in the largest and most industrialized cities. Since most people spend about 90 percent of their time indoors, the risks to health may be greater indoors than outdoors.

In addition, those who are indoors the most are often those most susceptible to the adverse effects of indoor air pollution. This includes the young, the elderly and the chronically ill, especially those with respiratory or cardiovascular disease. Fortunately, most households can reduce the risks from existing sources and can keep new problems from occurring.

Indoor pollution sources release gases or particles into the air and are the primary causes of indoor air quality problems. Poor ventilation can increase pollutant levels by not bringing in enough outside air and by not carrying indoor air pollutants out of the home. High temperature and humidity can increase concentrations of some pollutants.

Pollutant sources. These sources fall into several general categories:

1. Oil, gas, kerosene, coal or wood combustion sources.
2. Building materials as diverse as deteriorated insulation, wet or damp carpeting and carpentry or furniture made of certain pressed wood products.
3. Products for household cleaning and maintenance, personal care or hobbies.
4. Central heating and cooling systems and humidification devices.
5. Outside sources such as radon, pesticides and outdoor air pollution.

The relative importance of any single source depends on how much pollutant it emits and how hazardous it is. In some cases, the age of the source and its maintenance is significant. For example, an improperly adjusted gas flame emits much more carbon monoxide than a gas flame that is properly adjusted.

Some sources, such as certain household products and air fresheners, release pollutants continuously. Other activity sources release pollutants intermittently. Examples of activity sources are smoking, unvented or malfunctioning stoves, furnaces and space heaters. Other sources are cleaning solvents, paint strippers used in redecorating and cleaning products and pesticides used in housekeeping. High pollutant levels can remain in the house for a long period of time after the completion of some of these activities.

Ventilation. If too little outdoor air enters a home, pollutants gather to levels that can pose health and discomfort problems. Unless they are built with special ventilation, homes that are designed and constructed to minimize the amount of outside air that can leak into and out of them may have higher pollutant levels than other homes. Outside air enters and leaves a house in three ways:

1. Infiltration. Air flows through joints and cracks around windows and doors or in the foundation; or from crawl spaces beneath homes.

2. Natural ventilation. Air enters through opened windows and doors.

3. Mechanical ventilation. Air circulates from outdoor-vented fans, or systems with fans that mix outdoor and indoor air or remove polluted air from houses. The rate that outdoor air replaces indoor air is the air-exchange rate. When there is little exchange, the rate is low and pollutant levels increase. The average home exchanges air at 0.7 to 1 change per hour. A leaky house might exchange air as much as 2 changes per hour, while a tight house might run 0.2 to 0.3 changes per hour. An air change once per hour may not remove all pollutants in an hour. Pollutant release is slowed by air trapped in closed rooms, carpets and drapes.

Health effects. Health effects from indoor air pollutants fall into two categories: those that are seen immediately after exposure and those that don't appear for years.

1. Immediate effects. Immediate effects include irritation of the eyes, nose and throat, headaches, dizziness and fatigue. These are usually short-term and most can be treated, sometimes by simply stopping the exposure. Exposure to some indoor air pollution causes symptoms of some diseases, such as asthma, to appear immediately after exposure. This reaction depends on several factors, such as age or pre-existing medical conditions.

2. Long-term effects. Other health effects may become apparent years after exposure, or only after repeated exposure. These effects, which include emphysema and other respiratory diseases, heart disease and cancer, can be severely debilitating or fatal. It is not known exactly what the effects of indoor pollution will be on various people. There is much uncertainty about what concentrations or exposure levels produce specific health effects. People also react very differently to the same exposures.

Do you have an air quality problem? Signs of indoor air quality problems include some health effects, especially if they appear after moving to a new residence, remodeling a home or treating a home with pesticides. Reactions should be discussed with your doctor or health department to see if symptoms could be from indoor air pollution.

It is prudent to improve the quality of your indoor air, even if no symptoms are seen. Many of them may not appear for years, long after the exposure.

Another way to determine if you have a problem is to pinpoint sources of indoor air pollution. The presence of a source does not mean you have a problem, but knowing a source is present is a first step toward improving the quality of indoor air.

Look for signs of problems with the air flow through your home. These include stuffy or bad-smelling air, dirty central heating and air cooling equipment, damaged flues or chimneys, moisture condensation on windows or walls, signs of water leakage and areas where books, shoes or other items become moldy.

Measuring pollutant levels. The government recommends that you measure the radon level in your home. Inexpensive devices are available. For pollutants other than radon, measurements should be made when there are health symptoms or signs of poor air flow, as well as when specific sources or pollutants have been determined to be possible causes of air quality problems. Testing for pollutants can be expensive and you should consult with state or local health departments that have experience in solving indoor air quality problems.

Basic strategies

1. Source control. Eliminating air pollution sources or reducing their emissions is the best way to improve air quality. Some sources, like those with

asbestos, can be sealed or enclosed. Others, like gas stoves, can be adjusted to reduce emissions. Source control may be less costly than new ventilation or air cleaning devices, but the energy cost of added equipment should be considered. Source control is the most effective solution of the three listed in this section.

2. Ventilation improvement. Opening windows and doors when the weather permits may lower indoor concentrations of pollutants, by increasing the ventilation rate. Turning on outside vented bathroom or kitchen exhaust fans can lower pollution levels in the room in which the fan is located. If radon from the outside is a problem, open windows and doors only when the fans are in use. Other pollutant sources suitable for ventilation are painting, paint stripping, heating with kerosene heaters, cooking with unvented gas stoves or maintenance or hobby activities, such as soldering or sanding. Some heating and air conditioning systems provide the needed exchange of air. Before you buy a ventilation device or system for your home, you should do plenty of research and contact a reputable consultant or contractor.

3. Air cleaners. Some air cleaners, particularly whole-house systems, are very effective at cleaning polluted air. However, table-top models are effective only in their immediate area. How well an air cleaner works, depends on how well it collects pollutants. This is measured as an efficiency rate, based on the air drawn through the cleaner. A low flow of air through an effective filter will not do much to remove air pollutants, and neither will a high air flow by itself. Air-cleaner effectiveness also depends on the strength of the pollutant. Light-duty cleaners, such as table-top models, will not remove strong pollutants, especially near their sources. In

these cases, you must act to remove the source.

Biological contaminants

Biological contaminants include bacteria, mold, mildew, viruses, animal dander, cat saliva, mites, cockroaches and pollen. There are many sources for these pollutants. In fact, there is almost no end to the sources, some of which can become very potent under certain conditions. By controlling the relative humidity (30 to 50 percent is ideal), the growth of biologicals can be minimized.

Some biological contaminants trigger allergic reactions, such as asthma. Some transmit infectious illnesses, like influenza and measles. Others release disease-carrying toxins. Those who are older or more subject to disease and confinement, and the very young, are most susceptible. The best steps to reduce or keep biological contaminants under control include holding down the relative humidity, eliminating standing water and keeping the house clean.

Combustion products

Sources include tobacco smoke, unvented kerosene and gas space heaters, wood stoves, fireplaces and gas stoves. The main pollutants are carbon monoxide, nitrogen dioxide and particles. Some heaters emit hydrocarbons and aerosols. Unvented and improperly installed heating devices are major sources of the pollutants. All pollutants can be deadly in the right strength and circumstances.

Household products

Organic chemicals are common in household products because of their ability to dissolve substances and evaporate quickly. Many common household products release organic chemicals while being used and, to some degree, while being stored. Because of this, about a dozen organic chemicals are at much higher levels in the house than outdoors. Further, these chemicals can persist in the air long after their use. Exposure to household chemicals can be reduced by following these guidelines:

1. Follow label instructions carefully. If a label says to use the product in a well-ventilated area, go outdoors or to an area with a good exhaust fan.

2. Safely discard partly full containers of old or unneeded chemicals. Because gas may leak from closed containers, this helps rid the home of household chemicals. Keep chemicals in a well-ventilated area out of the reach of children.

3. Buy limited quantities. If you use products only occasionally or seasonally (such as gas for a lawn mower), buy only as much as you will use immediately.

4. Reduce exposure to emissions from products with methylene chloride. Products that contain this chemical include paint strippers, adhesive removers, aerosol spray paints and pesticide bombs. This chemical converts to carbon monoxide in the body and is thought to cause cancer. Use the products outdoors when possible and with good ventilation.

5. Keep to a minimum exposure to benzene. The main indoor sources of this chemical are tobacco smoke, stored fuels and paint supplies. To preventive exposure, stop smoking in the home, provide for maximum ventilation when painting, and discard paint supplies and fuels that will not be used at once.

6. Keep to a minimum exposure to perchloroethylene emissions from newly dry cleaned materials. Perchloroethylene is the chemical most widely used in dry cleaning. In the laboratory, it causes cancer in rats. Don't accept dry cleaning from the cleaners if the smell is too strong.

Formaldehyde

Formaldehyde sources in the home include smoking, household products and unvented fuel appliances, such as gas stoves or kerosene space heaters. Formaldehyde is combined with many other chemicals. It adds permanent-press qualities to clothes, is used in glues and preserves some paints. The most significant source in the home is likely to be pressed-wood products made for indoor use, such as plywood paneling and some fiber boards.

In the 1970s, many homes had urea-formaldehyde insulation (UFFI) in the walls and many of these homes had high concentrations of formaldehyde. However, because emissions decline with age, those homes are unlikely to have high concentrations now.

Health effects. Formaldehyde is a colorless, pungent-smelling gas, which can cause watery eyes, burning in the eyes and throat, nausea and breathing problems. In some people it may cause chemical sensitivity.

Reducing exposure

1. Before you buy, ask about the formaldehyde content of pressed-wood products, including building materials, cabinetry and furniture. If you experience adverse reactions to formaldehyde, you may want to avoid pressed-wood products completely.

2. Maintain moderate temperatures and humidity levels and provide good ventilation. Formaldehyde release increases with heat. Use dehumidifiers and air conditioning to control release, but drain and clean humidifiers often.

Pesticides

The amount of pesticides found inside homes is greater than can be traced to normal use. Possible sources include contaminated soil, or dust that floats or is tracked from the outside. Pesticides are dangerous if not used properly and can kill.

Health effects. Health effects of pesticides used at home are known, but the concentrations necessary to cause the effects are not. This is due to the many combinations and concentrations of pesticides and differences in consumers. Expect dizziness, headaches, muscle-twitching, weakness, tingling sensations and nausea from high levels of pesticides.

Reducing exposure in the home

1. Read the labels and follow directions. It's illegal and unsafe not to use pesticides as directed on the label. Never use pesticides that are for use only by state-certified pest control operators. They are too dangerous for most consumers to use.

2. Use in well-ventilated areas. Open windows when using pesticides indoors. Mix or dilute them outdoors or in well-ventilated areas, and only mix what will be needed at the time.

3. Use alternative, nonchemical methods of pest control. Pesticides can be found far from where they were used, so it is prudent to use them with care. Ask for a home inspection and a written control program before signing a contract. The program should list pests to be controlled and chemicals to be used, and should reflect your safety concerns. The contractor should have a proven record of competence.

4. Dispose of unwanted pesticides safely. Get rid of unused or partially used pesticide containers. Dispose of them, following directions on the labels, or on designated, special refuse-collection days.

5. Keep exposure to moth pellets to a minimum. The chemical in moth repellents is thought to cause cancer, and breathing the vapors has potential short-term toxic effects. Where possible, the containers (trunks, etc.) should be placed in areas separately ventilated from the home, such as attics and garages. Some of the same products are also used as air fresheners. Better to have a well-ventilated and clean area than to use air fresheners.

6. Call the National Pesticide Telecommunications Network for answers to your questions about pesticides and to receive certain EPA publications. The number is 1-800-858-PEST.

ELECTROMAGNETIC FIELDS (EMFs)

Two things are readily apparent about electromagnetic fields. Nearly everyone has concern about them and the answer to the damage they do is many years down the road of scientific inquiry, according to *Safety and Health* magazine.

EMFs are nearly everywhere. They come from power lines overhead, from electric lines buried under the ground and from wiring in building walls. They come from electronic appliances and other electrical devices that help us work and make life more pleasant. Because their intensity weakens quickly over distance and sometimes carry so little energy, they have long been thought harmless.

Several studies dating back to 1979 have found that children living near high-power lines were more likely to develop leukemia. Follow-up studies show the probability to be around one-and-a-half times as likely. More than 50 studies have tried to determine if low-frequency EMFs will harm people. Some researchers have found a statistical link with leukemia and cancer. The effects of EMFs from electric blankets, toasters and video display terminals have been studied frequently. Unfortunately, some of the studies are flawed because other factors that might influence the outcome of the studies were not considered.

Meanwhile, other workplace studies find no correlation between, for example, VDT use and pregnancy problems. One expert, Dr. Eleanor Adair, says, "If EMFs cause cancer, one might expect leukemia and other cancers associated with EMFs to have increased as electricity consumption has grown. The fact that these cancers have remained stable while electricity use soared in the last 50 years is very strong evidence against any kind of causal connection between the two." We cannot say for certain what could cause the problems.

Better information may be on the way. The National Institute for Health Sciences started a long-term study on the effects of EMF exposure on laboratory animals. The $65 million, five-year study will expose rats and mice to varying levels of electrical and magnetic energy. It will look for possible increases in leukemia, cancer, birth defects and developmental problems.

Until we have better data, most health experts advise prudent avoidance, which combines awareness with easy steps to reduce unnecessary exposure to magnetic fields. Do not worry about exposure that you cannot control, such as that from power lines. To use a childcare example, don't rip the wiring out of a wall near a baby crib. It might be prudent, however, to move the crib to another wall. Also, you can keep toddlers' and infants' sleeping places apart from VDTs. And you might use quilts instead of electric blankets.

If you have concerns about possible EMFs in your home, some utilities will measure them for you, or you can measure field strength with a gauss-meter (about $100). If you want to pursue the subject, two sources are: The Department of Engineering and Public Policy, Carnegie Mellon University, Pittsburgh, PA, 15213 has two booklets:

- *Measuring Power Frequency Fields* ($2.50).
- *What to Do About Possible Health Risks* ($3.50).

Fireside Books published Ellen Sugarman's *Warning: The Electricity Around You May Be Hazardous to Your Health.* After reading the Sugarman book, you might tend to stay away from the TV and microwave, but keep it in perspective.

Lead

Lead has long been known to be a harmful environmental pollutant. There are sources of lead exposure, including air, drinking water, food and contaminated soil or dust. Lead gets into the body when lead dust or particles are swallowed or breathed.

Lead-based paint, long recognized as a major lead source in the home, is seldom used now. However, there is a danger in older homes that lead paint may flake off and be ingested by occupants, particularly children. It can also be tracked into the home from areas where it is used, such as in soldering, electronics repair and stained glass work.

Lead in drinking water can only be detected by testing the water. Testing is conducted by most communities. Visual inspection of pipes and solder lines will not accurately determine lead content.

Health effects. Lead is toxic to many organs in the body. It can cause serious damage to the brain, kidneys, peripheral nervous system and red blood cells. Even low lead levels can increase blood pressure in adults.

Fetuses, infants and children are more susceptible to lead exposure than adults. Children also may have higher exposure, since they are more likely to get lead dust on their fingers and then put their fingers in their mouths.

Ways to reduce exposure

1. If you suspect that paint in your home contains lead, have it tested. Consult your health department for suggestions on how to have this done.

2. Leave lead-based paint undisturbed if it is in good condition and there is little likelihood that it will be eaten by children. Do not sand or burn off paint that may contain lead. If lead-based paint must be removed, then everyone, except those working on the removal, should leave the site.

3. If you may have been exposed to lead dust recently, you should have your blood tested by a doctor or local health department.

4. Keep surface areas clean with a wet mop or cloth to reduce the amount of lead dust that drifts or is tracked in from outdoors.

5. Choose well-ventilated areas to engage in activities that involve the use of lead. Consider using "no-lead" solder.

6. Have the drinking water in your home tested for lead. Certainly do not use solder that contains lead on drinking water systems. National Lead Watch (800-531-6886) offers lead testing kits and information for homeowners. Send a self-addressed envelope to: National Lead Watch, P.O. Box 2236, Fairfield PA, 52556.

BIBLIOGRAPHY

A Citizen's Guide to Radon, U.S. Environmental Protection Agency, August 1986.

A Home Buyer's Guide to Environmental Hazards, Washington, DC: Environmental Protection Agency, August 1990.

An Update on Formaldehyde, U.S. Consumer Product Safety Commission, October 1990.

Asbestos in the Home, U.S. Consumer Product Safety Commission and U.S. Environmental Protection Agency, 1990.

Asbestos in Your Home, American Lung Association, September 1990.

"Don't Use Solder That Contains Lead For Work On Drinking Water Systems," *Consumer Product Safety Alert,* U.S. Consumer Product Safety Commission, April 1988.

"The ELF in Your Electric Blanket," Farley, Dixie, *FDA Consumer,* Washington, DC: Government Printing Office, December 1992, pp. 23-24.

"Electric Current: A New Scare for the '90s?" Tritsc, Shane, *Safety and Health Magazine,* Chicago, IL: National Safety Council, Fall 1992, pp. 30-31.

The Inside Story—A Guide to Indoor Air Quality, U.S. Environmental Protection Agency and U.S. Consumer Product Safety Commission, September 1988.

HOME SAFETY CHECKLIST

Your home is safer if you can answer "Yes" to all questions in this checklist:

THERMAL HAZARDS

❑ Do space heaters, fireplaces and other heat sources have guards so that you can't touch the flames or heating elements?

❑ Do your children wear heat-resistant sleepwear (up through sizes 14)?

❑ Are drapes and furniture away from gas and electric ranges and baseboard heaters that could ignite them?

❑ Are matches and lighters kept out of reach of children?

❑ Are flammable liquids stored and used away from pilot lights?

❑ Are pot handles turned toward the back of the stove?

❑ Do you stay with preschool children when they are near hot water in the bathtub?

ELECTRICAL HAZARDS

❑ Are grounding type three-wire electrical appliances properly grounded?

❑ Are electrical appliances out of the bathroom so that you won't touch them while you're wet?

❑ Are extension cords, outlets and circuits not overloaded?

❑ Are electric cords out of reach so they can't be pulled or tripped over?

❑ Do unusual outlets have dummy plugs to keep children from getting shocked?

❑ Are appliance cords and extension cords in good repair?

MECHANICAL HAZARDS

❑ Are glass doors and walls marked with decals so that people can see them from both directions? Is safety glazing used?

❑ Are all drinking glasses used by children made from unbreakable materials?

❑ Are lawn mowers and other cutting machines in good repair with necessary guards?

❑ Are small rugs kept away from stairs?

❑ Is there a gate at the top of stairs to prevent small children from falling?

❑ Are there handrails all the way down the stairs?

❑ Is the furniture used for children stable and free of sharp edges?

❑ Are bicycles, playground equipment and other recreational equipment free of protrusions, sharp edges and other parts that could bruise or cut?

CHEMICAL HAZARDS

❑ Are all household chemical products locked up away from children?

❑ Are products that have safety packaging properly closed?

❑ Are all household substances bought in bulk (such as gasoline), or transferred from their original containers, kept in sturdy, clearly labeled, non-food containers?

❑ Are your gas appliances checked annually to ensure that they do not release carbon monoxide into the home?

CONSUMER PRODUCT HAZARDS

- ❏ Is the product right for the intended use and user?
- ❏ Are there some safer types of the same product that would be better?
- ❏ Did you read the label and follow the directions?
- ❏ Are there any possible hazards (such as flammability, toxicity and sharpness of parts) that you should know of?
- ❏ Are there some steps you can take to make the product safer?
- ❏ Should you keep children from the area in which you are using the product?
- ❏ Are there any broken, loose, worn or dirty parts to repair or replace?
- ❏ Is the product near a flame or heat source or within reach of children?
- ❏ Is it in a sturdy, nonbreakable container?
- ❏ Is the container clearly labeled?
- ❏ Is the storage place dry to prevent deterioration from dampness?
- ❏ Can the product be burned or should it be disposed of with nonburnable trash?

Many consumer letters and calls relate stories of accidents that result from the misuse of consumer products. Misuse leads to many serious injuries that require hospital emergency room treatment. Some types of misuse are so common that they deserve emphasis. The most common feature to these mishaps is the failure to read and follow instructions and warning labels. Be aware of:

1. Improper mixing. Some products are hazardous if mixed. For example, chlorine bleach mixed with ammonia, toilet bowl cleaners and drain cleaners may release hazardous gases, which can be deadly. The resulting solution may be caustic and can burn your skin. Although chlorine bleach must be clearly labeled with a warning not to mix it with ammonia or toilet bowl cleaners, some people either do not read the label or disregard it. Serious injuries occur when people put their hands into this mixture or breathe the gases.

2. Overuse. Some people think if a small amount is good, then a large amount must be better. That kind of logic can lead to hazardous situations. For example, too much acid-type drain cleaner can eat away drain pipes, and some cleaners can produce toxic fumes that, in large concentrations, can be deadly. Some aerosols can cause a lack of oxygen in the body, if too much is sprayed in a closed room. Always follow directions and don't use more than the recommended amount.

3. Haste. It is tempting to race through the preliminary steps in order to use a product and get a job done. However, if speed means you overlook a loose part on a power mower or a safety guard on a power saw, or you open a pressure cooker before it has been de-pressurized, or you step on a ladder without first leveling it, you can wind up with a serious injury. Take time to follow all steps.

4. Lack of maintenance. Failure to repair broken products and lack of maintenance contribute to serious injuries. Loose stair rails should be tightened. Broken electrical plugs or insulation should be replaced and broken ladders should be repaired. Watch out for warning signals, such as electrical sparks, flickering lights or gas odors and call for qualified service immediately. Complex machines, gas appliances and electrical appliances should be repaired by experts.

5. Improper storage. Highly flammable liquids may produce heavier-than-air vapors that can travel invisibly along the floor and be ignited by a distant pilot light in a gas furnace or water heater or by a discarded cigarette. Store flammable liquids outside your

living quarters, away from any ignition source. Store drugs, poisons and other hazardous products tightly closed and in an out-of-reach, locked location (such as a high cabinet). Children are resourceful and can get into cabinets that parents may think are safe. Keep products in their original containers and clearly labeled to prevent mistaking them for food or beverages. Store mechanical or electrical appliances in a dry place to prevent rust or other deterioration. Aerosols, too, always should be stored away from wet or damp areas; rust can lead to rupture or leakage of the aerosol contents.

It is easy to say "Be careful" and "Read the labels," but it is sometimes hard to put these general recommendations into everyday practice. It also is essential for parents to supervise children. It takes only a few minutes for a child to get into a hazardous situation that can lead to injury or death.

BIBLIOGRAPHY

"Misuse of Consumer Products," *Product Safety Fact Sheet,* April 1979.

"Sound Sense," Chicago: National Safety Council, 1990, 12 pages.

SENIOR AFFAIRS

Certain facts about old age must be faced by those of you who are seniors, as well as those of you who care for seniors. Families have the responsibility of providing care for their older members. And concerns about senior care increase as the population of those facing old age grows.

Home Safety Desk Reference includes this appendix on senior safety and health for several reasons:

1. Seniors are an ever-increasing group of consumer product users.
2. Consumers who have seniors living in their homes must approach safety and health from the viewpoint of seniors, as well as their own.
3. Senior caregivers face a new set of problems, due to the demands of caregiving.
4. Seniors who live independently must care for their own safety and health.

A study by the National Center for Health Statistics revealed these facts about a group of older people (who died in 1986) and their final year of life:

1. Most of the sample population's income was low.
2. About 35 percent were younger than 65 when they died.
3. Nearly half of those studied required special help or special equipment to perform the five basic activities of daily living (bathing, walking, dressing, toilet use and eating).
4. Three-quarters had stays in hospitals and about one quarter had nursing home stays.

5. Nearly all suffered from diseases that required extra care and hampered their lifestyles.
6. Only about 13 percent were still working at the time of their deaths. More than one-fourth had retired because of ill health or disabilities.

FALLS

The statistics on falls among seniors are staggering. Consider this:

1. More than one-third of those over age 65 will be injured by falls this year.
2. Falls are the leading cause of fatal injuries for those more than 65 years of age.
3. Half of all these people hospitalized due to falls die within a year.
4. More than half of falls happen at home, mostly in bathrooms or on stairs.
5. About half of the 200,000 seniors who suffer broken hips each year end up in nursing homes. In the state of Washington alone, this amounts to $53 million in hospital costs annually. One research organization (Harborview Injury Prevention Research Center in Seattle) believes 83 percent of hip fractures could be prevented if people would wear safe shoes.

• Lucille, in her 70s, was fixing lunch when she fell, fracturing her hip. Two years later she was still going twice a week for physical therapy and living with the fear she might fall again.

Falls are more threatening as you get older and more frail. Even minor falls may result in broken bones with overwhelming complications. You can reduce the danger of falls, and the deformities, disabilities or deaths that often accompany them, if you identify the changes related to aging. That way, you can act to prevent, correct or adjust for the changes.

Changes in eyesight. With age, it is more difficult to adjust to light (glare is most troublesome), to focus on objects and to differentiate between colors. The problems of age tend to reduce visual clarity, depth perception and peripheral vision. This, in turn, can causes you to misjudge steps or fail to identify hazards in your path.

As you get older, your eyes need as much as three times more light. Therefore, dim, money-saving bulbs may need to be replaced. Bulbs of 100 watts are better (if they do not give too much glare) for use in areas in which you move, work and play. One exception to this is where a fixture calls for a lower-wattage bulb or the wattage is not given. In that case, not more than a 60-watt bulb is recommended. Some vision problems can arise when lenses or eye glasses are not worn or when new ones are needed as your vision changes.

Slower reflexes. While your ability to do something may stay the same with age, the speed with which you do it slows. This may mean you're not able to react as quickly to hazards or to catch yourself if you trip or lose balance. Try to avoid timed activities or those that require fast responses.

Balance and coordination. Many falls happen when balance is lost. Stability is lessened by a variety of causes, including ear disorders, diabetes, thyroid disease and some drugs. Arthritis, strokes and Parkinson's disease can cause an unsteady gait. Many people become more stooped with age, which changes the center of gravity. Some tend to sway or shuffle, which, when combined with slower

reflexes and muscle weakness, can cause falls more easily.

If you suffer from such problems, avoid slippery walkways and wear sensible shoes. Avoid last-minute rushing, especially to answer the phone or door. Advise friends you may be slow to answer. If your gait is unsteady and you refuse to use an aid, such as a walker, you handicap yourself. Reduce your chances of a fall by discarding worn-out, loose-fitting shoes and slippers, no matter how comfortable they are. Remove scatter rugs or other items that may be hazardous.

Cardiovascular problems. With poor circulation, a sudden change of position can cause dizziness. Change positions from lying or sitting to standing, slowly and carefully. Don't stand in one position too long. Try to move around or even walk in place.

Drugs and alcohol. Alcohol and even prescribed drugs can cause weakness, dizziness, drowsiness and confusion, along with impaired balance, coordination and judgment problems. Long-acting tranquilizers, sedatives, narcotics and depressants remain in the system for 24 hours or more. Many more drugs also adversely affect you Your physician and your pharmacist can generally advise you about the side effects of medication or combinations of medications. Take only what you must.

Positive actions to avoid falls

1. Have regular eye checkups and use prescribed glasses.

2. If canes and walkers help you maintain balance, use them.

3. Don't carry objects that obstruct your view.

4. Don't stand on chairs, and avoid using ladders.

5. When on a step stool, be careful not to stretch beyond your reach.

6. Use step stools, preferably with handles and gripping devices, to reach high places.

7. Leave work that requires heights, such as window washing or gutter cleaning, to someone else.

8. Remove or fix physical hazards, such as area carpets, that might cause you to fall.

9. Make sure lighting is adequate by using bright bulbs and leaving lights on in the hallway or the bathroom at night. Consider your visitors as well. Lighting is critical for elderly visitors who must get up in the night.

10. Before going to bed, close all doors and dresser drawers. In a darkened room, they invite collisions and falls.

11. Keep yourself physically conditioned with regular exercise.

12. Have strong, stable railings and handles for getting in and out of bathtubs.

13. When you first awaken, sit on the side of the bed for a moment. Don't jump out of bed.

14. Use a LifeLine or other device. In case of a fall, you can press a button on the device, which can be worn around your neck, to call for assistance.

Minor head injuries. Older people are very susceptible to head injuries. Not only are falls more likely because of failing eyesight, reduced agility and degenerative disorders, such as Parkinson's disease, but the chance of brain injuries from falls increases in the elderly because the brain shrinks with age. This shrinking permits the blood vessels in the brain to be more readily strained, which can result in tearing. Tearing can be caused by a fall, or when the brain is jarred inside the skull, as it is from whiplash in a car accident.

If there are persistent headaches or confusion after a head injury, a CT scan or MRI is appropriate.

• After a former President fell from a horse, during a later medical checkup, a CT scan showed a collection of blood. The blood was drained, and he recovered nicely.

If you must fall. Learning to fall safely can pay great dividends.

1. When you feel yourself about to fall, put your arms over and close around your head.

2. When falling, try to roll forward. Don't try to catch yourself when falling backward, or you may do more harm.

3. When you begin to fall, relax as much as possible.

4. Direct your landing. Turn your body, to allow landing on a well-padded area, such as the buttocks, thigh or shoulder. Dropping backward into the sitting position can be hard on the spine.

5. If you fall in a standing position:
   • Retain the spring in your legs.
   • When falling from one level to another, it is best to hit the ground on the balls of your feet.
   • As you touch the ground, bend your knees and ankles and curl your body.

6. If you fall forward or fall on your hands or knees, reach out only moderately with your arms. Let your fingers help distribute the contact.

Older people are often involved in stairway accidents. Poor vision and slow physical response can contribute to accidents. Some people have trouble standing/balancing on one foot at a time and therefore have trouble on stairs or rough terrain. The following measures can reduce stairway accidents:

Selection

1. When buying a home, choose a house that requires minimal use of stairs. Good choices include single-level homes, homes with bedroom and bath on the first floor and homes without stairs at entrance ways.

2. If you buy an older home, examine all stairs and repair or replace any uneven or shoddy stairs.

3. Install handrails on both sides of each staircase. They should be firm, easy to grip and easy to reach.
4. Avoid stairs with long runs. An intermediate landing allows time to rest.
5. Avoid single-step changes in elevation between rooms, because they may be unexpected and cause falls.

Use of stairs

Since many stairway accidents are caused by distractions (carrying packages or slippery footwear) consider these measures:

1. Do not carry packages, groceries and laundry on the stairs and urge others who are older to avoid this also.
2. Do not place pictures and other objects on stairway walls, because they can distract and eliminate a touch or balance point.
3. Do not store items on stairs because they may not see be seen easily and can cause tripping.
4. Use and encourage the use of walk-in patio entrances that eliminate the use of stairs.
5. Do not wear slippery footwear, stockings or socks alone. They can cause falls.

Maintenance of stairs

1. When installing lights near stairways, minimize glare by using frosted or shaded bulbs. Glare can cause you to misjudge the location of the first or last step.
2. Remove shadows that commonly fall directly on stairs, by having lights at both the top and the bottom of the stairway. (A single light at the top of the stair casts a shadow down the stairs.) Place light switches where they are handy, at the top and bottom of the stairway.
3. Eliminate abrupt changes in light levels between stairs and surrounding rooms.

Allow enough time for your eyes to adjust to any differences.
4. Avoid slippery wax finishes on stairs and small rugs near stairs. The greatest hazards lie in unsuspected, slippery areas, either on stairs or in adjacent hallways and rooms. Uniform traction on walking surfaces is important.
5. Avoid carpeting on stairs. Carpet generally reduces the size of the step and can contribute to loss of balance. It may cause heels to catch or soles to slide.
6. Do not use indoor/outdoor carpet on stairs and ramps, because it can be slick.
7. When carpet is used, avoid large patterns that can cause depth-perception problems and can confuse or distract. The same consideration should be given to any flooring surface.
8. Inspect for splinters, loose rugs and carpet edges, loose handrails and broken concrete. Make thorough repairs quickly.
9. To reduce stairway use, consider relocating sitting, reading and other high-occupancy areas. Installing a first-floor bathroom or second-floor sitting room might be convenient and may help avoid accidents on stairways.
10. Provide rails and good lighting to make short flights of stairs more easily seen. Avoid installing short flights when a ramp or other means can be used.
11. Remove snow or ice quickly from exterior stairs or landings.

Entryways

1. Walkways to front entries should be level. Cracks and holes can be repaired with easy-to-use patching compounds, available from a building supply store.
2. Lighting is important, because people using an entryway may not be familiar with it. Further, it is necessary to have light to unlock the door. If there is not enough light, consider a battery-operated

light at the door or on your key chain. You must be able to see immediately, or at least, be able to turn on lights easily, after entering.

3. Have a place, other than the floor, to set packages while unlocking and opening a door.

4. The door should open and close easily. Many doors in apartment buildings require that keys be inserted at the same time that the handles are turned and pushed.

5. If the door handle is hard to grasp, wrap it with some tape. Better yet, replace round entry knobs with lever type handles.

6. Locks should turn smoothly. For protection, a deadbolt is desirable. The lock key should be easy to grasp and easy to locate in a purse or on a key ring. Imagine that this may have to be done with cold, perhaps gloved, hands in the dark. To avoid undue delay in opening an entry door, the key may need special markings or holders. For a better grip on keys, extend the key length by attaching it to a retractable holder.

7. Answering the door presents its own additional problems.

   - A doorbell or knocker should be easily heard from the inside. You may want to use a flashing light signal or a louder bell if this is a problem.

   - It is desirable to see who is outside without opening the door. Install a peephole device, if the entryway and door is solid. For those who use wheelchairs, locate peepholes at the proper height.

   - If the entry door requires a key to open it from the inside, a key should be kept near the door, but still out of reach of someone outside who might reach through a door or side window.

8. A sliding glass door requires a double lock for security. At least one should be a blocking device that must be removed from inside for entry. This does not work if you must remove it to leave and then return, but it does offer security when you are inside. Another problem with sliding glass doors is the difficulty in seeing the glass. Decals placed near eye level can be reminders that glass is present.

9. Most entryways, which may include various walkways, porches or patios, are a series of different-sized steps, ranging from ½ inch, to 3 to 5 inches. Each change of height is a hazard to be remembered or guarded against, and to be marked, perhaps with a strip of light tape or white paint.

10. Entryways are painted to resist weather more than to assure solid footing. In wet or icy weather, the entryway is likely to be slippery. And the smoother the paint, the more chance of slipping. Use rough-textured paint and nonslip strips to ease the problem. Arrange for the outside entry and steps to be kept clear of ice and snow, and keep a supply of sand or cat litter on hand to use on ice.

11. Outside exposure also means that outside steps and handrails will deteriorate quickly and may become loose and jagged with splinters. Be certain they are secure and easy to grasp without harm.

12. Entryways are no place for wearing socks, which can catch on nails or allow you to slip. Wear secure, smooth-toed slippers or shoes.

FIRE CONCERNS

People 55 and older account for about 40 percent of all burns and deaths due to fire. Adults 75 and older, and children 5 and younger, appear to be most victimized by fire. Residential fires account for 75 percent of all fires and there is a clear relationship between residential fires and older people.

Although fires are covered in detail in other parts of this book, the guidelines specific to seniors, and recommended by the U.S. Fire Administration, are listed here:

1. Have a licensed electrician examine the house wiring and all appliances, in addition to the capacity of the fuse and breaker systems.

2. If portable heaters are used, plug them directly into the sockets. Do not use extension cords, or a receptacle with several other appliance cords.

3. Don't leave portable heaters on while sleeping or away from the house. Unplug such heaters when you leave the house.

4. If you have an older, unplugged heater, bump or nudge it to see if it falls over easily. If so, it is best to replace it.

5. Don't run appliance cords over or under beds, or trap them between a bed and the wall, where heat could build.

6. Never place heat-producing appliances, such as curling irons, on beds.

7. Overheating, unusual smells, electrical shorts and sparks are all warning signs that an appliance needs to be repaired or replaced.

8. Don't wear loose-fitting clothing while cooking.

9. Avoid smoking in the house, especially in bed or on upholstered furniture. Make sure all cigarette butts are extinguished completely before discarding in the trash.

10. Have an approved chain ladder to climb out of rooms above the first floor.

11. Know at least two ways to escape from every room in the house.

12. Determine in advance what you are going to do about pets in case of a fire.

13. Know how to call for emergency help and know the location of the nearest phone away from your home.

14. Know the location of your fire extinguisher and how to use it. Your fire department will usually check the condition of extinguishers and show you how to use them.

COLD STRESS (Hypothermia)

Much like high blood pressure, hypothermia is a silent killer, in the sense that many of its victims are not aware of the threat. Elderly people may not become aware that they are getting cold as quickly as younger people. And their bodies may not adjust to the changes in temperature. The biggest threat comes from not understanding the nature of hypothermia.

Hypothermia is a condition of abnormally low internal body temperature. An abnormally low temperature is considered only 4 degrees below the body's normal 98.6°F. It develops when body heat is lost to a cool or cold environment faster than it can be replaced. Temperatures do not have to be below freezing for hypothermia to occur, especially to those who are more vulnerable. Hypothermia can set in at temperatures as high as 65°F. Many older people can develop low body temperatures after conditions of mild cold.

Who is at risk? Among the elderly, those most likely to develop hypothermia are the sick, the frail, the very old, those who can't afford enough heat and medically vulnerable people who do not know how to keep warm when exposed to the cold.

Others who are susceptible include those who: (1) live alone or in isolated areas; (2) do not shiver or react to cold; (3) take certain medications that prevent the body from regulating temperatures normally, such as anti-depressants, sedatives, tranquilizers and cardiovascular drugs; and (4) have fallen or are unable to get up for some time before they are found. (Check with a doctor or pharmacist for other drugs that increase susceptibility to hypothermia.)

Heat or eat. Many elderly people cannot afford to both heat and eat, thus the "heat or eat syndrome." They may set their thermostats at dangerously low levels, which aggravates some chronic health conditions, making it more difficult for them to recognize their hypothermia. An ordinary thermometer may be the best defense against hypothermia.

How to avoid harm from hypothermia

1. If you live alone, arrange for a daily check-in call with a friend, neighbor or relative. Or, if you can afford it and the system is available in your community, use LifeLine.
2. Insulate your home properly. Caulking is an effective and low-cost technique.
3. Wear warm clothing instead of tight clothing. Wear several loose, warm layers. Wear a hat and scarf to avoid heat loss through the head and neck. Stay dry. Moisture from rain, perspiration or melting snow can seriously reduce or destroy the insulating value of clothing.
4. Use extra blankets, because hypothermia can develop while sleeping.
5. Eat nutritious foods and exercise moderately. Proper diet and physical conditioning help protect against abnormal heat and cold.
6. Get proper rest. Fatigue makes you vulnerable to cold.
7. Drink enough liquids, such as water. Limit alcohol intake, which speeds up body heat loss.
8. Take your temperature in the morning, at noon and in the evening. If your temperature drops even 1 degree, you must have more warmth. If it goes below 95°, you need to seek medical help.

What to look for

1. Stiff muscles. In hypothermia, the muscles are often unusually stiff, particularly in the neck, arms and legs. This stiffness may be accompanied by a fine trembling, perhaps limited to a part or side of the body.
2. Shivering. This is a sign that the body is having trouble keeping warm. This response is often reduced or absent in older adults. The fact that a person is not shivering does not ensure that he or she is not cold.
3. Puffy or swollen face.
4. Difficulty walking or balancing. Both are slowed at low body temperatures.
5. Cool or cold skin. Pay special attention to the stomach, lower back, arms, legs, hands and feet. The skin color is usually very pale, but may have large irregular blue or pink spots.
6. Loss of consciousness. Consciousness may be lost as the body cools, but some victims stay conscious when body temperatures are as low as 80°.
7. Growing mental confusion. This is one of the first signs and becomes worse as the body temperature falls.
8. Strange behavior. Victims of hypothermia may behave strangely or become apathetic, irritable, hostile, mean or aggressive.

What to do. If you believe someone has hypothermia, call an ambulance or rescue squad immediately. It is a dangerous, complicated medical problem. While waiting for help to arrive, follow these suggestions:

1. Be very careful in handling the person. The heart is very weak when the body is cold.
2. Insulate the victim with available clothing, such as blankets, towels, pillows, scarves or newspapers.
3. Do not attempt to rewarm the victim at home. Hot baths, electric blankets and hot water bottles can be dangerous to someone with hypothermia.
4. Do not give the victim any food or drink.

5. If the victim is unconscious, do not raise the feet. This will cause blood from the legs to flow into the body "core" and further depress the body temperature.

HEAT STRESS

The body needs time to adjust to hot weather. A sudden increase in temperature can place a dangerous strain on the heart and blood vessels before the body acclimates itself. The elderly are more vulnerable to heat stress than younger people. They perspire less. They are more likely to have health problems requiring medicines that work against the body's natural defenses to adjust to heat. For example, diuretics (often used for high blood pressure) prevent the body from storing fluids and restrict the opening of blood vessels near the skin's surface. Certain tranquilizers and drugs used to treat Parkinson's disease interfere with perspiration. These and other chronic conditions often upset normal body responses.

Warning signs. Early symptoms—feeling hot, uncomfortable and listless—are mild and pose no threat, unless they persist. However serious signs of heat stress, which also are signs of other serious problems, usually precede milder symptoms. It is important to get medical attention if you experience any of the following:

1. Dizziness.
2. Rapid heartbeat.
3. Diarrhea.
4. Nausea.
5. Cramps.
6. Throbbing headache.
7. Dry skin (no sweating).
8. Chest pain.
9. Great weakness.
10. Mental changes.
11. Breathing problems.
12. Vomiting.

Keeping cool. The best advice for avoiding heat stress is to keep as cool as possible.

1. Air conditioning can provide lifesaving relief from heat stress, particularly if you have a heart condition. If you don't have air conditioning, spend as much time as you can in air-conditioned shopping malls, libraries, senior centers, movie theaters or the coolest room in your house.
2. Fans can draw cool air into your home at night or circulate air during the day. Air movement helps reduce stress.
3. Cool baths, showers, ice bags or wet towels provide relief from the heat, because water removes extra body heat 25 times faster than cool air.
4. Wear loose-fitting, lightweight, light-colored clothing.
5. Your body needs more water in hot weather. Don't wait until you are thirsty to have a drink of water. If you have a medical problem with water balance *check with your doctor* for advice on how much you should drink.

Special precautions

1. Reduce physical activity during extremely hot weather.
2. Avoid hot foods and heavy meals. They add heat to your body.
3. Watch salt use. Check with your doctor before increasing the amount of salt or potassium in your diet.
4. Avoid alcohol, which results in faster water loss.
5. If you live alone, make sure a friend or relative checks on you regularly.
6. Take the heat seriously. Pay attention to the danger signs and call your doctor at the first signs of trouble.

NUTRITION

Most seniors believe that nutrition is important for their health and well-being, but it appears that few act on their beliefs. At least 30 percent of them skip at least one meal per day. Seniors, particularly newly widowed men, may be vulnerable to poor nutrition, which adversely affects their health. To make matters worse, often the signs of malnutrition can baffle and mislead professionals. For example, weight loss, lightheadedness, disorientation, lethargy and loss of appetite are often diagnosed as illness, when actually they are signs that the person needs to eat better.

There is no single, simple solution. The aging process itself becomes a barrier. As many people age, their biological clocks wind down and they start to lose lean body mass. Although not a part of normal aging, their appetites may diminish, but requirements for nutrition do not. Some food requirements actually increase, such as certain vitamins or proteins.

The reasons some seniors shun balanced foods result from many factors other than natural metabolic changes. Loneliness, for example, can be a problem for a person who has always lived with a spouse or other family members. Depression, often linked to loneliness, may curtail a person's interest in food. Those who are single are more at risk. This seems to be especially true of older men. Sometimes, men who are without adequate cooking or shopping skills may eat less or skip meals. Women living alone may grow tired of cooking and lose interest in eating.

Another roadblock to eating well is the decline in sense of smell, which directly affects a person's sense of taste. The ability to taste remains largely intact with age, but the ability to smell is often responsible for taste complaints.

Money is another factor. After some people retire, their incomes may shrink, forcing them to make cutbacks in their budgets. The area that cuts most easily is food.

Other possible factors that contribute to poor eating habits: Some medications kill appetites or taste sensations. Perhaps ill-fitting dentures make chewing meats and fibrous vegetables difficult. Even failing eyesight may play a part, because meals can look less appealing, and reading labels is more difficult. Disease or broken bones limit mobility, and thus shopping. A frail person cannot readily carry home a heavy bag of groceries or make frequent trips to the grocery.

You can ensure a good nutrition level by using a senior food service, such as Meals on Wheels. Finally, begin early to learn and appreciate the benefits of nutrition for seniors.

CHOKING

For seniors, as well as young children, choking on food is a special hazard because often they are unable to help themselves solve the problem. The following food items most often cause trouble (listed from most problems to least):

1. Hot dogs and sausages.
2. Candy.
3. Nuts.
4. Grapes.
5. Hard cookies/biscuits.
6. Meat slices/chunks.
7. Raw carrot slices/sticks.
8. Peanut butter sandwiches.
9. Apples chunks/slices.
10. Popcorn.

MEDICATION MANAGEMENT

As you age, you tend to take more medicines to control common medical conditions, such as high blood pressure and heart disease. More medication—whether prescription or over-the-counter—increases chances for drug interactions and adverse reactions. Your body changes as you age and this affects your physiological responses to medicine. You may need to accommodate those changes and reduce the risk of adverse reactions and drug interactions. You should work closely with your doctor to ensure that you are taking the medications you need at the lowest possible doses.

DRUG OVERDOSE/MISUSE

This is not a discussion of intentional drug overdose, but overdose by misuse. Many symptoms of old age, such as forgetfulness, grogginess, unsteadiness and slurred speech, are also signs of senior drug overdose, better called drug misuse.

Drug misuse is a big problem. It is viewed as the fifth leading health threat to the elderly and accounts for 240,000 hospitalizations each year. Old age often is blamed for the estimated 63,000 elderly who, each year, experience severe mental impairment. Drug misuse may be the cause of or a factor in some impairments. And a report estimates that 32,000 of the falls that result in broken hips (the major injury experienced by the elderly) happen when the victims are under the influence of drugs.

All in all, an average individual over 65 years of age takes between two and seven prescription medications daily and fills 13 prescriptions yearly. Unfortunately, physicians may overlook signs of drug misuse or make the wrong diagnosis. Among the many possibilities for abuse are:

1. Some people double the dose, thinking more is better.
2. Some share drugs with family members or friends.
3. Patients see several doctors and "collect" prescriptions from each.
4. Patients may unwittingly combine drugs that interact dangerously.
5. Some may take alcohol or over-the-counter formulas with prescriptions.

What you can do. If you are experiencing confusion, don't think it is a necessary part of growing older. It may be unintentional drug misuse and your family doctor should be consulted. Ideally, doctors, pharmacists and patients work together on the problem.

1. Tell your doctor about all drugs you're taking, even off-the-shelf (over-the-counter) medications.
2. If you are seeing more than one doctor, make sure each knows what the other doctors are prescribing.
3. Keep a list of all medications you are taking and show it to the doctor at each appointment. Better still, take *all* your pills, including over-the-counter medications, to each appointment. Discuss your problems and seek answers to your questions. For each drug you take, know the name of the drug, the schedule for taking it, how it will interact with your other medicines and any possible side effects.
4. Deal with one pharmacy. By law, a pharmacy must keep a record on each customer.
5. Discuss any over-the-counter medications you take with your pharmacist.
6. Tell the pharmacist about drugs bought at other pharmacies. All medicines count.
7. When buying your drugs, ask your pharmacist to alert you to any possible complications with your other prescriptions or over-the-counter medicines.
8. Know the warning signs of drug misuse, overdose or complications from combinations of drugs, and report them to your doctor.
9. Don't stop taking a prescribed drug. But if you think you are experiencing unwanted side effects, see your doctor immediately.
10. Take the prescribed dosage. Too little medication may be the problem. Don't experiment on your own.
11. Understand tailor-made medications and how they work as low dose and slow release for the elderly. (See the section on tailor-made medicines.)
12. If you have trouble taking tablets, tell your pharmacist. He/she may be able

to supply a liquid or crush the tablets. Don't crush tablets unless directed by your pharmacist or doctor.

Getting it all together. Know what you have, know how to keep medications separated and have a systematic method to take a combination of medications.

1. Use a low-cost compartmentalized pill-box, which you can buy in a drugstore, that will allow you to organized your daily doses for a week or more.

2. Medicine cabinets and kitchen drawers sometimes are full of all kinds of medications in bottles, boxes and envelopes. Put them all in a bag, take them to your pharmacist or doctor and ask them to look them over and advise you. Don't be hesitant to ask them to do this. If, in the rare case, your doctor or pharmacist is not helpful, consult other health care professionals. It is a good idea to discard old prescriptions that you no longer need.

3. If you drink, even if it is only an occasional nightcap, let your physician know. Some medications simply won't work properly with alcohol and can be dangerous. The body's tolerance to alcohol decreases with age, so the drug-alcohol interaction is more significant.

4. Keep a written record of all your medications, so you can show it to your doctor or pharmacist. If your pharmacist cannot give you a chart to keep track of your medicines, consider one like this:

Medicine chart

Name of medicine	Color	Directions	Times	Purpose	Shape	Cautions

Tailor-made medicines. Many older patients cannot tolerate prescriptions in which one type is meant to fit all patients. Some drug manufacturers are making "low-dose" or "slow-release" versions of the standard drugs for the elderly. The slow release drugs reduce the number of pills or dose that need to be taken. This results in fewer pills per prescription. The safety benefit is that fewer drugs are taken and there is less chance of not taking enough, or taking too much, medication. Failure to follow the recommended regime is a major reason for adverse drug reactions.

Slow-release products include:

1. *Calan SR* to treat hypertension.
2. *Cardizem SR* for hypertension.
3. *Procardia XL* to treat angina and hypertension.
4. *Proventil Repitab* for asthma, a slow-release form of albuterol.
5. *Hismanal*, an antihistamine.

Low-dose products include:

1. *Cytotec* to counteract stomach damage caused by aspirin, ibuprofen and similar drugs.
2. *Tenormin* to treat hypertension.
3. *Halcion*, a sleeping pill.
4. *Coumadin*, a blood thinner and anticoagulant.
5. *MS Contin*, a slow-release version of morphine.
6. *Diflucan*, an anti-fungal agent.

New liquid versions include:

1. *Tagamet*, an anti-ulcer medication in liquid form.
2. *Zantac*, also used to treat ulcers.
3. *Prozac*, an antidepressant.
4. *Naprosyn*, nonsteroidal, anti-inflammatory drug.
5. *Pediaprofen*, nonsteroidal, anti-inflammatory medication for children, but suitable for the elderly.

DO YOU HAVE AN EMERGENCY?

The older you get, the more critical and difficult it becomes to know whether you have a medical emergency. There are obvious emergencies, like gunshot or stab wounds and bad eye injuries. But a change in mental status (confusion, delirium) in an elderly person over a few hours, a few days or a week or so, also is a medical emergency. Many other situations are more difficult to evaluate, especially if they were not considered emergencies earlier in life. The University of California, Berkeley's *Wellness Letter* provides a list of what doctors consider emergencies:

1. Difficulty breathing or shortness of breath.
2. Severe abdominal pains.
3. Slurring or loss of speech.
4. Convulsions.
5. Unconsciousness.
6. Uncontrollable breathing.
7. Bullet or stab wounds.
8. Head injuries.
9. Broken bones.
10. Eye injuries, sudden loss of vision.
11. Foreign substances in the eye.
12. Poisoning.
13. Drug overdose.
14. Choking.
15. Smoke inhalation.
16. Gaseous fume inhalation.
17. Heat stroke or dehydration.
18. Hypothermia.
19. Temperature 103°F or above.
20. Prolonged vomiting or diarrhea.
21. Snake or animal bites.
22. Insect stings that cause shortness of breath.

Eldercare options. In some corporate circles, child care concepts have expanded to include care for elderly relatives. The American Business Collaboration for Quality Dependent Care (ABCQDC), established in 1992, gives a new look to corporate benefits by adding care for elderly relatives to child care concepts.

The direction of elderly care as a corporate employee option may not clearly emerge for many years. Realize that safety and health concerns for elderly day care vary from those for child care. Also they present new situations and problems for caregivers and corporate sponsors.

CAREGIVER HELP

More than 7 million Americans care for an older, often mentally impaired, adult in their homes. To learn more about taking care of an older dependent, both at home and elsewhere, write:

Family Survival Project
425 Bush St., Suite #500
San Francisco, CA 94108

Alzheimer's Association
P.O. Box 5675HC
Chicago, IL, 60680-5675

You can call the National Council on the Aging at 1-800-424-9046 for referrals to local support agencies across the country. Eldercare through these agencies may include visiting nurses, physical therapy, housekeeping services, assistance with bathing, meal preparation, shopping or transportation, counseling and recreational activities.

LifeLine is a commercial service available throughout the U.S., which enables a person to wear a silver-dollar-sized button that can be pushed to summon aid. Obtain more information by calling 1-800-543-3546. In some communities, the service is subsidized locally. In some states, Medicaid covers all or part of the cost.

BIBLIOGRAPHY

"Household Falls: Keep Your Feet on the Ground," Abbot, Linda, *Family Safety and Health,* Itasca, IL: National Safety Council, Fall 1993, pp. 22-23.

"Sidewalk Savvy," Axe, Kevin, *Family Safety and Health,* Itasca, IL: National Safety Council, Winter 1992-1993, p. 10.

"Heat or Eat: Deadly Choice," Barnhill, William, *Healthwatch.*

"Be Alert to Signs of Drug Tampering," *Community Safety and Health*, Chicago, IL: National Safety Council, July/August 1991, pp. 4-5.

"Caregiving—When Caregivers Need Help," *Pacific Lifestyles,* Edmonds, WA: Pacific Medical Centers and Clinics, March 1993, p. 2.

"Safety and Health Watch," Castell, Jim, *Safety and Health*, Chicago, IL: National Safety Council, May 1993, pp. 151-153.

"Falls are Most Preventable," *The Third Age,* Everett, WA: p. 10.

"The Right Way to Take Medicine," Feldman, Debbie L. and Mick Hans, *Family Safety and Health*, Itasca, IL: National Safety Council, Fall 1993, p.8.

"Firms Join for Dependent Care." *Seattle Times,* Seattle, WA: Section B, pp. 1, 5, September 10, 1992.

"Getting Information From FDA," *FDA Consumer*, Washington, DC: Food and Drug Administration, December 1990, pp. 28, 30-31.

"Easy Ways to Fall-Proof Your Home," Grossman, Ellie, *Family Safety and Health,* Itasca, IL: National Safety Council, Fall 1991, pp. 14-17.

"Safety Suggestions for the Senior," Ignelzi, R. J., *The Journal,* Seattle, WA: February 9 to March 9, 1993, p. 21.

"Make Homes Safe for Elderly and Disabled," *Community Safety and Health,* Chicago, IL: National Safety Council, July/August 1992, pp. 3-4.

Medication Management Today (ADSB #951-8169), Vicks, 1991.

Medicine and You: A Guide for Older Americans, New York: The Council on Family Health, 13 pages.

"Nutrition and the Elderly," *FDA Consumer*, Washington, DC: Food and Drug Administration, October 1990, pp. 25-28.

"Older Consumers and Stairway Accidents," *Fact Sheet*, Washington, DC: U.S. Consumer Product Safety Commission, November 1975.

"Older People More Susceptible to Hypothermia," *Aide*, San Antonio, TX: October, 1991, p. 20.

"Pharmacists Help Solve Medication Mysteries," Washington, DC: Food and Drug Administration, January/February 1991, pp. 27, 29-34.

"Protect Your Eyes," *Community Safety and Health,* Chicago IL: National Safety Council, July/August 1991, pp. 2-3.

"Safe Shoe Prescribed to Prevent Epidemic of Broken Hips," Rhodes, Elizabeth, *Seattle Times*, November 8, 1992, p. K1.

Safety for Older Consumers: Home Safety Checklist, Washington, DC: U.S. Consumer Product Safety Commission, June 1986.

"Firms Try Harder, But Often Fail to Help Workers Cope With Elder-Care Problems," Shellenbacher, Sue, The Wall *Street Journal*, New York, NY: Wednesday June 23, 1993, pp. B1, B6.

"Tailor-Made Medicine," *Better Homes and Gardens,* September 1991, pp. 74, 76.

"The Road to Safety for Older Drivers," *Family Safety and Health,* Chicago, IL: Summer 1991, pp. 29-31.

CHILDREN AND PETS

Pets can be a source of joy and entertainment for families, but they can also be a source of illness for people—and people may be a source of illness for animals.

Buying a pet

When buying a pet keep these things in mind:

1. Be wary of buying more exotic pets—including wild animals, animals not readily treated by most veterinarians and animals that may carry unusual diseases.

2. Keep family allergies and your lifestyle in mind.

3. If children are in the house, consider the most suitable animal and more specifically, breed. Nervous or high-strung dogs, for example, are a poor choice.

4. Don't buy a pet to teach family responsibility. It never seems to work.

PROTECT YOUR PET

The Director of Chicago's Anti-Cruelty Society provides some tips on how to make your home safer for pets.

1. Keep your trash container under the sink so that pets cannot reach such foods as chicken, fish, or other foods that could cause them to choke.

2. Keep your vet's phone number and a nearby pet-emergency hospital phone number handy. Your regular vet has an immunization file on your pet.

3. Flush your toilet well and keep the lid down.

4. Be careful what human food you give pets. Chocolate can kill dogs and aspirin can kill cats, for instance.

5. Keep household cleaners, detergents, food wraps and plastic containers that can be poisonous away from pets, just as you would with children. (Remember that some pets can manage to open some door handles.)

6. Some plants have poisonous leaves. Keep the plants away from pets.

7. Cats like to enter washers, dryers and car hoods. Keep the doors closed and check before operating.

8. Puppies, rabbits, birds and rodents chew on electrical cords. Keep the cords high and away from them, and use safety plugs in unused outlets.

9. Fertilizers are harmful to animals, just as they are to humans. Keep pets out of the yard for at least two days after fertilizing.

10. Keep pets away from the stove. They can be burned by spills.

11. Keep your pets away from the Christmas tree and other artificial displays. Tree needles and some ornaments are poisonous or can cause them to choke.

12. People *cannot* get AIDS from dogs or cats, but cats can get FIV, a feline form of HIV, from other cats.

13. See that children know how to care for and respect dogs. They should be taught rules, such as: Never leave pets in hot or cold cars.

14. Don't let the family tease a dog, especially one that is tied.

15. Teach children not to go into a yard, where there is a dog, to retrieve balls and other toys. Knock on the door of the house first and get permission or help from an adult.

PROTECT YOUR FAMILY

Injuries from household pets are common. One of every 200 emergency room visits is for a dog-bite injury. Children should know safe procedures to follow when near animals (not to provoke them or take their food, etc.). Potentially dangerous or nonsocial animals, such as some pit bulls, should never be in the same physical space as children.

1. Any animal in the home, indoors or outdoors, should be in good health. It should show no evidence of carrying any disease and be a good companion, especially for children.

2. To help control transmittable diseases, dogs and cats should be immunized on a timely basis for diseases that can be transmitted to humans.

3. The living quarters of animals should be enclosed and kept clean of animal waste, to reduce the risk of human contact with the waste.

4. Animal cages with removable bottoms should be kept clean and sanitary.

5. Animal litter boxes should not be accessible to children. Immediately remove and dispose of all animal litter from areas where children may be.

6. Keep animal food supplies out of the reach of children. Animal food may become contaminated the same as human food. Temperature, insects and animals can contaminate standing pet food.

7. Live animals and fowl should be kept away from food preparation, storage and eating areas.

8. Special hand washing is required after handling animals. Wash with soap and warm, running water for at least 10 seconds to be effective.

9. Never leave infants or young children in a home alone with your dog or cat.

10. Ringworm is really a virus, not a worm. Dogs get it from other dogs and can pass it on to you. The person and dog must both be cured to stop the passing cycle.

11. Toxoplasmosis is a cat disease that can be passed on to anyone, mostly through animal waste. It is especially dangerous to pregnant women and can cause birth defects. Pregnant women should never change litter boxes.

12. Pets' fleas can bite you. Their bites are irritating, but seldom dangerous.

13. Worms, usually found in young puppies and kittens, are transferred to humans through animal waste. Children can catch the worms in sandboxes used by cats for litter.

14. If a pet bite breaks the skin, see a doctor immediately.

15. Sterilize your animal. It is estimated that 80 percent of the dog bites come from animals that are not spayed or neutered.

16. Train your dog to get along with people. Stay away from aggressive games. Tricks and frisbees are better than pulling and tugging.

17. Don't make guard dogs out of pets. Good guard dogs cannot tell friend from foe.

18. Make your dog part of the family. Care for the dog's welfare and don't leave the dog on its own any more than you would a child. When you don't care for dogs, they get in trouble.

ANIMAL BITES

Bites from animals, including pets, may be from rabid animals. The recommended action is to call a physician or medical facility and wash the wound gently and thoroughly with soap and water for 15 minutes. Keep track of the animal for further testing.

Dog bites. The Centers for Disease Control report that by the time they are 12 years of age, half of all U.S. children are bitten by dogs. The biting dogs are usually known to the neighborhood. A biting dog seems to have these characteristics: male, unneutered, free-roaming for extended periods, trained as an aggressor, family history of aggressiveness, very protective of property and may run in a pack.

WHEN A DOG CHARGES

1. If you are walking, stand still. Running threatens and excites the dog. Do not make eye contact.

2. If you are riding a bike, don't try to get away. Stop, put the bike between you and the dog and move slowly out of its territory.

3. If attacked by a dog or group of dogs, drop and "tuck." Drop to the ground, roll into a ball and place your hands and arms over your face and neck.

4. Don't scream. This upsets and excites the dog.

BIBLIOGRAPHY

Control of Communicable Diseases in Man, Benenson, A., Washington, DC: American Public Health Association, 1985.

Caring for Our Children, Washington, DC: American Public Health Association, 1992, pp. 98-99.

"Dogs That Bite: The Unseen Epidemic," Finney, Martha, and Deborah Dasch, *Aide Magazine*, San Antonio, TX: USAAA, August 1933, pp. 6-8.

Health in Day Care: A Manual for Professionals, Selma R. Deitch, Ed., Elk Grove Village, IL: American Academy of Pediatrics, 1987, pp. 212-213.

"Pets Can Be Great Friends," Pearlman, Cindy, *Family Safety and Health,* Chicago, IL: National Safety Council, Summer 1993, pp. 6-7

INDEX